FAMILY

Organization and Interaction

Chandler Publications in Anthropology and Sociology
LEONARD BROOM, EDITOR

Family

Organization and Interaction

by Bernard Farber

UNIVERSITY OF ILLINOIS

Chandler Publishing Company *San Francisco*

Contents

Preface

This book deals with sociology as applied to family life. It concentrates on the explanation of stability and change in the family. Its major focus is on the contemporary family in the United States.

I have chosen the problem of orderly replacement of family culture from generation to generation as the frame of my discussion of family life. This choice was made for strategic rather than ideological reasons. There is no implication of a desire for or belief in orderly replacement in the family. Instead, the tendency toward orderly replacement was postulated in order to provide a basis for examining the processes of change in family life from one generation to the next. Having made this assumption, I then ask: Which social arrangements facilitate orderly replacement? How do other social arrangements interfere with orderly replacement?

Though disorderly replacement might have been considered as the opposite of orderly replacement, the interference with orderly replacement is not simply the absence of continuity in the organization of family life. The study of change also involves the determination of direction of change. The major factor interfering with orderly replacement in contemporary society seems to be an increasing tendency toward permanent availability of adults for marriage with any cross-sex adult in the society. Permanent availability, which appears to be related to various aspects of kinship organization, not only disrupts family continuity but also provides a direction for change in norms relevant to family life. The interaction between tendencies toward orderly replacement and tendencies toward permanent availability seems to define the character of the contemporary family.

Ways of explaining change and stability in family life have shifted in the past century. Early family sociology, modeled after Darwinian biology, centered on the investigation of social origins and the evolution of the family. Later attempts at describing change focused upon the transition of the family from a basic institution in an agricultural, feudal society to an ephemeral small group in modern industrial society. This book will examine interaction and organization in the nuclear family as a reflection of basic changes in kinship rules.

In the first part of the book, the family is viewed as being essentially a cultural entity pertaining to marriage, kinship interaction, socialization of children, and housekeeping activities. The basic tendency in family life is described as the orderly replacement of this culture from one generation to the next. Whereas social scientists have sometimes focused on the family as the vehicle for transmitting the culture for the entire society, attention in this book is focused upon the family culture itself. The emphasis on orderly replacement leads to concentration upon those factors which limit or facilitate change in family life.

The second part of the book indicates how, in the interaction between family and other institutions, kinship patterns in contemporary society are being modified in ways which interfere with the orderly replacement of family culture. The different modes along which the family of the future may develop are investigated. Each mode of family organization has implications for personal destiny not only within the family but also in other aspects of social life.

The third part of the book concentrates upon the internal processes of family interaction relevant to orderly replacement. It describes predicaments faced in the contemporary family, changes during the family life cycle, family crises, socialization of children, and finally, mental health.

It is my belief that the purpose of textbooks in colleges has shifted in the past generation. Earlier, textbooks were used to provide the entire reading matter for a college course. Students did not have ready access to the original materials which were considered important in the area of study. Today, collections of journal articles and reproduction of individual articles have made original materials readily available to the student. My view is that a textbook now can organize the basic materials for a college course but permit the instructor flexibility in selecting articles for students from reproductions or published collections.

Writing a book is a collective enterprise. To claim individual authorship is to maintain a fiction. The ideas have come from the writings cited, from conversations with colleagues, and from teachers and students in the classroom. Even the words themselves cannot be considered as mine: quotations in the text, criticisms by students and colleagues, and editing by the publisher's office and by my wife, Annette, have made even the wording a collective enterprise. Since there are too many people who have contributed to the book in one way or another to try to enumerate them, I shall merely acknowledge my gratitude to all persons cited in the text. However, I must express my gratitude to Alexander L. Clark, University of Texas, for his very thorough and perceptive criticism of the manuscript.

Bernard Farber

PART ONE

Generic Aspects of Family Life

1 Study of the Family

What is happening to family life in contemporary society?

How are courtship and marriage practices changing?

What is the role of relatives in modern society?

What are the major trends in raising children?

These are questions with which this book is concerned. Later parts of the book discuss contemporary family life, courtship and marriage practices, interaction between relatives, and child raising, as well as other aspects of family relations. But before these topics can be discussed meaningfully, some preliminary ideas must be advanced to define terms, to indicate relevant aspects of family life, and to develop the particular viewpoint of the book. Part I of the book is intended to provide the general definitions and theoretical statements necessary for understanding the later discussion of contemporary family life.

This chapter has three tasks. First, to present a definition of the family. The family will be defined in terms of culture. In a sense, the remainder of the book is an

3

elaboration of this definition. Second, to describe the historical development of family sociology. Two major traditions will be indicated—the view of the family as an institution and the view of the family as a group. This historical discussion is intended to place the definition and approach to family life in this book in the context of what has occurred before. The third task is to indicate the focus of this book as that of the orderly replacement of family culture from one generation to the next. The concept of the closed system will be applied in explaining orderly replacement. Although the problem of orderly replacement is a traditional one in the study of social institutions, it has not been exploited in the investigation of the contemporary family.

Definition of the Family

What is the family?

In Western society, the family is a category of social life in which almost all individuals participate. Early in life, they learn to distinguish between those persons who are part of the family and those who are not. Individuals discover that they are supposed to act differently toward family members and toward outsiders. Each person develops a vocabulary and a set of selective perceptions relating to the identification of families and to norms and roles of family life. Each individual has an immediate understanding of his own family life and the family life of those with whom he is in contact.

The immediate comprehension of his own family life, however, does not explain to the individual how families emerge and how continuity of family life is sustained from generation to generation. The study of the family endeavors to make sense out of family life in a larger sense, that is, as a social category for the whole society rather than merely for the particular families with which the individual is acquainted. The study of the family thus seeks to enlarge understanding of the mechanics of social life.

Study of the family may begin with a provisional definition of the family as a social group. In Western society, the practical, day-to-day definition of the family group varies with the number of generations included. A single-generation family consists of husband and wife, *the married couple.* A two-generation family is made up of father-husband and mother-wife as well as sons and daughters, *the nuclear family.* A *three-generation family* ordinarily consists of grandfather-husband, grandmother-wife, father-husband, mother-wife, and sons and daughters. Since a family is usually regarded as "broken" or incomplete when either a father-husband or mother-wife is not present, these probably would be considered as the crucial family members.

In non-Western societies, the composition of the family may be different from that in Western society. In one society, the family may provide a basis for all occupations and power positions. Everyone in the society knows exactly who belongs to his family and who does not. In another society, membership in a particular family may make little difference with respect to occupation or power position. The individual may not even know which members in the society are related to him.

Murdock has suggested that the nuclear family is a

universal phenomenon, that in all societies—regardless of their form of kinship organization—observers can expect to find a distinct unit of father-mother-children.[1] Even with respect to the nuclear family, however, the composition of the family is not uniform. In societies where one man lives with several wives in a single household, do all of the wives and their progeny constitute a single nuclear family? Similarly, where one woman is married to several unrelated men, are they all members of the same nuclear family? In societies where the mother's brother is actively engaged in socialization of the children and in providing economic assistance, is he a member of the nuclear family also? These variations in family composition and activities present many difficulties in defining the family.[2]

If the category of the family differs in structure and composition among different societies, how then can an observer recognize family life when he sees it? In many non-Western societies, the category of family life may be intertwined with other aspects of social life so that the inhabitants themselves do not differentiate between family and nonfamily life. Perhaps, in many primitive societies, the family can be distinguished by the anthropologist only as an analytical construct rather than as an empirical entity.

However, focusing on certain categories of activities may help define what is meant by the family in any so-

[1] George Peter Murdock, *Social Structure*, New York: Macmillan, 1949.
[2] M. J. Levy, Jr., and L. A. Fallers, "The Family: Some Comparative Considerations," *American Anthropologist*, 61 (1959), pp. 647-651.

ciety. People are biologically alike in all societies: they grow up gradually, they mate selectively, they reproduce, and they raise children. We can regard as family those social arrangements which tie these activities together through procedures and rules pertaining to a small relatively permanent group. This group may be the married couple, the nuclear family, the three-generation family, or any other collection of persons entrusted with responsibility for these activities in a particular society. Pertinent procedures and rules would include regulation of marriage and divorce (nonrandom mating), legitimation of the birth of children (giving the child a complete family), courtship system (the selection process), kinship identity and obligations (relationship to other families), and biological and emotional family maintenance (provision for stability of the mother-father-child positions). Arbitrarily, these procedures and rules are viewed here as constituting family culture. This definition will receive elaboration in Chapter 2, Family and Kinship.

Family Sociology Viewed Historically

Attempts to make sense out of family life are not new. A brief summary of the history of family sociology indicates how separate viewpoints of the family (family as an institution and family as a group) have emerged. The discussion will also indicate how the group and institutional viewpoints have led to eclecticism in family sociology.

FAMILY AS INSTITUTION

Interest in the study of the family as an institution began to emerge in the middle of the nineteenth century. At that time there was much interest in the origin and evolution of both biological and social forms. Charles Darwin published his *Origin of Species* in 1859. In 1861, Sir Henry Maine published *Ancient Law*. Although Maine rejected the idea that "human society went everywhere through the same series of changes," he dealt with the evolution of society from *status* to *contract* as a basis for social relations. Herbert Spencer presented his work on the *First Principles* of sociology in 1862.

Frederick Engels dates the beginning of the study of the family as an institution as 1861 with the publication of J. J. Bachofen's *Das Mutterrecht*.[3] Before that time, Biblical history and Greek and Roman accounts of family life provided the basis for interpretations of family life in Western society. Bachofen, however, attempted to show a line of determinant evolution from an original sexual promiscuity to the modern family. He speculated that primeval promiscuity was followed by a rebellion of women. After asserting themselves initially, however, the women devoted themselves to a peaceful life and began to lose their superiority in domestic affairs as well as their political power in some regions. With this loss of power by women, paternity rather than maternity became the basis for family life. Thus, matrilineal descent (the tracing of family lines through women) took on importance for the understanding of family life as a survival from an earlier era and as a clue to family evolution.

[3] Frederick Engels, *The Origin of the Family, Private Property and the State*, New York: International Publishers, 1942, p. 8. The material on Bachofen is based upon Robert H. Lowie, *The History of Ethnological Theory*, New York: Holt, 1937, pp. 40-43.

The approach by Bachofen was heavily value-laden. Bachofen equated feminine dominance with the emphasis on the senses (bad) and male dominance with an emphasis on the spiritual (good). It fell to others like John F. McLennan to bring ethnographic material to bear upon the evolution of the family as an institution. Independently of Bachofen, McLennan "discovered" the importance of matrilineal descent for the evolution of the family.[4] McLennan believed that "all races of men have had, to speak broadly, a development from savagery of the same general character." He indicated that "wherever we observe symbolic forms, we are justified in inferring that in the past life of the people employing them, there were corresponding realities."

McLennan assumed that originally there were promiscuous hordes which were constantly at battle with one another. These tribes surrounded by enemies would find girls a source of weakness and hence would practice female infanticide. There being a shortage of women, eventually a small set of men would attach themselves to a particular woman in the tribe. The original promiscuity thus became an archaic form of polyandry without any ceremonial form of marriage. This archaic polyandry evolved into a fraternal polyandry when the sons of the same *mother* began to share a wife. Under both promiscuity and polyandry, kinship can be reckoned only through the mother because paternity is unknown. According to McLennan, under archaic polyandry the woman lived with her mother and brothers and her chil-

[4] The material on McLennan is based upon Lowie, *op. cit.*, pp. 43-49.

dren were born into this household. Lineage was traced through the household. In a later stage of fraternal polyandry, the woman was transferred from her own family into her husband's family and her children henceforth belonged to her husband's line. McLennan regarded the levirate (in which the mother marries a brother of her dead husband) as a survival of the polyandrous scheme.

Basic to McLennan's scheme were the concepts of endogamy and exogamy. McLennan defined exogamy as prohibition of marriage within the tribe. It was through the development of exogamy that family life emerged. Tribes with a shortage of women had to import wives from another tribe, at first through bride capture but later through exchange. McLennan suggested that all exogamous groups were originally polyandrous.

There was, however, little unanimity among students of the family concerning the course of evolution. Lewis H. Morgan did not consider marrying outside of one's clan as stemming from hostility between hordes but rather as resulting from natural selection. He regarded exogamy as enabling the clan to propagate itself over immense areas through the superior powers of an improved stock thus created. Utilizing classificatory kinship terms as survivals of the past (for example, calling all males of the parents' generation "father"), Morgan outlined the evolution of the family as proceeding from promiscuous intercourse to monogamous marriage. He outlined the steps as being (a) promiscuous marriage, (b) group marriage of brothers and sisters, who were then the consanguine family, (c) the organization of families into gentes, which prohibited brothers and sisters from marrying each

other as members of the same gens, (d) the emergence
of the marriage pair as a distinct social unit, (e) the patriarchal family and the establishment of lineal succession
to estates, and finally (f) the monogamous family.[5]

According to Morgan, each stage represented an attempt to define more clearly who was descended from
whom. Because of the certainty of identifying the mother,
lineage was first determined on the mother's side.

In the Engels interpretation of Morgan, matrilineal
organization was overthrown when men gained control
of the means of production and increased their economic
authority. Women were subjugated in family life. In the
course of its evolution, the family adapted to changes in
the division of labor in society and became the vehicle
for control over economic life and property. Engels speculated that in the next stage in the division of labor,
which would produce a socialist society, the family
would be characterized by its independence from property rights, by equal rights for women, and by its persistence only through the mutual consent of husband and
wife. He regarded these attributes as traditionally characteristic of the proletarian family.[6] In some respects,
Engels' predictions have come true in both socialist and
nonsocialist societies. For example, in the United States
the middle-class family is becoming more and more like
the proletarian family described by Engels. Since the Engels socialist-evolutionary hypothesis cannot account for
this change in the American family, other explanations
will be sought in this book.

[5] Lewis H. Morgan, *Ancient Society*, New York: Holt, 1878.
[6] Engels, *op. cit.*

In general, the attempts by evolutionists to place the forms of family life existing in primitive, feudal, and industrial societies on a single continuum resulted in establishing the central problem for sociological study of the family as an institution: What do the forms of family life in all societies have in common? The evolutionist hypothesis was that all forms of family life have a common sequence of development, with observed variations representing mainly different stages in development. The evolutionist formulation of the problem of universality of the family influenced especially the functionalist approach to the study of domestic life.

The work of Edward Westermarck formed a bridge between the evolutionist and the functionalist approach to the family as an institution. Asserting that "nothing is more difficult than to decide whether certain customs are survivals or not," Westermarck undertook to show that many lines of development may have occurred in the evolutionary process.[7] He suggested that "in all probability there has been no stage in the social history of mankind where marriage has not existed, human marriage apparently being an inheritance from some ape-like progenitor." Instead of postulating an earlier promiscuous stage, Westermarck began with the assumption that "the horror of incest is well-nigh universal in the human race" and believed that prolonged association dulls the sexual appetite.

He then regarded lines of familial descent and the practice of exogamy as developing from the incest taboo.

[7] Edward Westermarck, *The Origin and Development of the Moral Ideas*, London: Macmillan, 1917.

Aversion to the intermarriage of persons who live in intimate connection with one another has called forth prohibitions of the intermarriage of relations; and, as kinship is traced by means of a system of names, the name comes to be considered identical with relationship. This system is necessarily one-sided. Though it will keep up the record of descent either on the male or female side it cannot do both at once; and the line which has not been kept up by such means of record, even where it is recognized as a line of relationship, is naturally more or less neglected and soon forgotten. Hence the prohibited degrees frequently extend very far on the one side—to the whole clan—but not on the other. It should also be remembered that, according to primitive ideas, the name itself constitutes a mystic link between those who have it in common.[8]

In starting with the incest taboo, Westermarck foreshadowed Parsons, Murdock, and others of the functionalist approach. Moreover, Westermarck utilized the idea (if not the concept) of functional integration (and hence also foreshadowed Radcliffe-Brown) in discussing the problem of persistence of social forms. For example, Westermarck suggested that Christianity fostered monogamous marriage because the societies "on which Christianity was first engrafted" could accept only a religion which conformed to their own practices.

The functionalists concerned themselves with the same problem as the evolutionists, that of determining what is common to the family as an institution in all societies. However, instead of explaining the contemporary family on the basis of an evolution from particular origins,

---

[8] *Ibid.*, p. 369.

the functionalists focused their attention upon the organization of roles in family life. Granting that motherhood is a universally accepted cultural and biological fact, Bronislaw Malinowski raised the question: What is the role of the *father* in the kinship structure?[9] He concluded that without a "sociological" father as guardian and protector, the child does not have a legal status in the community. The father provides the legitimacy for the particular family even in a matrilineal society. Hence, Malinowski suggested that, in spite of the uncertainty of paternity, the assertion of sociological fatherhood by males forms the basis for maintaining kinship patterns. The problem raised by Malinowski with respect to the father was extended to other family activities. By asking "what does the family do," the functionalists have developed a variety of concepts and explanations to provide an understanding of the family as an institution. The functionalist approach will be discussed more fully in later chapters.

In the United States, study of the family as an institution showed a similar shift from emphasis on evolution to interest in functions. In 1889, C. N. Starcke published *The Primitive Family in Its Origin and Development.* Starcke, who was primarily a philosopher, was influenced by social evolutionism but indicated much skepticism about this approach.[10] In the first part of the twentieth

[9] Bronislaw Malinowski, "Parenthood, the Basis of Social Structure," in V. F. Calverton and Samuel D. Schmalhausen, eds., *The New Generation,* New York: Macaulay, 1930, pp. 113-169.

[10] Floyd N. House, *Development of Sociology,* New York: McGraw-Hill, 1936, p. 356.

century, much attention was given to the history of the family. However, many sociologists were pessimistic about the future of the family as an institution. An extreme position was taken by P. A. Sorokin, who viewed contemporary urban civilization as being inimical to family life. He predicted that "the main sociocultural functions of the family will further decrease until the family becomes a mere incidental cohabitation of male and female while the home will become a mere overnight parking place mainly for sex relationship."[11] Other sociologists were not so pessimistic over the future of the family, but most concurred that the family was declining as a vital institution through a transfer of its functions to other institutions. In 1929, W. F. Ogburn reported that trends in American society indicated that the economic, protective, recreational, educational, and religious functions of the family were being transferred to other institutions. The major function remaining in the family was affectional.[12] This trend toward shifting of family functions to outside agencies provided the basis for the Burgess classification of family types.[13] According to the Burgess scheme, the institutional family was characterized as one in which all the traditional family functions were present and the family was sustained by external, community pressures. The companionship family was characterized

[11] Pitirim A. Sorokin, *Social and Cultural Dynamics,* New York: Harper, 1937, Vol. IV, p. 776.

[12] William F. Ogburn, "The Changing Family," *Publications of the American Sociological Society,* 23 (1929), pp. 124-133.

[13] Ernest W. Burgess, Harvey J. Locke, and Mary Margaret Thomes, *The Family from Institution to Companionship,* New York: American Book, 1963.

by an absence of family functions (except affection) and was sustained by the emotional attachments among its members.

World War II was associated with a resurgence of interest in the family as an institution. Some of this interest probably came from the study by anthropologists of modern society. W. L. Warner and his associates applied to the study of Yankee City the concepts and methods that the anthropologist applies to a primitive society.[14] Warner indicated how family and lineage were closely interwoven in the social-class system in contemporary society. About this time also, interest in cross-cultural comparisons in kinship systems was stimulated by contacts with non-Western societies through occupying military forces. After the War, the rise in birth rate and the rapid growth in home ownership may have strengthened kinship ties in the United States. It is difficult to identify the specific influences in the increasing attention to the family as an institution. However, since the mid-1950's, there has been more study of the family as an institution without regard to specific family problems.

FAMILY AS GROUP

Let us return to the middle of the nineteenth century to observe another tradition in the study of the family. The evolutionists represented a highly speculative approach

[14] W. Lloyd Warner, *et al.*, *Social Class in America*, New York: Harper, 1960. See also Raymond Firth, ed., "Family and Kin Ties in Britain and Their Social Implications," *British Journal of Sociology*, 12 (1961), pp. 305-350.

to this study. Also emerging in the middle of the nine-teenth century was an empirical approach to the study of society. For example, E. B. Tylor published *Researches into the Early History of Mankind and the Development of Civilization* in 1865. Not only did Tylor insist upon an array of evidence to support his conclusions but he also introduced notions of probability and chance into his inferences.

Not all sociologists agree with Engels that family so-ciology begins with Bachofen. Many sociologists regard family sociology as starting in 1855 with Frédéric Le Play's work on *Les Ouvriers européens*.[15] LePlay was in-fluenced by Comte and was concerned with ways in which family organization varied with differences in so-cial and physical conditions, especially conditions relat-ing to poverty.

In his writings on social statics, Auguste Comte had maintained that the family is the basic social group in the study of society. Comte indicated that in the family "we get our first notion of the continuity of past genera-tions" and later notions "of the solidarity of living gen-erations." Moreover, he considered "families as the small-est societies capable of spontaneous endurance."[16]

Following Comte, LePlay used the family as his basic unit of study. To understand the nature of society, one

[15] See Pitirim A. Sorokin, *Contemporary Sociological Theories,* New York: Harper, 1928; and Carle C. Zimmerman and Merle E. Frampton, *Family and Society,* New York: Van Nostrand, 1935.

[16] Auguste Comte, *System of Positive Policy,* London: Long-mans, Green, 1875, Vol. 2, pp. 155-156. (First published 1851-1854.)

must understand the family. LePlay's basic formula was "place, work, family." LePlay's notion was that the general character of the physical environment (place) determines the economic life of the people (work), which in turn dictates the form of the family. The family, in turn, affects other characteristics of the society. LePlay chose the family budget as a quantitative expression of the various aspects of family group life.

LePlay influenced many sociologists in France and England. Paul Bureau, writing in 1923, indicated that although families in good economic circumstances can raise themselves above their immediate surroundings, the working-class family is more directly affected by its circumstances. Hence, the working-class family provides an entry for studying group process in the general society. LePlay's survey technique was applied by Booth, Rowntree, and others in their investigations of poverty and plans for social reconstruction in London and other areas of England. LePlay House was established in London and, until its merger in 1933 with the Sociological Society to form the Institute of Sociology, according to Becker and Barnes, it served to keep alive the name of sociology in Great Britain.[17]

One group tradition in American family sociology stems directly from the budget studies of LePlay. Rural sociologists (notably Carle C. Zimmerman, Carl C. Taylor, and Charles P. Loomis) utilized family budgets to investigate rural-family organization.[18] One of the fruits of their

[17] Howard Becker and Harry Elmer Barnes, *Social Thought from Lore to Science,* New York: Dover, 1961, Vol. 3.

[18] Charles P. Loomis, "Study of the Life Cycle of Families," *Rural Sociology,* 1 (1936), pp. 180-199.

studies was the finding that family organization varies as family composition changes and children mature. Out of their investigations, accordingly, came insight into the importance of the family life cycle as a variable in understanding family life. Within the past twenty years, there has been a growing emphasis upon the family life cycle in family research. This trend in treating the family as a group will be discussed in Chapter 9.

Another tradition in studying the family as a group emerged through a concern with problems in interpersonal relations in the family. Most of the investigations into family problems have taken place in the United States. In the 1880's an organization later known as the National League for the Protection of the Family was formed "to promote an improvement in public sentiment and legislation on the institution of the family, especially as affected by existing evils relating to marriage and divorce." House suggests that there is probably a relation between the League and a book by Charles F. Thwing and Carrie F. B. Thwing, *The Family: A Historical and Social Study,* published in 1887. In the early years of the twentieth century, interest in family problems increased. In 1908, the annual meeting of the American Sociological Society was devoted entirely to the family.[19]

In the United States, probably the greatest impetus to the study of the family as a group has come from Ernest W. Burgess. When Burgess joined the faculty of the University of Chicago in 1917, he was asked to teach a course on the family. Influenced by W. I. Thomas, Robert

[19] Arthur W. Calhoun, *A Social History of the American Family,* New York: Barnes and Noble, 1919, reprinted in 1960, Vol. 3.

E. Park, and George H. Mead at Chicago, Burgess reacted against the historical-institutional approach to the family. His course dealt with the family from the symbolic interactionist view in terms of "a unity of interacting personalities."

To be sure, Burgess was not the only family sociologist in the first quarter of the twentieth century to react against the historical-institutional approach. For example, Charles H. Cooley conceived of the family as a "primary group" (primary in time, in effect on socialization, and in sentiment).[20]

Yet, in terms of influence upon succeeding generations of graduate students in family sociology, Burgess appears unique. In his history of sociology, House regarded *Family Disorganization,* written in 1927 by Ernest Mowrer, a Burgess student, as "the first American book dealing with the family from a strictly sociological point of view to appear in a number of years."[21] Willard Waller acknowledged his "larceny" from Burgess of the basic conception of his textbook, *The Family, A Dynamic Interpretation.*[22] Burgess's work on marital prediction with Leonard Cottrell and Paul Wallin initiated longitudinal study of the family group on a large scale. Most major investigators and sociological commentators who received their graduate training in the family before World War II studied or worked with Burgess at some time in their career. In

[20] Charles H. Cooley, *Social Organization,* New York: Scribner, 1929.

[21] Floyd N. House, *op. cit.,* p. 364.

[22] Willard Waller, *The Family, A Dynamic Interpretation,* New York: Dryden, 1938.

addition to his academic influence, Burgess was instrumental in founding the National Council on Family Relations, which has been a clearinghouse not only for research information but also for family-life education.

Since World War II, there has been a proliferation of studies dealing with family problems and family interaction. Some studies have applied techniques used in small experimental groups; others have involved role-playing techniques. Investigators have dealt with family relations in connection with such problems as delinquency, handicapped children, mental illness, alcoholism, early marriage, working wives, birth planning, old age, family life-cycle progression, and marital adjustment. Many of these investigations will be described in Part III, Interaction between Family Members.

Generally, social scientists who emphasize group characteristics of the family have focused upon variations in the organization of family life in different social situations. Sociologists utilizing the group approach have not concerned themselves with the problem of universality of family functions. Indeed, it would not be consistent with their problem focus to hypothesize that forms of family organization persist because they are efficient in satisfying certain requisites such as reproduction or socialization. Frequently, it is precisely those families in which socialization problems occur which are the subject of sociological investigation. By investigating variations in family organization, group-approach sociologists attempt to uncover these factors which explain the persistence of problems in family life and, by implication, the inefficiencies of family organization.

ECLECTICISM IN FAMILY SOCIOLOGY

The history of family sociology briefly sketched in the above sections indicates that the study of the family, which developed in the latter half of the nineteenth century, arose from two concerns. The first concern was that of the theoretical evolution of the family. The second concern was practical, to initiate reforms in urban slums. Specific topics of investigation have changed and interpretations have been modified as family sociology has matured. Still, the two major reasons historically given for studying the family have remained the same: (a) to gain knowledge for its own sake and (b) to provide a basis for decisions in community policy and personal family life. Two separate approaches to the study of the family have developed. The first approach, based upon "knowledge for its own sake," is usually called the study of the family as an institution. The second approach, oriented toward serving immediate personal and community needs, has been the pragmatic study of the family as a group. The institutional approach looks to the development of a theory based upon simplicity of a "complete" explanation and assumes strict determinism; the group approach seeks utility of explanation and assumes possible manipulation. In the presence of these different aims in the study of the family, social scientists who attempt to organize information about the family tend to be eclectic, sometimes operating with the simplicity criterion and at other times with the utility criterion. They vacillate between regarding the family as an institution and viewing the family as a group.

The position taken here is that utility and simplicity in representations of family life do not necessarily conflict. Even so, a family theory developed on the basis of both criteria will not be the same as one constructed with either criterion alone. Instead of passing only one test (utility *or* simplicity) each theoretical statement must pass two. In addition, the representation of family life must admit both determinism *and* possible manipulation.

Orderly Replacement through Generations

This section focuses upon the approach taken in this book. Most major works in contemporary family sociology take as their point of departure the view that families fulfill essentially the same functions in all societies. Differences in family systems then occur in the ways that these universal functions are fulfilled. Since that position is not taken here, it is necessary to explain why a different approach was used. Below, the universal-functions approach will first be discussed and then the orderly-replacement position will be described.

THE UNIVERSAL-FUNCTIONS APPROACH

Social scientists who apply the universal-functions approach in studying the family raise the following question: How are organization and process in the family group related to the ways in which the family fulfills its functions? In this way, the family as a group is evaluated in terms of fulfillment of institutional functions.

Radcliffe-Brown has written that kinship systems, like language, are constantly made and remade in order to "work." A kinship system that does not do its work will not persist. Radcliffe-Brown did not imply that kinship systems "are normally constructed or changed by a process of deliberation and under control of a conscious purpose." He suggested that kinship systems must meet the minimum criteria of producing stability in the society or they cannot continue to exist.[23]

The position taken by the universal-functionalists is that if societies are to persist, certain requisites must be met. These requisites (or functions) are usually said to include reproduction, biological maintenance, socialization, economic cooperation, and status ascription. Murdock argues that the nuclear family performs the societal requisites more efficiently than do other institutions. Its efficiency in maintaining these requisites is regarded by Murdock as the basis for the universality of the nuclear family. Furthermore, the universal-functionalists argue that because the nuclear family is essential to societal persistence, all societies have developed protective devices to insure the continuity of the family. Among these protective devices are included the prohibition against incest within the nuclear family, provisions for the orderly distribution of sexual property, the principle of legitimacy of children, and the cultural regulation of jealousy and conflict.

Social scientists who apply the universal-functions approach in their study of the family face two general problems. First, the concept of efficiency in the performance of family functions has many value problems. Second, the functions usually ascribed to the family are more rele-

[23] A. R. Radcliffe-Brown, *Structure and Function in Primitive Society,* Glencoe, Ill.: Free Press, 1952, p. 62.

vant for maintaining personnel than for maintaining family culture. The discussion which follows will indicate value problems of the universal-functions approach and then will touch upon the family as a producer of personnel for the society.

Value problems

If the social scientist regards mere persistence of the family as the criterion of its efficiency, he does not encounter many value problems in his investigation. However, persistence of a social structure such as the nuclear family indicates only a minimum criterion of efficiency. This minimum criterion defines only the lower limit for persistence of the social structure; below that limit, the family will not persist. There is no logical basis, however, for the social scientist to restrict himself to the minimum criterion of efficiency in studying social structures. The universal-functionalist could (if he wished) seek to determine the character of the social structure under optimal conditions of efficiency. The study of optimal efficiency would be of major interest in the investigation of the process of change in family organization.

Problems in specifying optimal conditions with respect to universal family functions are indicated below. In many treatments of the family as an institution, it is regarded as fulfilling at least the following functions: reproduction, sex activities, socialization of children, and economic activities.

How many children are to be taken as the criterion for successful fulfillment of the family's reproductive function? Is it true that the larger number of children the greater the contribution of the family to other institutions in the society? If the family in economic straits has a large number of children, is it contributing to the welfare of society or is it merely placing a greater burden on the social services? The concept of reproduction must be considered in connection with the concept of social waste. Perhaps, in the absence of certain advantages in hereditary make-up and in educational facilities, giving birth to children can be regarded as contributing to the waste of society rather than as serving its personnel needs.

The sexual function can be fulfilled in a variety of ways. We can discuss either the satisfaction of sex life to the married pair or the efficiency of the sex life of the pair. Many groups regard sexual intercourse merely as a necessary act to provide reproduction and believe that people are misguided ethically when they regard the sex act as a symbol of love and companionship. Even sex activity as a criterion of family success is clearly not free from the value system of the observer.

The function of socialization in the family is sometimes viewed as the part played by the family in molding the personality of the individual and in preparing him for his adult roles. Again problems of value arise with the questions: What is a healthy personality? What is adequate preparation for roles in a changing society?

The economic function of the family in some societies is productive as well as consumptive. With the emphasis upon consumption in our society, not only is the economic factor to be evaluated in terms of efficiency in spending the family dollar but also in socioeconomic placement of children in the community. Determining which patterns of economic expenditure are most worthwhile constitutes a value problem.

Social scientists utilizing the universal-functions approach usually hypothesize that a family system adapts to changes in social conditions in ways which optimize its efficiency in performing its functions. Yet many changes in family organization cannot be attributed to optimization of the efficiency of the system. Many so-called irrational changes occur—fads, fashions, and other forms of collective behavior. Without specifying aspects of functions which he himself considers as crucial to the system, the social scientist cannot interpret which trends in family life are irrational and which contribute to the efficiency of the system. In his investigation of shifts toward the optimal efficiency of a particular family system, he must specify which is more crucial to the system: quantity or quality of reproduction, sexual satisfaction or fecundity, the happy person or the contributing person, production efficiency or consumption efficiency. His choice of one or the other alternative (or his weighting of their relative importance to system efficiency) will ultimately rest upon his own definition of "success" of the social system. Being concerned with optimal operation of the system, he can no longer regard persistence as a sole criterion of efficiency.

Probably, the efficiency of some social systems such as the economic system or the educational system is easier to evaluate than the efficiency of the family. The functions of the family, as they are presently defined by universal-functionalists, are diffuse in their content. Unlike the economic or educational system, the family is not organized on the basis of a scarcity such as goods or skills in the society. A scarcity implies that something should be optimized. Perhaps if the functions of the family were to be redefined in terms of scarcity, the universal-functions approach would be more useful in the study of persistence and change in family organization.

Personnel and culture

Murdock has proposed reproduction, sex, socialization, and economic cooperation as universal family functions.[24] As universals, these functions themselves have no content. They refer rather to the role of family life in fulfilling the personnel requirements of the general society. Hence, reproduction is concerned with the replacement of physical bodies in succeeding generations. Sex is important as a sustaining function for individuals because it provides enjoyment and avoidance of tension as well as the basis for reproduction. Socialization functions of the family are important insofar as they prepare the individuals for taking on institutional roles in the general society. Similarly, economic activities provide the basic source for physical subsistence. In sum, these functions refer more to how *personnel* is replaced than to how social institutions such as a family persist through time. These functions may account for the presence of *a* domestic life but not for the continuity of any *particular* form of domestic life. Indeed, the functions ordinarily regarded as universal would probably be fulfilled even if the family ceased to exist as a recognizable institution. Thus the universal-functions approach does not explain why the family con-

[24] Murdock, *op. cit.*

tinues to exist as a category of social life with a particular cultural content. The central concern of this book is the process by which a particular form of domestic life is sustained or changed.

THE ORDERLY-REPLACEMENT APPROACH

In this section, the general approach taken in this book will be described. The discussion will include (a) the problem of persistence of institutions, (b) the closed social system as explaining persistence, (c) the open social system as a problem for investigation, and (d) the relationship of orderly replacement to the institutional and group approaches to the family.

The problem of persistence of institutions

If cultural aspects rather than personnel aspects of family life constitute the central interests in family sociology, the essential question to be asked is: How does family life persist from one generation through the next as a social category with particular content? Consideration of the problem of persistence of social arrangements is not a new one. Simmel raised this question in his concern with how society can continue to exist.[25] Recently Parsons indicated that the maintenance of social patterns is one of the imperatives in the persistence of institutions.[26] Kirkpat-

[25] Georg Simmel, "Social Interaction as the Definition of the Group in Time and Space," in Robert E. Park and Ernest W. Burgess, *Introduction to the Science of Sociology*, Chicago: University of Chicago Press, 1921, pp. 348-356.

[62] Talcott Parsons, "An Outline of the Social System," in Talcott Parsons, Edward Shils, Kaspar D. Naegele, and Jesse R. Pitts, eds., *Theories of Society*, New York: Free Press, 1961, Vol. I, pp. 38-39.

rick has suggested that the family is unique in providing continuity of social life.[27]

To answer the question of persistence, we must first determine the *process* by which the family replaces itself in succeeding generations. By generational replacement we do not mean merely the replacement of personnel but also the transfer to the new personnel of the values and norms as well as the vocabularies which describe the social categories we ordinarily know as families.

Strictly speaking, for the family to persist through several generations as a continuity of norms, roles, and values, family culture would have to be transmitted from one generation to the next without change. That is, the norms and other rules of family life of one generation would be duplicated in each succeeding generation.

The family as a closed social system

What, then, are the logical conditions under which orderly replacement from one generation to the next would occur without change? A clue to the conditions necessary (although perhaps not sufficient) for orderly replacement to occur may be found in Robert Redfield's conception of the folk society.[28] Redfield regarded the folk society as a closed system of interaction which has persisted through numerous generations. The closed system is completely isolated from all contacts; all members are in intimate communication with one another; members of the system have a strong sense of belonging together; there is an oral

[27] Clifford Kirkpatrick, *The Family as Process and Institution,* New York: Ronald, 1955, p. 4.

[28] Robert Redfield, "The Folk Society," *American Journal of Sociology,* 52 (1947), pp. 293-308.

tradition; and the culture is transmitted from generation to generation without change. Insofar as the family resembles such a closed system it tends to duplicate itself from one generation to the next.

Under what conditions does the family social system tend in fact to become or remain a closed system? In other words, how are limitations on possibilities for change introduced? The Redfield discussion suggests that cognitive, evaluative, power, and sentimental or expressive factors are involved.

Cognitive factor. The closed system will occur when the vocabulary, norms, values, and other rules governing family life are simple and nonconflicting. Hence, there is only one set of rules that can be followed under any circumstances. If a group is isolated, no new perspective can be introduced to complicate the vocabulary and thought categories of the participants.

Evaluative factor. The closed system is reinforced when the norms, rules, and values of family life are supported by the conservative elements in the social system. Not only are these thought categories and words the only ones known but they tend to be regarded as sacred by the family leaders.

Power factor. One of the elements favoring orderly replacement by generations is the slow turnover in family members. Ordinarily family members enter and leave the nuclear family one at a time rather than in groups. Simmel has suggested that the continuity of group life can be maintained because only a small minority of the members of a society are inducted and socialized at any particular time. The cadre of society (the parents and other elders) therefore can devote much attention to the socialization of the young. It would be of interest to speculate how our society would change from generation to generation if most people were born in litters rather than as single births. With the necessity for caring for eight to ten young children at a time, the parents would find little time to exert their influence. Instead, the main interaction would occur among the children themselves.

Sentimental factor. Orderly replacement from one generation to the next is facilitated by the emotional ties of the younger generation to their elders. Cooley has indicated how the family acts as a major influence in creating the sentiments of individuals.[29] These sentiments arise mainly in parent-child relations. While much has been written about problems of identification and attachment in the modern American family, the parent-child relationship is still regarded as one dominated by close identification and sentimental attachment. Emotional ties to the previous generations bind the incoming generation to the norms and values of their elders.

Insofar as these four factors are operative, the family is a closed social system and the probability is enhanced that there will be orderly replacement of one generation by the next generation to carry on the family culture.

The family as an open social system

It would be unreasonable to expect that while one generation of personnel replaced another the family culture would in reality remain intact. Each factor operating to maintain a closed social system implies an opposite factor. With respect to each, conformity implies its opposite,

[29] Cooley, *op. cit.*

deviance; with deviance, other actions occur. Thus, some of the individuals may first merely reject the known social categories prevalent in the society and after a while invent new cognitive elements. The conservative individuals in the system may not be able to control the reformers who have invented new social categories. The reformers may no longer constitute a minority of those to be inducted into the society and they may seek power by leaving the old family groups and initiating new family cultures. And finally the younger generation may break away from the older generation and stratify the society on the basis of age groupings. All these possibilities amount to a set of assumptions opposite to those based on the closed social system, and they would provide an impetus toward change rather than duplication of family culture as this culture is transmitted from one generation to the next.

The probability of change is related to another problem, that of the direction of change. This book, in discussing the direction of change in American family life, will postulate a tendency for adults in contemporary society to optimize those norms and values in family life consistent with retaining permanently their availability for marriage with any other cross-sex adult in the society. This tendency toward permanent availability will be described as conflicting with the traditional tendency toward orderly replacement. Permanent availability implies certain cognitive, evaluative, power, and sentimental behavior diametrically opposed to behavior consistent with orderly replacement. Limitations imposed on orderly replacement by various social conditions not only eliminate certain traditional alternatives in family organization, but these limitations may also enhance family behavior considered as reprehensible in traditional family organization. Chapter 4 suggests that there exists a continued movement in contemporary society toward optimizing permanent, universal availability.

Orderly replacement and the family as institution or group

How is the conception of family life just discussed related to the institutional and group approaches to the family? As an institution, the family is defined in terms of its culture (the routinized and orderly patterns of social conduct). The question to be raised about the institutional patterns is: What are conditions under which the family as an institution (set of norms, rules, and values) persists through generations? As a group, the family is defined in terms of its personnel. The question to be raised about the family as a group is: How does the process of interaction among family members hinder or facilitate orderly replacement of family culture in the succeeding generation?

Part I of this book deals with variations in family organization from a cross-cultural perspective. Chapter 2 enumerates the logical possibilities in the variation of elements of family culture. These elements include the composition and stability of the marriage group, patterns of descent, rules of residence, the basic maintenance unit of family life, and the courtship system. On the basis of these variations, Chapter 3 indicates how courtship and marriage rules (as reflected in availability for sex relations) vary with different patterns of kinship identity and obligations. The relationship established between kinship patterns and availability for sex relations and marriage provides the basis for describing the American family in Part II of the book as tending toward universal, permanent availability.

Part II of this book discusses the problems of orderly replacement versus permanent availability mainly from the viewpoint of the family as an institution in American society. Part III is concerned with the family as a group and focuses upon the ways by which interaction among personnel influences orderly replacement.

Selected Readings

Probably the most informative general discussion of family and kinship is A. R. Radcliffe-Brown, "Introduction," in A. R. Radcliffe-Brown and Daryll Forde (eds.), *African Systems of Kinship and Marriage,* Oxford University Press, 1950, pp. 1-85.

There is much disagreement among sociologists and anthropologists over the definition of the family. Various definitions of the family are found in:

Burgess, Ernest W., Harvey J. Locke, and Mary Margaret Thomes. *The Family from Institution to Companionship.* American Book, 1963. See esp. Chapter 1, "The Nature of Marriage and the Family."

Fortes, Meyer. "Introduction," in Jack Goody (ed.), *The Developmental Cycle in Domestic Groups,* Cambridge University Press, 1958, pp. 1-13.

Hill, Reuben, and Donald A. Hansen. "The Identification of

Conceptual Frameworks Utilized in Family Study," *Marriage and Family Living*, 22 (1960), pp. 299-311.

Levy, Marion J., and Lloyd A. Fallers. "The Family: Some Comparative Considerations," *American Anthropologist*, 61 (1959), pp. 647-651.

Mogey, John. "Introduction," *International Social Science Journal*, 14 (1962), pp. 411-424.

Murdock, George Peter. *Social Structure*. Macmillan, 1949.

Redfield, Robert. "The Folk Society," *American Journal of Sociology*, 52 (1947), pp. 293-308.

Schrecker, Paul. "The Family: Conveyance of Tradition," in Ruth N. Anshen (ed.), *The Family: Its Function and Destiny*, Harper, 1959, pp. 488-510.

Historical presentations of the study of the family appear in:

Barnes, Harry Elmer. *An Introduction to the History of Sociology*. University of Chicago Press, 1948. See especially chapters on Morgan, Westermarck, and Briffault.

Becker, Howard, and Harry Elmer Barnes. *Social Thought from Lore to Science*. Dover, 1961. Passim.

Lowie, Robert H. *The History of Ethnological Theory*. Holt, 1937.

Discourses on family and kinship by Lewis Morgan, Alfred Kroeber, Bronislaw Malinowski, A. R. Radcliffe-Brown, and Max Weber have been reprinted in Talcott Parsons, Edward Shils, Kaspar D. Naegele, and Jesse R. Pitts (eds.), *Theories of Society*, Free Press, 1961.

2 *Family and Kinship*

In Chapter 1, the concept of the family was defined in terms of particular cultural elements. Family culture was presented as the procedures for regulating marriage and divorce, legitimation of the birth of children, courtship, kinship identity and obligations, father-mother activities in the socialization of children, and biological and emotional family maintenance. The present chapter elaborates upon this definition and indicates the wide variation theoretically possible in these procedures.

This chapter is concerned with three topics: First, the concept of culture as it is related to the family. The discussion emphasizes the evaluation placed upon the procedures for regulating family relations as well as the sources of these evaluations. Second, variations in the ways in which family culture (and kinship rules in particular) is maintained. Distinctions are drawn between prescribed and preferred activities and between ascribed and achieved family status. Third, the possible variations in the content of family culture and the implications of these variations for the continuity of this culture. Each of the elements of family culture in the definition of the family is analyzed with respect to logically possible alternatives. Examples are used to suggest ways in which the different alternatives in procedures affect the transmission of family culture from one generation to the next. Although the usefulness of some of the discussion for the study of the family may not be immediately apparent, the concepts introduced are necessary for understanding material in the chapters which follow.

The Concept of Culture

The family was called a cultural entity in Chapter 1. It is now in order to convey more clearly what is meant by *culture* and the relevance of the concept of culture to the study of the family.

Like many concepts in social science, the concept of culture defies the formulation of a precise, categorical definition. Instead, definitions of culture sensitize inquirers to view the social life of man in a certain way and lead them to focus upon certain aspects of social life. A. L. Kroeber focused upon things which are man-made and can be transmitted from generation to generation. His definition was formulated at a time when instinct psychology was prevalent. Kroeber's view of culture as "superorganic" sensitized social scientists to give attention to nonbiological explanations of social behavior.[1] Leslie White regards culture as a complex of symbols. He con-

[1] A. L. Kroeber, "The Superorganic," *American Anthropologist,* 19 (1917), pp. 163-213.

siders a symbol as a thing which has a value or meaning bestowed upon it by people who use it.[2] His definition implies that the central focus of studies of man's environment should be upon its *meaning* to men. Clyde Kluckhohn's definition covers essentially what is regarded as culture in this book:

Culture is not, strictly speaking, the visible act, the speech, or the product of these things. It is a *way* of thinking, feeling, believing. It is the knowledge stored up (in memories of men, in books and objects) for future use—patterns for doing certain things in certain ways, not the doing of them. We study the overt behavior, the speech and gestures and activities of people, and the tangible results of these things, such as tools, houses, cornfields, and what not. It has been customary in lists of "culture traits" to include such things as watches or lawbooks. This is a convenient way of thinking about them, but we must remember that they, in themselves, are nothing but metals, paper, and ink. What is important is that some men know how to make them, while others set a value on them, are unhappy without them, direct their activities in relation to them, or disregard them.

Culture, then, is one facet of human life. It is that part which is learned by people as a result of belonging to some particular group, and is that part of learned behavior which is shared with others. It is our social legacy, as contrasted with our organic heredity. It is the main factor which permits us to live together in a society, giving us ready-made solutions to our problems, helping us to predict the behavior of others, and permitting others to know what to expect of us.[3]

[2] Leslie A. White, *The Science of Culture*, New York: Grove, 1949.

[3] Clyde Kluckhohn, *Culture and Behavior*, New York: Free Press, 1962, p. 25.

Particularly relevant in the study of family life are the norms and values which people hold. Norms and values are elements of culture. Norms are patterns of conduct which people regard as right and proper. Ordinarily, they learn these norms in interaction with other people. They evaluate some norms as being more right and more proper than others. They thus regard norms of conduct in terms of certain criteria. These criteria, which consist of objectives, ends, aims, or goals of life, are called values. This discussion of the family considers those norms and values which people hold regarding courtship, marriage, divorce, socialization of children, kinship identity and obligations, residence, and household maintenance as elements of family culture.

Where do the norms and values of family life come from? There are three sources:

First, norms and values can be received from the previous generation of family members. Much of family culture is transmitted from parents and kindred to children.

Second, many institutions and groups in society which are not directly relevant to family life have developed norms and values pertaining to family behavior. Attempts by these institutions and groups to influence family life are quasi-family activities. Many institutions and groups perform quasi-family activities. For example, religious writings are explicit in rules regarding family conduct. People are variously told: Honor thy father and thy mother; thou shalt not commit adultery; the family that prays together, stays together; marriage should be restricted to persons of the same religious beliefs; divorce is improper. Law-enforcement agencies, schools, mass communication media, and even businesses also try to impose or encourage particular norms and values in family life.

The third source of family culture is the manipulation of previous norms and values to create new strategies of family organization. In Western society, since the household frequently consists of a relatively isolated small group, perhaps a good deal of family culture is created within the nuclear family. Thus patterns of culture are learned through imitation and teaching and are sometimes developed through innovation.

Variations in the Maintenance of Kinship Rules

There are wide variations in the extent to which individuals are expected by their relatives to adhere to rules and procedures relating to family relationships. These variations occur both within any society and between societies.

Major variations in rules of family life revolve upon the issue as to whether a given rule establishes what is prescribed or merely what is preferred. Other important variations in family relationships occur because in some societies (or some segments within a society) family membership is an ascribed status whereas in other societies or segments, membership in families is an achieved status. These terms will be discussed in the sections below.

PRESCRIBED AND PREFERRED ACTIVITIES IN THE FAMILY

In their attention to norms, individuals make a distinction between prescribed and preferred activities. Prescribed activities are those which the individual must (or must not) do.[4] Violations of prescriptions bring punishment. The incest taboo is a prescribed rule for virtually all mankind; parent-child intercourse or brother-sister intercourse is ordinarily regarded with horror and punishment is severe. An individual is rewarded for performing preferred activities but is not generally punished for nonperformance. In modern Egypt, a cousin is preferred to a stranger as a marriage partner, but not prescribed.

The nature of the act itself does not determine whether or not that act will be prescribed or preferred. In ancient Egypt, brother-sister marriage was practiced not only among royalty but also among commoners. The practice was more prominent among the wealthy, urban population than among the poor, rural population. Middleton suggests that incestuous marriage served the purpose of keeping family property intact from one generation to the next.[5]

Sometimes, there is little agreement among various segments of a society as to whether a particular act is prescribed or preferred. Endogamy (marrying within the group) within religious groups is merely preferred for most segments of American society; yet many families regard endogamy as prescribed and will cut off contact and "disown" a child who marries outside the religion. For example, in orthodox Jewish families, if a child marries out-

[4] The distinction between prescribed and preferred activities appears in numerous sociological and anthropological writings. For example, see Rodney Needham, *Structure and Sentiment,* Chicago: University of Chicago Press, 1962, pp. 8-9.

[5] Russell Middleton, "Brother-Sister and Father-Daughter Marriage in Ancient Egypt," *American Sociological Review,* 27 (1962), pp. 603-611.

side the religion, the parents may regard the child as dead and engage in ritual mourning (such as rending their clothes and observing a ten-day mourning period of prayer and seclusion).

The prescribed act has a tendency to drive the individual either back to the traditional family culture (and conformity) or into another culture (and violation); there can be no half-hearted commitment regarding prescribed acts. The preferred act, however, permits opening the family culture to other kinship units by introducing slight changes in norms and facilitates gradual change in family culture.

FAMILY AND KINSHIP STATUS AS ASCRIBED OR ACHIEVED

We can distinguish those societies in which membership in the kinship unit is an ascribed status from those societies in which, for all practical purposes, kinship membership is an achieved status. An ascribed status refers to a social position which an individual attains by birth or sometimes by marriage.[6] Age and sex expectations and traditional family obligations have been ascribed to individuals merely because they were born with a certain sex into a particular family. An achieved status refers to a social position which an individual attains through performing certain actions.

A study by R. Firth and J. Djamour suggests that in contemporary society, the relatives who are actively participating as kin to an individual (his kindred) can be better characterized as holding an achieved rather than

[6] Definitions of ascribed and achieved status based upon Ralph Linton, *The Study of Man,* New York: Appleton-Century, 1936.

ascribed status.[7] The Firth and Djamour investigation of
kinship patterns in London revealed three levels of participation. First, there were intimate kin who interacted
frequently and who could be readily relied upon for assistance. Second, the effective kin were those relatives who
interacted only occasionally (usually at ceremonial occasions such as weddings or funerals), but whose aid
could also be counted on in time of need. Finally, there
were the nominal kin who were seldom seen and with
whom no personal relationship existed. Among the families in the kinship network, interaction and assistance
were in the final analysis a matter of personal preference.
In a sense, the relatives had to earn the right of participation as intimate or effective kindred. In this sense, intimate or effective kinship status is achieved.

Relationships between kin in Western society (as suggested by the London study) can be contrasted with
those of the Gusii in Kenya. Among the Gusii, rights and
obligations between kin are determined by birth. The
Gusii trace descent through the male line and only men
are recognized as full members of the descent group (or
lineage). The descent group is clearly demarcated; a male
either belongs or does not belong to a kinship group descended from a particular ancestor. If he belongs to a particular group, he has certain rights and obligations in his
interaction with other members of that descent group.
Neither he nor the other members of the descent group
have to earn rights of participation in activities relevant

[7] R. Firth and J. Djamour, "Kinship in South Borough," in
R. Firth, ed., *Two Studies of Kinship in London,* London: Athlone
Press, 1956.

to the kindred; these rights accrue to them by virtue of their birth. For example, male descendants of the same grandfather constitute a single mourning group and perform the ritual of head-shaving at each other's funerals. Mourning groups combine to form a larger kin group in which there is much hospitality and intimacy. The male members of the larger kin group are generally descended from the same great-grandfather or the same great-great-grandfather. Several of the larger kin groups, united on the basis of a common ancestor, join together to form a clan. All clan members must marry outside the clan. With participation based on ascribed status, personal choice and personal preference are subordinated to rights and obligations attached to descent-group membership. With kindred membership as an ascribed status, the Gusii kindred has definite boundaries defined by rules of descent and clearly defined obligations with respect to any member.[8]

Variations in the Content of Family Culture

This section describes the possible variations in the content of family culture and suggests ways in which these variations are related to the continuity of family culture. Variations in patterns of family life are indicated with respect to marriage (variations in the composition of the marriage group), to kinship identity and obligations (patterns of descent), to biological-family maintenance (rules of residence), to social-family maintenance (basic main-

[8] Robert A. LeVine and Barbara B. LeVine, "Nyansongo: A Gusii Community in Kenya," in Beatrice B. Whiting, ed., *Six Cultures*, New York: Wiley, 1963, pp. 19-202.

tenance unit), and to the courtship system. Divorce practices are discussed in the course of characterizing other elements of family culture. Variations in the socialization of children are highly complex and will be described in Chapters 11 and 12.

COMPOSITION OF THE MARRIAGE GROUP AND CONTINUITY

Several possibilities exist for describing the composition of the marriage group: one man and one woman (monogamy), one man and more than one woman (polygyny), one woman and more than one man (polyandry), more than one woman and more than one man (group marriage). In some societies, the practice of concubinage or keeping a mistress is substituted for polygyny.

Ordinarily polygyny appears to be related to the status of women. The relationship between the contribution of women to the production of commodities for subsistence and the form of preferred family life has been the topic of some investigation. Using the Human Relations Area Files, Heath found that monogamy tends to occur more readily in those societies in which the woman's productive contribution is low and that polygyny tends to predominate when the woman's contribution is high. Similarly, the dowry, marriage without economic consideration, and mutual gift exchange tend to predominate where the woman's role in production is low; bride service, sister exchange, and bride price are found more often when the woman's contribution is high.[9] Hence, the woman's economic contribution appears to be a source of demand in

[9] Dwight B. Heath, "Sexual Division of Labor and Cross-Cultural Research," *Social Forces*, 37 (1958), pp. 77-79.

marriage. When her contribution is low, there is a smaller demand for women and monogamy rather than polygyny is the preferred form. When her contribution to production is high, she costs more (in the husband's services if not in money) and polygyny is preferred.

The most direct effect of the composition of the polygynous marriage group upon family continuity is to provide a large subsistence base and sufficient personnel for the succeeding generation. However, a secondary effect of polygyny is to expand the span of generations. This expansion of generations occurs when the wives are of different ages. Since brides are expensive, the older man may be in a better position to purchase brides than a younger man. A man who purchases wives both early and late in his life can have children over a forty- or fifty-year period instead of being restricted to the childbearing years of one wife. The husband is able to extend his authority during a longer period of time over the next generation of family members.

In contrast to polygyny, polyandry is rare. It tends to occur where conditions are harsh and wives contribute little economically.[10] In polyandry, there is ordinarily a specific husband who is designated as the father of a child. For example, the eldest brother may be arbitrarily designated as the father, or bestowing a gift upon the wife may establish one of the husbands as the father. Fatherhood in a polyandrous society is obviously a social category rather than a biological one.[11]

[10] *Ibid.*
[11] See William I. Thomas, *Primitive Behavior*, New York: McGraw-Hill, 1937, pp. 117-121; David Mandelbaum, "Polyandry

Group marriage is apparently a deviant marriage form
in any society. In addition to being practiced in a few
Utopian settlements, it was favored by Plato for the phi-
losophers in his ideal society.[12] The failure of group marriage to persist through numerous generations has suggested to many sociologists that this form of marriage is
incapable of orderliness in the replacement of generations.
However, other sociologists have suggested that the failure of group marriage to persist in these settlements has
resulted from hostile actions by the larger society as well
as from financial difficulty.

Monogamy is the prevalent form of marriage in almost
all societies. In contrast to polygyny, monogamy restricts
the influence of the older generation over the younger
generation to a shorter period.

LINEAGE AND DESCENT

Another variation in the forms of family life is that with
respect to the reckoning of descent. Reckoning of descent
is important for kinship identity and for defining obligations to others in the society. In many societies the problem of lineage or descent is of crucial importance. Line-

---

in Kota Society," *American Anthropologist*, 40 (1938), pp. 574-
583; and Marvin K. Opler, "Women's Social Status and the Forms
of Marriage," *American Journal of Sociology*, 49 (1943), pp. 142-
143; Stuart A. Queen, Robert W. Habenstein, and John R. Adams,
The Family in Various Cultures, New York: Lippincott, 1961,
pp. 18-43.

[12] "The Republic" in *The Works of Plato*, New York: Modern
Library, 1928, pp. 409-419; see William M. Kephart, *The Family,
Society and the Individual*, Boston: Houghton Mifflin, 1961, for
the discussion of Oneida Community, pp. 181-194.

age determines inheritance, authority, economic privilege, rights of participation in ceremonies and rituals, choice of marriage partner, and even whose side to take in a conflict. There are four possibilities for determining lineage: through the male members of the family (patrilineal), through the female members of the family (matrilineal), through both male and female (bilateral), and through either male or female lines (bilineal).

Membership in a lineage is indicated by the specific obligations and rights of the person in his interaction with other persons connected to him through "blood" or marriage. In the extreme unilineal systems, the patrilineal and matrilineal, there is much differentiation in obligations of the person toward his mother's and father's relatives. The person may act very formally toward members of his father's kinship group but very warmly toward his mother's kin (or vice versa). In the extreme case, the kin of one of his parents may have exclusive rights over his productive and reproductive powers. Most societies, however, probably require only moderate differentiation in interaction between mother's and father's kin. When there is no differentiation made between mother's and father's kin, we regard the kinship system as bilateral.

The complications of lineage are indicated by family relations in Greece.[13] In contemporary Greek village society, the formal reckoning of kinship is bilateral. Yet the husband's kin maintain control over the wife's activities and reproductive powers through patrilocal residence and the control of property (especially through male inheri-

[13] Ernestine Friedl, *Vasalika, A Village in Modern Greece*, New York: Holt, 1962.

tance). The wife almost becomes a member of the husband's kin group. However, by retaining control over the wife's dowry even after marriage, the wife's family can somewhat compensate for the control by the husband's kin. Thus, in the Greek family, the retention of control by the wife's family over the dowry given to the husband prevents the complete absorption of the wife into the husband's lineage.

In some societies, the relationship between lineage and family culture may be markedly affected by the presence of a clan or tribe system of social organization. An individual belongs not only to a certain family line but also to a particular clan or tribe. For example, the Kiowa Apache kinship system was marked by bilateral descent, and marriage within the tribe was preferred. Aside from the endogamous preference within the tribe, there was little restriction on marital choice.[14] Similarly, among the Cheyenne marriage was regulated not only by the immediate kinship network of families, but also by clan considerations. Marriage was not allowed within either the mother's or father's patrilineal clan groups.[15]

Variations in lineage are discussed below as if complications of tribal and clan rules relating to persons eligible for marriage do not exist.

Matrilineage is complicated by the fact that even

[14] J. Gilbert McAllister, "Kiowa-Apache Social Organization," in Fred Eggan, ed., *Social Anthropology of North American Tribes*, Chicago: University of Chicago Press, 1937, pp. 99-169.

[15] Fred Eggan, "The Cheyenne and Arapaho Kinship System," in Fred Eggan, ed., *Social Anthropology of North American Tribes*, Chicago: University of Chicago Press, 1937, pp. 35-98.

where lineage is determined through the female line, authority and responsibility for the maintenance of the line is ordinarily vested in the male (especially the mother's brother).[16] The biological father-husband is related to his own children only through bonds of affection established through intimate contact but he has little authority over them. The extent of obligation of the husband varies markedly in matrilineal societies. In some societies he returns to his lineage home only on feast days and during ceremonial periods; in other societies, he continues to spend most of his time with his own mother's kin group and is directly responsible for his sister's children. Divorce is fairly common in matrilineal societies, especially in those societies in which the woman continues to reside with her brother even after marriage.

In his discussion of African matrilineal kinship, Gluckman indicated that:

Here a man is socially reproduced, so to speak, not in his own son, but in his nephew by his sister. He is responsible for his sister's well-being, and his nephew inherits his property and position. But though his sister provides him with his heir, he may not, under the ban on incest, himself beget her children. He has to get some other man, or men, to cohabit with his sister in order that she have children, some of whom will be his heirs and successors.[17]

The Nayar of India present the extreme case indicating the transiency of marriage where the wife's family is

[16] Max Gluckman, *Conflict and Custom in Africa*, Glencoe, Ill.: Free Press, 1955, pp. 54-80.
[17] *Ibid.*, p. 67.

responsible for the socialization of the children. Among
the Nayar, the married couple lives together only three
days after the ceremony. Henceforth, the couple parts
and the husband no longer carries on any of the activities
associated with husband-father in American society. Instead, the wife's children are begotten by her lovers, and
her relatives form the basic domestic unit.[18]

In patrilineal societies, a cleaner break can be made
between the married woman and her own family of orientation. Unlike the male in a matrilineal society, the female in a patrilineal society does not retain supervisory
obligations in her own lineage. She is not expected to participate in the socialization of her sister's or brother's
children nor does she take part in the decisions of her
lineage after marriage. The woman can therefore become
more completely incorporated in the patrilineal group.
In some instances, continuity in the patrilineage is as-
sured through brother-sister marriage. In Egypt, marriage
records, genealogies, and even "a card of invitation issued
by a mother for the marriage together of her son and
daughter" indicate the encapsulation of the family possible (and sometimes preferred) in the patrilineage.[19]

In general, close relationships with the wife's consanguine kin outside the patrilineage would interfere with
her incorporation into her husband's family. In many

[18] E. Kathleen Gough, "Is the Family Universal?—The Nayar
Case," in Norman W. Bell and Ezra F. Vogel, *A Modern Introduction to the Family*, New York: Free Press, 1960, pp. 76-92;
reprinted from *Journal of the Royal Anthropological Institute*, 89
(1959).

[19] Middleton, *op. cit.*

patrilineal societies, ordinarily women can initiate divorce proceedings only with difficulty.[20] Perhaps restrictions on divorce prevent homesickness or personal attachments to old friends and family from taking precedence over commitments to the husband's family.

In the patrilineal society, the husband's kinship group gains the rights not only to the woman's sexual activity, but also the children produced by her. The rights to the children provide for the replacement of the personnel of the husband's family from one generation to the next. In addition, however, the children are raised in the social traditions and offices of the husband's lineage and in this manner the continuity of the patrilineal family culture is maintained. In contrast, in matrilineal societies, although rights to the wife's sexual activities are given to the husband, he does not have rights to his children. The children are ordinarily under the authority of the mother's brother. Control over the children by the mother's brother rather than by the husband enables the matrilineal family culture to continue from one generation to the next.

Even in unilineal societies, there are circumstances in which an individual may transfer by the device of "complementary filiation" to the lineage of the parent through whom his descent would ordinarily not be reckoned.[21] Complementary filiation generally occurs when there is insufficient personnel to occupy the offices of the kinship

[20] George P. Murdock, "Family Stability in Non-European Cultures," *Annals of the American Academy of Political and Social Science*, 272 (1950), pp. 195-201.

[21] Meyer Fortes, "The Structure of Unilineal Descent Groups," *American Anthropologist*, 55 (1953), pp. 17-41.

units. Because of high death rates and fecundity impair-
ment (perhaps through disease and insufficient diet), occasionally the kin group will not have a large enough
population to fulfill its duties and obligations. Murdock
cites instances of complementary filiation occurring among
the Mongo when a man has no sister (so that he is unable
to use her bride price for obtaining his own bride) and
among the Trukese when the woman has insufficient
"mothers" and "sisters" to maintain an efficient extended
family.[22] The Mongo, who are patrilineal and patrilocal,
permit the man without a sister to affiliate with his
mother's patrilineage and to receive a wife from his maternal uncle. Among the Trukese, who are matrilineal and
matrilocal, the woman with a shortage of "mothers" and
"sisters" can join her *father's* matrilineage. Thus, in spite
of personnel shortages, continuity of norms maintaining
unilineality and accompanying practices is ensured by
adopting the remaining personnel into existing lineages.

Another mechanism for maintaining lineage when
there is a shortage in personnel of the appropriate sex to
carry on the line is to reverse lineage rules for one generation. Among the Miao tribes of China, who were normally
patrilocal and patrilineal, when a man had daughters but
no sons, one daughter would remain at home and her husband would come to live with her. Her husband would
give up his lineage rights to the children.[23] A compara-

[22] George P. Murdock, "Cognatic Forms of Social Organization," in George P. Murdock, ed., *Social Structure in Southeast
Asia,* New York: Wenner-Gren Foundation, 1960, p. 12.

[23] Ruey Yih-Fu, "The Magpie Miao of Southern Szechuan," in
George P. Murdock, ed., *Social Structure in Southeast Asia,* p. 146.

ble situation occurs in maintaining the English throne. In the absence of a male heir, Queen Elizabeth II ascended the throne and maintained the paternal line. Her son will assume his rights and duties as a member of his *mother's* patrilineage. In this way, not only will the personnel of the family line be replaced, but the rights and duties of the lineage will continue to remain in operation.

In the bilineal society the married pair can affiliate with either the husband's or the wife's family. In some cases, this affiliation may be related to joining the family enterprise. For example, the society may be organized on the basis of family corporations. The young husband and wife are then required to join the corporation of either his or her parents. The corporation assumes the supervisory task over the maintenance of lineage and socialization of children. The divorce rate in the bilineal society organized on the basis of corporations tends to be high.[24]

The bilateral system appears to characterize contemporary urban society. Characteristics of this system constitute the major content of this book. Research on other societies (China, USSR, Greece, India and the Arab countries in northern Africa and the Middle East) suggests that changes in family systems in those societies are occurring in the direction of the bilateral system characteristic of American society.[25]

[24] J. D. Freeman, "The Iban of Western Borneo," in George P. Murdock, ed., *Social Structure in Southeast Asia*, pp. 65-87.

[25] C. K. Yang, *The Chinese Family in the Communist Revolution*, Cambridge, Mass.: Technology Press, 1959; "Family Research around the World," *Marriage and Family Living*, 23 (1961), No. 2; "International Issue on the Family," *Marriage and Family Living*, 16 (1954), No. 4.

RESIDENCE AND CONTINUITY

Another source of variation in family forms related to the problem of continuity is that of residence. There are two patterns of residence—by marriage and by generation.

Marital rules of residence

Where does the married couple go to live? Murdock suggests the following alternatives: With the wife's family (matrilocal or uxorilocal residence), with the husband's family (patrilocal or virilocal residence), with either family of orientation (bilocal residence), or to a residence of the couple's own choice regardless of location (neolocal residence). Rarely, the rule of residence is that of living near an uncle (avunculocal residence).[26]

The importance of marital residence for family continuity is found in the supervision and socialization of children. If the wife goes to live with her husband's family, she is a stranger and at a general disadvantage in maintaining control over her children. If the husband lives with his wife's people (matrilocal residence), he too is at some disadvantage. However, if the couple does not live far from the husband's own family, he is less a stranger. The bilocal rule again provides some choice to the married couple and the residence may be chosen on the basis of least disadvantage. The rule believed to exist in contemporary American society is that of neolocal residence. Since this rule has not been systematically examined, it is possible that for different groups, matrilocal, patrilocal, or bilocal tendencies exist.

[26] George Peter Murdock, *Social Structure*, New York: Macmillan, 1949.

The description of normal residential patterns in a society is complicated by changes in the composition of the domestic group over time. Fortes suggests that there are three major phases in the developmental cycle of the domestic group. The first phase is one of expansion lasting from the marriage of two people to the adulthood of the last child. The second phase is one of dispersion. This phase begins with the marriage of the first child and ends with the marriage of the last child. The third phase, which Fortes calls the replacement phase, is one in which the domestic group consists of the old married couple. The third phase "ends with the death of the parents and the replacement in the social structure of the family they founded by the families of their children, more specifically, by the family of the father's heir amongst the children."[27]

Various changes in residential patterns can occur over the years. In societies in which the husband provides a bride service as payment for his wife, the married couple may reside with the wife's family until the husband has completed his obligations. This matrilocal period would occur in the expansion phase. Early socialization of children would involve the wife's relatives; the norms and values imparted to the children would be influenced by the matrilocal residence. After the husband has completed his bride service, the couple may then move to the husband's family. The dispersion and replacement phases would take place under conditions of patrilocal residence. The husband's relatives would be involved in the marriage of the children. Another complication in describing

[27] Meyer Fortes, "Introduction," in Jack Goody, ed., *The Developmental Cycle in Domestic Groups,* Cambridge: Cambridge University Press, 1958, p. 5.

residence patterns of domestic groups involves the beginning and the end of the dispersion phase. Freeman found
that among the Iban of Borneo, the oldest brother would
reside with his wife's family upon marriage; the youngest
son would remain on the family property and his wife
would move in.[28] The Iban are clearly bilocal in residence;
yet the term bilocal residence does not in itself suggest
the effect of birth order upon residence at marriage. Thus,
although the number of basic possibilities of residence at
marriage are few (matrilocal, patrilocal, bilocal, neolocal
and avunculocal), the time factor introduces many complications in norms for residence of married couples prevalent in a society.

Generational rules of residence

Several possibilities also exist with respect to rules of residence of children. Not all children are expected to live
with their mother and father as a single unit. In some societies, the children are supposed to live with their
mother; in other societies with their father; in still other
societies with other relatives; and in various societies with
groups of other children. Among the Fulani of the Sudan,
the homestead is arranged in such a way that the women
and girls sleep in shelters on one side of the compound,
while on the other side, separated by a leather rope, the
men and boys sleep. Even during the day, entry into the
female section of the household is forbidden to males and
the females are restricted to their side. Only the husband
and wife have a right of limited access to the other side.[29]

[28] Freeman, *op. cit.*
[29] Derrick J. Stenning, "Household Viability among the Pastoral

In the Israeli kibbutz, the children are raised by nurses and teachers; parents have only limited contact with the children. Only when the kibbutz children reach maturity do they cease living in age-graded dormitories.[30] Among the Tiwi of North Australia boys from the age of 14 to about 22 lived in the bush in small bands under the authority of their older male cross cousins (their fathers' sisters' sons).[31] Thus, the rules of residence for children vary greatly from society to society.

Eisenstadt has suggested that separate residence for the younger generation has important implications for family continuity.[32] In those societies in which there is marked differentiation by age groups and much authority in the family (as in Southeast Asia or in Scandinavia), separate residence of youth prevents conflict between younger people and their parents. In some societies each generation of young men forms its own village. The younger boys at first do not live entirely in the new village but as they mature they separate from the parental village. In the United States, in contrast, the young unmarried are generally expected to live at home except for short periods of military service or college. Frequently, however, completion of schooling or military service sig-

---

Fulani," in Jack Goody, ed., *The Developmental Cycle in Domestic Groups*, pp. 92-119.

[30] Y. Talmon-Garber, "Social Change and Family Structure," *International Social Science Journal*, 14 (1962), pp. 468-487.

[31] C. W. M. Hart and Arnold R. Pilling, *The Tiwi of North Australia*, New York: Holt, 1960.

[32] S. N. Eisenstadt, *From Generation to Generation: Age Groups and Social Structure*, Glencoe, Ill.: Free Press, 1956.

nifies adult status and the single individual may leave his parents' residence.

PRIORITIES IN FAMILY MAINTENANCE AND CONTINUITY

The manner by which family relations are maintained is important to the orderly replacement of one generation by another.

Two questions are pertinent. First: Which family relationship is the one emphasized as the basic unit of family maintenance in a particular society? The basic relationships defining rules of family maintenance (authority, property rights, emotional support, status in community) can be either the father-child unit, the mother-child unit, or the husband-wife unit in the family. The "basic maintenance unit" is also the pair whose relationship is the most *stable* in the family. The second question concerns the consequence of this unit for the maintenance of the family society: Does this pair as the basic unit for family maintenance promote continuity or discontinuity of the family?

In a society in which the father-child units form the basis for lineage definition, location, social status, and property inheritance, the mother-child form can be introduced as the *basic* family unit to maintain family life without continuity. In the Roman empire, a form of *connubium* known as *concubinatus* was practiced. If the man were married, *concubinatus* was not permitted nor was the unmarried man allowed to have more than one *concubinatus*. This "marriage" form was used mainly when a wealthy man wished to have family life for a time, but wanted to avoid some complications. In *dignitas* (official marriage), the man would be concerned with permanence of family life, inheritance problems, children, and *potestas* (authority). These problems did not arise in *concubinatus*. The children of *concubinatus* were not under the father's *potestas* (but instead were under their mother's *potestas*), nor could they inherit their father's property. The children belonged to the mother. In time of need, the children had to support their mother and, in turn, inherited their mother's property, which could not be inherited by the father. Hence, *concubinatus* permitted a sexual relationship outside of marriage, and at the same time, provided the children with rights in the mother-child unit. *Concubinatus* functioned without interfering with the basic patrilineal continuity of Roman society.[33]

When the mother-child relationship as the basic maintenance unit is carried into the matrilineal society (such as the Ashanti), this relationship does not interfere with family group continuity. The secondary father-child relationship is associated with discontinuity. According to Meyer Fortes, in Ashanti society (in Ghana, West Africa):

When a man marries, he acquires legal rights to his wife's marital fidelity and to domestic services such as the regular provision of his meals. If a wife commits adultery, her husband can claim damages from the other man and apologies and a gift of placation from the wife, even if, as often happens, he does not divorce her. He can and will insist on divorce if his wife neglects her household duties or refuses to sleep with him. The husband is in turn obliged to provide food, clothing

[33] Description based on Carle C. Zimmerman, *Family and Civilization*, New York: Harper, 1947.

and general care for his wife and children. If he fails in these duties, his wife can divorce him. In fact, divorce is very common among the Ashanti. Usually, it is free of acrimony, for it does not involve the splitting of a household. What an Ashanti man does not acquire by marriage are rights over his wife's reproductive powers, that is, over the children she bears him. These belong to her lineage, as opposed to his. An Ashanti man cannot demand help from his sons, for example in farming or in the payment of a debt, as he can from his sister's sons. He can punish his nephew, but not his sons. He can order his nieces to marry a man of his choice, but not his daughter. . . .

By the rule of matrilineal descent, a man can will no property to his own children; they belong to another household and another clan: his wife's. A man's heirs and successors are his sisters' sons. . . . In the Ashanti tradition the individual comes under the authority of the mother's brother, not the father.[34]

There are several similarities between the Roman *concubinatus* and the Ashanti marriage (as well as some differences). In both family forms, the relationship between mother and child forms the basic definition of the child's role in the society, the father has little control over the children, the children do not inherit the father's property, and neither form of "marriage" is necessarily permanent. A significant difference between the two forms, however, is that in *concubinatus* the mother-child unit is isolated from all other kinship structures whereas in the Ashanti form the mother's brother acts as a liaison between the mother-child unit and the rest of the kinship group. Al-

[34] Meyer Fortes, "Primitive Kinship," *Scientific American,* 200 (1959), pp. 147-156.

though the Ashanti people are matrilineal, the authority, inheritance obligations, assistance obligations, and permanent relationship of the mother's brother enable the mother-child unit to maintain continuity of the family group. The analysis indicates not only the consequence of the mother-child unit as the basic unit in defining property of the children, inheritance, and authority in a patrilineal versus a matrilineal society, but also the necessity of mother's brother role to maintain continuity in the Ashanti family. In his relations with his sister and her children, the brother finds stature, respect, and authority sustaining his role in maintaining the continuity of the lineage.

MATE SELECTION AS A CRITICAL POINT
IN FAMILY CONTINUITY

Rules regarding mate selection in a society are of crucial importance in determining the extent to which family culture will be preserved. Because of incest taboos, with only few exceptions, individuals must marry outside the domestic group. In some societies, the domestic group is defined as the nuclear family; in others, the domestic group may consist of the village, the tribe, or the compound. Since the bride and groom must come from different domestic groups, marriage seems to be the point at which new norms and values can most readily enter into family culture. If the norms and values of a particular family constitute a closed cultural system, then interchange of its family members with a member of another family would provide an opportunity for opening the system to external influences. Thus, at the point of marriage of the child both parental families are in danger of having their culture interrupted in transmission by the introduction of possibly contradictory values from the other family. Restrictions in the society on mate selection would delimit the direction of change in family cultures from one generation to the next. If certain families will permit marriage only with other families very similar to themselves in norms and values, then a general continuity of the cultures of both families can be expected.

Goode has approached the problem of restriction in mate selection not from the point of view of cultural transmission but from the point of view of maintaining the social classes in a society.[35] He has described patterns of control over courtship and mate selection in various societies. Amount of control is probably related to the extent to which financial consideration and social status are involved. The degree of control by parents over courtship has been described as: (a) child marriage (complete parental control), (b) definition by the parents of a class of eligible spouses, (c) isolation of young people from potential mates not of the parents' choice, (d) close supervision by relatives in courtship, and (e) informal control by parents and peer groups. In the last category the free selection of mates is preferred. Where kinship ties and social class lines are most blurred, the weakest parental control over mate selection would be expected and much discontinuity would occur.

Goode's discussion of restrictions on mate selection

[35] William J. Goode, "The Theoretical Importance of Love," *American Sociological Review*, 24 (1959), pp. 38-47.

does not take into account the great variety of marriage forms, the composition of marriage groups, the distinction between legitimate and nonlegitimate birth, or the distinction between sex relations and love. However, Goode does focus upon a crucial problem with respect to the continuity of family culture.

Summary

This chapter has been concerned with the definition of family culture. Culture is regarded as a concept which sensitizes us to look at "patterns for doing certain things in certain ways." The culture provides ready-made solutions to problems and enables people to predict the behavior of others. Aspects of culture which are particularly relevant to the study of the family are norms and values. The norms and values which people hold regarding courtship, marriage, divorce, kinship identity, and obligations, socialization of children, residence, and household maintenance are the elements of family culture. There are wide variations in the extent to which individuals are expected by their relatives to adhere to rules and procedures relating to family relations. Prescribed activities are those which the individual *must* perform; he is punished for failing to perform these activities. Preferred activities are those for whose performance an individual is rewarded but for whose nonperformance he is generally not punished. Kinship relations can be ascribed (attained merely by birth or sometimes marriage) or achieved (earned by performing certain activities). There are also wide variations in the content of culture. Each variation in the content of culture has particular implications for the orderly replacement of family culture in the succeeding generation.

The contemporary American family can be characterized as monogamous, bilateral, neolocal with respect to the married couple, having the nuclear family as the basic residential unit (i.e., the parents and their unmarried children), having the husband and wife as the basic maintenance unit, and having mate selection relatively uncontrolled by the parents. Part II of this book examines the implications of this combination of cultural attributes for orderly replacement.

Selected Readings

Variations in family organization in different societies are discussed in:

Gluckman, Max. *Conflict and Custom in Africa.* Free Press, 1955, pp. 54-80.

Goode, William J. "The Theoretical Importance of Love," *American Sociological Review,* 24 (1959), pp. 38-47.

Gough, E. Kathleen. "Is the Family Universal?—The Nayar Case," *Journal of the Royal Anthropological Institute,* 89 (1959). Reprinted in Norman W. Bell and Ezra F. Vogel (eds.), *A Modern Introduction to the Family,* Free Press, 1960, pp. 76-92.

Heath, Dwight. "Sexual Division of Labor and Cross-Cultural Research," *Social Forces,* 37 (1958), pp. 77-79.

Kluckhohn, Clyde. "Variations in the Human Family," in *The Family in a Democratic Society,* Columbia University Press, 1949, pp. 3-11.

Spiro, Melford. "Is the Family Universal?" *American Anthropologist,* 56 (1954), pp. 839-846. Reprinted with revisions in Bell and Vogel, *op. cit.,* pp. 64-75.

Specific cultural forms of family organization are described in:

Anshen, Ruth N. (ed.). *The Family: Its Function and Destiny.* Harper, 1959. (Negro-American, Latin American, Russian, Chinese, Indian, Negro-African, Islam.)

Burgess, Ernest W., Harvey J. Locke, and Mary Margaret Thomes. *The Family from Institution to Companionship.* American Book, 1963. (American rural and urban, Negro, Russian.)

Kenkel, William F. *The Family in Perspective.* Appleton-Century-Crofts, 1960. (Hebrew, Roman, early New England colonies, Trobriand, Russian, Israeli kibbutz.)

Kephart, William M. *The Family, Society, and the Individual.* Houghton Mifflin, 1961. (Experimental family organization—Mormon, Oneida community; Minority family types—Amish, Negro, Italian-American.)

Queen, Stuart A., Robert W. Habenstein, and John B. Adams. *The Family in Various Cultures.* Lippincott, 1961. (Toda, Hopi, Baganda, Chinese, Israeli kibbutz, Hebrew, Roman, early Christian, Anglo-Saxon, English, and colonial American.)

3 *The Incest Taboo and Its Extensions*

The prohibition of sexual intercourse between members of the same family who are not married to each other is generally called the incest taboo. Murdock suggests that by preventing the same family from being both a family of orientation (the nuclear family into which the individual is born) and a family of procreation (the nuclear family in which the individual is a husband or wife), the incest taboo provides a basis for the institution of marriage. An understanding of the basis of the incest taboo provides many insights into the operation of family and kinship systems.

This chapter will first define the concept of the incest taboo and will suggest that the incest taboo refers primarily to family and kinship relationships and only incidentally to sex. Second, the basis for the incest taboo will be discussed. The explanations offered by the traditional functionalist approach and the exogamy approach will be compared and an explanation based on the concept of orderly replacement will be proposed. Third, extensions of the incest taboo will be discussed. This discussion will consider (a) the relationship between lineage and the incest taboo, (b) situations in which sex relations occur between persons who cannot marry one another, and (c) prohibition of sex relations between persons who can marry. The discussion will suggest that extensions of the incest taboo are consistent with an explanation developed on the basis of the concept of orderly replacement.

The Incest Taboo

This section presents an elaboration of the definition of the incest taboo. An explanation of its basis follows.

DEFINITION OF THE INCEST TABOO

Many definitions of the incest taboo have been offered by social scientists. One difficulty in trying to define this taboo is that the prohibition of sex relations does not always refer to the same categories of persons. Murdock includes many distant kin in his definition. According to Murdock, incest is heterosexual intercourse which "takes place outside of marriage between two persons . . . related to one another by a real, assumed, or artificial bond of kinship which is culturally regarded as a bar to sex relations."[1] In contrast, Radcliffe-Brown restricts the incest taboo to the nuclear family. He indicates, "Incest is properly speaking the sin or crime of sexual intimacy between immedi-

---

[1] George Peter Murdock, *Social Structure*, New York: Macmillan, 1949, p. 261.

ate relatives within the family, father and daughter, mother and son, brother and sister."[2] This book will follow the Murdock definition although, to be sure, the term incest is most frequently applied to members of the nuclear family.

The Murdock definition is preferred here because of the close affinity between prohibition of sex relations and prohibition of marriage. In meaning, the incest taboo is not identical with the prohibition of marriage. Incest deals with a specific physical activity. Marriage is concerned with norms and values which define duties and obligations of the husband and wife as members of the nuclear family. Norms and values relating to marriage almost universally prescribe sexual access between the spouses but deny such access between members of any other combination in the nuclear family. In particular societies, this prohibition of sexual access may be extended to other kin. By this extension, the incest taboo becomes not merely a nuclear-family phenomenon but is associated also with rules of marriage. The major immediate significance of the incest taboo is seen here as lying in its influence upon marriage practices in a society.

The incest taboo refers primarily to family and kinship relationships and only incidentally to sex relations. In rules regarding incest, the same kind of avoidance behavior appears for both males and females; there is no role differentiation by sex. Moreover, if we regard the incest taboo mainly as a prescription relating to family and

---

[2] A. R. Radcliffe-Brown, "Introduction," in A. R. Radcliffe-Brown and Daryll Forde, eds., *African Systems of Kinship and Marriage*, Oxford University Press, 1950, p. 69.

kinship relationships, then we must also recognize the existence of rules permitting sex relations in situations which are isolated from a family and kinship context.

Is all incest equally serious in threatening the existing norms and values of family life in a society? Incest is more serious at certain times and with certain persons. Leach suggests that an individual's relationships with his relatives change over time and that individuals who are considered as "prohibited" relatives in youth may be considered as marriageable relatives at a later time.[3] However, Goody indicates that, among the LoDagaba of the African Gold Coast, having intercourse with a clanswoman before her marriage (that is, before her sexual powers had been committed to a member of another clan) was of minor importance; intercourse with the same woman after her marriage was severely punished. Among the Ashanti, sexual intercourse with the wife of a kinsman carries sanctions which are much lighter than intercourse with a blood relative. He points out that having sex relations with a member of the person's own clan would be punished by death or expulsion whereas having illicit relations with the wife of a clansman would demand only a special payment to the husband.[4] In contemporary society, incest between siblings would probably not arouse as much concern if the brother and sister were young adolescents engaging in sexual experimentation as it would if they

[3] E. R. Leach, "Concerning Trobriand Clans and the Kinship Category Tabu," in Jack Goody, ed., *The Developmental Cycle in Domestic Groups,* Cambridge: Cambridge University Press, 1958, pp. 120-145.

[4] Jack Goody, "A Comparative Approach to Incest and Adultery," *British Journal of Sociology,* 7 (1956), pp. 286-305.

were mature adults living together. Similarly, people would not be as concerned over sex relations between unmarried cousins as they would over incest between siblings. Presumably, the more distant the relationship (as distance between kin is defined in a particular society), the less does sexual access pose a threat to the stability and continuity of family norms and values.

On the basis of the Murdock definition of incest, the term "incestuous marriage" is a paradox. Since by definition incest occurs between persons of the same family who are not married to one another, how can there be incestuous marriage? Yet incestuous marriage will be discussed later in this chapter. By incestuous marriage is meant the marriage between nuclear-family members who are related by birth (brother-sister, father-daughter, or mother-son marriage). Incestuous marriage is prohibited in almost all societies. In those few instances where incestuous marriage is permitted, the privilege is reserved for a select few (for example, royalty and wealthy commoners in ancient Egypt, and the Azande royal clan).

THE BASIS FOR THE INCEST TABOO

The existence of a relationship between marriage regulations and the incest taboo suggests the question: What is the basis for the incest taboo? Understanding the basis for the incest taboo may provide additional insight into the workings of the contemporary family. Social scientists have suggested numerous explanations for the prevalence of the incest taboo. In the past, some anthropologists suggested that the incest taboo was instinctive.

However, with the decline of instinct as an explanation for the development of social phenomena, few anthropologists today hold this view. Instead, many of them follow Lowie in regarding the "horror of incest" as a very deeply rooted aspect of culture. At one time Lewis Morgan suggested that the incest taboo was developed because of the biological degeneration produced through inbreeding. However, the numerous exceptions to degeneration with inbreeding have led social scientists to disregard this theory. Still other anthropologists, Linton for one, acknowledge the existence of incest regulations but admit that they are unable to explain them.[5] This section will compare the traditional functionalist and exogamy explanations of the incest taboo.

From the point of view of orderly replacement, incestuous marriage would facilitate efficient transmission of family culture. Specifically, the orderly replacement of one generation of family life by the next could take place most efficiently if the only marriages permitted were those between brother and sister. There would then be no opportunity for the introduction of contradictory routines and practices into the particular family. Nevertheless, very few societies permit brothers to marry their sisters.

This section will also speculate upon family life in an imaginary society in which incestuous marriage is prescribed. This imaginary construct is intended to show that the incest taboo is in reality necessary for the orderly replacement of family culture from one generation to the next.

[5] See the summary of explanations presented in Leslie A. White, *The Science of Culture,* New York: Grove, 1949, pp. 303-329.

Functionalist and exogamy approaches

Perhaps the most plausible explanations of incest prohibition that have been offered are those formulated in terms of prehistoric permissiveness of incest. There are two general approaches—the traditional functionalist position emphasizing the unity of the nuclear family and the exogamy position emphasizing relationships between families.

As a functionalist, Malinowski regarded the sexual impulse as disruptive to stable social relations. Sex relations among all members of the nuclear family would not only foster jealousy and competition within the family but would also inhibit cooperative activities necessary for the security of the group. Parsons has indicated that specialization of roles in the nuclear family would be impeded if incest were permitted. Following Durkheim's suggestion that a division of labor creates solidarity among the individuals in a cooperative endeavor, Parsons reasoned that role differentiation in the family eases competitive pressures among family members and produces a sense of solidarity. The erotic relationship of the husband and wife symbolizes both their solidarity as a couple and their specialized roles in the family. The marital relationship thus embodies the generational and sexual role differentiation in the family. If parent-child marriage were permitted, marriage would no longer serve to solidify family relationships and to distinguish roles associated with generation and sex. Incest would thereby diminish role differentiation and, consequently, family solidarity. One may speculate that in Parsons' view the prohibition of incest would have become more rigorous as the family emerged as an institution. Inasmuch as Parsons sees the nuclear family in contemporary society as increasing rather than decreasing in role specialization, he would probably forecast an increase in the "horror" of incest in the modern world. In brief, social scientists in the functionalist tradition (such as Malinowski and Parsons) see the incest taboo as generated to maintain the unity of the nuclear family.[6]

Many social scientists have regarded the incest taboo as developing parallel to the practice of exogamy. White regards mutual security and aid in primitive groups as requiring cooperation not only of the family members but also of other groups in the territory. Intermarriage between families provides a basis for alliances which maintain cooperation.[7] Levi-Strauss has suggested that the incest prohibition is founded on a principle of reciprocity. He viewed marriage as an exchange in which one lineage becomes a debtor and the other lineage a creditor in a perpetual mutual obligation to supply women in marriage. Assumptions made by Levi-Strauss were that women in prehistoric society were regarded as property and that there was a scarcity of women for marriage. He based his assumption of a scarcity of women upon a putative polygamous nature of males and the greater attractiveness of some females than others. The welfare of the individual family is enhanced by its having women as a commodity to exchange with other families. However, more

[6] Talcott Parsons, "The Incest Taboo in Relation to Social Structure and the Socialization of the Child," *British Journal of Sociology*, 5 (1954), pp. 101-117, and Talcott Parsons and Robert F. Bales, *Family, Socialization and Interaction Process*, Glencoe, Ill.: Free Press, 1955.

[7] White, *op. cit.*

important for Levi-Strauss is the establishment of alliances for the purpose of sustaining creditor-debtor reciprocities between families. Through the creation of women-trading alliances, the incest taboo lays the basis for the development of groups larger than the individual family.[8]

The Levi-Strauss conception of marriage and incest is somewhat similar to that of McLennan. As was indicated in an earlier chapter, McLennan suggested that girl babies were killed to enhance the ability of a particular horde to defend itself. The resultant shortage of females required the horde to develop exogamous practices to maintain itself. The major difference between Levi-Strauss and McLennan is that whereas McLennan posits a warlike existence, Levi-Strauss assumes the presence of an exchange system. Unintentionally perhaps, Levi-Strauss appears to be operating with a social-contract view of society. This social contract, like that proposed by Locke, is developed for the mutual security of individuals by placing limits on the freedom of man to engage in conflict and exploitation. McLennan, on the other hand, appears to have used a Hobbes-like assumption of a natural state of war with exogamy (marrying outside the group) as a means for limiting this warlike state of existence. In exogamy not only do groups set up obligations with one another but they also donate women as hostages to each other. At any rate, both views suggest an original state out of which emerged a social contract involving exogamy and the taboo of brother-sister marriage.

[8] J. P. B. De Josselin De Jong, *Levi-Strauss' Theory on Kinship and Marriage,* Leiden: Brill, 1952.

There is a tendency, on the part of the functionalists who stress intrafamily factors in explaining the incest taboo, to focus upon parent-child sex relations whereas the social scientists who utilize the exogamy explanation emphasize sibling sex relations. In support of the traditional functionalist explanation, Brenda Seligman has pointed out that if a girl in a matrilineal society has sexual intercourse with her father she is doing so with a person outside her lineage. By rules of exogamous marriage, sex relations between persons of different lineages are permitted. Hence, according to Seligman, this father-daughter case would not be incest since membership in different lineages permits persons to have sex relations. She concludes that exogamy cannot provide an explanation for the taboo on incest.[9] However, in support of the exogamy explanation it may be noted that in many domestic units both in primitive and contemporary societies the parents share their abode with married children and the presence of subfamilies does not interfere with the authority and roles of the parents. Conceivably, the nuclear family could remain intact with brother-sister incest permitted. Hence, contrary to Parsons' discussion, the restriction of erotic relationship to the parents may not be necessary for maintaining the role differentiation and solidarity of the nuclear family. Both the traditional functionalist and exogamy explanations are open to criticism when the possibility of parent-child incest is discussed in relation to exogamy and when sibling incest is discussed in relation to role differentiation in the family.

[9] Brenda Z. Seligman, "The Problem of Incest and Exogamy: A Restatement," *American Anthropologist*, 52 (1950), pp. 305-316.

Prescribed incestuous marriage—
an imaginary construct

Instead of assuming that an original state of family life existed from which the incest taboo developed, let us imagine that a society exists in which brothers and sisters can marry only one another. What would be the characteristics of family life in such a society? The imagined construction of a society based on incestuous marriage may provide a perspective for viewing the contemporary family.

1. In the imagined society, each individual is obviously very much limited in marriage choice. Since the list of eligible spouses will generally comprise no more than three or four other individuals, little ceremonial courtship behavior can be expected. There being no economic considerations (such as dowry or bride price), girls probably marry upon puberty. To maintain clear distinctions between family lines, monogamy is the prescribed form of marriage.

2. If an average of six children in a family reach adolescence, only half of the families can expect to have an equal number of boys and girls to be matched as mates.[10] Because of the relatively small number of families able to marry off all children to siblings, rules must be developed covering the marriage of extra brothers or sisters. Inasmuch as there are only boy children or only girl children in some families, the society must accept the phenomenon of bachelorhood and solve the problem of what to do

[10] Wilson D. Wallis, "The Origin of Incest Rules," *American Anthropologist*, 52 (1950), pp. 277-279.

with the family property when the last of the bachelor children die. In addition, in a single-sex set of siblings, there are problems with regard to the division of labor. In this society, roles must be assigned on some basis other than sex, perhaps birth order.

3. Since marriage is permitted only with siblings, there are few chances for divorce and remarriage. Remarriage is feasible only if two pairs of siblings are dissatisfied at the same time. Another difficulty is that upon remarriage, a number of half-sibling relationships are established. Can these half-brothers and half-sisters marry? If the society sticks rigorously with its brother-sister marriage system, they cannot. The practice of divorce will then restrict the number of eligible spouses very severely. Since divorces, as in most societies, take place when the couples are relatively young, numerous children have no siblings available for marriage (having only one sibling of the same sex or being only children).

4. Since marital relationships are kept strictly within the family, the individuals have little opportunity for familiar or joking relationships which characterize intimate relatives in many societies. In order to maintain a given marriage, a family can rely only upon avoidance relationships between brothers and sisters who are not married to one another. There is thus little opportunity for carrying on flirtations, love affairs, and sex play either within or outside the family. Within-sex familiarities are encouraged at the expense of those between the sexes. This emphasis upon single-sex solidarity fosters latent and manifest homosexual activities. Most individuals in the society are restrained and socially withdrawn, especially from

outsiders. The restraint must be exercised because individuals outside the nuclear family can easily disrupt the pattern of social relations in the incestuous family.

Evidence for the above characterization of interpersonal relations in the incestuous family exists in materials relative to the Vongara royal clan of the Azande people in central Africa. Evans-Pritchard found that this clan encouraged father-daughter and sibling intercourse among its members. A common practice was for a Vongara to marry a half-sister by a different mother. Divorce was difficult and the women took male and female lovers. Since the clan was a military unit, solidarity among males was important. In the clan, homosexuality was widespread and, particularly among males, it was openly practiced and recognized. Unlike the commoners in Azande society, members of the Vongara clan were reserved and suspicious in their relations with outsiders. Whereas the commoners practiced blood-brotherhood to maintain alliances, members of the Vongara clan did not. Although the Azande material does not pertain specifically to a society practicing incestuous marriage exclusively, the characteristics of the Vongara are generally consistent with those to be expected in a society practicing prescribed incestuous marriage.[11]

[11] The materials on the Vongara clan of the Azande people are based upon Thomas, *op. cit.*, and the Human Relations Area Files. References in the HRAF include Charles G. Seligman and Brenda Z. Seligman, *Pagan Tribes of Nilotic* Sudan, London: Routledge, 1932; Edward E. Evans-Pritchard, "Social Character of Bride Wealth, with Special Reference to the Azande," *Man*, 34 (1934), pp. 172-175; P. M. Larken, "An Account of the Zande," *Sudan Notes and Records*, 9 (1926-1927), pp. 1-55 and 85-134; Edward

The severe limitations on interpersonal relationships where brother-sister marriage is the prescribed form suggest that a family system based on incestuous marriage would be difficult to maintain. There would be many discontinuities in family life through (a) childlessness and the presence of superfluous unmarried siblings, (b) much tension because of the difficulties in breaking off a marriage fraught with conflict, (c) high incidence of homosexuality, and (d) much restraint necessary in interaction to avoid the mingling of families. The maintenance of the incestuous marriage system would require close supervision by parental authorities and a system of harsh sanctions for violation of the marriage rules prescribing incest.

While the maintenance of an exclusively incestuous marriage system would be difficult, the continuity of family culture through a completely closed social system could not occur on any other basis. If divorce were readily allowed, if superfluous siblings were permitted to marry outside the family, if half-siblings could marry, and if dalliance and flirtations were allowed, family continuity would be threatened. Once the exclusively incestuous relationship is violated in the practice of marriage, there is no basis for maintaining the nuclear family as an independent descent group. The organization of the Vongara as a *clan* rather than a number of royal family lines stems from the fact that they did permit departures from incestuous marriage. Perhaps this departure from prescribed incestuous marriage occurred because of the dif-

E. Evans-Pritchard, "Witchcraft (Mangu) Among the A-Zande," *Sudan Notes and Records,* 12 (1929), pp. 163-249.

ficulty in maintaining such a system. Only in exceptional cases where the transmission of property or power is at stake would the severe limitations of incestuous marriage be worth the personal sacrifices entailed.

Although the discussion of prescribed incestuous marriage was presented mainly in terms of brother-sister marriage, parent-child marriage offers more than comparable difficulties. With a short life span prevalent in most primitive societies, few parents would survive long enough to produce offspring with all of their children.[12] In addition, as Davis has indicated, many problems would arise in developing role expectations for a child born in a father-daughter marriage. The child would be his mother's half-brother, his mother's mother's stepson, his mother's brother's half-brother, and paradoxically his father's grandchild. Numerous contradictions in authority and role would arise. Should the child act toward his mother as a half-brother or as a son? Should he act toward his uncle as a half-brother? Being a member of two generations simultaneously might produce many conflicts for the child in his relations with the rest of the family. Because of these contradictions, regulation of family life would be difficult.[13]

In summary, the marriage system in which brother-sister or parent-child marriage is the only prescribed form as a completely closed kinship arrangement in the society exists nowhere in reality. This system would entail an

[12] Mariam Kreiselman Slater, "Ecological Factors in the Origin of Incest," *American Anthropologist*, 61 (1959), pp. 1042-1059.

[13] Kingsley Davis, *Human Society*, New York: Macmillan, 1949, p. 403.

extremely limited set of potential spouses for any individual; family culture would tend to remain intact from generation to generation until the line became extinct; numerous prohibitions would exist with respect to male-female social relationships; and social relationships would be stable. However, because of personnel problems incestuous marriage is unworkable.

Since incestuous marriage as the prescribed form of marriage would be unworkable, society must look for the next-best plan for orderly replacement of family culture from one generation to the next. If incestuous marriage cannot exist because of personnel problems, at least families can restrict marriage of their members to other families whose norms and values resemble their own. By intermarrying with culturally duplicate families, a particular family can maintain orderly replacement of its culture and avoid the personnel difficulties of incestuous marriage.[14] Accordingly, lineages, clans, and other similar kinship arrangements operate as mechanisms for establishing clear family and kinship identities of individuals (by prescribing exogamy) and for promoting orderly replacement (by intermarriage with culturally similar lineages or clans).

[14] The practice of cross-cousin marriage is of interest here. A cross cousin is the child of a father's sister or of a mother's brother. A parallel cousin is the child of a father's brother or a mother's sister. Under a matrilineal or patrilineal system, cross cousins would not belong to the same lineage; parallel cousins, however, would belong to the same lineage. The practice of cross-cousin marriage, a preferential arrangement in many primitive societies, would ensure intermarriage with a culturally similar family group which has a separate kinship identity.

This section has explained the relevance of the incest taboo for the development of lineages and other kinship arrangements on the basis of the unworkability of incestuous marriage and the tendency of orderly replacement in family life. Attention is now directed to the extensions of the incest taboo beyond the nuclear family.

Extensions of the Incest Taboo

Many societies permit nonmarital sex relations. Of the 250 societies described in the Human Relations Area Files established by Murdock, 65 permit unmarried and unrelated persons complete freedom in sexual matters, and 20 others give qualified consent, whereas only 54 (about a fifth) forbid or disapprove premarital liaisons between nonrelatives, and many of these allow sex relations between specified relatives such as cross cousins.

Even after marriage, many societies permit sexual intercourse with a person other than the spouse. In 126 (roughly half) of the societies in the Human Relations Area Files, sexual intercourse between persons who are married but not to each other is forbidden. Such intercourse is permitted freely in only 24. However, a married man can have sexual intercourse with one or more of his female relatives, including his wife's sister, in 41 societies.[15]

If there were a perfect correlation between availability for marriage and sexual access outside marriage, the task of determining extensions of the incest taboo would be simple. We would merely have to examine which particular persons could participate in nonmarital sex relations and which could not. However, in each society there

[15] Murdock, *op. cit.*

are provisions for sex relations between persons who are not allowed to marry (or with whom marriage is not preferred) and there may be restrictions on sex relations between persons who can marry one another.

The discussion in this section includes (a) the relationship between lineage and extensions of the incest taboo, (b) situations in which sex relations occur between persons not eligible or not preferred for marriage with one another, and (c) prohibition of sex relations between persons who can marry one another. The discussion is intended to indicate that lineage, which exists to facilitate orderly replacement, is a major factor in particular prohibitions of sex relations. Those societies in which matrilineage or patrilineage dominates individual activity will be found to present certain characteristic restrictions on nonmarital sex relations. On the other hand, sex relations between persons who are ineligible for marriage tend to be isolated from the kinship system.

LINEAGE AND NONMARITAL SEX RELATIONS

Control of nonmarital sex relations would be most urgent when the child born of such a union interferes with kinship relations in a society. Under the permissive norms of societies, cross-sexual intimate relations (including coitus) tend to occur between individuals who are available for marriage according to kinship rules and tend to be restricted between individuals for whom marriage is forbidden. Availability for intimate relations can occur either prior to marriage (premarital availability) or after marriage (postmarital availability). Since lineage to a large extent determines marriage rules, the problem with which inquirers are concerned becomes: How is variation in availability (both premarital and postmarital) related to kinship lineage?

Murdock has surveyed premarital availability and has, in general, found it related to extensions of the incest taboo in the extended family.[16] Availability after marriage can occur, as Murdock has indicated, when the cross-sex partner is a potential secondary spouse in polygamy. In addition, a high divorce rate suggests that in a bilateral lineage system, even marriage may not remove any individual from availability as a potential mate. Hence, in a bilateral system, tabooed (and avoidance) relationships are at a minimum, availability at a maximum, and there is no need for an elaborate classification of kinship arrangements. In contrast, unilineal systems set up a complex arrangement of restrictions.

Several illustrations can be given to indicate the relationship between variation in intimate relations and lineage.

For example, Hoebel has found that among the Cheyenne, who at the time were tending toward matrilinearity and were normally matrilocal, a man should never speak to his mother-in-law, he should never be alone with her, and he should cover his head in her presence. This norm eliminates opportunities for familiarity, on the one hand, or conflict, on the other. Although a daughter-in-law is permitted to speak and to be in the same lodge with her husband's father, she must show respect to him. In contrast, since every sister-in-law is potentially a second wife

16 *Ibid.*

(with preferential levirate and sororate marriage), familiarity and courtship behavior between the man and his sister-in-law are encouraged.[17]

The Cheyenne can be compared with the Miao. The Magpie Miao, originally from the Yangtze plain of China, but later spreading into various parts of Southeast Asia, are ordinarily patrilineal and patrilocal. Monogamous marriage is the rule.

A son-in-law defers to the opinions of his wife's parents, and his respect for them approaches avoidance in the case of his mother-in-law. Avoidance also prevails between a daughter-in-law and her husband's father.[18]

The avoidance patterns of the Cheyenne and Miao also suggest that in unilineal societies, both avoidance and familiarity patterns tend to be highly specific with respect to potential sexual partners. In Miao society, marriage between consanguineal kin or parallel cousins is forbidden. However, cross-cousin marriage (FaSisDau and MoBroSon) is favored and sex relations between unmarried cross cousins are "freely permitted and taken as a matter of course." How is the cousin sex relationship reflected in social relationships among the Miao?

The interaction of cousins, both cross- and parallel-cousins and regardless of sex, is characterized by privileged familiarity which permits teasing and mild joking. This takes a much

[17] Edward A. Hoebel, *The Cheyennes: Indians of the Great Plains,* New York: Holt, 1960.

[18] Ruey Yih-Fu, "The Magpie Miao of Southern Szechuan," in George P. Murdock, ed., *Social Structure in Southeast Asia,* New York: Wenner-Gren Foundation, 1960, pp. 154-155.

more extreme form between cross-cousins, where such behavior becomes obligatory and finds expression in singing and
dancing, in practical jokes, and in sexual play.

A man is more restrained in his behavior toward his maternal parallel-cousins than with his cross-cousins . . . and he
can neither marry nor have sex relations with his mother's
sister's daughter.[19]

Chahar society in Mongolia, like the Magpie Miao
group, is monogamous, patrilineal, and patrilocal. Among
the Chahar people, a symmetrical cross-cousin marriage
was permitted (FaSiSon to marry MoBrDau) as was
marriage between maternal first cousins (MoSiSon to
marry MoDau). In social relationships:

Cross-cousins were treated with less reserve than paternal
cousins. Maternal cousins were treated with complete freedom—"They are more like friends than relatives and you can
do anything you want with them." . . . The relationship between a married woman and her husband's parents was somewhat like that between a daughter and her own parents, but
more reserved and "distant." . . . With her husband's brothers
[whom she could marry], a married woman had a differential
relationship depending upon the relative age of her husband
and his brothers. An elder brother could not . . . remain alone
in her presence; in a group of people he could never joke
with her—"The elder brother never sees the younger brother's
wife." On the other hand, a younger brother might remain
alone with an elder brother's wife and joke freely with her,
during the day; after dark, however, he should never be alone
with her.[20]

[19] *Ibid.*, p. 155.
[20] Herbert Harold Breeland, III, *Mongol Community and Kinship Structure,* New Haven: Human Relations Area Files, 1957,
pp. 174-175.

How is the avoidance-familiarity pattern related to type of lineage? In the bilateral family, the nuclear family is generally a highly differentiated kinship unit which tends to live independently of kin. Moreover, little distinction is made in social relationships between affinal (in-laws) and consanguine (blood) relatives. Hence, the major distinctions of avoidance and familiarity are made with respect to persons inside and outside the nuclear family and there is little reason for strict regulation of familiarity and avoidance among various classes of relatives. Familiarity between the sexes, assortive mating, a high status of women, and high divorce rate in the bilateral family reflect the high degree of availability after marriage as well as before marriage.

In the bilateral system, restrictions on intimate relationships, even when they occur, do not seem to be clearly defined. The kinship system of the Chiricahua Apache was bilateral, but residence was matrilocal. All relatives of the opposite sex of the same generation were called a common term and were expected to have a formal, reserved, or avoidance relationship. Such a relationship was considered a privilege. However, children and adolescents were not expected to participate in a polite or avoidance relationship. With sororal polygyny permitted, the married adult sisters of the wife *tended* to use the polite form of speech with their sister's husband, while unmarried sisters did not. Most important for availability as potential spouses was the following: Although the use of the polite form was expected among opposite-sex relatives of the same generation, this formal relationship could be terminated by mutual consent. Frequently, use of the polite form was theoretically possible, but did not take place in practice.[21] This feature of the Chiricahua Apache system suggests that restrictions on intimate relationships among bilateral societies tend to be abandoned when these restrictions interfere with regulations concerning availability for marriage. The restrictions on intimate relationships among relatives do not appear to be crucial for maintaining the bilateral kinship system.

In a unilineal society, however, care must be taken to preserve the "purity" of the lineage. Where the nonlineage member of the family (wife in the patrilineal system and husband in the matrilineal) is not yet well integrated into the spouse's social world, family members have little loyalty to this outsider. Intimate behavior with this outside member is to be avoided. Intimacy would violate the "social placement" of children and engender jealousy and conflict within the kinship group. Most avoidance rules seem to center about the spouse outside the lineage. On the other hand, to ensure the continuity of preferred lineage relations, intimacy is stimulated among potential mates. Thus, the polygamous Cheyenne permitted familiarity between the husband and his wife's sisters, the patrilineal Miao encouraged familiar behavior among cross cousins, and the patrilineal Chahar permitted intimate behavior with maternal cousins.

In summary, the discussion has suggested that residence, composition of the marriage group, and especially lineage are related to availability under marriage rules

[21] Morris E. Opler, "An Outline of Chiricahua Apache Social Organization," in Fred Eggan, ed., *Social Anthropology of North American Tribes,* Chicago: University of Chicago Press, 1937, pp. 173-239.

and intimacy of cross-sex nonmarital relationships. Bilateral kinship, minimum restriction of residential location, and multimarriage (for example, polygyny) are related to high availability of individuals for cross-sex intimate relationship.

The fact that nonmarried persons who are eligible for marriage with each other are permitted to have nonmarital sex relations does not imply that the elders of the society regard premarital and extramarital sexual intercourse as *preferred* forms of interaction for younger people. Instead, it means that participants in nonmarital sex relations are not punished severely (if they are punished at all) when they are eligible for marriage to each other. A high value placed upon premarital virginity will generally counteract this permissiveness. Premarital chastity will be discussed later in this chapter.

SEX RELATIONS BETWEEN PERSONS NOT ELIGIBLE TO MARRY EACH OTHER

Sometimes a society will permit sex relations between persons who are not eligible mates according to the rules of marriage prevalent in that society. The persons may be ineligible for marriage by law or because their respective social groups strongly discourage such a marriage. The norms governing sexual intercourse between ineligible persons tend to be such that this intercourse has little or no direct consequence for family and kinship relations. Four of the possible situations in which sex relations are permitted between ineligible persons are prostitution, secret and anonymous affairs, concubine-mistress arrangements, and periods in which conventions are suspended.

Prostitution[22]

A prostitute is defined as a woman who engages in sex relations for payment. Prostitution as an organized set of practices has occurred for religious purposes, for raising a dowry, for government financing, and as a commercial enterprise. Regardless of purpose, however, there has always been a tendency to isolate practicing prostitutes from the kinship system. From earliest times, the religious or commercial brothel and the "red light" district or its equivalent have isolated prostitutes residentially. Prostitutes have also been isolated from kinship and family life by compulsory distinctive appearance. According to Flexner, licensed prostitutes in medieval Europe were sometimes forced to wear special clothes. In ancient Rome, prostitutes not only had to wear distinctive dress, but also to dye their hair or wear wigs. Moreover, isolation from normal family life is enhanced by the fact that prostitution is often more than an occupation; it is a way of life inconsistent with the norms and values associated with family and kinship. The impression of the writers of the British Wolfenden Report was that "the great majority of prostitutes are women whose psychological make-up is such that they choose this life because they find in it a style of living which is to them easier, freer and more profitable than would be provided by any other occupa-

[22] This section is based upon Abraham Flexner, *Prostitution in Europe*, New York: Century, 1914; T. E. James, *Prostitution and the Law*, London: Heinemann, 1951; Committee on Homosexual Offenses and Prostitution, *The Wolfenden Report*, New York: Stein and Day, 1963.

tion." However, prostitution is not a lifelong occupation. "Prostitutes disappear rather than die." A large proportion of prostitutes eventually marry and participate in the normal family and kinship life of the society.

Secret and anonymous affairs

A second form of sexual liaison between persons who are not eligible for marriage to one another is the secret and/ or anonymous affair. Secret and anonymous affairs are generally of short duration. If they are prolonged, nonparticipants become aware of the situation and, if anonymity is involved, the participants may learn each other's identity. By the very maintenance of secrecy and anonymity, these affairs are effectively isolated from family and kinship relationships.

Although the anonymous affair is by definition restricted to strangers, the secret affair frequently occurs in small communities. In many primitive groups, secret meetings take place either in isolated quarters in the dark of night or in dense vegetation by day.

Concubine-mistress arrangements

The term mistress is used here as a general term to describe a woman who maintains a sexual liaison ordinarily of indefinite duration outside of marriage. Either or both partners may have a spouse. If the mistress is unmarried and is being "kept" by the man, her home or apartment ordinarily serves as a rendezvous, isolated from his family life. Especially in the case of the concubine, the man provides the necessary economic means for maintaining the woman. The concubine in Roman society was juridically isolated from the rights and duties of family life associated with the patrilineage. The concubine and her children had no inheritance rights, the man had no power over her children. If the mistress is married, other means are usually found for segregating the love relationship from family life. In some societies where divorce is not permitted (such as Italy), there is often a tacit understanding between husband and wife that the husband will have a mistress, but at the same time, he is expected to be "discreet" in handling his extramarital affairs.

Liaison with a mistress differs from the irregular marriage among many groups of low socioeconomic status in that: (a) in the low socioeconomic groups the woman at least hopes that the arrangement will be a permanent one while the mistress knows that the relationship will last only as long as mutual erotic interest is maintained; and (b) in the low socioeconomic groups the issue of children is taken for granted whereas in the man-mistress relationship children are inimical to the sexual bond. The liaison in the low socioeconomic groups is intended to merge with other family and kinship activities; the man-mistress relationship ends when the erotic interest is gone and familial and kinship duties enter into the relationship.[23]

Periods in which conventions are suspended

In many societies, there are certain periods during which

[23] See Hyman Rodman, "Marital Relationships in a Trinidad Village,'" *Marriage and Family Living*, 23 (1960), pp. 166-170; and

the restrictions and norms governing everyday life are suspended. Usually these occur during festivals, funerals, initiation rites, and other occasions when there is much emotional fervor generated. W. I. Thomas has reported that among the Fiji islanders, where brothers and sisters have avoidance relationships with one another, they may join in the orgiastic celebration accompanying initiation rites and at this time may even have sexual intercourse with one another. After the celebration, of course, they must again resume their avoidance relationship.[24] Frequently, in defloration rites which precede marriage, men who are ordinarily forbidden sexual access by incest taboos may have intercourse with the girl.[25] The suspensions of sexual restrictions in these examples are isolated from the rules of family and kinship relations by their occurrence at a particular time which everyone in the society regards as "separate" from the conventional rules of living.

This section has discussed various situations in which persons who are ineligible for marriage to one another participate in sex relations. These situations are prostitution, secret and anonymous affairs, concubine-mistress arrangements, and periods in which the ordinary conventions of the society are suspended. In each situation, the participants and the society developed modes of conduct

---

"On Understanding Lower-Class Behavior," *Social and Economic Studies*, 8 (1959), pp. 441-450.

[24] William I. Thomas, *Primitive Behavior*, New York: McGraw-Hill, 1937, p. 265.

[25] *Ibid.*, p. 270.

which isolate the sexual liaison from family and kinship relations. The incest taboo is essentially a norm related to kinship and not to sex as such. These exceptions to the positive relationship between marriage availability and nonmarital sexual accessibility represent activities outside the realm of family relations. Hence, these exceptions are not directly relevant in dealing with problems of orderly replacement of family culture from one generation to the next.

PREMARITAL CHASTITY AND AVAILABILITY FOR MARRIAGE

However general the tendency for persons eligible for marriage with each other to be sexually accessible, a high value placed upon virginity prior to marriage places a restriction on this tendency. In feudal Chinese society, many precautions were taken to segregate unmarried girls so that their virginity would be protected. In the Philippines, as in other Catholic countries with a Spanish background, the chaperone is used to guard the girl's chastity. Although Philippine parents do not actually choose the spouse for their children, there is parental pressure to marry a "well-liked second cousin" and some parental attempt to control mate selection.[26] Similarly, among the ancient Hebrews, virginity of girls in high-status families was highly valued. Proof of lack of virginity at marriage could lead to severe sanctions, including the girl's being stoned to death (Deuteronomy 22:20-21). These three

[26] William F. Nydegger and Corinne Nydegger, "Tarong: An Ilocos Barrio in the Philippines," in Beatrice B. Whiting, ed., *Six Cultures*, New York: Wiley, 1963, pp. 697-867.

examples have been drawn from diverse cultures. Yet they have in common the active role played by parents in selecting a mate for their child. This similarity suggests that premarital virginity is connected with avoidance relationships of eligible young people in societies in which marriage is arranged by parents. If sexual liaisons were permitted before marriage, the young people could form personal commitments which would interfere with the parent's choice. Premarital chastity is then merely one aspect of the avoidance relationships which facilitate parental choice. The tradition of premarital chastity in contemporary society will be sustained to the extent that parents participate in the mate selection of their children. Premarital chastity is in effect an adjunct to the incest taboo in facilitating orderly replacement.

Summary

This chapter has discussed the incest taboo and its extensions. The incest taboo is the prohibition of sexual intercourse between males and females who are related to one another by a bond of kinship which is regarded as a bar to sex relations. The strongest restrictions are placed upon sex relations between father and daughter, mother and son, and brother and sister. However, the incest taboo can be extended to cover any kinship relationship. Because rules of marriage involve sex relations, there is a correlation between prohibition of sex relations and prohibition of marriage. The basis for the incest taboo may lie in the difficulty of providing for orderly replacement by incestuous marriage. Because of personnel difficulties in maintaining incestuous marriage, patterns of intermarriage between culturally similar families have developed. These patterns refer to lineages which intermarry with one another. The practice of intermarriage with particular culturally similar lineages has the effect of facilitating orderly replacement without the personnel problems of incestuous marriage. The extension of the incest taboo to other members of the lineage appears to have developed to maintain kinship identity and thereby to avoid some of the difficulties of incestuous marriage.

If there were a perfect correlation between prohibition of sexual access to another person and prohibition of marriage, then the incest taboo could be employed to explain all variations in marriage availability. However, there are some situations in which sex relations are permitted but marriage is not; other situations exist in which marriage is permitted but nonmarital sex relations are not. Prostitution, secret and anonymous affairs, concubine-mistress arrangements, and periods during which ordinary conventions of the society are suspended were noted as situations in which sex relations between ineligibles could occur. In each situation, the participants developed modes of conduct which isolated the sexual liaison from family and kinship relationships. Hence, these situations are not directly relevant to problems of the orderly replacement of family culture from one generation to the next.

Availability for marriage coupled with sexual inaccessibility occurs in societies where a high value is placed upon premarital chastity. This restriction on sexual access between unmarried persons may be related to the control over mate selection by parents. Avoidance relationships between unmarried persons facilitate the ability of the parents to engage in mate selection for their children. Premarital chastity is one aspect of this avoidance relationship, and thus an adjunct to the incest taboo in facilitating orderly replacement.

The following chapter on the contemporary American family utilizes the approach to the incest taboo developed here to indicate how changes in the American kinship system are related to various trends in availability for marriage.

Selected Readings

The relationship between the incest taboo and kinship arrangements is discussed in:

De Jong, J. P. B. De Josselin. *Levi-Strauss' Theory on Kinship and Marriage*. Leiden: E. J. Brill, 1952.

Goody, Jack. "A Comparative Approach to Incest and Adultery," *British Journal of Sociology*, 7 (1956), pp. 286-305.

Middleton, Russell. "Brother-Sister and Father-Daughter Marriage in Ancient Egypt," *American Sociological Review*, 27 (1962), pp. 603-611.

Murdock, George Peter. *Social Structure*. Macmillan, 1949.

Parsons, Talcott. "The Incest Taboo in Relation to Social Structure and the Socialization of the Child," *British Journal of Sociology*, 5 (1954), pp. 101-117.

Slater, Mariam Kreiselman. "Ecological Factors in the Origin of Incest," *American Anthropologist*, 61 (1959), pp. 1042-1059.

White, Leslie A. "The Definition and Prohibition of Incest," *American Anthropologist*, 50 (1958), pp. 416-435.

Contemporary Family and Kinship

4 A Conceptual Model
of the Contemporary Family

This chapter is intended to provide a framework for the study of the family in contemporary society. A conceptual model of the contemporary family is described and, to some extent, evaluated through comparison with other views of the family.

Various conceptual schemes have been developed to describe the major features of contemporary family life.[1] These approaches, however, regard family relationships either as an adjunct of other institutions or as a result of the interplay of psychological forces.[2] The family is not

[1] For example, Ernest W. Burgess, Harvey J. Locke, and Mary Margaret Thomes, *The Family*, New York: American Book, 1963; Kingsley Davis, *Human Society*, New York: Macmillan, 1949; Talcott Parsons and Robert F. Bales, *Family, Socialization and Interaction Process*, Glencoe, Ill.: Free Press, 1955.

[2] See William J. Goode, "The Sociology of the Family," in Robert K. Merton, Leonard Broom, and Leonard S. Cottrell, Jr., eds., *Sociology Today*, New York: Basic Books, 1959, pp. 179-

conceived in these approaches as a functionally autonomous institution which interacts with other institutions in the society.

The conceptual model described here does not require specific assumptions about other institutions in the society; instead, it is based upon the relationship between lineage system and availability of individuals for marriage. First, this chapter will discuss the assumptions contributing to the model. Some of the assumptions are consistent with orderly replacement (closed system); other assumptions are consistent with universal, permanent availability of persons in a society as mates (open system); and still other assumptions are concerned with the conflict between orderly replacement and universal, permanent availability. Second, evidence will be presented to indicate the relevance of the model to contemporary American society. Third, the permanent-availability model will be compared with the concept of companionship family developed by Burgess and with the functional-differentiation view of Parsons.

Assumptions Contributing to the Model

ASSUMPTIONS CONSISTENT WITH ORDERLY REPLACEMENT

This section will review briefly assumptions about orderly replacement presented in Chapter 1. It will indicate the kinds of norms and values consistent with orderly replacement and the kinds of social control required to maintain the family as a closed social system from one generation to the next.

---

186. An exception is Carle C. Zimmerman, *Family and Civilization,* New York: Harper, 1947.

If orderly replacement of the family culture is to occur, each family of orientation must be organized to produce in its children's families of procreation patterns of
norms and values identical to its own. This organization
of family life implies:

1. Values and norms relating to patterns of behavior
in the family remain constant from one generation to the
next.

2. Socialization of children is aimed at making children duplicates of their parents as these children achieve
adulthood.

3. Because of its part in duplicating succeeding generations, the family and its auxiliary kinship system do
not initiate change in society; the family is a force for
conservatism in social arrangements.

For the family system to retain its constancy, various
controls would have to be instituted:

1. With each generation duplicating its predecessor
and a replacement process described as *orderly*, this constancy could be maintained most efficiently if an individual outside the particular nuclear family were given authority and responsibility for judging and directing replacement within the family (the patriarch in a patrilineal society or mother's brother in a matrilineal society).

2. Marriage would be restricted to individuals who
come from families with identical norms and values of
family behavior. Indeed, to avoid cultural contamination,
contact (both before and after marriage) with persons
with different cultural backgrounds would be kept at a
minimum.

3. Since the essence of family life and kinship is maintenance of the traditional patterns relating to ancestors and origins, authority is time-based rather than skill-based—with older generations in authority.

Up to this point, the family as described above is similar in many characteristics to the folk society of Redfield.[3] As was indicated in Chapter 1, the folk society is unchanging in its culture, is based on retribution when its values are challenged, is composed of a homogeneous population (both culturally and genetically), and actively resists all change.

ASSUMPTIONS CONSISTENT WITH UNIVERSAL, PERMANENT AVAILABILITY AS A MATE

In this section, the part played by marital practices in interfering with orderly replacement will be discussed. The suggestion will be made that in the bilateral kinship system lineage considerations in mate selection are at a minimum and kinship control over marriage dissipates. As a result, individuals become avaliable for marriage with anyone and at any time during their adulthood.

The concept of lineage is important to the discussion of permanent availability. As used here, the term *lineage* has a broader connotation than simply the designation of formal lines of descent. Lineage is regarded as the totality of the particular ancestors, contemporaries, and descendants in whom an individual, by the rules of his society, can claim a property right. By a property right is meant the right of the individual (a) to claim these per-

[3] Robert Redfield, "The Folk Society," *American Journal of Sociology*, 52 (1947), pp. 293-308.

sons as belonging to him in terms of certain criteria of kinship and, (b) within certain restrictions, to use these persons to perpetuate the criteria for claiming others as belonging to the kin group. Hence, lineage as used here refers to such criteria as the rules of inheritance and authority, designation of the parent to whom the children belong, and the right to appropriate the spouse's relatives as one's own.[4]

In the previous section, it was assumed that control of replacement is instituted in the kinship system of which the nuclear family is a part. Accordingly, variation in the type of kinship system reflects the ways in which the nuclear family's activities related to its replacement in time are controlled by the larger kinship unit.

In the unilineal system (matrilineal or patrilineal) there is a need to restrict the list of the potential mates available to any individual. Moreover, if there were to be familiarity and intimate behavior among those whose marriage would contaminate patterns of lineage, such behavior would interfere with the maintenance of lineage continuity. Hence, in a unilineal system, there is a need for specific restrictions as well as obligations of intimate relationships between relatives of various kinds.[5] In addition, there is need for an office (such as the patriarch) or council in which authority over kinship affairs resides.

In the bilateral kinship arrangement in a complex society, lineage considerations must be modified.[6] With high concentrations of population and freedom of move-

[4] See George P. Murdock, *Social Structure,* New York: Macmillan, 1949, pp. 46 ff.

[5] *Ibid.,* pp. 235-236 and 243.

[6] See Davis, *op. cit.*

ment, it would be difficult to maintain "clean" lineage systems. Moreover, in the control of continuity of family culture, various problems would be faced. Since each individual belongs to two lineages with equal rights and obligations, which lineage is responsible for maintenance of the norms and values in the nuclear family? Under conditions of modern urban life, how can kinship authority be maintained? How can mate selection be regulated? The discussion below suggests the relationship between problems of control of continuity of family culture in the bilateral kinship system and mate selection.

1. Since there is no need to consider lineage (that is, the perpetuity of a given class of person-property) in the bilateral family, there is no need to restrict the available list of potential mates beyond the persons subject to the incest taboos in the nuclear family. If patterns of intimate behavior are admitted between all persons who are potential mates, there will be a tendency for much intimate interaction to occur in cross-sex relationships in all parts of the society. There is no necessity to restrict patterns of intimate behavior to specific individuals. The absence of these needs obviates the need to restrict availability for marriage to individuals from kinship units with identical values and norms of family behavior. As a result, homogamy with respect to social characteristics declines in importance for mate selection.

2. Since there is no need to consider lineage arrangements for marriage in a society with a bilateral kinship system, the maintenance of marriage is personal rather than a kinship problem. Assortive mating is expected and a marriage need not last beyond the desires of the par-

ticular individuals. Thus, we expect love marriages rather than arranged marriages. We also expect a high rate of divorce. Since the size of a domestic unit in the bilateral system tends to be small, there is neither an immediate kinship authority to control occurrence of divorce nor extra relatives in the home to be interested parties in the divorce.

3. Since there are neither restrictions on patterns of intimate behavior nor imperative lineage considerations, each individual, at least theoretically, is permanently available as a potential mate to all other cross-sex individuals. An important point here is that being married does not restrict an individual with respect to his future potentiality as a mate in later marriages.

This third item is the statement of universal, permanent availability of mature individuals in the bilateral kinship system. Each adult individual, regardless of his current marital status, is available as a potential mate to any other cross-sex individual at any time.

ASSUMPTIONS CONSISTENT WITH CONFLICTING NORMS

The assumptions consistent with orderly replacement conflict with the assumptions consistent with universal, permanent availability in structuring family relationships. Orderly replacement reflects a closed system characterized by unilineal kinship arrangements and permanent availability an open system associated with bilateral kinship arrangements.

The conflict between orderly replacement and permanent availability is a continuing one because, in reality, (a) each nuclear family is to some extent a closed system isolated from other families and (b) some restrictions do exist with regard to availability as a mate even in bilateral systems. Yet the conflict tends to be resolved in favor of permanent availability. The basis for suggesting the tendency for permanent-availability characteristics to triumph in contemporary society is as follows: Orderly replacement operates most efficiently when the kinship group holds property rights in the individual and has a stake in controlling his family of procreation. Control can be maintained by a representative who has authority and can invoke sanctions. The bilateral system makes control of the nuclear family by the larger kinship unit difficult. Thus, when norms appropriate to the bilateral system conflict with those of orderly replacement, the bilateral-kinship norms will predominate. With the predominance of bilateral-kinship norms, the practices appropriate to universal, permanent availability practices take precedence over those of orderly replacement in the structuring of family relationships.

The family operating in terms of universal, permanent availability of individuals as potential mates can be expected to have the following characteristics:

1. The family group takes the form of a voluntary association in which a person continues membership as long as his personal commitments to the other family members exceed his commitments elsewhere.

2. If the individual is to sustain a high desirability as a potential mate, he is motivated to develop and maintain certain personal skills and attributes enhancing his ability to perform family activities and his appeal to members of the opposite sex.

3. The concurrent assumptions of universal, permanent availability and orderly replacement suggest that the socialization of children be aimed at maximizing their market position in permanent availability (to the degree that permanent availability becomes the traditional norm). As a perennially marketable product, the child is required to develop (a) a pleasing personality, (b) competence in interpersonal relations, (c) a pleasant appearance, and (d) occupational career skill regardless of sex (not only to secure a good marriage but also to facilitate disengagement from an "unsatisfactory" marriage). The parents are correspondingly obligated to provide appropriate aid to enhance the market position of their children during childhood and adulthood.

4. Having children is a voluntary pledge by the parents to maintain their marital relationship. This pledge emerges as a consequence of attempts to develop norms capable of handling the predicament of orderly replacement versus permanent availability. Orderly replacement implies that children be born in the family. Yet, ideally, for a person to be completely flexible in forming and dissolving marital relationships, he should be free from other personal commitments and unencumbered by children. The solution to this predicament is a norm which permits orderly replacement, but which gives priority to permanent availability in case of direct conflict. The compromise solution involves the married couple's regarding children as an expression of their commitment to one another, a symbol of the endurance of their love. The presence of the children diminishes flexibility in changing marriage partners; the children provide additional considerations

to be taken into account in decisions. Hence, implicit in the decision to have children under these conditions is a pledge by the parents to restrict their own marital availability voluntarily. However, at time of divorce, permanent availability is given priority over orderly replacement and the pledge to restrict availability is revised. The marital commitment which the children were supposed to symbolize no longer exists. Ordinarily, the basis for revising the pledge to restrict availability is that continuing the marital relationship would be detrimental to the welfare of all of the family members.

5. Without temporal or marital-status restrictions on availability, neither premarital chastity nor marital fidelity have bearing on availability as a potential mate. Hence, recrimination for nonmarital sex relations is at a minimum and lack of chastity does not diminish the individual's market position as a potential mate.

6. Since neither time nor prior marriage (including current married status) reduces the availability of the individual as a potential mate, there is no incentive to delay marriage. On the contrary, to fulfill personal needs and maintain intimate relationships in an impersonal world, persons are under pressure for both early marriage and remarriage later in life. Remarriage, moreover, provides the children of an earlier marriage with a full complement of relatives. Thus both early marriage and a pressure to remarry are expected in the society characterized by bilateral kinship.

These characteristics are elaborated upon in later chapters.

Evidence Relevant to the Model

The conceptual model's utility for providing insight into the functioning of an institution lies, in part, in the extent to which characteristics described in the model correspond to empirical data. This section focuses upon trends and characteristics found in contemporary American society which correspond with the permanent-availability model. Some of the evidence presented will be given in greater detail in later chapters. The material discussed in this section includes: (a) age at marriage, (b) rates of divorce-remarriage, (c) children and divorce, (d) premarital chastity and marital fidelity, (e) homogamy, (f) interpersonal competence, (g) employment of married women, and (h) emphasis upon youthfulness and glamour.

1. Age at first marriage has been steadily decreasing. In 1890, the median age at first marriage for men was 26.1; by 1961 the median age was 22.8. For women, the median age at first marriage declined from 22.0 in 1890 to 20.3 in 1961.[7] In addition, marriage among teen-agers is increasing not only among the lower socioeconomic groups but also among middle-class individuals.[8] These

---

[7] Paul C. Glick, "The Life-Cycle of the Family," *Marriage and Family Living*, 17 (1955), pp. 3-9, and U.S. Bureau of the Census, *Statistical Abstract of the United States: 1962*, Washington, D.C., 1962, p. 72.

[8] Lee G. Burchinal, "Adolescent Role Deprivation and High School Age Marriage," *Marriage and Family Living*, 21 (1959), pp. 378-384; Samuel H. Lowrie, "Early and Late Dating: Some Conditions Associated with Them," *Marriage and Family Living*, 23 (1961), pp. 284-291.

findings are consistent with the expectation in the permanent-availability model that delay in marriage does not enhance the individual's potential as a mate.

2. Rates of divorce-remarriage are increasing. Of the people who married in 1950, 17 per cent had been previously divorced. By comparison, 2 per cent of the men and 3 per cent of the women who married in 1900 had been divorced.[9] Although the percentage of persons who divorce and remarry in any particular year is a relatively small minority, the cumulative percentage of divorced-remarried persons is growing to a sizable number. The increase in divorce-remarriage suggests a change in the role played by the family in an individual's life career. Much has been written concerning the unwillingness of the contemporary young person to take risks in the business world and of his preference for a secure position in a large corporation. He has been called such names as "organization man" and "bureaucratic personality." Yet, if occupation is compared with marriage practices, a different pattern emerges. In earlier years, the heyday of the business entrepreneurs, marriage and family life among the middle class were relatively stable and secure; divorce rates were low and the man's home was his private domain. Possibly the current emphasis upon security in occupational career is a result of an entrepreneurial view toward marriage and the family. Whereas risk-taking was once to be found in business, current risk-taking may be found more and more in marriage and family life.

3. Traditionally, the presence of children has been

[9] Paul H. Jacobson, *American Marriage and Divorce*, New York: Rinehart, 1959, p. 71.

regarded as inhibiting divorce and reducing chances for remarriage. Many marriages have been maintained "for the sake of the children." Yet, data on divorce show that since World War II there has been a growing proportion of divorces involving children. In 1940, prior to the War, 36 per cent of divorces involved children; by 1945, children were involved in 41 per cent of the divorces issued; in the period from 1945 to 1955, the figure rose steadily to 47 per cent.[10] There are no indications of a reversal in trend after 1955. The steady increase in percentage suggests that the presence of children is declining as a deterrent to divorce. (Glick has shown that, contrary to popular belief, remarriage rates, standardized by age, indicate that the number of children is not a crucial variable in remarriage. According to standardized rates of remarriage, a woman with three or more children has about the same chance of remarriage as a childless woman.[11]) These data indicate trends consistent with the permanent-availability model. The model assumes that marriage is not maintained for purposes of orderly replacement but exists instead for personal welfare. Children cease to be the prime consideration in making decisions regarding family life. At most, in terms of the permanent-availability model, having children can be understood as a voluntary pledge to restrict one's availability as a potential spouse. However, pledges are often revised and, in time, the children may cease to have their symbolic cohesive effect on the parents.

[10] *Ibid.*, p. 131.
[11] Paul C. Glick, *American Families*, New York: Wiley, 1957, p. 138.

4. There has been a decline in premarital chastity and marital fidelity in American society.[12] Both of these trends are in accordance with the expectations of permanent availability concerning chastity and fidelity as desirable traits. Moreover, sex relations outside of marriage occur less frequently in channels which compartmentalize sex relations away from marriage—prostitutes are visited less frequently and amateurs are more readily available. This trend is found both among lower socioeconomic classes and also among the middle classes, in association with the breakdown in formality of cross-sex relations. This breakdown in formality is consistent with the proposition that patterns of familiarity tend to be associated with availability for marriage. This decline in nonmarital chastity is reflected in rising illegitimacy rates even though the widespread use of contraceptive devices might be expected to reduce them. Table 1 demonstrates the increasing rate of illegitimacy in American society. In 1940, only seven illegitimate births per thousand unmarried women ages 15-44 were reported. In 1959, twenty-two illegitimate births per thousand unmarried women were reported. Although this rise in the illegitimacy rate may represent an increasingly more efficient reporting system, it is unlikely that *all* of the increase can be thus explained.

5. There is a decline in homogamy with respect to such social characteristics as ethnic background and re-

[12] Ira L. Reiss, "The Double Standard in Premarital Sexual Intercourse," *Social Forces*, 34 (1956), pp. 224-230. See also Alfred C. Kinsey, *et. al., Sexual Behavior in the Human Female*, Philadelphia: Saunders, 1953.

Table 1

NUMBER OF ILLEGITIMATE CHILDREN BORN PER 1000
UNMARRIED FEMALES AGED 15-44 IN THE
UNITED STATES, 1940-1959*

Year	Illegitimate birth rate	Year	Illegitimate birth rate
1959	22.1	1949	13.3
1958	21.0	1948	12.5
1957	20.9	1947	12.1
1956	20.2	1946	10.9
1955	19.3	1945	10.1
1954	18.3	1944	9.0
1953	17.0	1943	8.3
1952	15.6	1942	8.0
1951	15.1	1941	7.8
1950	14.1	1940	7.1

* Based on estimated number of illegitimate live births.
Source: Department of Health, Education and Welfare, *Vital Statistics of the United States: 1959*, Volume I, p. 3-29.

ligion,[13] both of which are related to family values and norms. The restriction of availability to specific groups with similar family norms and values consistent with orderly replacement is thus decreasing. Here is an instance of the decline of the controls necessary for orderly replacement, and it raises the question: If homogamy is abandoned, then what do individuals do in order to maximize their availability as potential spouses at different points in their life cycle?

[13] Burchinal, "Research on Young Marriage," *op. cit.*, p. 8; John L. Thomas, "The Factor of Religion in the Selection of Marriage Mates," *American Sociological Review*, 16 (1951), pp. 487-492.

6. There is a growing emphasis on competence in interpersonal relations and on getting along with others. Various studies have documented this trend. For example, Harris found that from 1935 to 1957, there was an increase among adolescents in their interest in getting along with other people.[14] Some observers have suggested that this trend in emphasis on interpersonal relations is related to bureaucracy in large-scale organizations.[15] It is equally plausible to regard the emphasis on a pleasant personality as a result of universal, permanent availability. Possibly, there is an increasing tendency in both marriage and occupation to extend the current limits of availability with respect to age, social characteristics, and personality variables.

7. There is a continual increase in the labor-force participation of married women. In 1940, there were about 5 million women in the labor force; by 1961, the number had risen to 14.6 million. Moreover, only 36 per cent of the women in the labor force in 1940 were married whereas 60 per cent in 1961 were married.[16] Some of this increase represents labor-force participation of married women as secondary workers in the family to earn "extra" money. Regardless of kind of economic motivation, the employment itself permits married women a measure of independence and takes them out of the home. Contact with

[14] Dale B. Harris, "Sex Differences in the Life Problems and Interests of Adolescents, 1935 and 1957," *Child Development,* 30 (1959), pp. 453-459. See also Daniel R. Miller and Guy E. Swanson, *The Changing American Parent,* New York: Wiley, 1958.

[15] Miller and Swanson, *op. cit.*

[16] U.S. Bureau of the Census, *Statistical Abstract of the United States: 1962,* Washington, D.C., 1962, p. 225.

others at the place of employment provides married women with information about current fashions in marriage and divorce and keeps them in touch with the cosmetic and interpersonal needs of the marriage market. The married working woman is not necessarily consciously shopping around for a spouse; inadvertently, she is "keeping in shape" (or keeping up her "resale value") in case the contingency arises.

8. The increasing emphasis upon youthfulness and glamour in American society is consistent with the permanent-availability model. Larger and larger amounts of money are expended annually upon cosmetics and toilet preparations. The retail excise tax on toilet preparations alone totaled $108 million in 1959, $120 million in 1960, and $131 million in 1961.[17] The amount spent on television advertising for cosmetics and toiletries shows a comparable increase—from $99 million in 1958 to $127 million in 1961. In 1950, approximately 10 per cent of money spent on television advertising pertained to toilet preparations; by 1961, toilet preparations accounted for 17 per cent of the amount spent for television advertising.[18] Other indices of services and activities related to youthfulness and glamour would probably show comparable increases. If the content of television commercials reflects reality, both young and old, single and married, women and men pursue youthfulness and glamour. Glamour-conscious individuals are not necessarily actively seeking new mates (although some admittedly are); but, like the work-

[17] *Statistical Abstract of the United States: 1961,* p. 373, and *Statistical Abstract of the United States: 1962,* p. 386.
[18] *Statistical Abstract of the United States: 1962,* p. 853.

ing wives, they are maintaining their availability. More-over, since the spouse is also potentially available, the in-dividual is stimulated to apply the techniques for main-taining glamour and youthfulness to sustain the spouse's interest in the existing marital relationship. As in the case of competence in interpersonal relations, some observers have suggested that the increased interest in youthfulness and glamour is related to the needs of the occupational career. However, office flirtations, occasional testing of one's own availability, remarriage to a younger spouse—all of these suggest that the emphasis upon glam-our and youthfulness is related rather to permanent availability as a potential spouse than to career mainte-nance. In contrast to the stress on glamour in American society, a negative cosmetic effect is sometimes attempted in some patriarchal societies. For example, among the eastern European Jews, after marriage the wife donned an unattractive wig. The wig served both to show that she was already married and to reduce her physical attrac-tiveness.

In summary, the evidence supports the application of the permanent-availability model to American society. The age span at which people get married is widening, the rate of remarriage is increasing, children are ceasing to be an impediment to divorce, there is a decline of pre-marital chastity and marital fidelity, homogamy in social characteristics is decreasing, there is a growing emphasis upon competence in interpersonal relations, women are growing more independent financially, and the emphasis upon youthfulness and glamour is increasing.

Comparisons with Other Conceptions of the Contemporary Family

The model of the contemporary bilateral family with universal availability of all adults as potential spouses is compared below with two other conceptions of the modern family—one by Ernest W. Burgess and the other by Talcott Parsons. Both the Burgess and the Parsons conceptions are consistent with many of the empirical findings which the permanent-availability model is presumed to explain. The discussion below concentrates on the differences between them and the permanent-availability model. The Burgess and Parsons conceptions are briefly described before the differences between them and the permanent-availability model are discussed.

Burgess conceives of the family as capable of description on a continuum from purely institutional to purely companionship extremes.[19] In terms of social control, the completely institutional family is buttressed mainly by outside forces such as community opinion and kinship relations whereas the extreme companionship family is held together only by the internal bond between husband and wife. Burgess associates the following with the companionship family: interpersonal compatibility, freedom in the choice of mate, freedom in social relations before marriage, love and companionship before marriage, stress on the primacy of personal relations, the institution of divorce, and appreciation of children as persons rather than as economic assets.

The contemporary middle-class family described by

[19] Burgess, Locke, and Thomes, *op. cit.*

Parsons is similar to the Burgess companionship family. However, whereas Burgess bases his typology on the source of the family bond, as affected ultimately by mobility and technological change, Parsons utilizes functional differentiation of the various parts of society as the basis for his description of the American family.[20] Parsons suggests that the American family is an adjunct of the economic system and tends to become more and more specialized as society increases in complexity. He predicts continued differentiation between roles of husband and wife in an independent nuclear family; the husband-wife bonds hold the family together.

The Burgess and Parsons conceptions of the family are both discussed more fully in later chapters.

THE COMPANIONSHIP FAMILY OF BURGESS

Although there are many similarities in the propositions generated by the conception of the companionship family and by the permanent-availability model there are also differences.

1. The nature of companionship as a marital bond is ambiguous and is only tenuously related to the function of affection ascribed by Burgess as a specialized family function in contemporary society. As such, the concept of companionship family is essentially based in contemporary society, that is, in history, and is, therefore, not a general model for analysis. It corresponds more to the Weber notion of the historical individual than to a generalized ideal type. As a kind of historical individual, the

[20] Parsons and Bales, *op. cit.* .

companionship family has limited usefulness in cross-cultural analysis. Burgess used the patrilineal family as his principal reference for constructing the companionship family. Hence, comparisons between the American kinship system and bilateral and matrilineal systems in preliterate societies cannot be made directly on the basis of his typology of institution versus companionship. However, inasmuch as the permanent-availability model is formulated in terms of general characteristics of kinship systems, it should be capable of being applied to non-Western societies.

2. Whereas the Burgess conception of the companionship family treats divorce as a negative element in terms of failure to attain the companionate ideal, the permanent-availability model regards divorce as an integral part of the kinship system. The companionship family could possibly exist in a society in which divorce was forbidden.[21] The bilateral system with universal, permanent availability requires the institution of divorce for its existence.

3. Each scheme treats the socialization of children in a different way. The emphasis on personality development of children and achievement by them cannot be deduced from the assumption of companionship in mar-

---

[21] An arrangement like that of the Nayars could be used in companionship marriage with a ritualistic marriage to give the children a legitimate position in the family and kinship structure. The Nayars, however, are matrilineal (in the sense that lineage has been defined in this chapter). Such an arrangement would be inconsistent with a bilateral system. See E. Kathleen Gough, "Is the Family Universal?—The Nayar Case," in Norman W. Bell and Ezra F. Vogel, eds., *A Modern Introduction to the Family*, New York: Free Press, 1960, pp. 76-92.

riage. The logical outcome of the companionship family
is not to have children at all. In the companionship family, there is no essential need for the parents to emphasize
their children's personality development, especially since
this development may occur at the expense of their own
companionship. The American family seems to have
reached its closest approximation to the companionship
family in the 1920's and early 1930's when the birth rate
was declining and a very small family was considered
optimum. The assumptions relating to the bilateral system with universal, permanent availability of potential
spouses, however, interpret having children as a pledge
by the parents to maintain their commitment to each
other. Preparing children for a life of permanent availability requires in addition that much emphasis be placed
upon being socially facile as well as highly motivated to
achieve success in an occupation. Social facility and occupational success would enhance the individual's ability
to be permanently available. The permanent-availability
model thus accommodates the maintenance of relatively
high birth rates and emphasis upon being both congenial
and achievement-oriented.

In general, comparison between the permanent-
availability model and the companionship model reveals
that the permanent-availability model derives its characteristics from the concept of the bilateral kinship system
whereas the companionship model is based upon empirical data describing trends in American society; the ideal
companionship family persists without divorce whereas
permanent availability requires divorce as an integral

part of family practices; the ideal companionship family would have the minimum number of children to provide maximum personal attention for all members of the family to one another, whereas under conditions of permanent availability parents would tend to have a large number of children as a pledge to maintain their marriage. Comparison between the two models suggests that the permanent-availability model has advantages over the companionship model in cross-cultural analysis, in explaining the prevalence of divorce and remarriage, and in interpreting high birth rates and parental emphasis on social facility and achievement.

FUNCTIONAL DIFFERENTIATION: THE PARSONS VIEW OF THE FAMILY

Some of the differences in the propositions consistent with the Parsons position and the permanent-availability model are described below:

1. With bilateral kinship, according to Parsons, the nuclear family tends to be independent. According to Parsons, this independence places a great strain on the marital relationship so that the need for complementarity of husband's and wife's roles is extremely important. The high divorce rate, according to Parsons, results from a failure to maintain this complementarity. A question may be raised as to whether marital strain is a sufficient explanation. Parsons, as well as Burgess, has not explained why divorce rather than an alternative solution has been developed in contemporary society to handle incompatibility in marriage. For example, in some bilateral socie-

ties, networks of family corporations or elaborate legal contracts inhibit divorce.[22] Parsons' view is that since the family tends to be a self-adjusting system, sooner or later families will develop practices to reduce the strain on the marital bond. This reduction in marital strain would, in turn, decrease the probability of divorce. With the assumption of universal permanent availability, however, the necessity for the institution of divorce becomes apparent.

2. The Parsons conception of the contemporary family as a highly specialized group taking its form from other institutions (notably economic) does not provide an institutional basis for having children. Parsons must introduce psychological mechanisms to explain why people have children. He suggests that adults desire children "to express what are essentially 'childish' elements of their own personality."[23] In contrast, the assumptions of the model of the bilateral family do provide an institutional basis for having children; a basic postulate is that under all conditions the family tends to duplicate itself generationally. The discussion has also suggested that having children is regarded as a pledge by the parents to restrict voluntarily their availability as potential spouses.

3. The Parsons view of the family suggests a trend toward an increased specialization of marital roles. How-

[22] For example, J. D. Freeman, "The Iban of Western Borneo," in George Peter Murdock, ed., *Social Structure in Southeast Asia*, New York: Wenner-Gren Foundation, 1960, pp. 65-87. See also C. Ackerman, "Affiliation: Structural Determinants of Differential Divorce Rates," *American Journal of Sociology*, 69 (1963), pp. 13-20.

[23] Parsons and Bales, *op. cit.*

ever, United States Census data indicate that the husband is the only recipient of income in only 44 per cent of those families in which both husband and wife are present. Both husband and wife work in 43 per cent of the families. In only 53 per cent of the families in which the husband is under 35 is the husband the only recipient of income.[24] Thus, Parsons' characterization of the American family as one in which the husband goes out to work while the wife stays at home is no longer accurate.

4. The Parsons conception of the family is especially strong in explaining whatever differentiation exists in husband and wife roles. It is especially weak in explaining the popularity of marriage. If the occupational structure has a dominant influence on family life and if requirements for jobs are becoming more rigorous, why are teen-age marriages among middle-class people increasing? The Parsons conception fails to explain this trend. The need for additional training should produce, if anything, an increase in age at marriage. Moreover, if the strain on the marital bond is great, Parsons' functional position leads to the prediction that marriage will decline in popularity. Only the assumption that people will marry when they have an opportunity and that availability as a potential mate does not change over time can explain the increase in the popularity of marriage. People are not reducing their later chances of marriage by risking a particular marriage (early or late) when the opportunity arises.

[24] U.S. Bureau of the Census, "Family Characteristics of Persons: March, 1959," *Current Population Reports*, Series P-20, No. 112, December 29, 1961.

Table 2

PER CENT OF WOMEN AGED 15-44 EVER
MARRIED WHO WERE CHILDLESS

Year	Per cent of women childless
1959	14.8
1957	15.9
1954	18.1
1952	20.7
1950	22.8
1940	26.5

Source: U.S. Bureau of Census, *Current Population Reports*, Series P-20, No. 108, July 12, 1961, pp. 17–18.

5. With an increasing number of women in the labor force, the Parsons position would lead us to expect a corresponding increase in the number of married women who are childless. A mother cannot both work and take care of the house and children, even with assistance, without some conflict in role. Children may become ill, overtime work may be demanded, and at times she may not be able to obtain assistance. Yet population data do not support the view that married women decide in favor of their occupational commitments over having children. An examination of Table 2 concerning American women who were childless indicates that from 1940 to 1959 the percentage of women who had ever been married but had not had children declined steadily from 26.5 per cent to 14.8 per cent.[25]

Nor is this decrease in childlessness to be found pri-

[25] U.S. Bureau of the Census, "Marriage, Fertility, and Child-spacing: August, 1959," *Current Population Reports*, Series P-20, No. 108, July 12, 1961.

Table 3
NUMBER OF CHILDREN EVER BORN PER 1,000 WOMEN FOR
WOMEN EVER MARRIED, AGED 15-44, 1950-1959, BY
LABOR-FORCE STATUS, UNITED STATES

Year	Number of children per 1,000 women (standardized for age)		
	Women in the labor force (a)	Women not in the labor force (b)	(a)/(b)×100
1959	1,805	2,534	71.2
1957	1,657	2,456	67.5
1950	1,268	2,083	60.9

Source: U.S. Bureau of Census, *Current Population Reports*, Series P-20, No. 108, July 12, 1961, p. 20.

marily among women not in the labor force. Table 3 shows the number of children (standardized for age of mother) by labor-force status of the mother. In 1959, among women in the labor force, 1,805 children had been born per 1,000 women as compared with 2,534 cumulative births per 1,000 women not in the labor force. Although the proportion of births was higher for women not in the labor force, the birth rate for women in the labor force increased much faster from 1950 to 1959 than the rate for women not in the labor force. Hence, labor force participation of women appears to be declining as a deterrent to childbearing.[26] The data do not appear consistent with the contention that having children is inimical to the participation of women in the labor force.

[26] *Ibid.*

In summary, the comparison between the Parsons view of the family and the permanent-availability model indicates that (a) whereas the Parsons conception regards divorce as marital failure and suggests that, with more experience at marital adaptations, divorces should decline in prevalence, the permanent-availability model requires a high incidence of divorce; (b) while Parsons explains having children on the basis of irrational needs of parents, the permanent-availability model interprets having children as a pledge to maintain the marriage; (c) Parsons' view is that specialization of marital roles will increase, whereas the permanent-availability model requires little specialization so that the marriage can be readily dissolved; (d) while the Parsons conception favors late marriage, the permanent-availability model predicts early marriage; and (e) whereas the Parsons position calls for a minimum number of children per family and childlessness for working women, the permanent-availability model makes having children a personal choice which is independent of the working status of the wife. The permanent-availability model has the following advantages over the Parsons position in that it explains (a) the tendency for divorce rates to remain high, (b) having children as part of the general family norms without recourse to another source of explanation, (c) the increasing tendency for married women to work, (d) the trend toward early marriage, (e) the continuation of relatively high birth rates, and (f) the increasing tendency for working women to have children.

Conclusion

A model of contemporary family life was developed by superimposing the assumption of universal, permanent availability of all adults as potential spouses upon an initial assumption that each family tends to duplicate its culture in the next generation. Specific implications of the model are described above. Some general considerations are:

1. Inasmuch as the assumptions did not require specific characteristics of other parts of the society, the model implies a functional autonomy of the family system. Although the particular family system may flourish more readily under some conditions rather than others, the conservative commitments fostered by the family system are sufficient to sustain it in a variety of situations. Hence, the model provides a basis for familial determinism as an independent variable in the development of social structure.

One of the assumptions was that change is not initiated in the family. However, once a trend is set into operation in the family system, further modification is required in the other institutions. Although change in occupational structure (for example, separation of home and work) may provide an initial impetus for changing family forms, the changed form would tend to be self-sustaining because of the pressure toward generational duplication. Moreover, the introduction of a second assumption (permanent availability) brings with it a possibility that the two tendencies in family life may be inconsistent in particular areas of activity. To resolve these inconsistencies, families may invent ingenious strategies. Hence, although the family cannot be viewed as initiating major social changes through family-life education or a family-reform movement, it can be seen as a force to which other institutions must adjust their norms and values.

2. The conceptual model of the family was presented as if the entire population in contemporary society preferred norms consistent with universal, permanent availability over those relating to orderly replacement of family culture from one generation to the next. Actually, norms appropriate to orderly replacement and to permanent availability can co-exist in a society. There are three segments of the married or potentially married population: (a) those who choose orderly-replacement norms over universal-availability norms at all times, (b) those who choose universal-availability norms over orderly-replacement norms at one time or another, and (c) those who rank orderly replacement and universal availability as equally important in their evaluation of norms.

In the third segment of the total population, in which both orderly replacement and universal availability are ranked equally in preference, some individuals alternate in their use of orderly-replacement and permanent-availability norms. It may be of interest to determine the circumstances under which they apply orderly-replacement norms and the circumstances they consider appropriate for permanent-availability norms. Other individuals in the third segment develop compromise norms embodying elements of both orderly replacement and permanent, universal availability.

The chapters which follow will expand upon the tendencies described in this chapter. They will indicate how the trend of contemporary society toward the increasing prevalence of characteristics of bilateral kinship affects mate selection, kinship relations, and interaction within the nuclear family.

Selected Readings

The views of Talcott Parsons on the American family are expressed in:

Parsons, Talcott, and Robert F. Bales. *Family, Socialization and Interaction Process*. Free Press, 1954. (Notably in Chapter 1, "The American Family: Its Relations to Personality and to the Social Structure.")

Parsons, Talcott. "The Social Structure of the Family," in Ruth N. Anshen (ed.), *The Family: Its Function and Destiny*, Harper, 1959, pp. 241-274.

The views of Ernest W. Burgess on the American family are found in:

Burgess, Ernest W. "The Family in a Changing Society," *American Journal of Sociology*, 53 (1948), pp. 417-422.

Burgess, Ernest W., and Paul Wallin. *Engagement and Marriage*. Lippincott, 1953. Especially Chapter 1, "Marriage in Transition."

Burgess, Ernest W., Harvey J. Locke, and Mary Margaret Thomes, *The Family from Institution to Companionship*. American Book, 1963.

Other discussions of the contemporary American family include:

Arensberg, Conrad M. "The American Family in the Perspective of Other Cultures," in Eli Ginzberg (ed.), *The*

Nation's Children, Columbia University Press, 1960, Vol. 1, pp. 50-75.

Sirjamaki, John. "Culture Configurations in the American Family," *American Journal of Sociology,* 53 (1948), pp. 464-470.

5 Courtship and Mate Selection in Contemporary Society

Rules of mate selection in a society are of crucial importance in determining the extent to which family culture will be preserved from one generation to the next. Because of incest taboos, individuals in Western societies must marry outside the nuclear family. Since the bride and groom come from different families, new norms and values can readily enter into family culture at marriage. If the norms and values of a particular family constitute a closed cultural system, then marriage of one of its members provides an opportunity for opening the system. Marriage of children presents to each family the possibility of having the transmission of its culture interrupted by the introduction of contradictory values from the other family. If in the extreme case of bilateral kinship structure each adult individual is a potential mate of any other adult of the opposite sex, this universal, permanent availability of adults should have a profound influence upon mate selection.

Availability for marriage has two dimensions: (a) To whom is the individual available for marriage? (b) When is the individual available for marriage?

In unilineal systems individuals are restricted in their choice of potential mates to a particular field of eligible persons. Since lineages place great emphasis on continuity of family practices, those lineages which practice marriage with one another tend to be alike in their norms of family life. As a consequence of limiting marriage to a restricted number of lineages over several generations, individuals mutually eligible as potential mates in unilineal systems have a definite kinship status in relation to one another and are similar in their views of family rights and duties. The marrying lineages then are part of the same general culture system. From the viewpoint of culture groups, the set of lineages is considered as related through *in*marriage (or marriage within the system). In bilateral systems, with less emphasis on continuity, fewer restrictions are placed on potential mates with respect to kinship status. In bilateral systems, therefore, a greater tendency probably exists for people to marry outside their particular culture system. Marrying outside the culture system is *inter*marriage.

Time is another dimension to be considered in the analysis of mate selection. The welfare of the families in the lineage is a major consideration in marriage in patrilineal or matrilineal societies. The best time for a child to marry is either (a) when he (or she) can bring the highest bride price or dowry to the family or (b) when the child's worth to the lineage into which he (or she) is marrying is at a maximum. (The child's worth can be reckoned in terms of ability to produce material goods or children or in terms of beauty.[1]) In the bilateral system, a child cannot be regarded as "investment capital" for the lineage and there is less pressure upon him to marry at any particular time. A wide variation in marriage rates by age can therefore be expected in bilateral societies.

This chapter will discuss several aspects of courtship and mate selection in contemporary American society:

1. *To what extent is intermarriage occurring?* Different practices are expected in courtship and mate selection for intermarriage and for inmarriage. Thus, if the incidence of intermarriage is increasing, appropriate modifications of norms in courtship and mate selection are to be anticipated.

2. *To what extent are marriage rates changing at the extremes of youth and mature adulthood?* Courtship practices change as individuals mature. An increase in the participation of persons at both extremes in age would entail a modification in courtship practices and mate selection for the society.

3. *What are specific implications for orderly replacement from the increased incidence of intermarriage and the widening of the span of years in which people par-*

[1] The value of a girl's beauty to her lineage is suggested by Levi-Strauss' contention that in most societies one basis for the scarcity of women desired for marriage is the variation in attractiveness. Generally, there is not a sufficient supply of attractive women to satisfy the demand. In marriage-exchange practices between kin groups such as bride price or bride service, the kin group can capitalize upon the bride's beauty. See J. P. B. De Josselin De Jong, *Levi-Strauss' Theory on Kinship and Marriage,* Leiden: Brill, 1952.

ticipate in courtship? Ways in which changes in rates of intermarriage and incidence of early and late marriage affect divorce rates will be indicated first. Examples of ways by which non-Western bilateral societies have provided stability for the kinship structure will be presented thereafter.

Intermarriage

What are the commonly recognized kinds of intermarriage? Categories used by people in describing intermarriage include:

1. Race ("She's Negro, but her husband is white.")
2. Social class ("She was raised in the poor section of town, but she sure married into a fine family with lots of money.")
3. Ethnic-group membership ("Her parents are Irish, but she married a man whose family comes from Italy.")
4. Religion ("They had a civil ceremony because he's a Catholic and she's a Methodist.")

Trends in American life for each category of intermarriage are described below. Because there have been relatively few systematic large-scale investigations of intermarriage, estimates of national trends are based upon studies limited to small segments of the population. Even so, interpretations of these trends appear to be consistent with findings of studies of other institutions in American society.

RACIAL INTERMARRIAGE

The major problems of racial intermarriage in the United States are best exemplified by Negro-Caucasian intermarriage and this discussion deals mainly with this type of marriage. Other combinations exist (for instance, Negro-Oriental; Oriental-Caucasian).

Attitudes with respect to racial intermarriage reflect visual and historical criteria for classifying human beings. Couples living in racially mixed marriages are highly visible to outsiders. For example, in his study of Negro-white marriages in Philadelphia, Golden found that the Negro member of the mixed couple tended to be dark and Negroid in appearance and could not "pass" easily.[2] Differences in the culture of Negroes and whites in any segment of society are not crucial in the sentiments of people against racial intermarriage as they may be with reference to social class, ethnic group, and religion. Rather, an outdated view of genetics has rationalized a historical injunction preventing slave owners (male and female) from marrying their slaves. Regardless of the inadequacy of such a rationale, more than 30 states in the United States have laws prohibiting racial intermarriage of Caucasians not only with Negroes but sometimes also with Orientals and Indians.[3]

In those states where intermarriage is illegal, the state itself attempts to prohibit miscegenation and to punish those

[2] Joseph Golden, "Characteristics of the Negro-White Intermarried in Philadelphia," *American Sociological Review*, 18 (1953), pp. 177-183.

[3] Irving Mandell, *The Law of Marriage and Divorce*, New York: Oceana, 1957.

who violate the proscription. In those states, however, where no such law exists, there is no official agency or institution to uphold the mores of racial endogamy. There it is the family which, more than other institutions, assumes the responsibility for preventing miscegenation, especially in the form of inter-marriage. [In a study by Golden], although many of the persons interviewed had few and not very strong family ties, a significant proportion related that their interracial marriage was preceded by family discussion. Their parents, siblings, and other relatives offered advice, pointed out the dangers of mixed marriage, and warned of the prejudice they would encounter. Some appealed to their loyalty. . . . Several white wives stated that they had never informed their parents of the marriage.[4]

Racial *inter*marriage remains as proscribed in many American cultural groups. However, there is evidence that the rate of intermarriage is increasing. Most Negro-white marriages take place between Negro men and white women.[5]

Data on racial intermarriage are not readily available. In those states which prohibit racial intermarriage, probably some Negroes (or perhaps the white partners) "pass" in order to obtain a marriage license. These unacknowledged intermarriages would generate other unrecorded intermarriages when the children in these marriages themselves mature and mate. However, even in those states which permit intermarriage, the rate of Negro-Caucasian

[4] Joseph Golden, "Social Control of Negro-White Intermarriage," *Social Forces*, 36 (1958), pp. 267-269.

[5] John H. Burma, "Interethnic Marriage in Los Angeles, 1948-1959," *Social Forces*, 42 (1963), pp. 156-165. Golden, "Characteristics of the Negro-White Intermarried in Philadelphia," *op. cit.*

intermarriage is low. Less than three per cent of the Negro marriages are officially acknowledged intermarriages.[6] Intermarriage between whites and other races is only slightly more prevalent. Possibly, most racial intermarriages are not officially acknowledged.[7]

SOCIAL-CLASS INTERMARRIAGE

The importance of the rules of mate selection for maintaining the existing social order in a society is suggested by Warner:

By extension or limitation of the usual rules of descent and marriage, the control of sexual accessibility or its prohibition and of descent of the offspring (together with economic controls) provides the powerful foundations for many general systems of rank. Crucial questions for understanding this problem of the relation of the moral statuses which control the species environment and rank order are: Are all unmarried males and females of mature sexuality potential mates, unfettered by any rules other than those of incest prohibition? Or is the choice of mates bounded by, and limited to, sharply defined ranked categories? . . . [In closed class systems,] statuses which fix the position of the individual sharply divide the biological group by social prohibitions and boundaries. Full access between all members of the sexes for marriage purposes is forbidden. The physical life of the individual is confined within narrow boundaries; mates do not come from diverse but within similar statuses. . . . [On the other hand, the open type of status system] provides a "mating" system

[6] Harold A. Phelps and David Henderson, *Population in Its Human Aspects*, New York: Appleton, 1958, p. 161.

[7] Milton L. Barron, *People Who Intermarry*, Syracuse: Syracuse University Press, 1946, pp. 113-119.

where the two members of the marriage pair may come from most diverse or very similar backgrounds.[8]

Norms of accessibility then govern the ability of a society to maintain a particular social structure. Warner includes both sexual accessibility and accessibility in social intercourse as criteria for determining the openness of a class system. If individuals at any particular status level are accessible *only* to one another for sexual and social intercourse, they will develop common interests, common perspectives, and eventually a value system in common. To the extent to which accessibility among people of different social rank is limited in a society, to that extent separate cultures will develop within each social class. In transferring concepts of the intimate, "joking" relationship versus the avoidance and highly formal relationship from the analysis of kinship to the analysis of social stratification, Warner has shown the similarities between lineage and social class as social entities. Both systems are maintained (or disrupted) by rules governing accessibility and avoidance both within the system and in relations with outsiders.

What are the trends in American life with respect to marriage of individuals originating in different social classes? Findings on social-class intermarriage indicate that:

1. Generally, people choose their mates from others of the same social class. In 1949, Hollingshead found that in New Haven, Connecticut, 83 per cent of all marriages

[8] W. Lloyd Warner, with Marchia Meeker and Kenneth Eells, *Social Class in America,* New York: Harper, 1960, pp. 269-270.

in his sample occurred between men and women of similar social-class levels.[9]

2. Women tend to marry upward in social class to a greater extent than men.[10] A basis for this upward mobility is suggested by a study in Aberdeen, Scotland. There, girls of working-class origin who married upward had more education and tended more often to work in white-collar occupations than girls who married within the working class. This study indicates that the girls who marry upward generally assume middle-class views and develop interests and aims compatible with those of a middle-class husband.[11]

3. The tendency to select mates from within social classes appears to be stable rather than decreasing. Dinitz, Banks, and Pasamanick studied the socioeconomic characteristics of marriage applicants in Columbus, Ohio, from 1933 to 1958. They found that propinquity had decreased as a factor in mate selection but that people still tended nevertheless to find mates in areas somewhat similar to their own in socioeconomic characteristics. Their results indicated that "persons who selected spouses from radically different socioeconomic areas appeared to decrease consistently from the earlier to the later time period." The

[9] August B. Hollingshead, "Cultural Factors in the Selection of Marriage Mates," *American Sociological Review*, 15 (1950), pp. 619-627.

[10] *Ibid.* See also Julius Roth and Robert F. Peck, "Social Class and Social Mobility Factors Related to Marital Adjustment," *American Sociological Review*, 16 (1951), pp. 478-487.

[11] Cited in Seymour M. Lipset and Reinhard Bendix, *Social Mobility in Industrial Society*, Berkeley: University of California Press, 1960, p. 235.

investigators interpreted their findings as possibly more indicative of the "blurring of class distinctions in the middle range than of increasing class fluidity."[12]

Like race, social class does not appear to be declining noticeably as a criterion (and barrier) for intermarriage. The apparent increase in specialization as well as the professionalization of the labor force has probably served, on the one hand, to increase obstacles to informal cross-sex relations between people at the extremes and, on the other hand, to extend middle-class values to large sectors of the population. This extension would enlarge the field of potential mates considerably without breaking down traditional social-class lines.

Perhaps, if more unmarried persons were to move away from their parents and live an independent existence, social-class intermarriage might occur on a greater scale. Coombs found that social-class intermarriage was *most* likely to occur when neither the bride nor groom in his sample of married university students had lived at home with parents during the courtship period; intermarriage was *least* likely to occur when both had lived at their parents' home during courtship.[13]

ETHNIC-GROUP INTERMARRIAGE

Ethnic groups develop their unique ethical and moral rules through regional isolation. Ethnic groups frequently

[12] Simon Dinitz, Franklin Banks, and Benjamin Pasamanick, "Mate Selection and Social Class: Changes During the Past Quarter Century," *Marriage and Family Living*, 22 (1960), pp. 348-351.

[13] Robert H. Coombs, "Reinforcement of Values in the Parental Home as a Factor in Mate Selection," *Marriage and Family Living*, 24 (1962), pp. 155-157.

become nations. However, where ethnic groups persist within nations, we regard them as cultural islands. Examples of North American cultural islands are the hillbillies, the Pennsylvania Dutch, and the French Canadians.

Most information on ethnic intermarriage pertains to members of ethnic groups who have migrated to the United States.[14] Findings on intermarriage of ethnic groups originating outside the United States indicate:

1. The trend toward marriage of members of ethnic groups with those outside their particular group is generally low among first-generation immigrants, but intermarriage steadily increases with each succeeding generation (all other things being constant).[15] The longer the ethnic group's residence in the community, the greater is the incidence of intermarriage.

2. The basis for intermarriage is undergoing change. Barron found that the larger the size of the ethnic group in the community, the lower is the incidence of intermarriage. The factor of size counteracts the tendency for the rate of intermarriage to increase with each succeeding generation. Rate of intermarriage in the early generations may be inflated not so much by individuals' breaking away from tradition but perhaps more by a shortage of potential spouses within the ethnic group. As time goes on and the ethnic group increases in size and improves its financial status, intermarriage resulting from scarcity of spouses within the ethnic group apparently declines. The basis for intermarriage would then more often be the loss

[14] Unless otherwise indicated, the findings reported on ethnic-group intermarriage are taken from Barron, *op. cit.*

[15] Phelps and Henderson, *op. cit.*, p. 152.

of ethnic identification by the individuals involved.

3. Ethnically intermarrying people frequently select as spouses those whose ethnic background is somewhat similar in cultural values to their own. Such marriages would meet with minimal parental opposition. This tendency suggests that ethnic inmarriage is ordinarily preferential rather than prescribed. Like ethnic inmarriage, intermarriage also tends to become traditional. Children of ethnic intermarriage intermarry more often than children of parents who married within the ethnic group.

Cultural islands will probably disintegrate as communication media are expanded, as educational requirements (accompanied by more state control and less local control of schools) are increased, and as transportation facilities are improved. The breakdown of these cultural islands is difficult to measure; however, the decline of the isolated rural community and the cityward migration of the marginal farmers decimate cultural islands.

RELIGIOUS INTERMARRIAGE

Pressures against religious intermarriage are probably greater than pressures against ethnic intermarriage. Chapter 4 suggested that orderly replacement can be maintained most efficiently if an individual outside the particular nuclear family is given authority and responsibility for judging and directing replacement within the family. Incidence of ethnic intermarriage depends mainly upon members of the kinship unit (perhaps the parents of the bride and bridegroom). Religious intermarriage, however, eventuates in the face of opposition by representatives of church groups committed to maintaining particular values in succeeding generations. Each major religious group accepts the possibility of intermarriage, but tries to exert whatever pressure it can to maintain continuity. For example, in a marriage between a non-Catholic and a Roman Catholic, the non-Catholic "must promise that the Catholic party will be permitted to practice his or her Catholic religion. Both persons must promise that all children resulting from the marriage will be brought up in the Catholic religion."[16] Similarly, statements of the Reform Jewish position reaffirm a commitment to the preservation of Judaism and the Jewish people and therefore these statements reflect an effort to discourage marriage between a Jew and non-Jew. Some rabbis perform wedding ceremonies between mixed couples on the condition that the couples "promise either that the children be brought up as Jews or the couples join a Jewish congregation, or both."[17]

Protestant views on intermarriage generally have been formed in response to the Catholic stand. On the assumption that religion is essentially a personal matter, the dominant Protestant position is that members of different faiths who intermarry should decide on a particular church and raise their children in the church of their own choosing. In Europe, Protestant countries in the past created regulations regarding the upbringing of children of Protestant-Catholic marriages. In 1825, the Prussian government stipulated that children should be brought up in

[16] Barron, *op. cit.*, p. 41.
[17] *Ibid.*, p. 31. See also *The Central Conference of American Rabbis Yearbook*, 1962.

the religion of their father. In 1868, Austrian law gave the parents the right to make any arrangement they desired about the religion of their children and, if no arrangements were made, boys were to be raised in the father's religion and girls in the mother's religion. Polish laws also provided for boys to follow their father's religion and girls their mother's in Protestant-Catholic intermarriage.[18] Thus although the major religious groups admit the possibility of intermarriage, they try to minimize its effects upon the norms and values of the succeeding generation (through sanctions imposed either by religious officers or by the government).

In the United States, there has been sustained interest in research on religious intermarriage. Research findings suggest the four following trends:

1. Although ethnic intermarriage tends to occur primarily within religious groups, the amount of intermarriage between religious groups is increasing. Thomas found several indications of the increase in rate of religious intermarriage.[19] His data suggest that the earlier Hollingshead study of New Haven underestimated the amount of intermarriage.[20] Although Hollingshead found only 6.2 per cent of Catholics marrying outside their religion, information for the entire state of Connecticut showed an intermarriage rate by Catholics of 40.2 per cent. Hollingshead also found little Jewish-Christian in-

[18] Barron, *op. cit.*, pp. 48-49.
[19] John L. Thomas, "The Factor of Religion in the Selection of Marriage Mates," *American Sociological Review*, 16 (1951), pp. 487-491.
[20] Hollingshead, *op. cit.*

termarriage; later studies of Jewish families in urban centers suggest that at least 15 to 25 per cent of the Jewish brides and grooms are marrying non-Jews.[21] Thomas observed that the rate of religious intermarriage depends upon the extent to which predominantly Catholic and Jewish ethnic groups are close-knit; the closer-knit the ethnic groups, the lower are the religious intermarriage rates. As ethnic groups in the community lose their identity, there is an increase in religious intermarriage. Thomas further observed that the higher the socioeconomic level the greater is the rate of religious intermarriage. He found that the percentage of Catholic-to-non-Catholic marriages in the highest socioeconomic areas in a metropolitan area was more than twice the percentage in the lowest areas. Heiss also found that Protestant-Catholic intermarriage increased with socioeconomic status.[22] As the general educational and economic well-being of the Catholic population continues to increase, a corresponding increase in religious intermarriage may be expected.[23]

An investigation of Canadian marriages by Heer provides support for expectations of increased religious intermarriage. Although there are probably minor differ-

[21] For example, see Stanley K. Bigman, *The Jewish Population of Greater Washington in 1956,* Washington: The Jewish Community Council of Greater Washington, 1957.

[22] Jerold S. Heiss, "Premarital Characteristics of the Religiously Intermarried in an Urban Area," *American Sociological Review,* 25 (1960), pp. 47-55.

[23] See Lee G. Burchinal and Loren E. Chancellor, "Ages at Marriage, Occupations of Grooms and Interreligious Marriage Rates," *Social Forces,* 40 (1962), pp. 348-354. Burchinal and Chancellor found that in Iowa Protestant-Catholic intermarriage was inversely related to socioeconomic status.

ences in mate-selection practices in the United States and Canada, the two countries are similar in most aspects of culture. The lack of comparable information for the United States necessitates reliance upon the Canadian investigation. Heer found that, even when the distribution of Catholics, Protestants, and Jews was held constant, the ratio of religious intermarriage to all marriages showed a fairly steady increase from 1922 to 1957 for each Canadian province.[24] Thus, the existing evidence suggests an increasing amount of religious intermarriage in contemporary society.

2. Rates of intermarriage tend to increase as parental opposition to religious intermarriage declines or is ineffective in controlling mate selection. In his study of intermarriage in Manhattan, Heiss found the following tendencies were more pronounced among intermarried than inmarried respondents: (a) Religion was not important to the parents. (b) Parents never attended church. (c) Ties with family had been tenuous when the respondent was young. (d) Grandparents did *not* live with the family.[25] Barron also reported that children of religious intermarriage were more likely to intermarry than children of inmarried parents.[26]

3. As the marriage rates of persons under 20 or over 30 years of age increase, the incidence of religious intermarriage will probably also increase. Burchinal and Chancellor found that religious intermarriage tended to

---

[24] David M. Heer, "The Trend of Interfaith Marriages in Canada: 1922-1957," *American Sociological Review*, 27 (1962), pp. 245-250.

[25] Heiss, *op. cit.*

[26] Barron, *op. cit.*

occur among teen-agers and those over 30 years of age in Iowa.[27] Heiss confirmed their finding on late marriages (after the age of 30) in his Manhattan sample.[28]

4. As the incidence of remarriage increases, there will be more religious intermarriage. In both the Iowa and Manhattan studies, those persons who had been married previously tended to intermarry with greater frequency than those persons entering their first marriage.

The general loss of ethnic identity, the rise in socio-economic level of Catholics, the decline of the effectiveness or motivation of parents to limit intermarriage, and the increasing frequency of early and late marriage (and remarriage) all suggest a continued trend toward increased religious intermarriage.

SUMMARY OF TRENDS IN INTERMARRIAGE

The findings of studies relating to racial, social-class, ethnic-group, and religious intermarriage suggest a slow trend toward an increase in intermarriage in contemporary society. Racial and social-class intermarriage rates show least change. However, the trend toward intermarriage does not appear to be one of an increased *willingness* or *tolerance* by people in different segments of society to intermarry with people in other segments. Rather, the change is occurring in the significance of these categories in contemporary life. Social-class lines themselves are becoming blurred; ethnic groups are losing their specific identity as their members are diffused among the various socioeconomic statuses and institutions of the so-

[27] Burchinal and Chancellor, *op. cit.*
[28] Heiss, *op. cit.*

ciety; religious identity is increasingly amorphous. (Herberg suggests that we are developing an "American" church.[29]) Hence, intermarriage is occurring not only because of a breakdown in parental control over mate selection, but also because the traditional social categories for inmarriage are themselves becoming vague and diffuse. As the various segments of the population lose their visibility, barriers to intermarriage are dissolved. This interpretation of intermarriage trends is supported by the persistence of racial intermarriage taboos; racial intermarriage is recognized primarily by visible physical attributes and such intermarriage probably occurs most often through "passing."

In spite of the tendency for old social categories to persist, other categories of mate selection will likely increase in relative importance. Inmarriage is merely one form of homogamy (a person marrying another person like himself). Other aspects of homogamy are not so much concerned with traditional categories of social life (like race, religion, social class, and ethnic group) as with community background, personal interests, personality characteristics, and physical characteristics of the couple. For example, homogamy tends to occur for the following characteristics:[30]

1. *Community background.* Couples tend toward homogamy in the size of the community in which they were

[29] Will Herberg, *Protestant—Catholic—Jew: An Essay in American Religious Sociology,* New York: Doubleday, 1955.

[30] Ernest W. Burgess and Paul Wallin, *Engagement and Marriage,* New York: Lippincott, 1953, pp. 204-211.

raised. Urbanites tend to marry other urbanites; ruralites tend to marry ruralites.

2. *Personal interests.* There is a tendency for people who marry to agree on whether the wife should work, the number of children they desire, whether divorce is permissible, who is to be head of the house, drinking and smoking habits, and leisure-time activities.

3. *Personality characteristics.* Homogamy generally occurs for neurotic tendencies and specifically for day-dreaming, for being touchy, and for having feelings easily hurt.

4. *Physical characteristics.* The healthy tend to marry the healthy; the good-looking tend to marry the good-looking.

As homogamy based upon such social categories as social class, religion, ethnic group, and race declines, homogamy based on personal characteristics can be expected to become the primary factor in mate selection—community background, personal interests, personality characteristics, and physical characteristics. With an increased emphasis upon personal characteristics of the potential spouse, individuals are expected to make a *personal commitment* in marriage; family pressure (either from the parental family or the extended family) is unable to enforce such a commitment. This system of mate selection must allow for the possibility that individuals will withdraw their personal commitment in one marriage *and* form new marital commitments. Divorce and remarriage are necessary concomitants to the marriage based upon personal commitment. Individuals thus remain permanently available to all persons of the opposite sex as potential mates.

The Widening Time Span of Courtship Behavior

It was suggested earlier in this chapter that under unilineal descent systems courtship which eventuates in marriage occurs at the most propitious time in the individual's life. The descent group profits by retaining the individual until he or she can bring the greatest bride price or dowry, or the most productive spouse. The female may have to develop household and field skills as well as accumulate property to become valuable "capital" for the descent group. The male may have to prove his skills in warfare, hunting, agriculture, and government.

In the bilateral system, with marriage based upon mutual personal commitment, individuals have little to "sell" except their commitment and little to "buy" except the commitment of the potential spouse. What then is the most propitious time for marriage or for courtship which eventuates in marriage? If the degree of personal commitment is the criterion for marriage, the individual may well begin as early as possible to develop this personal commitment. And if the personal commitment upon which the marriage is based has been lost, then a new personal commitment may be developed. The process can continue as long as the individual is able to stay in the competitive market. In a marriage market of this kind, young people tend to enter marriage as early as possible and older persons tend to make themselves available for marriage as long as possible.

With the limits of availability extended at both upper and lower extremes of age, an aura of optimum age must be maintained. If the individual is to show that he is capable of fulfilling marital expectations, he must present himself as a youthful yet mature person with much potential to fit the personal needs, congenial relations, and style of life associated with a satisfactory marriage. To maintain a self concept of high availability, an individual is required to think of himself as youthful, but not too youthful. If he regards himself as too youthful, he will not be taken seriously as a potential mate. If he presents himself as elderly, his value as a potential mate is also diminished. Hence, the young person must present himself as a mature sixteen-, seventeen-, or eighteen-year-old while the older individual must present himself as a young forty-, fifty-, or sixty-year-old. While older people are constrained toward maintaining an impression of youthfulness, the young must strive for an appearance of some maturity. Within this extended range of maturity, the individual is at the peak of his availability and, if he can find an appropriate mate, has little reason not to marry. The consequences are emphasis on maturity with early marriage among adolescents and stress upon youthfulness with companionate remarriage among older people.

Traditionally, the ages roughly between twenty and thirty have been considered as the "appropriate" years for marriage in Western society (especially for men). The norm has been that men should be slightly older than their wives, or the same age. An extension of the time span of courtship and marriage implies that early marriage takes place when the couple is below twenty and late marriage occurs when the couple is over thirty. This chapter considers *early marriage* as marriage between teen-agers and *late marriage* as marriage between persons thirty or over.

The following sections of this chapter are concerned with the implications of the increased time span of courtship behavior for early marriage and for marriage late in life.

Early Marriage

In this section, data on early dating and marriage are described and analyzed. The incidence of early marriage, courtship and early marriage, and factors in mate selection are discussed.

INCIDENCE OF EARLY MARRIAGE

On the basis of United States Census data on marriage in ages 15-19 and 20-24, Jacobson reported that there has been an increase in the percentage of married persons for both age groups.[31] During the period 1890 to 1950, he found that married males 15-19 increased from 0.5 to 3.0 per cent of all males in that age group and married females 15-19 increased from 9.5 to 16.8 per cent. In the same period, married males 20-24 increased from 18.9 to 39.5 per cent of the age group and married females 20-24 increased from 46.8 to 65.8 per cent. By 1962, 47.0 per cent of males 20-24 and 68.8 per cent of females 20-24 were married.[32] These data evince a fairly constant increase in marriage rates among the young.

[31] Paul H. Jacobson, *American Marriage and Divorce,* New York: Rinehart, 1959.

[32] U.S. Bureau of Census, *Current Population Reports,* Series P-20, No. 122, March 22, 1962.

Analyzing marital status for whites and nonwhites separately, Burchinal found that although nonwhite teenage marriage has shown little (if any) increase from 1910 to 1950, the percentage of white teen-agers who are married has risen fairly steadily. However, in the period 1950-1959, the percentage of married teen-agers showed little rise, with increases mainly in the 18-19 age categories.[33] Burchinal's analysis indicates that the decline in age at first marriage is reaching its lower limit. This change in rate of teen-age marriage among whites suggests that the basis for getting married is shifting. Findings of various studies will be examined to determine the nature of this change.

COURTSHIP AND EARLY MARRIAGE

In general, those who regard themselves as possessing fewer traits marketable in mate selection will marry at a younger age than will others. Traditionally, the less attractive, the uneducated, and especially the poor marry at a younger age than other individuals.

Martinson indicated that more persons who regard themselves as being deficient in a variety of ways tend to marry young than those who are well adjusted.[34] He found that girls who marry soon after graduation from

---

[33] Lee G. Burchinal, "Research on Young Marriage: Implications for Family Life Education," *Family Life Coordinator*, 9 (1960), pp. 6-7.

[34] Floyd M. Martinson, "Ego Deficiency as a Factor in Marriage." *American Sociological Review*, 20 (1955), pp. 161-164; and Floyd M. Martinson, "Ego Deficiency as a Factor in Marriage —A Male Sample," *Marriage and Family Living*, 21 (1959), pp. 48-52.

high school show less favorable scores on health adjustment, emotional adjustment, self reliance, sense of personal freedom, and social-integration tendencies than girls who remain single longer. His study of marriage patterns for boys showed comparable findings.

Similarly, Burchinal found that girls from families with lower socioeconomic backgrounds have a greater tendency to marry at high-school age than do girls of higher socioeconomic levels.[35] Data presented by Glick also indicate that the median age at marriage for low socioeconomic groups is lower than that for high socioeconomic groups.[36] Possibly, low-status girls have decided at an earlier age than high-status girls that they have reached their full potential in marital availability. Moreover, Lowrie found that children who come from families in which parents had little education, were of foreign origin, and lived in low-status neighborhoods tended to start dating later but to go steady earlier than children of other backgrounds.[37] These observations suggest that individuals who regard themselves as bringing little to the marriage market tend to marry at the first opportunity.

Does this suggestion then imply that middle-class individuals, in tending to marry earlier than before, now regard themselves as less attractive as marriage partners?

[35] Lee G. Burchinal, "Adolescent Role Deprivation and High School Age Marriage," *Marriage and Family Living*, 21 (1959), pp. 378-384.

[36] Paul C. Glick, *American Families*, New York: Wiley, 1957, p. 118.

[37] Samuel H. Lowrie, "Early and Late Dating: Some Conditions Associated with Them," *Marriage and Family Living*, 23 (1961), pp. 284-291.

Not necessarily; instead, findings of studies relating to dating among high-school students suggest a change in courtship norms of adolescents.

In a study of social climates in high schools, Coleman found that the central feature of the value system of girls was to be popular with boys and to be desirable for dates.[38] The overriding characteristics for membership in the leading crowds of nine high schools studied by Coleman were a pleasant personality, good looks, and clothes. These characteristics overshadowed the matter of a good reputation for girls. However, even a good reputation did not imply a lack of "cooperative" behavior on dates. The definition of a good reputation was concerned more with the way the girls handled themselves than with what they actually did. Hence, popularity (regardless of means for maintaining this popularity) rather than stability of commitments was important.

The growing emphasis upon popularity and dating in norms of courtship among high-school students is supported in Lowrie's study. His investigation showed that frequent daters are those who begin early dating. Those students who began dating early play the field more frequently (as opposed to going steady). Playing the field would serve to develop techniques for increasing one's attractiveness as a potential marital partner, for testing one's own marketable value, and for determining what is desirable in a mate.[39]

[38] James S. Coleman, *Social Climates in High Schools,* U.S. Office of Education Cooperative Research Monograph No. 4 (OE-33016), Washington: U.S. Government Printing Office, 1961.

[39] Lowrie, *op. cit.*

Courtship is ordinarily considered as the period during which individuals prepare for married life. In adolescence, boys and girls learn how to get along with each other as *members of the opposite sex*. Concepts of "good" and "bad" girls (and boys) are formed in that period. Anticipatory concepts of marital roles are formed in the courtship process. In societies in which formal relations between husband and wife are maintained after marriage, courtship behavior is generally also formal. The traditional Chinese, Japanese, and Spanish marriage systems reflect the formality of male-female relations. In societies in which the companionate relationship between husband and wife is stressed, courtship behavior is also an acquaintance process marked by informality. Thus, courtship and marriage may be deemed as a continuous process in the development of husband-and-wife interaction. If the husband-wife relationship develops as a continuous process, norms of courtship behavior will tend to be consistent with the marital roles that follow.

The spread of the pattern of early dating to middle-class groups suggests a direction in the change for criteria for marriage. Burgess and Locke described the stages of courtship in American society as: Dating, keeping company, going steady, a private understanding between the man and woman to be married, and engagement.[40] Of these stages, keeping company is no longer in the courtship vocabulary and going steady no longer implies a

[40] Ernest W. Burgess and Harvey J. Locke, *The Family from Institution to Companionship*, New York: American Book, 1953, pp. 331-337. Compare with 1963 edition of Burgess and Locke (with Thomes), pp. 224-231.

prelude to a private understanding. Instead, going steady merely refers to the person with whom the individual is currently involved. For some people, going steady does not even connote exclusiveness. The system of mate selection of the 1920's and 1930's, in which there was a continual narrowing of the field of prospective spouses, has given way to a series of personal involvements. One of these involvements eventuates in marriage.

One consequence of the courtship career as a series of involvements rather than a continual narrowing of the field of prospective mates is a decline of the romantic notion of there being one and only one true love possible in the lifetime of an individual. If the young person does not believe that there is a unique person with whom he or she is to fall in love, what reason is there for delaying marriage? Since marriage is a preferred state of existence in our society, the individual may reasonably marry at the first opportunity provided in a relationship in which he feels sufficiently involved.

A second consequence of the trend in courtship careers toward a series of involvements is a change in the handling of sexual aspects of courtship. On the premise that there is one true love that lasts forever and that marriages are made for a lifetime, virginity until marriage served to symbolize withholding the significant commitment; giving up virginity at the time of marriage then became an act of eternal commitment. Such beliefs held by women reinforced the double standard of sexual behavior, wherein men would have premarital and extramarital intercourse with women who were ineligible as spouses (prostitutes; women of a different social class or race).

When premarital intercourse between potential mates did occur, it was generally with the engagement partner.[41] However, with a change in the courtship career, premarital sex patterns are shifting. Kinsey found that at least half of the married women in his sample had premarital intercourse and slightly less than half of these had intercourse only with their fiances.[42] The Ehrmann study suggests that the extent of personal involvement is the norm now emerging to define conditions under which premarital intercourse is permissible. Ehrmann reported that girls in his sample regarded as "unthinkable" the possibility that they would engage in physical lovemaking with anyone with whom they were not going steady at the time.[43] The shift in the courtship career from an elimination process to a series of personal involvements thus reduces the symbolic significance of premarital virginity in courtship and marriage.

A third consequence of the trend toward the courtship career as a series of involvements lies in the socialization process. Under traditional courtship customs, the individual progressively eliminated people from courtship until he was able to confine his attention to the one person he was to marry. In terms of socialization, the elimination process provided a training experience for maintaining a courtship relationship with only one person. But,

[41] Burgess and Wallin, *op. cit.*, p. 331.

[42] Alfred C. Kinsey, Wardell B. Pomeroy, Clyde E. Martin, and Paul H. Gebhard, *Sexual Behavior in the Human Female*, Philadelphia: Saunders, 1953, p. 336.

[43] Winston Ehrmann, *Premarital Dating Behavior*, New York: Holt, 1959, pp. 141-142.

what happens when the family system incorporates "playing the field" or courtship as a series of commitments into its institutional structure? The Coleman and Lowrie findings describe the kind of courtship behavior that appears appropriate to a set of norms involving potential permanent availability as a mate. The custom of playing the field or having a series of personal involvements then becomes something more than testing for characteristics desirable in a mate (in the elimination process). Playing the field and becoming involved in a series of courtship relationships provide training experiences for considering other persons, regardless of their current marital status, as potential mates. (Kinsey found that wives with a history of premarital intercourse were more likely than others to indulge in adultery.[44]) In the series of personal involvements, the youth develop skills for maintaining continual availability through the years.

FACTORS IN MATE SELECTION

Different factors operate in selection for a permanent mate and selection for a mate under conditions of permanent availability. The most appropriate process of mate selection under conditions of permanence would be to determine one's own needs and to seek a mate in terms of reciprocal needs. The meshing or complementarity of personality needs is crucial to permanent mating because of the decline of external pressures to keep the nuclear family together in contemporary society. A good meshing is necessary in that conditions affecting family life continually shift—change in stage of family cycle, upward or

---

[44] Kinsey, *et al., op. cit.,* p. 438.

downward social mobility, frequent geographic mobility. Since the social situation cannot remain constant in contemporary society, the focus for permanent mating is upon the complementarity of the basic, stable patterns of personality.

The classical picture of the boy seeking a mother image or a girl looking for a father image in mate selection illustrates in an obvious way the tendency for one generation of family life to duplicate the preceding generation. Strauss suggests, however, that parent images may operate in mate selection either to encourage or discourage marrying someone like the parent. If experiences with the parent had been especially disturbed, the person may try to avoid marrying anyone like his parent. On the average, though, evidence points *toward* rather than *away from* marrying a parent image.[45]

The role of complementary personality needs in mate selection has been described by Winch.[46] According to Winch, one task of courtship is to eliminate individuals whose needs do not complement one's own needs. After the elimination process, individuals whose needs are complementary can achieve a mutual satisfaction in their relationship.

Winch's work is based on the premise that a person seeks a mate who shows greatest promise of "maximum need gratification." The hypothesis which he tested is that

[45] Anselm Strauss, "The Ideal and the Chosen Mate," *American Journal of Sociology*, 52 (1946) pp. 204-208, and Burgess and Wallin, *op. cit.*, p. 198.

[46] Robert F. Winch, *Mate-Selection: A Study of Complementary Needs*, New York: Harper, 1958.

the need pattern of one partner will be complementary (rather than similar) to the need pattern of the other partner.

Winch performed an intensive study of a small sample. His sample consisted of 25 young married couples, students at Northwestern University, who formed a relatively homogeneous group with respect to social characteristics. He derived five sets of ratings on the personality needs of these young people from: (1) a content analysis of a "need interview," (2) a holistic analysis of this interview, (3) a holistic analysis of case histories, (4) a Thematic Apperception Test, and (5) the consensus of a panel of judges after they had studied both need interviews and case histories.

Winch found that his interspousal correlations on three of the ratings supported the theory of complementary needs, while there was neither evidence in support of nor evidence against the theory in the holistic analysis of case histories and TAT ratings. Winch concluded that "the bulk of evidence, therefore, supports the hypothesis that mates tend to select each other on the basis of complementary needs."

Through factor analysis, Ktsanes, who was Winch's associate, was able to determine patterns of needs.[47] Ktsanes' first hypothesis was in terms of heterogamy rather than complementarity, namely, that two mates would represent different psychological types, and he found support for this expectation. A second hypothesis,

[47] Thomas Ktsanes, "Mate Selection on the Basis of Personality Type: A Study Utilizing an Empirical Typology of Personality," *American Sociological Review*, 20 (1955), pp. 547-551.

aimed directly at complementarity, was: "Persons who show high loadings on a factor tend to select as mates persons who show low or negative loadings on the same factor." Ktsanes found statistically significant support for this hypothesis only on the factors of "hostile dominance" and "mature nurturance."

Turner has criticized Winch's work on the grounds that those personality traits for which complementarity has been shown are those which would also reflect patterns of accommodation in a relationship. Dominance and nurturance patterns, according to Turner, would have to develop in a stable relationship regardless of the "needs" of the individuals prior to marriage. He has suggested that Winch studied the development of role expectations after marriage and, from these, inferred basic personality needs which existed prior to marriage.[48]

To test Winch's theory of complementary needs on samples of couples prior to their marriage, several investigators have sought to determine needs expressed by couples during courtship. Using a sample of courting couples, Bowerman and Day found little evidence in support of either complementarity or homogamy with respect to needs. Ten of the fifteen needs in their list were comparable to those studied by Winch.[49] Schellenberg and Bee, concentrating on nurturance and dominance in their study of both married and courting couples, found little support for the complementary-needs theory. Inasmuch

[48] Ralph Turner, review of Robert F. Winch, *Mate-Selection*, *Social Forces*, 37 (1958), pp. 175-176.

[49] Charles E. Bowerman and Barbara R. Day, "A Test of the Theory of Complementary Needs as Applied to Couples During Courtship," *American Sociological Review*, 21 (1956), pp. 602-605.

as Winch has regarded nurturance and dominance as major needs involved in complementary mate selection, the Schellenberg and Bee results suggest that perhaps the role of complementary needs in mate selection is no more than chance.[50]

A study by Kerckhoff and Davis provides an exception to investigations which reported negative findings with regard to complementary needs as a factor in mate selection.[51] They found that courting couples who had become closer in a six-month period following their initial interview (as opposed to remaining the same or drifting apart) tended to fall into two groups: (a) Those who had a relatively short courtship but had a high consensus on values related to family success, and (b) those whose courtship was longer and showed much complementarity in personality needs.

Kerckhoff and Davis interpreted their findings in terms of the traditional conception of courtship. They characterized courtship as a "filtering process" in which different factors operate at successive points in mate selection. The initial filtering consists of the elimination as eligible mates of those individuals who lack certain social characteristics (racial qualifications, religious qualifications, socioeconomic status qualifications, and ethnic qualifications). The next stage in the filtering process is to determine those individuals whose values and interests

[50] James A. Schellenberg and Lawrence S. Bee, "A Re-Examination of the Theory of Complementary Needs in Mate Selection," *Marriage and Family Living*, 22 (1960), pp. 227-232.

[51] Alan C. Kerckhoff and Keith E. Davis, "Value Consensus and Need Complementarity in Mate Selection," *American Sociological Review*, 27 (1962), pp. 295-303.

are congenial. At this stage there may be an idealization of the lover. The third stage, according to Kerckhoff and Davis, is that of determining complementarity of personality needs.

The Kerckhoff and Davis conceptualization of the courtship process assumes that the couple aims ultimately at a complementarity of need fulfillment (consciously and unconsciously). This complementarity may be necessary under conditions of permanent mating, but under conditions of permanent availability, interests and congeniality of goals and values may override personality complementarity and other traditional mate-selection factors. For example, Huang reports that in Communist China "compatible political enthusiasm" is considered more important in mate selection than similarity in education or social class.[52] Hence, the process of courtship for permanent availability may differ markedly from that for lifetime mating.

Permanent availability implies that the basic needs of the individual may change in the course of his life and that meeting personality needs at an early age may not suffice to maintain the marriage. To prepare himself for marriage under conditions of permanent availability, the individual does better if he plays the field (or goes steady sequentially) and develops his competence in interpersonal relations than if he settles upon a spouse who complements his personality needs at an early period in his life. By playing the field (as suggested by the Lowrie and

[52] Lucy Jen Huang, "Attitude of the Communist Chinese Toward Inter-Class Marriage," *Marriage and Family Living*, 24 (1962), pp. 389-392.

Coleman studies), the individual may develop a greater tolerance for "incompatible" personality needs in a spouse. Greater tolerance with respect to personality complementarity would make possible a more adequate selection on the basis of congeniality of interests and values. Hence, the courtship process need not progress in the filtering of undesirable traits to the extent necessary under permanent mating.

In the light of this discussion on permanent availability, the Kerckhoff and Davis findings can be interpreted as follows: People become committed to others who display congenial interests and values. In establishing a relationship, they work out a compatible arrangement in accordance with personality needs. Personality needs are not magnetlike selectors in the mate-selection process, but merely factors in accommodation. If the couple cannot develop a workable system of accommodations, they break up. In this interpretation, complementary personality needs are not the primary selection factors but merely operate in situations when conflict between the individuals is generated. The emphasis is thus upon compatibility and upon tolerance of the personality needs of the marriage partner rather than upon specific complementarity of needs.

As defined by Foote and Cottrell, the elements of competence in interpersonal relations consist of health, intelligence, judgment, autonomy, creativity, and empathy.[53] With the development of these elements of competence,

[53] Nelson N. Foote and Leonard S. Cottrell, Jr., *Identity and Interpersonal Competence*, Chicago: University of Chicago Press, 1955.

personal growth and development become the primary criteria for marriage. Competence in interpersonal relations stresses the development of an ability to accommodate differences in personality needs. Because competence in interpersonal relations and the procedures for training individuals in competence refer mainly to socialization rather than mate selection, the development of interpersonal competence will be discussed in a later chapter.

EARLY MARRIAGE: SUMMARY

Generally the evidence supports the contention that there is a growing pressure for age at first marriage to decrease. This trend appears indicative of a change in the basis for marriage. Under past criteria for marriage, early marriage was related to low market value of the individual. Hence, the unattractive, the poor, and the neurotic tended to marry early. Changes in courtship practices, however, indicate that dating begins early and generally persists through both playing the field and a series of personal involvements rather than progressive settling on a closed relationship. Under conditions of permanent availability, playing the field seems to be incorporated into the family system. Accordingly, criteria for mate selection are not those appropriate for permanent mating. Mate selection for lifetime mating requires a meshing of basic personalities which persists through numerous social situations. Instead, courtship and marriage on the basis of permanent availability take place through the development of congenial interests and values and focus upon the maintenance of personal commitments in the relationship. Emphasis is focused upon the continual development of the relationship and the development of competencies to accommodate potentially incompatible differences in basic personalities.

Late Marriage

Although much has been written about trends in courtship among adolescents and young adults, relatively little has been done with regard to courtship among the older population as such. This section will discuss the incidence of late marriage, factors in late marriage, and mate-selection and courtship practices.

INCIDENCE OF LATE MARRIAGE

The increased life span of the American population has created a situation in which the never-married, divorced, or widowed individual faces a long life of loneliness and sometimes hardship if he does not enter into a marriage even after the age of thirty. With increased leisure time, early retirement, and resources for maintaining good health, there is a high probability that home life will become progressively more important to people. In addition, the large number of divorced individuals provides a reservoir of unmarried persons in the population. The increased span of life, the leisure time, and the pool of divorced persons facilitate late marriage.

Jacobson has shown that for the years 1940 to 1948 there was an increase in the rate of marriage for all age groups—the old as well as the young. Whereas the increase in marriage rates for those under 30 can be attributed in part to the war years, the increase for individuals who were over 55 cannot. For example, in the 65-74 age group, the marriage rate per 1000 population was 12.5 in 1940 and 18.2 in 1948.[54] Thus, the rate of marriage for older age groups appears to be on the increase.

FACTORS IN LATE MARRIAGE

Several factors are probably responsible for the increase in late marriage. Three of these factors are: increased life expectancy, remarriage, and perpetuation of adulthood status.

Life expectancy

The average length of life in the United States has been steadily increasing. An individual born in 1960 can expect more than 70 years of life on the average. The estimated average length of life for individuals born in 2000 is 82 years of age.[55] However, this increase in expected life span will represent mainly a decline in people's dying at a young age rather than any marked extension of the upper limits of survival. That is, the age at which people die will cluster more around the average length of life than it does now. At present, the adult life span covers more than 50 years. An individual who was 35 years of age in 1950 generally had not yet lived half his life; he could expect to live another 38 years.[56]

This long period of adulthood increases the significance

[54] Jacobson, *op. cit.*

[55] Phelps and Henderson, *op. cit.*, p. 209; estimate by Eugene Lyman Fisk, "Possible Extension of the Human Life Cycle," *The Annals of the American Academy of Political and Social Science*, 145 (1929), p. 165.

[56] T. Lynn Smith, *Fundamentals of Population Study*, New York: Lippincott, 1960, pp. 358-362.

of active adult status for the population. Adult status becomes something to be lived for and retained as long as possible. The bilateral kinship system is consistent with this conception of adult status. In the bilateral system, participation in courtship and marriage is to be extended indefinitely. To maintain their potential for courtship and marriage, mature individuals continue to present themselves as youthful.

The proposition that older individuals tend to regard themselves as relatively youthful and try to maintain an aura of youthfulness is supported in a study by Jacobson. Although women do not generally marry men who are younger than they are, the tendency to marry younger men increases with age. In 1948, fewer than 4 per cent of all brides were older than their groom by five or more years. Yet, 10 per cent of the brides who were 30 years of age and more than 20 per cent who were past 65 married grooms at least five years younger than themselves. The situation is similar for men. Although men at all ages tend to marry women younger than themselves, the greater the age of the man the more of an age spread is generally found between his age and his wife's. For example, Jacobson reports that in 1948 when the groom was 22 the median age of the bride was 20. However, when the age of the groom was 79, the median age of the bride was 65.[57] Marrying downward in age may be interpreted as an attempt to maintain youthfulness.

Remarriage

A second factor in late marriage is remarriage. Most late marriages are remarriages. Glick reports that in 1953, the

[57] Jacobson, *op. cit.*

median age at remarriage when the spouse had also been previously married was 37 years for the wife and 42 years for the husband.[58] In contrast, the median age of those in their first marriage approached 20.

Marriage rates, age by age, are highest for divorced persons, intermediate for widowed persons, and lowest for single persons. However, about two-thirds of the marriages of divorced and widowed persons occur among those above 30 years of age. . . . It is estimated that, under current conditions, close to one out of every five marriages is likely to end in divorce and that about two-thirds of the divorced women and three-fourths of the divorced men will eventually remarry.[59]

With a life expectancy of 70 to 75 years, individuals who remarry can anticipate 30 or 40 years of married life (with their current spouse or another). With such a long time span of married life likely, the incidence of remarriage can be expected to increase.

Perpetuation of adulthood status

The third factor in late marriage is also related to life span and to retention of active adult status. An independent living arrangement (as opposed to living with married children or other relatives) is a symbol of active adulthood for older people. For an individual who expects to live another twenty or thirty years to move in with relatives as a *single* individual signifies abrogation

[58] Glick, *op. cit.*

[59] *Ibid.*, pp. 198-199. As of 1959, there was one divorce for every 3.8 marriages. "Population: Marriages, Divorces, and Rates with Percent Changes From Preceding Years: United States, 1920-1959," *Vital Statistics of the United States: 1959*, Part 2, p. 2-17.

of adulthood. Remarriage extends adulthood status, companionship, and personal assistance in an independent establishment. Most of the reasons given for remarriage in the Bernard study relate to the retention of the active adult status. Reasons given by individuals for having remarried were (a) being in love (which has been traditionally considered as inappropriate for people in their "middle years"); (b) missing the companionship of a marital partner (loneliness, need for companionship, habit, desire for stability); (c) need for support or care (to look after one another); (d) conformity to the expectations of family and friends (who organize their social life on the basis of married couples rather than singles); and (e) upward mobility (by successively marrying spouses of higher social status than the previous spouse).[60] Thus, it appears that perpetuation of the adult role provides a basis for continuing participation in courtship and marriage long after the traditional period of marriageability.

MATE SELECTION AND THE COURTSHIP PROCESS

There has been little systematic investigation of courtship and mate selection in late marriage. Findings related to remarriage may provide some insight into courtship practices among older persons, however, inasmuch as people who remarry tend to be older than the population marrying for the first time. Many of the courtship practices of the remarried may be related to age rather than to previous marital status.

[60] Jessie Bernard, *Remarriage,* New York: Dryden, 1956, pp. 118-135.

Hollingshead compared the wedding behavior of individuals who married for the first time and those who were previously married.[61] The persons previously married were older than those marrying for the first time. Although the specific findings probably reflect the unique characteristics of the 900 couples living in New Haven, Connecticut, in 1949-1950, the general trends may have broader applicability. Hollingshead found that:

1. The period of courtship tends to be shorter for those who are remarried than for those who are married for the first time, especially when the woman has been previously married. For example, when the woman had been previously married but the man was marrying for the first time, the couple dated a mean of 13 months before engagement and the engagement lasted about 7 months. On the other hand, when a single woman married a man who had been previously married, Hollingshead found that the period of dating lasted about 17 months and the engagement about 9 months.

2. A smaller proportion of couples who have been previously married than of couples being married for the first time have a formal engagement. Where both members had been married previously, only about half were formally engaged whereas almost 90 per cent of the couples being married for the first time had a formal engagement. Couples who had been previously married tended to have a less formal engagement, they spent less on engagement rings, and a smaller proportion had bridal showers or

[61] August B. Hollingshead, "Marital Status and Wedding Behavior," *Marriage and Family Living*, 14 (1952), pp. 308-311.

bachelor parties. There is less ceremonial investment in remarriage than in first marriage.

3. Not only are courtship practices simpler for the previously married, but the wedding itself is less complex. A smaller proportion of the previously married than of those who had not been married before had a church wedding or other formal type of wedding, a smaller proportion had a double-ring ceremony, the number of guests was smaller, and a smaller number had a reception. After the wedding, a smaller number of the previously married took a wedding trip.

4. The courtship of the previously married also begins in a different manner from the courtship of those couples being married for the first time. The previously married persons in the Hollingshead study tended more often than the individuals being married for the first time to meet on the job or at a friend's home and less often to meet as a pick-up, at a dance, at church, or on a blind date. One of the reasons for the difference in meeting place may be the social circles of the previously married as compared with the younger never-married individuals. The previously married had at one time been accepted into a circle of friends who themselves were married and whose social and family lives were centered around activities of the married. For an older person, the pick-up or the dance signifies an easy mark for nonmarital sex relations and hence the individuals would neither seek nor be sought as potential mates in such a way. On the other hand, the job or the married friend provides a suitable social contact for meeting another mature individual.

In summary, the Hollingshead study indicates that, as compared with persons entering first marriages, individuals who had been married previously have shorter courtship histories, show less ceremonial investment in courtship and marriage, and meet initially in more "prosaic" ways. Hollingshead's data suggest that remarriage is more consciously directed at a voluntary, voidable association than is the first marriage. They support the inference that as the rate of remarriage among the older population increases, practices reflecting permanent availability will also increase among older people.

LATE MARRIAGE: SUMMARY

Marriage after the age of thirty is increasing steadily. The lengthened span of life, leisure time, and a reservoir of divorced persons facilitate late marriage. These factors, coupled with the extension of active adult status under conditions of a trend toward permanent availability as a potential mate, encourage mature individuals to present themselves as youthful for as long as possible. The increasing popularity of remarriage results from this trend. Courtship and mate selection in remarriage show less personal investment than in first marriages: The period of courtship is shorter, there is less attention given to ceremonials and rituals such as showers or formal engagements, weddings are simpler and honeymoons are rarer, and finally the initial meeting is more frequently "arranged" by a friend or relative. Emphasis in matchmaking is upon common interests and common experiences rather than upon complementary emotional needs. The process of courtship and mate selection in remarriage (which is generally late marriage) thus appears to reinforce the tendency toward permanent availability.

Implications of Trends in Courtship and Mate Selection for Family Stability

The trends in intermarriage as well as the increasing time span for potential participation in courtship and mate selection have various implications for the stability of family life. This section will discuss these trends as they affect the incidence of divorce and remarriage and will suggest the possibility of instituting controls over family stability in bilateral societies.

DIVORCE AND REMARRIAGE

The trends relating to religious intermarriage, age at marriage, and remarriage are themselves associated with such diverse factors as religious training of children and premarital sex relations. These trends present a complex of factors that affect the incidence of divorce and remarriage. Implications of these trends for the stability of family life include the five following:

1. The incidence of cross-religious marriage will increase. A study by Burchinal and Chancellor in Iowa showed that interreligious marriages had a lower survival rate than either Protestant or Catholic inmarriages.[62] Summarizing investigations in Michigan, Maryland, and Wash-

[62] Lee G. Burchinal and Loren E. Chancellor, "Survival Rates Among Types of Religiously Homogamous and Interreligious Marriages, Iowa, 1953-1959," *Social Forces*, 41 (1963), pp. 353-362.

ington state, Landis also found that in each study there was a greater percentage of divorces resulting from religious intermarriages than from inmarriages.[63] Thus, as religious-intermarriage rates increase, tendencies toward high divorce rates will probably be sustained.

2. The median age at first marriage will continue to decline or to remain low. Glick found that, until the age of 22, the lower the age at marriage of women, the greater was the probability of their being divorced and remarried. Women who had married for the first time before their eighteenth birthday had triple the probability of divorce and remarriage for women first married in the age range of 22-24. This tendency held regardless of whether the first marriage took place in the 1920, 1930, or 1940 decade.[64] Burchinal and Chancellor also found that the survival rates of marriages were smaller for younger than older brides and bridegrooms.[65] The trend toward early marriage then reinforces high rates of divorce.

3. The rate of marriage of persons over 30 is also increasing. Glick found that even first marriages contracted at the age of 30 or over tend to be of relatively short duration.[66] Here again the likelihood of divorce is increased.

4. The rate of remarriage of the United States population will continue to increase. Monohan found that divorced persons who remarry have a greater probability of

[63] Judson T. Landis, "Marriages of Mixed and Non-Mixed Religious Faith," *American Sociological Review*, 14 (1949), pp. 401-407.

[64] Glick, *op. cit.*

[65] Burchinal and Chancellor, "Survival Rates . . . ," *op. cit.*

[66] Glick, *op. cit.*

another divorce than do persons who are in their first marriage.[67]

5. The number of persons participating in premarital sexual intercourse is increasing. Divorced persons are more likely than happily married persons to have had premarital sexual experiences.[68] The same factors that lead to premarital intercourse appear to increase the probability of divorce.

The above discussion of intermarriage, age at marriage, divorce and remarriage, and premarital sex relations suggests a convergence of these factors to sustain the individual's permanent availability as a potential spouse in American society. Persons who remarry are more likely than those persons entering first marriages to intermarry with someone from another religion. Irreligiosity and tolerance of premarital sex relations are associated.[69] As was indicated in a previous section, Burchinal and Chancellor also found that interreligious marriage is related to age at marriage; in their Iowa sample, intermarriage rates between Protestants and Catholics were highest for persons under 20 (early marriage) or 30 and over (late marriage). Divorced individuals ordinarily remarry. Hence, the fac-

[67] Thomas P. Monohan, "The Changing Nature and Instability of Remarriages," *Eugenics Quarterly,* 5 (1958), pp. 73-85.

[68] Harvey J. Locke, *Predicting Adjustment in Marriage,* New York: Holt, 1951.

[69] Frank Lindenfeld, "A Note on Social Mobility, Religiosity, and Students' Attitudes towards Premarital Sexual Relations," *American Sociological Review,* 25 (1960), pp. 81-84; Jean Dedman, "The Relationship between Religious Attitude and Attitude toward Premarital Sex Relations," *Marriage and Family Living,* 21 (1959), pp. 171-176; Kinsey, *et al. op. cit.*

tors of intermarriage, age at marriage, premarital sex relations, divorce, and remarriage reinforce one another in
promoting universal availability.

THE POSSIBILITY OF CONTROL OF FAMILY STABILITY

Various corporate structures have been developed in non-
Western bilateral societies to restrict or compensate for
universal, permanent availability of the adult population
as potential spouses. For example, in the Philippines, according to Fred Eggan, unilineal kinship systems have not
developed. Instead, kinship is reckoned bilaterally. Among
the Sagada Igorots, a territorial ward-organization system
has been instituted for continuity and stability of social
structure. The ward is associated with a territory for
houses, gardens, public buildings, and ceremonial plat-
forms, with rights and obligations for residents, and with
a traditional history and ceremonial roles. Individuals who
are members of a particular ward can change wards only
through obtaining consent. Prior to marriage, there is much
sexual freedom. Before the birth of children, there is a possibility of divorce. Indeed, if no children are born, the
marriage ordinarily breaks up. However, once children
are born, divorce is difficult. Regulation of divorce is
maintained by the ward. The ward thereby replaces the
centers of authority which would ordinarily be found in
the unilineal kinship system. The restrictions of availability as a potential spouse are primarily temporal and are
applied at the point where orderly replacement of the
generations begins to occur, that is, at the birth of the first
child.[70]

[70] Fred Eggan, "The Sagada Igorots of Northern Luzon," in
George Peter Murdock (ed.), *Social Structure in Southeast Asia,*

Similarly, the Iban utilize a corporate family system to maintain continuity and orderly replacement of generations of nuclear families. Among the Iban, (a) the descent system is bilateral and marriage is monogamous, (b) there is no substantial bride price or dowry, (c) there is assortive mating with little restriction by specific kinship relations, (d) any married couple can be divorced by mutual consent, (e) divorce is a common occurrence, (f) the intimate tie between husband and wife is the basic social structure of the corporate family, and (g) residence at marriage is bilocal (to either the husband's or wife's corporate establishment). In this society, the corporate system permits divorce even after children have been born. The continuity of the family from one generation to the next is to be found in the extended family corporation. Although the relatives of the individual who marries into a corporate group are affines (in-laws), they are personal kindred for his children. Since kinship is reckoned bilaterally, the children have as consanguine relatives the members of the corporate families of both their mother and father. Through marriage between corporate families, a network of stable, congenial kinship units is maintained in the society without disturbing the permanent availability of persons as potential mates. The

New York: Wenner-Gren Foundation, 1960, pp. 24-50. A cross-cultural analysis by Ackerman has indicated the importance of territorial organization in maintaining family stability in societies with bilateral kinship organization. He found that those preliterate bilateral societies in which marriage is restricted to persons already living within the community tend to have lower divorce rates than societies practicing community exogamy. Charles Ackerman, "Affiliations: Structural Determinants of Differential Divorce Rates," *American Journal of Sociology*, 69 (1963), pp. 13-20.

major point to be emphasized is that continuity lies in the corporate structure rather than in the individual nuclear family, where permanent availability of the parents is maintained.[71]

The characteristics of the Sagada Igorot and Iban kinship systems have implications for the future of the family in Western societies. These non-Western systems indicate that corporate social structures can be developed to handle both orderly replacement and permanent availability under bilateral kinship. To compensate for the maintenance of permanent availability, continuity among the Iban is to be found not in the nuclear family but in the corporate structure. In contrast, among the Sagada Igorots, where continuity does occur through the nuclear family, *temporal* restrictions on availability as a spouse are considered necessary. In contemporary western society, there is neither a ward corporate organization nor a family corporate organization. Perhaps at some future time some sort of corporate structure may develop to provide continuity. However, if current trends continue, permanent availability will come to characterize the American courtship and marriage system to a greater extent than at present.

Selected Readings

The research literature on courtship and mate selection is voluminous. Some reports, like Ernest W. Burgess and Paul Wallin, *Engagement and Marriage*, Lippincott, 1953, are concerned with numerous facets of the courtship and mate-selec-

[71] J. D. Freeman, "The Iban of Western Borneo," in Murdock, ed., *Social Structure in Southeast Asia, op. cit.* in note 70, pp. 65-87.

tion process in studies of large samples. Most investigations, however, are limited in scope in such areas as social and cultural factors in mate selection, dating practices, premarital sexual behavior, and complementary needs in mate selection.

Social and cultural factors in mate selection:

Golden, Joseph. "Social Control of Negro-White Intermarriage," *Social Forces*, 36 (1958), pp. 267-269.

Hollingshead, August B. "Cultural Factors in the Selection of Marriage Mates," *American Sociological Review*, 15 (1950), pp. 619-627.

Katz, Alvin M.,and Reuben Hill. "Residential Propinquity and Mate Selection: A Review of Theory, Method, and Fact," *Marriage and Family Living*, 20 (1958), pp. 27-35.

Locke, Harvey J., Georges Sabagh, and Mary Margaret Thomes. "Interfaith Marriages," *Social Problems*, 4 (1957), pp. 333-340.

Thomas, John L. "The Factor of Religion in the Selection of Marriage Mates," *American Sociological Review*, 16 (1951), pp. 487-491.

Vincent, Clark E. "Interfaith Marriages: Problem or Symptom," in Jane Zahn (ed.), *Religion and the Face of America*, University of California (Berkeley), 1959. Reprinted in Marvin B. Sussman (ed.), *Sourcebook in Marriage and the Family*, Houghton Mifflin, 1963, pp. 349-359.

Dating practices:

Burchinal, Lee G. "Research on Young Marriage: Implications for Family Life Education," *Family Life Coordinator*, 9 (1960), pp. 6-24. Reprinted in Sussman, *op. cit. s.v.* Vincent.

Herman, Robert D. "The 'Going Steady' Complex: A Reexamination," *Marriage and Family Living*, 17 (1955), pp. 36-40.

Hollingshead, August B. *Elmtown's Youth*. Wiley, 1949.

Lowrie, Samuel H. "Factors Involved in the Frequency of Dating," *Marriage and Family Living,* 18 (1956), pp. 46-51.

Premarital sexual behavior:

Christensen, Harold T. "Cultural Relativism and Premarital Sex Norms," *American Socialogical Review,* 25 (1960), pp. 31-39.

Ehrmann, Winston W. *Premarital Dating Behavior.* Holt, 1959.

Ehrmann, Winston W. "Premarital Sexual Behavior and Sex Codes of Conduct with Acquaintances, Friends, and Lovers," *Social Forces,* 38 (1959), pp. 158-164.

Reiss, Ira. "The Double Standard in Premarital Intercourse— A Neglected Concept," *Social Forces,* 34 (1956), pp. 224-230.

Complementary needs in mate selection:

Kerckhoff, Alan, and Keith E. Davis. "Value Consensus and Need Complementarity in Mate Selection," *American Sociological Review,* 27 (1962), pp. 295-303.

Rosow, Irving. "Issues in the Concept of Need-Complementarity," *Sociometry,* 20 (1957), pp. 216-233.

Winch, Robert F. *Mate-Selection: A Study of Complementary Needs.* Harper, 1958.

The relationship between courtship practices and divorce is suggested in:

Ackerman, Charles. "Affiliations: Structural Determinants of Differential Divorce Rates," *American Journal of Sociology,* 69 (1963), pp. 13-20.

Burchinal, Lee G., and Loren E. Chancellor. "Survival Rates among Types of Religiously Homogamous and Interreligious Marriages," *Social Forces,* 41 (1963), pp. 353-362.

Christensen, Harold T., and Hanna H. Meissner. "Premarital Pregnancy as a Factor in Divorce," *American Sociological Review,* 18 (1953), pp. 641-644.

6 Kinship and Social Criticism

The permanent-availability model presented in Chapter 4 was based upon the interaction between tendencies toward orderly replacement and tendencies toward permanent availability. Whereas the previous chapter focused upon empirical evidence in courtship and mate selection relevant to tendencies toward permanent availability, this chapter is concerned with kinship groups in contemporary society as vehicles of orderly replacement. The suggestion will be made that because of their composition, the functioning kinship groups in contemporary society are not sufficiently powerful to counteract the development of norms appropriate to permanent availability.

The view that kinship relations in modern society are mainly "expressive" and diffuse is widespread in sociological literature. For example, Paul Reiss in his study of relations among kin wrote:

The expressive nature of extended kinship contact is most clearly seen in one type of extended kinship interaction—the large family gatherings. . . . All the large family gatherings occurred either on a holiday or on the occasion of a family event.[1]

Similarly, Parsons contrasts the domination of the social structure by kinship in primitive societies with the loss of functions by kinship structures in contemporary society.[2] The reduction in the importance of extended kinship structures in contemporary societies implies that they continue to exist mainly for "emotional" and sentimental reasons. Indeed, if the nuclear family actually exists as an independent unit, then no "rational" or "instrumental" function can be defined to justify continued loyalty to extended kin. There is then justification for thinking of extended kinship in contemporary society as a social category somewhat like friendship.

However, Homans and Schneider have provided empirical evidence for regarding kinship and friendship as distinct social categories in contemporary society rather than regarding "functioning" or "effective" relatives as a subcategory of friends. In their study of kinship terminology among 209 Harvard students and faculty, Schneider and Homans distinguished between a person-to-person relationship and a kinship relationship.[3] They found that when a particular "uncle" was called by his first name only, the informant dwelt upon personal qualities (for ex-

[1] Paul J. Reiss, "The Extended Kinship System in the American Urban Middle Class," Ph.D. Dissertation, Harvard University, 1960.

[2] Talcott Parsons and Robert F. Bales, *Family, Socialization and Interaction Process,* Glencoe, Ill.: Free Press, 1955, p. 9.

[3] David M. Schneider and George C. Homans, "Kinship Terminology and the American Kinship System," *American Anthropologist,* 57 (1955), pp. 1194-1208.

ample, mean, unpleasant, pleasant, nice, many things in common). These qualities dominated the relationship. The first-name relationship tended to occur between age and generation equals or when the speaker was the senior. Garigue also noted the informality of relations between generation equals in French Canada.[4] (Otherwise, when the kin term was used, the kinship character of the relationship was dominant.) The Homans and Schneider study suggests that the kinship system in contemporary society is not merely a sentimental survival of the past.

The model of the contemporary American family presented in Chapter 4 was developed in response to the question: "What would happen to American family life if nothing were done to counteract the discontinuities of universal availability in the bilateral kinship system?" It was suggested in the model that an essential for the continuity of family culture from one generation to the next is the presence of a social critic who can intervene in family relationships. The social critic then stimulates the development of family organization strategies to counteract events fostering discontinuity in family culture. The present chapter deals with kin as social critics of family life in contemporary society.

The role of the social critic in maintaining the organization of activities in various areas of social life has received little scrutiny. The theater represents one of the few areas in which the critic has become recognized as part of the institution. Walter Kerr, the drama critic of the *New York Herald Tribune,* has indicated:

The critic is part of the running argument [with regard to

[4] Philip Garigue, "French Canadian Kinship and Urban Life," *American Anthropologist,* 58 (1956), pp. 1090-1101.

the lack of vitality in the American theater]. There must always be someone detached from the [theatrical] process to comment on it. A playwright may have four successes in a row. The first one may be excellent, the second quite good. The third and fourth may be decidedly inferior but be successful for extraneous reasons, perhaps because the first two had been, or because of a star or because of some sentimentality in subject-matter that just happens to catch the fancy of the public.

Since all four of those plays are more or less equally successful at the box office, the playwright himself has no way of knowing which time he did well and which time he may have worked opportunistically. *The real value of a commentator who stays outside the process is to tell the playwright what he is doing this time.* The critic can be wrong, too. But it is essential always that someone stand apart from the box-office receipts, from the popularity of the play—or from the unpopularity of the play—and offer his idea of an objective measurement. This is important to the writer, to the director, to the actor, and to the theater in general. Otherwise one simply gets swallowed up in "what works" and comes to measure one's product by "what works."[5]

Similarly, in family life, a social critic who is outside the nuclear family may be required to evaluate the strategies developed by the family members in terms of their long-run effects (that is, effects on orderly replacement of generations). Otherwise, the nuclear family tends to judge adequacy of its strategies in organization by "what works" in coping with short-run problems.

[5] Walter Kerr, in *Stage and Screen* (one of a series of interviews on the American Character), Santa Barbara: Fund for the Republic, 1962, p. 27.

The discussion by Kerr suggests that the role of the critic, regardless of the social arrangements being evaluated, tends to have four characteristics:

1. *The social critic is located outside the social arrangement he is criticizing.* In the theater, the critic does his actual criticism away from the theater; however, he must have access to the events he is evaluating. Although the critic role depends upon the existence of a theater, the person acting as critic obtains his financial rewards and acclaim from another source (newspaper, magazine). The location of the theater critic outside the theater suggests a similar location with respect to the effective family critic. It is to be expected that the effective family critic will be someone who is outside the particular nuclear family he is criticizing (as a mother criticizing practices in her child's family of procreation). We would also anticipate that the effective family critic will be financially independent and live in a residence apart from the nuclear family he is evaluating.

2. *The social critic has developed clear standards for performance in the unit he is evaluating.* The "objective measurement" offered by the critic results from a long period of involvement with performances in comparable situations. This long experience and high involvement provide the critic with his credentials. In the theater, the critic ordinarily has had a background of academic or theatrical training and has served as apprentice or substitute to an established critic before he is accepted as competent by playwrights, directors, and actors. The family critic would gain his (or her) credentials through high involvement in family affairs from childhood in a family

in which the norms and values of the family culture were explicitly defined. He would also anticipate a period of informal apprenticeship before eventual acceptance as competent.

3. *The social critic communicates to the unit he is criticizing the discrepancies between standards he would like to maintain and actual performance.* Until the critic communicates his evaluation to the participants in the unit which is the object of his criticism, he has not taken part in the interaction tying him to the unit. The role of the critic thus includes his providing "feedback" to the unit he is evaluating. Otherwise, he cannot influence the performance of the members of the unit. In the theater, the performers anxiously await the critical reviews following the initial performance of a play. In the family, no institutionalized form of criticism such as the review exists. Instead, the family critic must resort to more informal means: gossip, "the grapevine," a friendly talk, or an argument. Occasionally, the family critic submits his evaluation of the deviant behavior for review by a professional critic dealing in interpersonal relations. This professional critic may be either a marriage counselor or one of the newspaper critics who comment on family problems (Ann Landers, Edan Wright).

4. *The social critic attempts to minimize the amount of deviant behavior in the unit he is evaluating.* Theater critics, in their attempt to influence the theater, may try to influence the reputations of the performers (including playwrights and directors as well as actors) and the box-office receipts for a play—adversely or advantageously. The family critic may also try to reduce deviant behavior

through his known capacity to influence the reputation of the person in the extended family or to impose economic sanctions. Frequently, the members of the criticized nuclear family may view such attempts at control as "interfering" in their personal life. However, the overt or implicit threat of sanctions may be strong enough to stimulate the criticized person to conform with expectations in the family culture.

Various family sociologists have indicated that the social critic is important for maintaining family life (although they may have used terms other than "critic"). According to Zimmerman, without powerful leadership in the kinship system, there may be insufficient pressure to prevent the members of the nuclear family from pursuing their individualistic wants and desires. The power of the Roman patriarch exemplifies the large amount of control exerted over the nuclear family when the head of the extended family held all authority and property of the entire group in trust. Zimmerman contrasts the stability of the patriarchal "trustee" family with the instability of the urban "atomistic" family in which values of individualism predominate over those of familism.[6] Similarly, Burgess, Locke, and Thomes point out that "the most extreme conceptual formulation of the institutional family would be one in which its unity would be determined entirely by the . . . social pressure impinging on family members."[7]

[6] Carle C. Zimmerman, *Family and Civilization,* New York: Harper, 1947.

[7] Ernest W. Burgess, Harvey J. Locke, and Mary Margaret Thomes, *The Family from Institution to Companionship,* New York: American Book, 1963, p. 3.

By contrast, in the extreme formulation of the companion-ship family, the family members are bound together by "bonds of affection, congeniality, and common interests." Burgess, Locke, and Thomes regard the "diminishing control of the kinship group and of the community over the family unit" and the increasing dependence upon internal "bonds of affection, temperamental compatibility, and mutual interests" as contributing to the instability of families of the companionship type.[8]

This chapter focuses upon the role of members of kinship units as social critics in developing and maintaining organization of family life through generations. The sections comprising this chapter discuss the three following problems:

1. *What do relatives actually do in their role of social critics with respect to other relatives?* Not all relatives act as social critics to their kin. Because a social critic must earn his credentials, an individual is not as a matter of course actively engaged in critical interaction with his relatives. A distinction must be made between effective kin who are actively engaged in kinship relations and "nominal kin." Being a member of the kindred or the effective kin becomes an achieved status rather than an ascribed status. The section The Kindred will examine activities associated with the kindred and factors in selecting and maintaining the kindred.

2. *In which phases in the family life cycle is the kindred most active?* How does interaction with the kindred change over the course of the family life cycle? The

[8] *Ibid.*, p. 4.

changing character of the kindred over time may provide additional insights into the character of kinship in contemporary society. If the kinship system operates to provide social criticism for orderly replacement, then in contemporary society the interaction between relatives would be greatest when the children are growing up. The relationship between changes in family composition and interaction with relatives is indicated in the section on The Family Life Cycle and the Kindred.

3. *If membership in the kindred is an achieved rather than ascribed status, is it then possible for nonrelatives to take on the activities of the kindred?* Many families have friends who are regarded as "being in the family." Moreover, large-scale organizations can also assume activities normally associated with the kindred (here, specifically, criticism of family life). The section The Large-Scale Organization as a Quasi Kindred will take note of ways in which large organizations sometimes provide a locus for the performance of activities appropriate to a kindred.

The Kindred

In contemporary society, individuals differ widely in their interaction with relatives. One class of relatives actively particpates in an individual's kinship system. These relatives constitute the individual's effective kin and include those with whom the individual has intimate contact. Relatives achieve effective-kin status by their participation in the individual's kinship system. The activity of effective kin most relevant to orderly replacement is their role as social critic with respect to family matters. A sec-

ond class of relatives has kinship ties with the individual
by birth or by marriage but little involvement in his personal life. The second class of relatives constitutes the individual's nominal kin. All members of the individual's
kinship unit (including nominal kin) constitute the universe from which the effective kin, the kindred, are drawn.[9]

ACTIVITIES OF THE KINDRED

What does the kindred do? The concept of effective kin
suggests an enterprise in which the kinship unit is engaged. The enterprise of the kinship system is the reproduction of the family culture in the next generation.
Ideally, the kindred attempts to conserve existing patterns
of family behavior and to minimize the amount of disruption among relatives. Characteristics of ideal kindred relations include norms relating to participation in rituals
and ceremonies, to promotion of the welfare of family
members, to making personal resources available, to trust
in the kindred, and to a maximum of communication.

Participation in rituals and ceremonies

Numerous rituals and ceremonies are associated with traditional transitions in the life cycle of family members.
Participation in festive rituals and ceremonies (such as

[9] Sometimes the kindred is called "intimate relatives" or "effective relatives" or a "close-knit kinship network" or simply "family." See Lorraine Lancaster, "Some Conceptual Problems in the
Study of Family and Kin Ties in the British Isles," *British Journal of Sociology,* 12 (1961), pp. 317-333, and J. B. Loudon, "Kinship and Crisis in South Wales," *British Journal of Sociology,* 12
(1961) pp. 333-350.

weddings, naming of infants, religious confirmation ceremonies, or academic graduation rites) enables the kindred to reinforce the parents for having done well in
launching the offspring along the traditional patterns of
family life, and, through gifts and congratulatory remarks,
to reward the offspring for adhering to these patterns. At
funerals and other bereavement affairs, the presence of
the kindred serves to reassure the bereaved that only one
link in the kinship chain has been lost and that the living
will continue as they always have done. In disruptive situations such as divorce or disgrace (for example, illegitimate motherhood, prison), when the relatives "stand by"
the individual, they are offering their support for him providing he will resume his responsibility in the kinship enterprise.

For the kindred to operate effectively, there must be
consensus that a particular relative belongs in the kindred. Since ceremonies related to life-cycle transitions
permit the celebrants to reaffirm their reciprocal status as
kindred, failure to meet expectations with respect to participation in these ceremonies may result in fissions among
kin. Leichter and Mitchell report that:

One feud, which resulted in an eight month fission between siblings, was over the failure to include a woman's
daughter as bridesmaid at her [the mother's] sister-in-law's
[daughter's] wedding. . . . The girl's mother explained: "Everyone walked up to me and said, "How come Cheryl wasn't in
the ceremony?' and I said, 'Well, she just doesn't rate,' and I
was very angry about it. . . . There are only three grandchildren in the family. . . . Two granddaughters walked in the

wedding procession . . . and my daughter didn't. . . . My daughter was most certainly insulted and hurt.[10]

This feud was precipitated by the implicit suggestion that although the girl was a "close" relative, she was not a member of the intimate kindred. The excluded girl and her mother apparently believed that all relatives of a given kinship position should be given equal opportunity to assume the rights and duties of the kindred. Distinguishing kindred from nonkindred evidently involves not only how distantly two individuals are related but also whether the equal-opportunity principle is operating.

Promoting the welfare of the family members

A traditional kinship norm is that welfare of kindred has priority over the welfare of nonkindred. This welfare priority includes assistance in economic matters. For example, a retailer may give a discount to a relative, or a consumer may patronize a relative, or a proprietor may hire a relative. In case of need, relatives ideally are expected to provide aid within the limits of their resources. Such aid may include residence, nursing, advice, free professional service, or financial aid.[11] Finally, the welfare norms include the performance of favors. For example, a gift to a kindred member should be larger than a gift to a

[10] Hope J. Leichter and William E. Mitchell, "Feuds and Fissions within the Conjugal Kindred," paper presented at annual meeting of American Anthropological Association, Minneapolis, Minnesota, 1960.

[11] Marvin B. Sussman and Lee Burchinal, "Kin Family Network: Unheralded Structure in Current Conceptualizations of Family Functioning," *Marriage and Family Living*, 24 (1962), pp. 231-240.

nonmember. The welfare principle in kinship provides for reciprocation when resources are sufficient. Leichter and Mitchell reported that "being taken advantage of" was one of the common issues over which feuds and fissions developed among kin in their sample of New York Jewish families. Many of the relatives felt that they were being exploited by other relatives.[12]

Making personal resources available

If an individual is to promote the welfare of his kin, he must make his personal resources available to them. However, the individual and his kin must consider the welfare position of the relative as inferior to the individual's own position before his assistance is expected. Since resources vary with socioeconomic position and with age, kinds of assistance given depend upon the comparative status and age of the giver and receiver of aid. Middle-class families provide a greater amount of financial aid and a larger supply of costly gifts than working-class families.[13] Similarly, mature persons have greater financial resources and experience to impart than younger people. The important point is that the individual is expected to make these resources available to his relatives who might require them. Conversely, the individual lacking resources is not expected to sacrifice to assist a relative. Most people do not ask relatives with many problems of their own (such as infirmity or poverty) for assistance in times of illness or financial crisis.

[12] Leichter and Mitchell, *op. cit.*
[13] Sussman and Burchinal, *op. cit.*

Trust of kindred

Operating in conjunction with the norm of promoting the welfare of kindred is another norm of placing trust in effective kin. The kindred can best accomplish the transmission of family culture to the next generation in an atmosphere of congeniality and trust. For the giver of aid or favors, the trust norm prevents cheating a relative or misrepresenting actions. Since two relatives can seldom enter into a simultaneous exchange of favors, receipt of aid and favors implies an obligation for the recipient to reciprocate later should the opportunity arise. Deviations from the norm of trust leave relatives feeling "cheated," "made a fool of," or "humiliated."[14]

A maximum of communication

Interaction based upon mutual trust implies that all information pertinent to the kindred will be communicated. The content of communication among kin concerning still another relative includes gossip, rumors, and any news about the particular relative which might determine modes of action: Is the relative "deserving" of aid or favors? Is the relative to be trusted? Is the relative conforming to traditional kinship expectations? Is someone in the relative's family approaching a marriage, divorce, birth, or other life-cycle transition? The content of communication between two relatives generally involves discussion of problems concerning socialization of children (if the relatives are parents), life-cycle transitions, allocation of funds, or other business of the kinship unit. Politics, business, sports, fashions, science, or humanistic mat-

[14] Leichter and Mitchell, op. cit.

ters are used mainly as fillers in the conversations. However, since the kinship system operates in spite of differences in view on matters not related to the reproduction of the family culture, where differences of opinion would interfere with the family enterprise, the controversial topics are generally avoided. Because of this avoidance, families with members scattered in social status, education, religion, and interests are marked by a blandness in interaction. The symbolic importance of open communication among kin is suggested by the "refusal to talk" with relatives who have not maintained their kinship obligations (for example, have exploited or slighted the individual).

SELECTION OF KINDRED

Who belongs to the kindred? Without corporate bodies such as family businesses, cousins' clubs, family circles, or other associations to define membership in the kindred, each individual in a bilateral system may have innumerable, vague kinship obligations to maintain. Under a unilineal system, membership in the lineage can be easily identified. Under a bilateral system, membership in a family corporation can identify recipients and givers of kinship aid and favors. However, contemporary society is characterized by neither unilineality nor family corporations. As a result, each individual must select his functioning relatives from a reservoir of nominal relatives; at the same time, these relatives also select or reject the individual as a functioning relative. This selection process introduces the question: What are the factors in the selection of kindred?

With each generation, there is a breakdown and then a re-forming of the kindred. Any individual in a society has prior generations of kindred to orient him in his socialization. Although the orienting generation of kin is generally immediately ascending (the generation of his parents), the generation of his grandparents also participates in his orientation. In addition, kin of the individual's own generation (his lateral kin) are involved in orienting the individual in the family culture. However, the kin of the individual's own generation also constitute the emerging generation. Eventually, the emerging generation matures and the individual and his lateral kin become the main orienting generation for their descending kin (later generation). The descending kin now constitute the emerging generation and continue the process.

The participation of the lateral kin in both the emerging kindred and orienting kindred of the individual provides continuity in kinship relations. As the older generations of orienting kindred die off, individuals must mutually select an orienting kindred from their lateral kin for transmitting the family norms and values to the newly emerging generation.

How is the kindred of an individual selected? Litwak found that loss of face-to-face contact did not reduce identification with extended family.[15] On the other hand, Reiss did find that degree of relationship as well as characteristics related to friendship was associated with the frequency of interaction between kin.[16] Probably selec-

---

[15] Eugene Litwak, "Geographic Mobility and Extended Family Cohesion," *American Sociological Review*, 25 (1960), pp. 385-394.
[16] Reiss, *op. cit.*

tion for kindred membership is associated with frequency of interaction and intensity of friendship relationships. These criteria for kindred selection will now be considered.

1. Frequency of interaction among kin varies inversely with the distance of the kinsman's residence. Propinquity provides numerous opportunities to reinforce a friendly relationship and, thereby, becomes an important element in the maintenance of friendly relations. Time, cost, and distance were mentioned frequently in Reiss's study as reasons for differential contact with kin (that is, for seeing some kin more often than others).[17]

2. Similarity in age, sex, and life experiences increases the probability of a high degree of solidarity and interaction among kin. Individuals with common experiences and similar interests tend to "hit it off." The Reiss study indicated that common interests were often reported as a reason for differential contact among kin.[18] Garigue found that personal preference played a large role in selecting affines (in-law relatives) or cousins with whom contact was maintained.[19] In interaction among kin of the same generation (lateral kin), men interact more with other men and women with other women.[20] (Presumably, in contemporary society with its minimum of restraints on who can be regarded as a potential mate, assistance and control among kin could suffer under the pressure of cross-sex jealousy, lack of trust, and anxiety over a fairly close

[17] *Ibid.*
[18] *Ibid.*
[19] Garigue, *op. cit.*
[20] Reiss, *op. cit.*

relative as a possible rival. In this respect, modern urban families are somewhat similar to the bilateral Chiricahua Apache among whom relations tend to be intimate between same-sex siblings and cousins but formal between cross-sex relatives.[21])

3. Congeniality in personality traits increases the probability of friendly relations between kin. In the Reiss study, personal characteristics of specific kin were given as the most frequent reason for differential contact with various kin.[22]

4. The role of a semblance of equality in the relationship as a prerequisite for friendship is suggested by Reiss's finding that a close relationship between parent and child is destroyed with the increasing senility of the parent.[23]

The findings thus suggest that friendly relations among kin in contemporary society will occur under conditions comparable to those among nonrelatives. Friendly relatives who also have considerable personal resources are likely to be in a position of being effective social critics of family relations.

In different ethnic groups, establishing priorities for membership in the kindred may involve such criteria as sex, age, socioeconomic status, and personal achievement or ability as well as consanguinity or distance of the relationship (for example, first cousins versus fifth cousins). For instance, the comparative importance given to age as

[21] Morris E. Opler, "An Outline of Chiricahua Apache Social Organization," in Fred Eggan, ed., *Social Anthropology of North American Tribes*, Chicago: University of Chicago Press, 1937, pp. 173-242.

[22] Reiss, *op. cit.*

[23] *Ibid.*

opposed to sex as a basis for authority may affect kinship relations. Strodtbeck found that Jewish mothers apparently have more power than Italian Catholic mothers in family interaction and that the power dispersion is greater in Italian Catholic families.[24] This finding suggests that sex is not an important criterion for authority among Jewish families but may be among Italian Catholic families. Applied to kinship relations, this suggestion implies that priority among kindred is developed on the basis of sex in the Italian Catholic family whereas age differences may explain major kinship priorities among the Jewish families.

Since age is ordinarily associated with development of independence and with achievement, where age is the criterion for authority and kindred selection, child-raising practices tend to be more permissive and independence is encouraged. Where sex category is the criterion for authority and kindred selections, emphasis is placed upon minimizing risks in raising conforming, obedient children.

Formal membership in the kinship unit is not a necessary criterion for participation in the kindred. Many individuals are isolated from their kin either by residence or by difference in social status. Since the advantages of having a kindred are many, isolated nuclear families will often utilize their friends as kindred.[25] Inasmuch as selection of a functioning kindred occurs informally even among biological relatives, these kindred by complementary filiation do not require a specific position in the kinship

[24] Fred L. Strodtbeck, "Family Interaction, Values, and Achievement," in David C. McClelland *et al.*, *Talent and Society*, Princeton: Van Nostrand, 1948, pp. 135-194.

[25] Loudon, *op. cit.* in note 9.

structure (as uncle or mother's brother). The nuclear family can simply regard the friend as being "like a close relative."

FEMALE INVOLVEMENT IN KINSHIP

In unilineal societies, the major pressure for maintaining the lineage appears to be found in the male. Gluckman's discussion of African kinship suggests that even in matrilineal societies the males retain the property rights to their sisters' children.[26] Indeed, the mother's brother in the matrilineal society holds much authority over his sister and her children. In contrast, several studies have indicated that women in contemporary society tend to maintain a closer relationship with their immediate family and kin than do men:

1. In his investigation of Boston families Reiss found that married women have greater contact with their consanguine (blood) relatives than do married men with their relatives. Consistent with this finding, married men have a greater frequency of contact with their in-laws than do married women with their in-laws.[27] Stryker found that women are more likely than men to be more dependent upon their mothers and that the adjustment of the wife to her mother tends to be higher than her adjustment to her mother-in-law.[28]

[26] Max Gluckman, *Custom and Conflict in Africa,* Glencoe, Ill.: Free Press, 1955, pp. 54-80.

[27] Reiss, *op. cit.* See also Elizabeth Bott, *Family and Social Network,* London: Tavistock Publications, 1957.

[28] Sheldon Stryker, "The Adjustment of Married Offspring to their Parents," *American Sociological Review,* 20 (1955), pp. 149-154.

2. The findings on kinship relations of women as compared with men are complemented by results of studies on interaction with male and female relatives. Reiss found that people are in more contact with female extended-family members than with male members. His respondents of both sexes also reported that in interaction with kin they had closer relationships to female than to male relatives of the same degree of relationship (except for lateral-generation relatives).[29] In her sample of Jewish families in New York, Hope Leichter indicated that women more than men reported "a great deal" of interaction with their kin, lists of relatives seen by respondents contained more women than men, and more couples lived with the wife's family than with the husband's family.[30] Robins and Tomanec found that young adults generally felt closer to maternal grandparents, aunts, uncles, and cousins than to comparable paternal relatives. Moreover, they felt closer to aunts than to uncles and to female cousins rather than male cousins.[31]

In sum, there is general agreement in research that women tend to be more involved in kinship obligations and activities than do males.

Ordinarily, involvement in particular kinds of interpersonal relations facilitates the internalization of norms pertaining to those relations. Since women are more in-

[29] Reiss, *op. cit.*

[30] Hope J. Leichter, "Normative Intervention in an Urban Bilateral Kinship System." Paper read at annual meeting of the American Anthropological Association, December 30, 1959.

[31] Lee N. Robins and Miroda Tomanec, "Closeness to Blood Relatives Outside the Immediate Family," *Marriage and Family Living*, 24 (1962), pp. 340-346.

volved than men in participation with kin and in carrying out kinship obligations, they would be expected to internalize to a greater extent the norms and values related to kinship. The assumptions concerning orderly replacement emphasize tradition rather than change in family and kinship norms. In internalizing these norms, females would be expected to be more conservative than males with respect to family life. Findings in various investigations support the expectation of greater conservatism of females in matters related to the family:

1. Boys more often than girls condone drinking, gambling, and dishonest business practices.[32]

2. Girls more often than boys believe that having children is necessary for a happy marriage.[33]

3. Girls are more reluctant in attitude than boys to participate in cross-religious dating and marriage.[34]

4. Women are less inclined than men to have premarital sexual intercourse.[35]

[32] Albert J. Reiss and Albert L. Rhodes, *A Sociopsychological Study of Conforming and Deviating Behavior Among Adolescents,* U.S. Office of Education Cooperative Research Project 507, 1959.

[33] Ernest W. Burgess, "A Study of the Development of the Child in the Family," in Nels Anderson, ed., *Studies of the Family,* Volume 2, Goettingen: Vandenhoeck and Ruprecht, 1957, pp. 17-45.

[34] Lee G. Burchinal, "Membership Groups and Attitudes toward Cross-Religious Dating and Marriage," *Marriage and Family Living,* 22 (1960), pp. 248-253.

[35] Ernest W. Burgess and Paul Wallin, *Engagement and Marriage,* New York: Lippincott, 1953; Harold T. Christensen and George R. Carpenter, "Value-Behavior Discrepancies Regarding Premarital Coitus in Three Western Cultures," *American Sociological Review,* 27 (1962), pp. 66-74.

5. Women more often than men adhere to traditional religious practices and beliefs.[36]

6. More men than women remain unmarried.[37]

The tendency for women to participate in kinship relations, however, may under certain conditions produce a willingness to change patterns of family life. When families are comparatively isolated from their biological kindred and develop a quasi kindred of friends, the women members of the quasi kindred may reinforce in each other the view that different norms of family life are more appropriate than the traditional norms. Quasi kindreds of friends tend to develop in middle-class suburbs such as Park Forest or Crestwood Heights. According to Riesman, in Crestwood Heights the mothers rather than the fathers have adopted a more progressive outlook in family life. The men remain "somewhat imbedded in older entrepreneurial values." He suggests that "with respect to child-rearing and other values, *educated* upper-middle-class women are somewhat readier to change, more fashion-prone, more open, in ideas as well as in dress, than their menfolk."[38]

In summary, women appear to be both more highly involved in kinship relations and more conservative in family matters than men. The development of a quasi

[36] Bernard Lazerwitz, "Some Factors Associated with Variations in Church Attendance," *Social Forces*, 39 (1961), pp. 301-309.

[37] David M. Heer, "The Marital Status of Second-Generation Americans," *American Sociological Review*, 26 (1961), pp. 233-241.

[38] David Riesman, "Styles of Response of Social Change," *Journal of Social Issues*, 17 (1960), p. 85.

kindred of friends may provide an exception to these tendencies. In general, however, the findings support the contention that the essential character of kinship is orderly replacement of the family culture from one generation to the next. In the extreme case, orderly replacement implies exact duplication and complete conservation of social values and norms relating to the family. Generally, as critics in the kinship system, women attempt to establish conservative opposition against tendencies toward family discontinuity.

Various interpretations may be offered concerning the involvement of women in American kinship groups. Two of these interpretations are presented here.

One interpretation is based upon the premise that in contemporary society any particular nuclear family persists as a recognizable unit throughout the lifetime of its members—the mother, father, sons, and daughters. This persistence occurs despite the fact that the family may no longer live together. Goode suggests that in American society close kinship relations are maintained primarily between families of adult siblings and between parents and their children's families of procreation.[39] This emphasis upon sibling and parent-child ties implies that kinship relationships in contemporary society tend to be extensions of roles in the nuclear family. A woman acts toward her sister-in-law as she would toward a sister; she acts toward her parents-in-law as she would toward her own parents. The functionalist view is that the role of women in the nuclear family focuses upon maintaining integra-

[39] William J. Goode, *World Revolution and Family Patterns,* New York: Free Press, 1963.

tion and solidarity. By extending this role to in-laws and their families, women become the integraters of the kindred. This interpretation would attribute the involvement of women in kinship groups to the emergence of the nuclear family as the predominant kinship unit in contemporary society.

A second interpretation of the involvement of women in relationships with kindred in contemporary society is based upon the separation of the location and personnel in economic production from the location and personnel in consumption activities. According to this interpretation, with the emergence of industrialization and urbanization in Western Europe, the place of work and the work group were separated from the place of residence and the family group. The husband became highly involved in production and the wife retained her involvement in the residence and domestic matters. Those activities which were associated primarily with residence and domestic relationships were regarded as falling into the wife's province. Domestic affairs and residence pertain mainly to nonproductive activities (especially to patterns of consumption) and to the maintenance of relationships not related to economic production. These nonproductive relationships in contemporary society generally include the kindred. Patterns of providing help and promoting the welfare of the kindred act mainly to increase the capacity to consume goods and services (either luxuries or necessities) in related families. Industrialization and urbanization hence have acted to make the kinship group (except in family-controlled businesses) primarily a consumption unit considered to be in the woman's province. This interpretation suggests that as married women become more involved in the productive processes in society through their increased participation in the labor force, specialization in kinship relationships by sex may decline. With this decline in specialization, men might be expected to increase their involvement in kinship matters.

EFFECTIVENESS OF THE KINDRED

Is the kindred effective in the transmission of family culture from one generation to the next? In this chapter, the kindred has been regarded as composed of relatives drawn from the kinship groups to which an individual belongs. The enterprise of the kindred is to reproduce the family culture in the succeeding generation. Kindred membership, informal as it may be, is a status achieved rather than ascribed. The kindred participates in rituals and ceremonies associated with traditional transitions in the life cycle of family members, promotes the welfare of the family members, utilizes a norm of mutual trust, and is characterized also by open communication among its members. Insofar as there is agreement among the kindred that these norms of kinship participation are appropriate for family life, orderly replacement tends to be sustained. The findings relating to kinship relations, however, reveal two factors which decrease the effectiveness of the kindred's performance as a social critic.

The first factor affecting the effectiveness of the kindred is its indefinite composition. With kindred membership an achieved status rather than an ascribed status, members can withdraw voluntarily and the individual can change the membership of the group he accepts as kindred in order to meet his needs as critical situations arise. Indeed in times of crisis the individual would call only upon those relatives or quasi relatives who have the particular resources demanded by the specific critical situations. Resources may include emotional support, congenial ideas and values, or material goods. These relatives may leave the kindred as soon as the crisis is over. The kindred is thus unstable as a collective enterprise because the individual can manipulate its membership and membership is voluntary. The instability of the kindred interferes with its effectiveness for invoking sanctions to enforce its criticism.

The second factor influencing the effectiveness of the kindred is the greater involvement of women than men in kinship matters. In societies in which the kindred is capable of enforcing its social criticism, men make the major decisions not only with respect to kinship matters but also in economic and political affairs. They are therefore in a position to impose sanctions in case of deviance from traditional family norms. This situation is found both in patrilineal and matrilineal societies. In contemporary societies, however, although men are responsible for major decisions in productive and political affairs, women tend to be social critics in family and kinship relations. Lacking authority to enforce economic or political sanctions upon deviants, the women are limited in the extent to which they can control orderly replacement of family norms and values from one generation to the next.

The two factors—indefinite composition of the kindred and the greater involvement of women in kinship affairs—indicate that the structure of the contemporary bilateral kindred itself interferes with its operation as an enterprise aimed at orderly replacement.

The Family Life Cycle and the Kindred

When is the kindred most active in its operation as a collective enterprise? Kinship roles and obligations as well as amount of interaction with kindred appear to differ at various points in the family life-cycle. As individuals get married, have children, and in time raise these children, they regard their relatives in a series of different ways.

Paul Reiss investigated patterns of kinship obligations and interaction among 161 individuals in the Boston area.[40] He classified phases of the family life cycle as follows: (1) the unmarried adult; (2) the early years of marriage or the childbearing phases, which Reiss regarded arbitrarily as the first fifteen years of marriage; (3) the mature family or the child-raising phase; (4) the stage after the children had left home; and (5) widowhood. Reiss distinguished between phase 3 and phase 4 according to whether or not most of the children had left home. The discussion of the family life cycle and kinship in this section will focus upon the childbearing phase (phase 2) and the later stages (phases 4 and 5) in order indicate how interaction and obligations are related to the orderly replacement of the family from one generation to the next.

THE CHILDBEARING PHASE

Reiss found that the greatest sense of obligation to maintain contact with kin occurred in the childbearing phase.[41]

[40] Paul Reiss, *op. cit.*
[41] *Ibid.*

During this phase, and no other, respondents considered relatives as more important than friends. This was the period during which most aid was received in the form of home service. By home service Reiss meant providing a home, helping with the housework, nursing the sick, and minding children. More than other individuals, respondents in the childbearing phase reported their having kin as advantageous to them. To these respondents in the childbearing phase, kin represented not only a sense of belonging (as they did for other phases) but also a source of security and advice. None of the respondents in the childbearing phase reported no advantages to their having kin. However, the respondents in the childbearing phase were also comparatively high in indicating that they found specific disadvantages to having kin. More than those in later phases, the respondents in the childbearing phase saw relatives as prone to take advantage of people and especially as interfering in family affairs. This interference presumably comprised voluntary giving of advice, suggestions, or perhaps material aid to the young family when the members of the young family did not want this assistance.

It is noteworthy that the nuclear family's greatest involvement with kin occurs in the childbearing stage (at least for the Reiss sample). This is the period of the family life cycle in which the nuclear family is most actively engaged in the replacement of one generation by the next. During this period of most intensive socialization of the children, the nuclear family relies upon aid from relatives. Along with giving aid, however, kin apparently "interfere" with the operation of the nuclear family and make claims upon it. After the childbearing stage of the family cycle, there is a continual decrease in reports on relatives as a source of help, on relatives as taking advantage of people, and on interference by relatives.[42]

The childbearing phase in the family life cycle ordinarily coincides with the period during which upward mobility in social status also occurs. Contrary to the common belief that kinship ties are generally broken when a couple moves upward, Garigue found that loss of contact occurred mainly with lateral kin (same generation) at the lower status level. In his sample, a new kin group formed rapidly at the higher status level. This segmentation of kinship groups also resulted when his Montreal families moved from French to English culture.[43] This movement apparently represents a shift from one set of orienting kin to another.

Increase in kinship solidarity during the childbearing phase even when the children have "moved" to a different culture is also indicated by Campisi's investigation of the children of Italian immigrants.[44] Campisi interprets this renewed solidarity as the realization of the immigrant parents that they have moved to America and that the children have established independent households. It is equally plausible that the presence of grandchildren has influenced the attitudes not only of the immigrants but also of their married children.

[42] *Ibid.*

[43] Garigue, *op. cit.* See also Eugene Litwak, "Occupational Mobility and Extended Family Cohesion," *American Sociological Review*, 25 (1960), pp. 9-21.

[44] Paul J. Campisi, "Ethnic Family Patterns: The Italian Family in the United States," *American Journal of Sociology*, 53 (1948), pp. 443-449.

THE LATER PHASES OF THE FAMILY LIFE CYCLE

Do grandparents constitute a superannuated generation which plays little or no role in the transmission of family culture? Or do grandparents continue to participate as an orienting generation?

In some societies, grandparenthood has been institutionalized as controlling and assisting; in other societies, the grandparent role is characterized by warm and friendly actions. Dorrian Apple studied the ethnological reports of 75 societies to determine the relationship between the authority of grandparents and the extent to which the grandparents were on warm and friendly terms with their grandchildren.[45] She found that:

1. In societies where the grandparental generation exercises considerable authority over the parental generation (after the birth of grandchildren), the relationship between the grandchildren and grandparents is generally not one of friendly equality.

2. When parents hold unequal household authority in the nuclear family, the grandchildren will be more friendly with those grandparents associated with the parent who has less authority than they will with the grandparents on the side of the greater authority.

The Apple findings suggest that authority and friendliness are incompatible with each other. That is, authority is a superordination-subordination relationship whereas friendship is a relationship between equals. However, the results of other studies indicate that in the Amer-

[45] Dorrian Apple, "The Social Structure of Grandparenthood," *American Anthropologist,* 58 (1956), pp. 656-663.

ican kinship system, a different kind of reciprocity may be involved. For example, a 1950 study by Sussman in New Haven, Connecticut, provided information on assistance by parents in the early years of their child's marriage.[46] The sample consisted of 97 Protestant, middle-class couples with married children. Sussman found that:

1. Parents gave as reasons for wanting to help their children the desire to continue to grow and develop with their children as well as the "privilege for companionship with grandchildren." The parents regarded themselves as still youthful and not yet ready for retirement from family roles. Moreover, they did not want the children to begin married life at a reduced socioeconomic position.

2. Where there was a help pattern established with the married children, the majority of parents indicated that this pattern included nursing care and assistance in vacations for the married children. Nursing care occurred mainly as caring for the grandchildren during the mother's illness or confinement, or at vacation time.

3. The parents expected their children to reciprocate by continued show of affection, joint participation in some activities, and personal service and attention.

The findings by Sussman suggest that the American grandparent provides an indulgent, companionate relationship with his children and grandchildren. In return, the grandparent expects his children to accord him an elder-statesman role which contains a right to assist and control the younger generation.

[46] Marvin B. Sussman, "The Help Pattern in the Middle-Class Family," *American Sociological Review*, 18 (1953), pp. 22-28.

Similarly, Reiss reports that in each successive phase in the family life cycle, there was an increase in the proportion of respondents reporting companionship as a specific advantage of kin. At the same time, there was also an increase in describing as a disadvantage of kinship the obligation to supply residence and financial aid to other relatives.[47]

The close relationship between parents and their married children and grandchildren is further indicated in a study by Streib and Thompson. They found that the large majority of grandparents report frequent interaction with their children and grandchildren. Moreover, the elderly tend to see their children and grandchildren more often and to feel closer to them than to their own siblings.[48]

Taken together, the studies by Sussman, by Reiss, and by Streib and Thompson show two kinds of orienting activity of grandparents: the authority style and the indulgent style. These studies suggest further that these styles are not incompatible in kinship relations in American society. Instead, these styles appear in their combined form to be a continuation of the conditional love relationship in parent-child relations in which the parent rewards the young child for behaving properly. Affectionate behavior (indulgence) is withheld when the child misbehaves. Viewed in this way, the indulgence-authority pattern of American grandparents represents an attempt to retain an active adult status in the parent-child relationship as

[47] Paul Reiss, *op. cit.*

[48] Gordon F. Streib and Wayne E. Thompson, "The Older Person in a Family Context," in Clark Tibbits, ed., *Handbook of Social Gerontology*, Chicago: University of Chicago Press, 1960, pp. 447-488.

long as possible. This emphasis on extending adulthood status is consistent with the permanent-availability conceptual model presented in Chapter 4. Sooner or later, the social and material resources of the grandparent are exhausted and reluctantly the grandparent becomes superannuated. This reluctance is suggested by the fact that even at the age of 75 three-fourths of the elderly population do not live in the household of their children or of other relatives.[49] The older person is also hesitant about seeking help from his adult children.[50] Perhaps in accepting assistance (and by implication a lower intrafamily status) the older person feels that he is jeopardizing his own indulgent-authority role with his children and grandchildren.

To summarize, kinship relationships are strongest during the active periods of replacement of one generation of family groups by the next. There is much assistance especially during the early years of marriage and through the childbearing years (defined operationally as the first fifteen years). Indulgent behavior of grandparents, too, apparently has an influence in controlling behavior in their children's families of procreation and extends active adult status for as long as possible.

The Large-Scale Organization as a Quasi Kindred

This section deals with the tendencies of large-scale organizations to assume the role of social critic in family

[49] H. D. Sheldon, *The Older Population of the United States,* New York: Wiley, 1958, p. 96.

[50] William H. Smith, Jr., Joseph H. Britton, and Jean O. Britton, "Relationships within Three-Generation Families," University Park: Pennsylvania State University, 1958 (cited in Streib and Thompson, *op cit.*).

life. The geographical movement of individuals away from their kindred may sometimes result in the development of a quasi kindred of friends, as was suggested in an earlier section. Large-scale work organizations and communal organizations are also capable of displacing the biological kindred in assuming control over family life.

Stated more generally, this section is concerned with the control over family life exerted by larger social systems in which the family participates. Helmut Schelsky (discussing family and community) and Elizabeth Bott (describing nuclear-family relationships and kinship networks) converge upon a similar perspective in their analysis of the relationship between the family and larger social systems.

Schelsky studied the German family following World War II.[51] He found that many of his families, though living in a highly disorganized society, were actually more integrated and solidified than they had been before the postwar period. He distinguished between the open community and the closed community as well as the open family and the closed family. An open community is one in which there is much flow both inward and outward of population. In the closed community there is little turnover in population through migration or through temporary, routine movement. Similarly, the open family is one which admits outsiders into close contact and intimate relations, whereas the closed family excludes outsiders from personal interaction. Schelsky suggested that in the closed community, with each family well acquainted with other inhabitants of the community, there is little threat

[51] Helmut Schelsky, *Wandlungen der Deutschen Familie in der Gegenwart,* Stuttgart: Ferdinand Enke, 1955.

found in personal relations with others in the community. The open family, with its frequent interaction with outsiders, is amenable to controls instituted by these outsiders; the closed family is less vulnerable to external control. Schelsky suggested that the closed community tends to be associated with the open family system and the open community with the closed family.

In her study of kinship in London, Bott described the relationship between nuclear-family interaction and the extent to which tightly organized kinship and friendship networks existed. She described networks as close-knit or loose-knit. Close-knit networks are those in which there is much interconnectedness among the persons in the network of relationships (that is, almost everyone knows and interacts with almost all other persons in the network). Bott found that in close-knit networks, many friends and relatives knew each other and exerted informal pressures on one another to conform to norms. Husbands' and wives' close-knit networks tended to be segregated from one another and each spouse received emotional satisfaction and assistance from his relatives and friends rather than from his mate. Close-knit networks tended to develop when the husband and wife and their friends and relatives grew up in the same area and continued to live there after their marriage. In these situations, the marriage was more or less engrafted upon existing social relationships. In contrast, loose-knit networks of social relationships are those in which there is little interconnectedness among persons in the network. Couples participating primarily in loose-knit networks are relatively insensitive to external opinions. The Bott study indicated that hus-

bands and wives in loose-knit networks received emotional satisfaction and assistance from their spouses rather
than from persons in the network. Husbands and wives
generally participated in the same network of friends and
relatives. Loose-knit networks tended to develop through
the couple's residential or occupational mobility.[52] Like
the families associated by Schelsky with the closed community, the families described by Bott as participating in
close-knit networks of relationships with friends and relatives were highly vulnerable to pressures to conform. Like
the families linked by Schelsky to the open community,
the families in loose-knit networks tended to be the more
encapsulated.

The analyses by Schelsky and by Bott suggest that the
larger social system (such as community or kinship network) dominates the smaller social system (the nuclear
family) when the larger system consists of a tightly knit
network of social relationships. The network in which the
nuclear family participates can be organized on the basis
of bureaucratic hierarchy as well as on the basis of informal friendship and kinship relationships. The view expressed by Schelsky and Bott suggests that severe limitations on patterns of family organization can be introduced
by corporate structures.

The large-scale organization assumes quasi-kindred
functions in two ways: (a) formally through the development of organization policy concerning the family life
of its members, and (b) informally through the formation
of relatively closed social networks created through the

[52] Elizabeth Bott, *Family and Social Network*, London: Tavistock Publications, 1957.

bringing together of specialized personnel (for example, families of university faculties, families of military personnel).

The development of an organization policy concerning the family life of employees produces the "organization family." The "organization man," as described by Whyte and others, conforms to many of the attitudes and values generally accepted by middle-class American society.[53] The large-scale organization puts great stress upon interpersonal relations among its organization men. The family of the organization man must then become an organization family.

A study by William Henry indicates that the organization requires a breakdown of extended-family commitments. According to Henry:

In a sense the successful executive is a "man who has left home." He feels and acts as though he were on his own, as though his emotional ties and obligations to his parents were severed. It seems to be most crucial that he has not retained resentment of his parents, but has rather simply broken their emotional hold on him and been left psychologically free to make his own decisions. [Henry has] found those who have not broken this tie to be either too dependent upon their superiors in the work situation, or to be resentful of their supervision (depending, of course, upon whether they are still bound to their parents or are still actively fighting against them).[54]

[53] William H. Whyte, *The Organization Man,* New York: Simon and Schuster, 1956.

[54] William E. Henry, "The Business Executive: A Study in the Psychodynamics of a Social Role," *American Journal of Sociology,* 54 (1949), pp. 286-291.

Furthermore, the large-scale organization not only requires adherence to a set of standards, it also acts as an agent in defining what the positive values of family life ought to be. The ideal organization wife is one who is very adaptable, is gregarious, and accedes to the organization's assumption that the husband's primary commitments are to it and not the nuclear family.[55]

By screening devices, the socially "unfit" families are eliminated from the upper echelons of the organizational hierarchy. Large-scale organization thereby generates mobility for the nuclear family, not so much as a consequence of individual freedom to move, but rather as an agency assuming authority over "family" activities which are associated with organizational aims and its public images. Thus, the large-scale organization assumes a quasi-kinship role when it develops policies affecting the selection of family groups for membership in the organization "lineage" and the control of socialization activities within families.

The large-scale organization also operates to control family life in a more informal way. Large-scale organizations bring together numerous specialists who are uprooted from the communities in which their kindred live. As these specialists reside over a long period of time in the community, there is a tendency for their families to form a closed subcommunity. Various community divisions are formed in this way: town versus gown, military versus civilian, company cliques. In the closed subcommunity, according to Schelsky's view, the family would tend to become open with respect to the other members

[55] Whyte, *op. cit.*

of the subcommunity. The open family would then be vulnerable to the controlling influences of the subcommunity.

Informal control is not restricted to members of the same organization. Whyte has suggested that organization men who are highly socially mobile tend to live in newly built suburbs which surround the large urban centers. Webs of friendships tend to develop between "organization families" and people are expected to be outgoing in personality. The openness of family life in these suburbs is indicated by Whyte's statement that "privacy has become clandestine." The consequence of this openness of the family is that the community of "organization families" serves as quasi kindred:

The suburban group also has a strong effect on relations between husband and wife, and in many ways a beneficent one. The group is a foster family. In the transient organization life the young family has to take a good part of its environment with it; no longer is there the close complex of aunts and uncles and grandparents to support the couple, and when they come to their first crisis this absence can have a devastating effect. Thus the function of the suburban group. All the other young couples are in the same boat, and in a sort of unspoken mutual assistance pact they provide for one another a substitute for the big family of former years.[56]

Granted that the large-scale organization influences family life, the question remains: Does the large-scale organization as a quasi kindred operate to maintain orderly replacement? The studies concerning the "organization man" suggest that large-scale organizations generally sus-

[56] *Ibid.*, pp. 392-393.

tain traditional patterns of family life. Insofar as the quasi kindred rewards practices consistent with traditional patterns of family life, orderly replacement is fostered. However, if the quasi kindred is oriented toward a deviant form of family living (for example, a religious sect), the quasi kindred can interrupt the process of orderly replacement. Two examples are offered of organizations that disrupt traditional forms of family life. One of these examples is the Israeli kibbutz and the other is the "total institution."

A kibbutz is a communal organization for operating an agricultural settlement in Israel. Each kibbutz has its own government to manage the living arrangements of the inhabitants and the production and marketing of agricultural and manufactured goods. The kibbutzim were developed to meet the hardships of agricultural life in the Palestinian desert and were designed to eliminate many of the inequities of Eastern European Jewish family life. The kibbutz has communal eating facilities and its children are raised through communal efforts. Ordinarily, the kibbutz children are housed and cared for apart from their parents. There is no housewife role and every woman is expected to be a full-time worker in the kibbutz. Marriage is formed through personal preference and divorce is relatively easy. According to persons raised in a kibbutz, prior to marriage there are permissive sex relations. However, children in the same school classes ordinarily regard each other as quasi siblings and incest taboos are likely to arise. Apparently, cross-sex companions are sought among other age classes or in different kibbutzim. Most adult members of kibbutzim are married and, as in other bilateral systems, marriage is regarded as a preferred way of life. Parents have no official authority over their children in the kibbutz, but are expected to be affectionate and indulgent to them.[57]

Thus, in the kibbutz, the rules and regulations regarding socialization as well as the performance of socializing activities are handled by individuals as agents of the kibbutz rather than by the family. As an extreme bilateral system exists, there is little restriction on availability of adults as spouses regardless of current marital status. However, the limit of the authority of the kibbutz over the socialization of children is constantly tested by the parents and especially by the grandparents of the children. For example, parents may visit their children at any free time and, being able to observe child-raising practices, they may exert pressure for a revision of these practices either on the nurses or teachers or on the responsible committee in the kibbutz. To the extent that the kibbutz is solidary and well organized it can maintain control over the marital practices and over socialization practices ordinarily dominated by kinship groups. The family-life practices now traditional in the kibbutz represent a radical departure from the family norms of its European founders.

Extreme domination over family life occurs in what Goffman has described as "total institutions."[58] Ordinarily,

[57] Discussion based upon Melford E. Spiro, *Kibbutz: Venture in Utopia,* Cambridge: Harvard University Press, 1956, and Melford E. Spiro, *Children of the Kibbutz,* Cambridge: Harvard University Press, 1958.

[58] Erving Goffman, "On the Characteristics of Total Institutions," in *Asylums,* New York: Doubleday (Anchor Books), 1961, pp. 1-124.

in American society, people tend to sleep, play, and work in different places, in each case with a different set of people, under a different authority, and without an all-over plan directing activities in all these places. In a total institution, however, there are no barriers separating these activities. All of these activities are carried out in the same place and under a single authority. The rules governing these activities cover all participants and activities tend to be carried out by batches of individuals at each time. Since there are rules covering all activities, daily activities are tightly scheduled for each individual and are coordinated through a rational plan developed to fulfill the official aims of the institution. The essential features of Goffman's discussion are that the organization's authority is extended over "nonrational" activities, that the organization appropriates control over its members' total life according to a rational plan to fulfill its particular aims, and that this total control is inimical to family life. Family life requires some measure of autonomy so that it can maintain itself as a recognizable subsystem. Complete control by a bureaucratic organization obliterates any tendency for an autonomous family tradition to develop within the total institution.

Thus, the large-scale organization operates at some times to promote and at other times to inhibit orderly replacement of family culture from one generation to the next. The appropriation of quasi-kinship activities such as social criticism of family life tends to occur especially when the individual's actual kindred is ineffective and kinship networks are loose-knit. The structure of the kindred in contemporary American society contains elements interfering with its effective operation (indefinite composition and greater involvement of women than men) and kinship networks are, if anything, tending to become more loose-knit. Only the grandparents consistently act to sustain close-knit kinship ties. In the light of these tendencies, there is a high probability that in the future large-scale organizations will take on more quasi-kinship activities either formally by formulating policies or informally by the creation of comparatively closed (tight-knit) social networks.

Selected Readings

The role of kinship in contemporary society is discussed in the following references:

Aldous, Joan. "Urbanization, the Extended Family, and Kinship Ties in West Africa," *Social Forces,* 41 (1962), pp. 6-12.

Apple, Dorrian. "The Social Structure of Grandparenthood," *American Anthropologist,* 58 (1956), pp. 656-663.

Bott, Elizabeth. *Family and Social Network.* London: Tavistock Publications, 1957.

Cumming, Elaine, and David M. Schneider. "Sibling Solidarity: A Property of American Kinship," *American Anthropologist,* 63 (1961), pp. 498-507

Faris, Robert E. L. "Interaction of Generations and Family Stability," *American Sociological Review,* 12 (1947), pp. 160-164.

Garigue, Philip. "French Canadian Kinship and Urban Life," *American Anthropologist,* 58 (1956), pp. 1090-1101.

Litwak, Eugene. "The Use of Extended Family Groups in the Achievement of Social Goals: Some Policy Implications," *Social Problems,* 7 (1959-1960), pp. 177-187.

Reiss, Paul J. "The Extended Kindship System: Correlates of

and Attitudes on Frequency of Interaction," *Marriage and Family Living*, 24 (1962), pp. 333-339.

Robins, Lee N., and Miroda Tomanec. "Closeness to Blood Relatives Outside the Immediate Family," *Marriage and Family Living*, 24 (1962), pp. 340-346.

Schneider, David M., and George C. Homans. "Kinship Terminology and the American Kinship System," *American Anthropologist*, 57 (1955), pp. 1194-1208.

Sussman, Marvin B. "The Isolated Nuclear Family: Fact or Fiction?" *Social Problems*, 6 (1959), pp. 333-340.

Sussman, Marvin B., and Lee G. Burchinal. "Kin Family Network: Unheralded Structure in Current Conceptualizations of Family Functioning," *Marriage and Family Living*, 24 (1962), pp. 231-240.

Sussman, Marvin B. "Family Continuity: Selective Factors Which Affect Relationships between Families at Generational Levels," *Marriage and Family Living*, 16 (1954), pp. 112-120.

Sweetser, Dorrian Apple. "Asymmetry in Intergenerational Family Relationships," *Social Forces*, 41 (1963), pp. 346-352.

Young, Michael, and Peter Willmott. *Family and Kinship in East London*. London: Routledge and Kegan Paul, 1957.

7 *The Future Family*

What characteristics will the family of the future have? Forecasting future developments in family life entails many uncertainties. Accuracy of forecasts depends upon three factors: the relevance of information about trends in the society, the adequacy of conceptual schemes for organizing this information, and the extent to which new elements (unanticipated in the forecasts) will modify future events. The first section of this chapter will describe current trends in American society which appear relevant to family life. In the second section, forecasts will be made on the basis of three different conceptual approaches as applied to these trends. The three approaches are the idealistic, the functionalist, and the interactionist explanations of social change. The forecasts made on the basis of these explanations of change will pertain to the near future (the next decade or so). The third section will speculate about new elements in society which make difficult the forecasting of trends of family life in the more distant future.

Short-Run Trends

Within the next few years, in what kind of social situation is the modal American family most likely to find itself? Which explanatory schemes appear to be most adequate for forecasting the organization of family life in the near future?

The discussion will indicate various trends anticipated over the next decade or so and then demonstrate how several explanatory schemes relate these trends to family life.

In the next ten or fifteen years, if current trends continue, six significant changes may be expected in the United States. These changes are decline of manpower in agriculture, increased automation, increased manpower in service occupations, increased social density, increased employee-entrepreneur ratio, and continued advances in medicine. These changes are interdependent; modification of one trend will affect all others.

DECLINE OF MANPOWER IN AGRICULTURE

The percentage of the labor force in agricultural occupations will continue to decrease until a point of stabilization is reached. Kuznets has shown that the percentage of persons engaged as entrepreneurs or employees in agriculture has decreased steadily from 26 per cent of the total labor force in 1909-1913 to 7.5 per cent in 1958-1960.[1] A reversal of this trend is not forecast for the immediate future. Clague suggests that the number of

---

[1] Simon Kuznets, "Income Distribution and Changes in Consumption," in Hoke S. Simpson, ed., *The Changing American Population*, New York: Institute of Life Insurance, 1962, pp. 21-58.

"farmers and farm workers will shrink until they constitute no more than about 6 per cent of the entire labor force in 1975."

But this trend will not go on indefinitely. Sooner or later, productivity in agriculture will catch up with that in industry and in the services. . . . From then on, the farm labor force will remain stable or actually might increase.[2]

How might the trend toward a diminishing agricultural labor force affect the social environment in which the family finds itself? Agricultural activity in the past has been associated with seasonal labor, heavy physical effort, stability of residence, limited educational attainment, and either an isolated residence or life in a closed community. With 90 to 95 per cent of the labor force engaged in non-agricultural activities, fewer people will be tied to the routine and location associated with agricultural occupations. The change will permit wider variation in labor-force activity with respect to the spread of work through the year, physical exertion, mobility of residence, educational attainment, and interaction with people of different occupations and social backgrounds.

INCREASED AUTOMATION

There will be a continued increase in the use of automated devices in processing raw materials, manufacturing, and providing services. Automation of industry means less handling of goods, less physical exertion, and a tremendous increase in productivity through a completely ra-

[2] Ewan Clague, "Demographic Trends and Their Significance," in Simpson, ed., *The Changing American Population, op. cit.*, pp. 19-20.

tional manufacturing process. With an almost infinite production capacity, plants will operate below capacity and will be able to increase or decrease production without a corresponding change in manpower; employment levels can remain relatively constant. Automation will permit a short work week, short hours, and careful but not exhausting work (for which women will be capable even in traditionally "heavy" industry) and it will encourage a high educational level for workers. Noland forecasts that:

Family life doubtless will change. In a recent survey report by William Faunce, 96.8 per cent of the interviewees, when asked what more leisure would mean to them, looked to "working around the house," and 76.8 per cent anticipated "spending more time with family." It seems likely, therefore, that the family will become less matriarchal. There is the possibility, however, that some employees will be working, say, four straight days and will be away from work three days at a time. An employee with this work arrangement might have two homes—one for his family, quite removed from the work place, and the other a "bachelor apartment" near his job. Whether or not this arrangement would promote family solidarity and proper child socialization is open to question.[3]

Automation will accelerate at least temporarily the trend toward greater participation of women in the labor force, result in more families in which both husband and wife work, and markedly increase the number of families which by income and education characteristics can be classified as "middle class."

[3] William Noland, "Technology's Impact on Culture and Work," in Simpson, ed., *The Changing American Population, op. cit.*, p. 74.

INCREASED MANPOWER IN SERVICE OCCUPATIONS

There will be an increase in the percentage of persons in the labor force performing professional and personal services. From 1948 to 1961, the percentage of white professional and technical workers in the labor force increased from 7.2 per cent to 12.7 per cent. Over that period, the percentage of nonwhite professional and technical workers grew from 2.4 per cent to 4.8 per cent.[4] Clague estimates that by 1970, the number of professional and technical workers will have increased about 40 per cent over the 1960 workers. He anticipates that this group will experience the greatest increase of any segment in the labor force over the 1960-1970 decade.[5]

Like the trend in increased automation, the increase in professional and personal services will open more positions to women and to those persons with higher education. The educational level of the population will continue to rise. In 1960, the median number of school years completed in the United States was 10.8. By 1980, the anticipated median number of years of schooling completed will be at least 12.0 if short-term trends over the past few years are continued. Estimates based on long-term trends are higher.[6] Trends in the increase of percentage of professional workers will tend to reinforce those labor-force trends created by the increase in automation.

INCREASED SOCIAL DENSITY

There will be a continued increase in the social density of American society. Durkheim pointed out the relationship

[4] *Statistical Abstract of the United States: 1961*, p. 216.

[5] Clague, *op. cit.*, p. 19.

[6] *Statistical Abstract: 1961, op. cit.*, p. 113.

between social density and the heterogeneity of urban life. He indicated the character of high social density:

Social life, instead of being concentrated in a multitude of little centres, distinctive and alike, is generalized. Social relations . . . consequently become more numerous. . . . The division of labor develops, therefore, as there are more individuals sufficiently in contact to be able to act and react upon one another.[7]

Richard Dewey suggests that, when social density increases in a large-scale population, other characteristics associated with urban life follow: anonymity, heterogeneity, impersonal and formal relationships, and the presence of status symbols which are independent of personal acquaintance.[8]

There can be little doubt that the social density of the United States will continue to increase. This increase will follow from greater use of radio and television, technological improvements in long-distance and local telephone equipment, development of local and interstate highway systems (both tollway and freeway), and mass transportation by jet airplanes. An increase is expected in the four types of mobility which Burgess, Locke, and Thomes have regarded as breaking down the traditional norms and values relating to family life: residential mobility; vertical mobility through change in social or socioeconomic status; spatial mobility facilitated by modern means of transportation; and ideational mobility facilitated by mass com-

[7] Émile Durkheim, *The Division of Labor in Society*, Glencoe, Ill.: Free Press, 1947, p. 257.

[8] Richard Dewey, "The Rural-Urban Continuum: Real but Relatively Unimportant," *American Journal of Sociology*, 66 (1960), pp. 60-66.

munication media, by increased educational attainment,
and by residential and spatial mobility.[9]

INCREASED EMPLOYEE-ENTREPRENEUR RATIO

There will be a decrease in the percentage of the
labor force who are entrepreneurs and a corresponding
increase in the percentage of the labor force who are employees. Kuznets has indicated several trends in employment. From 1909-1913 to 1958-1960, the ratio of employees to entrepreneurs in the total labor force has risen
markedly. In 1909-1913, employees comprised 75 per cent
of the labor force and entrepreneurs the remaining 25 per
cent (ratio of 3.0). In 1958-1960, employees made up 86
per cent of the labor force and entrepreneurs 14 per cent
(ratio of 6.1). Over this period, the percentage of non-
agricultural entrepreneurs has varied little (between 8
and 10 per cent of the total labor force). The change in
the employee-entrepreneur ratio has come mainly from the
decrease in agricultural entrepreneurs and employees during the period studied.[10]

The significance of the increase in employee-entrepreneur ratio for family life lies in the stabilizing influence of corporate enterprise on family continuity. Family
ties are maintained in operating a business or farming enterprise and in passing this family property from generation to generation. The shift from entrepreneurial to bureaucratic economic organization eliminates the possibility of using the family corporation as a mechanism for

[9] Ernest W. Burgess, Harvey J. Locke, and Mary Margaret
Thomes, *The Family from Institution to Companionship*, New
York: American Book, 1963, pp. 365-374.

[10] Kuznets, *op. cit.*, p. 26.

orderly replacement and substitutes the more precarious controls of a large-scale organization whose policies and leadership may change frequently.

CONTINUED ADVANCES IN MEDICINE

There will be an increase in medically relevant discoveries in human biology and an accompanying increase in the application of these findings to health-service agencies. The net result of this trend will be an increase in the ability to control illness and disease in ways previously considered fantastic. As a consequence of this control, there will be longer life expectancy, fewer incapacitating illnesses, and an increase in the ability of individuals to make long-range plans.

Several developments will influence the length of life. Preventive medicine will be widely practiced. Medicines yet to be invented will be more efficient in counteracting diseases. Techniques will be perfected for replacing diseased or crippled vital organs. Obstetrical techniques to prevent birth injury are being steadily improved. Infant mortality rates have continued to decline. In 1940, the infant mortality rate was 47.0 deaths per 1000 live births; by 1961, this rate was 25.2.[11] At the other extreme in age, there have been phenomenal increases in the population 85 or older, and whereas in 1920 there were fewer than 5 million persons 65 or older, estimates for the year 2000 are around 30 million in that age range.[12] Death rates have decreased for all ages. The death rate adjusted

[11] *Statistical Abstract of the United States: 1962*, p. 63.

[12] Eighty-seventh Congress, Special Committee on Aging, "New Population Facts on Older Americans, 1960," Washington, D.C.: U.S. Government Printing Office, 1961.

for the age distribution of the population was 17.8 in 1900 and 7.7 in 1959-1960.[13] There is no indication that the downward trend in death rate will be reversed in the foreseeable future.

Not only length of life, but also the level of health in the population will improve. With more efficient medical services and improved medical knowledge, the number of people incapacitated by illness will decline (barring catastrophe). However, the same techniques which will prolong the health and life of so-called normal individuals will also cause individuals born with metabolic disorders and central-nervous-system deficiencies to survive in larger numbers.

Finally, control over physiological functions is being increased not merely in connection with illness, but also in normal day-to-day activities. The tranquillizer tides people over critical emotional situations; benzedrine derivatives change "energy levels." Oral contraceptives are coming into use.

These developments concerning length of life, health, and control over illness will inevitably have various effects on family life. Grandparenthood and great-grandparenthood will be more common and older people may exert greater control in family and kinship relationships; invalidism and illness will be less important factors in preventing participation of people in "normal" life activities; control over day-to-day living will be improved.

Explanations and Forecasts of Change in Family Organization

The trends cited above concerning the composition of the labor force, automation of production, social density, and

[13] *Statistical Abstract: 1962, op. cit.*, p. 63.

medically relevant discoveries and applications indicate the conditions under which family life will operate in the future. These conditions will create predicaments for individuals in their family life. Family members—indeed, all members of society—will have to decide as they have in the past which alternative courses of action are most appropriate.

Social scientists have developed schemes which presumably reflect the ways in which people define their problems and react to them. Specifically, these explanations of change indicate how family members (and governments) will define their predicaments related to family life and how they will choose courses of action. Each explanatory scheme focuses on certain aspects of social conditions as creating particular kinds of problems for the family; two schemes may utilize the same trend for determining family predicaments, but this trend may have different implications for the two explanatory schemes. Accordingly, two questions are pertinent for each explanatory scheme:

1. What is the basic predicament in the organization of family life according to this scheme? That is, which courses of action must families adopt in order to continue their existence as a social category meaningful to their members?

2. What specific forecasts can be made with respect to family organization by applying the explanatory schemes to the trends listed in the previous section?

This discussion will consider three major classes of explanatory schemes concerning change in family organization. The *idealist* explanation bases change in the organization of norms and values on the modification of men's ideas. The *functionalist* explanation seeks the stimulus for change of family norms and values in the other institutions in the society and indicates the direction of change in terms of adaptation. The *interactionist* explanation views change in the organization of norms and values of the family as reflecting change in the other institutions of the society and in turn stimulating change in those institutions. These explanatory schemes and the forecasts they evoke are described in the following sections.

THE IDEALISTIC EXPLANATION

This approach emphasizes the role of ideas in social change. Some students of the family, such as Anshen and Zimmerman,[14] regard change in family organization as occurring through idealistic causation as opposed to materialistic causation. Both Anshen and Zimmerman regard the family as a set of roles or positions defined and sustained by moral and ethical beliefs. The family is thus a normative pattern of relations reflecting the moral strength of society. Implicitly this view pictures a "natural man" motivated toward satisfying his wants in the most direct, immediate, and "sensual" ways possible. The task of social groups is to control these "natural" impulses. When the family exists as a moral force in the society, the members of the family can control one another to act in accordance with familistic norms. However, when social conditions are such that familistic control declines, the family disintegrates and individualistic, self-indulgent

[14] Ruth N. Anshen, "The Family in Transition," in Ruth N. Anshen, ed., *The Family: Its Function and Destiny*, rev. ed., New York: Harper, 1959, pp. 3-19; Carle C. Zimmerman, *Family and Civilization*, New York: Harper, 1947.

norms predominate. Resurgence of familistic norms occurs through legal control and education of the population to return to the religious and traditional ideas endorsing familistic values.

In one sense, the Anshen and Zimmerman approach to change in family organization does not explain change: Essentially their argument is that change occurs in social relations when men want to change social relations. However, their approach does not specify conditions under which the "natural man" reverts back to the "moral man."

The experiences of Communist China and the U.S.S.R. suggest the extent to which family policy can influence social change.

Traditional Chinese society had as its base the family organization characterized by Burgess, Locke, and Thomes as "institutional."[15] Marriage was arranged by the parents, great power and authority, were given to the patriarch, the patriarch and his sons' families lived in joint households, and emphasis was given to the father-son relationship through which the family could continue to persist through generations. Confucian doctrine, which lay at the core of family values, stipulated that the father command the esteem of his descendants and the mother be given their love.[16]

The coming of the Republic in the early twentieth century weakened the patriarch's control over family life. Parents began to face opposition in arranging marriages,

[15] Burgess, Locke, and Thomes, *op. cit.*
[16] Shu-Ching Lee, "China's Traditional Family: Its Characteristics and Disintegration," *American Sociological Review*, 18 (1953), pp. 272-280.

filial piety began to lose its sacred and binding character, the women's movement for improved educational and social rights developed. Confucian ethics, which sought solution of problems in the self-sacrifice of the individual for the preservation of the group, was losing its hold on family life.

In the early years of the Communist assumption of power in China, the Communists attempted to break the old family ties by encouraging young people to rebel against their parents and to leave home to work for the revolution in distant places. The Communists ridiculed filial piety, emphasized the conflict and differences between generations, and encouraged spying at home and denunciation of parents. The 1950 marriage laws provided for free choice in marriage; equal family status for men and women; and equal rights of husband and wife to choose an occupation, to possess, manage, and inherit family property, and to use his or her own family name. The 1950 laws permitted divorce when official attempts at reconciliation failed. The law also stipulated the duties of divorced parents toward their children.[17]

By removing the rigorous parental controls on marriage and family life, the Communist People's Republic of China furthered the development of what Zimmerman would regard as the "atomistic" family. Individualism rather than familism was dominant. By 1956, the Communist authorities became alarmed at the unrestrained behavior and lack of self-discipline among the youth. There had been an increase in juvenile delinquency. Boys

[17] C. K. Yang, *The Chinese Family in the Communist Revolution,* Cambridge, Mass.: Technology Press, 1959.

and girls were engaging in multiple sexual relationships. Quick marriage and divorce was becoming popular. In school, students did not study hard and follow school regulations. A society cannot achieve stability under these conditions. The Communist regime launched a propaganda campaign to revive family loyalties. The policy was intended to promote filial respect by the children and at the same time to curb parental authority.[18] Beginning in 1956:

Newspaper and magazine articles preached the virtue of parental care and respect. Members of youth organizations were asked to set good examples for the nation. Many arguments were put forth to show the necessity of taking good care of parents. Parental love is now extolled as beautiful and deserving of continued gratitude on the part of the children. Youth are told to love their parents because they will be the parents of tomorrow. It is also argued that old people are often helpful at home. Young people are exhorted not only to feed and clothe the old people but to love and respect them in order to make them happy.[19]

Yang reported that as of 1958 the Communist Chinese policy was to develop a family form comparable to the stem family in France, in which one of the sons continues to live with the parents after marriage while the other sons and daughters leave the family unit upon marriage.[20]

The U.S.S.R. followed a similar course. In the early years of the Russian revolution, the Communists made

[18] Theodore Hsi-En Chen and Wen-Hui C. Chen, "Changing Attitudes toward Parents in Communist China," *Sociology and Social Research*, 43 (1959), pp. 175-182.

[19] *Ibid.*, p. 182.

[20] Yang, *op. cit.*, pp. 214-215.

marriage and divorce easy, fostered communal living, and tried to provide separate quarters for children and to remove socialization of children from the sphere of the family. However, by the 1930's, divorce rates were extremely high, there was much delinquency, and the number of abortions was intolerably large. In 1936, family laws were revised to stabilize family life. With this stability has come a conservative movement in Soviet society:

As the family is strengthened in the Soviet Union, kin relations . . . play an increasingly important role in determining Soviet youths' opportunities for mobility. . . . Stories about persons in responsible positions exerting influence to favor their kin have appeared with considerable frequency, both in the Soviet press and in the reports of first-hand observers. There is now a large group of people who have achieved high status by means legitimate within the existing social system, and who wish to pass some of their benefits and privileges to their children.[21]

The breakdown of traditional authority in both China and Russia follows the course indicated in the Zimmerman-Anshen view of social change. Beginning with the trustee family, both societies experienced a steady movement toward atomization of family life. When the point was reached where the atomization of the family no longer served to destroy the unwanted traditional institutions and practices in the society but instead was preventing the stabilization of the new social structure, both China and the U.S.S.R. formulated national policies for promoting the conservation of family values. The part played by

[21] Alex Inkeles, "Social Stratification and Mobility in the Soviet Union: 1940-1950," *American Sociological Review*, 15 (1950), pp. 477-478.

totalitarian control over the Chinese and Russian people is not known, nor the extent to which the population itself was inclined to conserve the "collective" institutions of the Communist regimes. Probably both elements were involved in the success of the family policies. At any rate, the relative effectiveness of these policies in revitalizing family life provides some evidence that the idealistic explanation of Zimmerman and Anshen can account for change in the content of family norms and values.

THE FORECAST: IDEALISTIC APPROACH

There is an increasing probability that the United States will develop explicit national policies on family relations. Various trends in social and economic life will produce problems for family life: the changing sex ratio in the labor force, the increase in leisure, the mounting pressure for university education, and increased demand for health and educational facilities. Increased pressure will be placed on governmental agencies to handle these problems. To do so, the government will have to devise policies for supporting certain values in family life. These policies are likely to involve the following elements:

1. *Protection of the male as the primary breadwinner in the family.* This policy is implicit in current governmental practices. In census and income-tax returns, the male is listed as family head. The practice of providing federal insurance on home mortgages (FHA) only when the husband's income is sufficient to cover monthly payments also recognizes the male as the "legitimate" breadwinner. A well-developed policy in this respect would give greater job security to the male than to the female.

2. *Protection of family norms and values in mass media, commercial entertainment, and recreational facilities.* Toward this end, increased pressure would be placed upon television and movie producers to provide "wholesome" subject-matter and to adhere to "codes of decency." Emphasis would be placed upon providing "wholesome" recreational facilities for youth and encouragement of family recreation as a unit (for example, the further development of family camping sites, "family rates" in commercial transportation systems).

3. *Increased aid to students for university education.* Although previous governmental aid to educational institutions has emphasized the improvement of instructional facilities and programs, the high costs of a university education will ultimately have to be borne collectively by the nation rather than by parents. Otherwise, the colleges and universities will be unable to produce trained people in sufficient numbers to meet the needs of industry and the professions. The effect of defining "student" as an adult occupation will be to keep young people off the labor market. Emphasis can then be given to quality of training in a highly automated and professionalized world rather than to length of productive life.

4. *Responsibility for standards of physical and mental health.* A national policy governing health insurance (covering doctors' fees, medicines, and hospital care) will probably be formulated in the foreseeable future. Increased emphasis will be placed upon public-health measures (such as mass innoculations). In addition, construction of clinical and medical-research facilities may be expected to continue.

Many people consider a national policy necessary to conserve a "healthy," "normal" family life in the United States. Individual citizens must expect to contribute to the decisions leading to the formulation and maintenance of a national policy on the family.

FUNCTIONALIST EXPLANATION

The functionalist explanation of social change focuses upon the adaptation of one institution to changes in another. Implicit in this approach is the assumption that the parts of society tend toward maintaining consistency with one another.

The functional approach assumes that man is essentially an imperfectly "rational" being. Man wishes to live for as long as possible under the best material and social conditions. He must adapt his social commitments to his "needs." In adapting, he must first be the "economic man" and try to maximize his production and consumption of material and social goods to fulfill his "needs"; second, he must minimize conflict with his fellow humans and be the "political man." Being imperfect, man is not always rational. To the extent that man departs from his rationality, crises occur. Insofar as man is economically rational, differentiation in society occurs (so that the division of labor will maximize production to fulfill material and social needs) and new social and material inventions are developed (to utilize resources fully in man's adaptation to his environment). Insofar as man is politically rational, he seeks to adjust the various segments of his own life and to reduce the probability of conflict through an integration of the various segments of society. Thus, the differentiation of tasks, the development of adaptations, and the attempts at integration of the various elements of society appear as efforts to create a rational existence. The functionalists view tendencies against orderly differentiation, adaptation, and integration as "irrational" or "dysfunctional."

In his concern over order and change in social life, Max Weber utilized "rationalization" as an historical process to explain how societies are stabilized following cataclysmic events. He regarded bureaucracy as the extreme case of "rational" organization. "Bureaucracy has a 'rational' character: rules, means, ends, and matter-of-factness dominates its bearing."[22] As bureaucracies outlive their usefulness and cease to exist for rational purposes, they begin to exist more on a traditional basis (such as patriarchal structures). As traditional structures, these organizations may become dysfunctional with respect to the welfare of the population, and they may be overthrown and more rational structures instituted.[23] In family life, this functional drama of traditionalism, rebellion, and rationalization would be played an infinite number of times each generation. This rationalization of family life repeated each generation in all families in the society would provide a constant evolution of organization of family life.

Many social scientists have applied the functional approach to explain change in family life. Explanations have included urbanization (Burgess), economic devel-

[22] H. H. Gerth and C. Wright Mills, eds., *From Max Weber: Essays in Sociology,* New York: Oxford University Press, 1946, p. 244.
[23] *Ibid.*

opment (Parsons), and change in residence rules (Murdock).

Using the ideal-type method, Burgess and Wallin attempted to describe the nature of marriage under conditions approaching the folk society, which they designated as "rural life conditions," as contrasted with marriage under "urban life conditions." The Burgess and Wallin description is found in Table 4. The characteristics listed under rural life conditions correspond to the "institutional family" and the characteristics under urban life conditions describe the "companionship family."

Just as Burgess chose urban life conditions as the stimulus for change in the family, Parsons sought the motivating factor for change in the economic system. Parsons indicated that the contemporary American occupational system "and its structural correlates in the society places severe limitations on the kind of kinship structure which is compatible with such a system."[24] According to Parsons, a closely knit extended family would hamper occupational mobility and motivation toward achievement.

The process by which the family adapts to a changed role in society is indicated more specifically by the work of Murdock.[25] His position is that the crucial factor in the change of kinship systems is a modification in the rules of residence at marriage. For example, according to Murdock's view, prior to the breakdown of a matrilineal and matrilocal kinship system, the married couples would have

---

[24] Talcott Parsons, "The Social Structure of the Family," in Ruth N. Anshen, ed., *The Family: Its Function and Destiny, op. cit.*, p. 263.

[25] George Peter Murdock, *Social Structure*, New York: Macmillan, 1949.

Table 4

THE IDEAL-TYPICAL NATURE OF MARRIAGE UNDER RURAL
AND URBAN LIFE CONDITIONS, AS DESCRIBED
BY BURGESS AND WALLIN*

Aspect of marriage	Rural life conditions	Urban life conditions
1. Definitions of obligations	Primarily a status of formally defined reciprocal rights and duties	Obligations defined on personal basis with norms based on compatibility and satisfaction of personality needs of the couple
2. Marital selection	Marriage arranged by parents (or by couple in accordance with parental standards of mate selection)	Freedom of young people in choosing their mates
3. Pre-marital social interaction and courtship practices	Segregation of children and youth of different sexes before marriage or only formal relationships under strict chaperonage	Freedom in choice of social relationships before marriage with decline of parental supervision and control
4. Role of love	Love after marriage	Love and companionship as prerequisites to marriage
5. Primary aims	Emphasis upon the economic and legal aspects of marriage to maintain the family as an institution	Stress on the primacy of congenial personal relations
6. Role of children	Children valued as potential workers, economic assets, and bearers of the family line	Children appreciated as *persons*, with interest in their personality development
7. Permanence of marriage	Marriage relatively indissoluble	Divorce resorted to if marriage regarded as failure

* Adapted from Ernest W. Burgess and Paul Wallin, *Engagement and Marriage*, New York: Lippincott, 1953, p. 31.

to cease living near the wife's parents. Freed from control by the members of the old lineage, the married couple could eventually affiliate with the husband's lineage. The husband's lineage would become the main source of kinship identification and would attain control over the couple's property. In India, the newer pattern of residence is for the children to disperse upon reaching maturity. However, "in most cases the obligations and relationships of the joint family are emotionally and morally *retained* in varying degrees."[26] The movement away from tradition is slow. Murdock's view suggests that the change in residential pattern provides a stimulus for a chain of events leading eventually to modification of the manner in which lineage is reckoned.

The changes occurring in Africa as it becomes more Westernized suggest the appropriateness of the functionalist approach in explaining modification of the family culture.

In Africa, marriages, which were "formerly primarily the concern of the larger family, lineage, or clan, are now increasingly arranged by the individuals themselves. Such marriages often lack the traditional sanctions including bride-price or bride-service, and the kinsmen of each spouse are less effective in helping to maintain the stability of the union."[27]

This change exists as part of a more general modifica-

[26] Ben Schlesinger, "The Changing Patterns in the Hindu Joint Family System of India," *Marriage and Family Living*, 23 (1961), p. 175.

[27] Nancie L. Solien de Gonzalez, "Family Organization in Five Types of Migratory Wage Labor," *American Anthropologist*, 63 (1961), p. 1271.

tion of the relationships between kin. Where many Africans migrate recurrently as wage labor, the authority of parents over adult children has decreased tremendously. The "young men are increasingly reluctant to divide their cash wages among a large group of people according to traditional customs along kinship lines." In some societies in Africa, where husbands are absent from their wives a long time while working in town, adultery has become a problem. The instability of marriage and family life in Africa at the present time is probably related to the "general lack of sanctions to enforce stability and sexual faithfulness under the new patterns of living which include labor migration." This breakdown in relations with the tribal community is fostered by the practices of management:

Recurrent migrants tend to return home as often as possible, and especially for important native rituals and ceremonies, family crises, etc. In addition, many may feel obligated to return to help with various economic and domestic activities, such as clearing fields, harvesting, fishing, house-building, and slaughtering. From the point of view of management, a worker who frequently leaves the job to return home on visits is a less desirable employee than one who works steadily for longer periods of time. For this reason, workers are often encouraged to travel farther away than the nearest labor center to obtain work. They may be lured by the promise of higher wages, free one-way transportation, and other supposed benefits. Obviously, the farther away a man is from his home, the less often he will be able to return there.[28]

The changes in family life in Africa suggest that the subordination of the family to the economic system fol-

[28] *Ibid.*, p. 1269.

lows the pattern of industrialization of Western society. The willingness of both management and labor to place production efficiency and wages above the welfare of family and kinship is primarily a Western style of thinking.

The problem of functional integration (meaning efficient integration) of family and kinship, however, does not refer only to norms of family life as related to economic institutions. Rationalization of life implies also making consistent rules and procedures within the category of the family. Turner, in his study of the Ndembu of Northern Rhodesia, points out the consequences for the lives of the Ndembu of having inconsistent rules of residence and of descent:

The nuclear residential group consists of male matrilineally related kin. To remain together this set of kinsmen must import their wives from other village lineages and export their sisters. But with maternal descent as the basis of village continuity a contradiction arises between the role of men as fathers who wish to retain their wives and children with them, and their role as uterine brothers and uncles who wish to recover the allegiances of their sisters and sisters' children. Without that allegiance men cannot found enduring villages. . . . Thus both marriages and villages are inherently unstable and in-laws struggle continually for control over women and their children. . . . Radical incompatibility, then, between maternal descent and virilocality [patrilocal residence] gives a keen edge to conflicts between uterine kinsmen and husbands of women, which result in quarrels between villages; to marital conflicts, producing a high divorce rate; and to conflict of loyalties between . . . maternal descent groups.[29]

The trends in African society toward a money econ-

[29] V. W. Turner, *Schism and Continuity in an African Society*, Manchester, Eng., Manchester University Press, 1957, p. xix.

omy and the problems raised by matrilineage are patently different from the trends and problems in American society. Yet, by their contrast, they emphasize the universality of rational process in family life.

THE FORECAST: FUNCTIONAL APPROACH

Given the trends in American society described earlier in this chapter, what "rational" adaptations can be anticipated in the family?

1. *The continual increase of the proportion of women in a labor force which also requires higher education will probably affect the family in several ways.* First, women can be expected to have increasing power in family relations. Accompanying this increase in power will be a greater tendency toward divorce, and, because of high productive potentials of women, remarriage. The birth rate may be affected, for, as might be expected, working women are more frequently users of contraceptive methods than are nonworking women and tend to have smaller families.[30] Increased participation in the labor force will probably also bring a greater pressure toward university education for women. University education most likely will decrease the influence of the woman's parents upon her selection of a mate, her style of family living after marriage, her child-raising practices, and her residence after marriage. The demands made upon the working

[30] Ronald Freedman, Pascal K. Whelpton, and Arthur A. Campbell, *Family Planning, Sterility, and Population Growth*, New York: McGraw-Hill, 1959. Data presented in Chapter 4, however, indicated that the difference in birth rate between employed women and housewives is decreasing.

wife's time will also operate to decrease parental influence upon her family of procreation.

2. *The increase in the amount of leisure anticipated in future years will also require an adjustment of family life.* With less time committed to occupation, the husband and wife will have greater choice in spending their free time. The increase in uncommitted time will make possible much more interaction between husband and wife. While some couples will adjust to the additional free time by filling it with companionate interaction, other couples will probably use this time to better their social and economic position. Thus, many couples will attend adult-education classes or will "moonlight" on a second job to increase income. Whether the time is used for recreation or work, family members will probably perform a greater variety of activities in daily life.

3. *The increase in the social density of society will probably lead, on the one hand, to a greater diversity of styles of family life because of an accompanying increase in occupational specialization and, on the other, to a standardization of family life because of increased communication and visibility of family life.* Toward diversity: Ethnic, religious, and perhaps racial intermarriage will increase and with the increasing importance of occupational specialization, there will be many different styles of family living. However, there may be a decline of marriage across social-class lines. For though increased university attendance by all segments of the population will serve to facilitate cross-class marriage somewhat, the trend toward early marriage will diminish the effects of the university in mate selection since an increasing proportion of stu-

dents will already be married. Toward standardization: The convergence of norms as social density increases is evidenced by the number of children desired by women. The investigation by Freedman, Whelpton, and Campbell of a national sample of 2,713 young married women concerning the prospective growth of population showed that the various sectors of society are converging upon a common set of values regarding family size. Women in the sample reported that they expected to have from two to four children. There was very little difference in expected number of births by income, by husband's occupation, or by urban or rural residence except that farm families expected a slightly higher average number of births. The average number of births expected was 3.0 for the total sample.[31]

4. *The anticipated increase in health services by agencies outside the family will bring a further decline in the practice of family medicine and nursing services.* The experience with national health insurance in Great Britain and in the Scandinavian countries attests to the increased reliance upon professional medical care; correspondingly, it projects a marked decrease in another family "function."

5. *The increase in life expectancy may place even more emphasis upon companionate relations between husband and wife.* The length of life will be increased for the average American. In his analysis of changes in the family life cycle, Glick has shown that whereas in 1890 most parents were widowed by the time that their last child was married, by 1950, most parents could expect at least fourteen years of married life after the marriage of the

[31] *Ibid.*

last child.[32] With a continual increase in life expectancy, the time may come when the period of marriage after the children have matured and left the home will be as long as the child-raising years.

6. *A rise in the amount of education can facilitate an acculturation process in which the students will appropriate the norms of family life ordinarily associated with professional groups in society.* This acculturation would provide further support to the "companionship" basis of family life. The family which stresses companionship norms is considered by some sociologists as "functional" to people of high socioeconomic levels (white-collar occupations and high educational level).[33]

7. *The high unemployment rates which automation may bring would require severe adaptations in patterns of family life for the population at the low socioeconomic levels.* The affected classes will be stimulated toward a continuation of maternal dominance, a decline in marriage and birth rates, and perhaps a greater alienation than at present from the norms associated with middle-class society. The educational and conformist requirements for jobs will confront many young people at low socioeconomic levels who are unable either to assume adult occupational roles or to qualify for college education. This inability may foster the development of deviant patterns of family life. The unskilled may face a repetition of the experiences of the family in the Depression of the 1930's.[34]

[32] Paul C. Glick, "The Life Cycle of the Family," *Marriage and Family Living*, 17 (1955), pp. 3-9.

[33] Robert O. Blood, Jr. and Donald M. Wolfe, *Husbands and Wives*, New York: Free Press, 1960, pp. 168-172.

[34] See Ruth Shonle Cavan, "Unemployment—Crisis of the Common Man," *Marriage and Family Living*, 21 (1959), pp. 139-146.

THE INTERACTIONIST EXPLANATION

The central concept in the interactionist approach to social change is personal commitment. In making commitments, people bind or pledge themselves to perform or pursue a given course of action. When they commit themselves to another person, they give that person their pledge to do something for him. Some commitments, such as contracts, are specific as to course of action. Other commitments are vague and imply that those who make them bind or pledge themselves to pursue any course of action they consider beneficial to the welfare of that person. Either kind establishes a connection between the act to which the actor is committed and the person to whom he is committed.[35]

When courses of action are specified by the commit-

---

[35] The view of man as a set of commitments is limited by the extent to which he is also a rational being who is aware of a restriction on the number of courses of action possible under given circumstances. A major difference between the functionalist and interactionist approach is one of emphasis. Whereas the functionalist approach focuses upon rational adaptation, the interactionist approach focuses upon the role of personal commitments in adaptations. However, even when irrational elements are studied in the functionalist approach (for example, the use of psychoanalytic concepts), emphasis is upon efficient adaptation to psychological needs. The functionalist approach explains the existence of several different courses of action appropriate to a particular complex of social and psychological needs and characteristics as "functional equivalents." In the interactionist approach, on the other hand, commitment and rationality frequently appear as opposing forces in determining action, each setting limits on the other. The interactionist approach takes for granted the existence of "functional equivalents" and explains them on the basis of differences in personal commitment. A question suggested by

ment, any two people in interaction are said to strike an action bargain. When this action continues over a period of time, the exchange of specific commitments constitutes a *role bargain*.[36]

However, much interaction among family members is not part of any role bargain. Many decisions and leisure activities in family life go beyond role bargains. Most family interaction appears to be based upon vague commitments to pursue whatever courses of action the person considers beneficial to other family members or to the family as a group and to refrain from acting in ways detrimental to the others. The vague commitment as to courses of action is nevertheless specific as to the persons for whom the acts are performed. Thus, most family interaction occurs on the basis of these *welfare commitments*.

When the person is not highly committed to others in the family, he continues to perform at the minimum expectations set by the role bargains and in that way to stabilize courses of action in the family. In families in which there is an unequal commitment, the actor who is more highly committed can be exploited readily by his fellow family members.[37]

---

the interactionist approach is: In any given situation, why are there not more functional equivalents?

[36] Cf. William J. Goode, "A Theory of Role Strain," *American Sociological Review*, 25 (1960), pp. 483-496. Trends toward increased leisure time suggest that instead of overcommitting their time, people tend to fill time in accordance with Parkinson's view that the performance of any activity is extended to cover the amount of time available.

[37] Willard Waller, *The Family, A Dynamic Interpretation*, New York: Dryden, 1938, pp. 239-255.

The interactionist approach assumes that man is characterized by the composition of his commitments. In turn, sentiments (such as love, hate, envy, adoration) define the nature of the commitments of one person to another.[38] In the process of forming sentiments regarding another person, the actor commits himself to pursue courses of action with respect to that person. Depending upon the sentiment, the courses of action may be specific or diffuse. If the actor is indifferent to the other person, he will tend to pursue carefully delineated actions in accordance with a minimum role bargain and hence develop courses of action in accordance with self-gratification norms. If the actor's dominant sentiment is love, affection, adoration, or other "positive" sentiment toward the other, he will feel committed to perform a wide variety of actions beneficial to the other; this actor is committed to a welfare norm in developing courses of action appropriate to his sentiments. Finally, if the actor views the other person with envy, spitefulness, hate, or other "negative" sentiment, he will act in ways he regards as harmful to the other; this actor is committed to a destructive norm in developing courses of action appropriate to his sentiments. Thus, the nature of the commitment determines at least in part the courses of action which family members develop in their interaction.

[38] In his discussion of "human nature," Cooley focused upon the development of sentiments in interaction. See Charles H. Cooley, *Human Nature and the Social Order*, New York: Scribner, 1902, and *Social Organization*, New York: Scribner, 1908. See also Nelson N. Foote, "Identification as the Basis for a Theory of Motivation," *American Sociological Review*, 16 (1951), pp. 14-21, and George Herbert Mead, *Mind, Self and Society*, Chicago: University of Chicago Press, 1934.

According to the social-interactionist explanation, however, participants in family life have only partial control over their interaction. Social conditions have a limiting effect upon the number of lines of action remaining open to them. For example, unilineal kinship can be maintained (controlled) only when a social critic is given authority and responsibility for judging and directing generational replacement in the family, when availability of marriage partners can be restricted to particular kinship units, and when older generations in authority maintain traditional patterns of family life. If these conditions are met, the family members can readily develop strategies for maintaining lineage commitments. If the conditions are not met, access to one set of alternatives for kinship maintenance is denied to the participants. Thus, social conditions are determinate in interaction insofar as they inhibit certain kinds of kinship strategies (rather than promote certain adaptations as suggested by the functionalist explanation).

The alternatives for family organization available in the presence of industrial organization may be many. Bennett and Despres have cited several examples to show that while family organization is modified in some societies in the interest of rationalization of politics and industry, in other societies industry and political organization develop in such a way as to accommodate the existing kinship organization. They noted that the work group in Japanese industry may adopt family rituals and terminology to maintain cohesion and authority. In the Philippines, candidates for high provincial and national offices have been chosen from factions organized on the basis of numerous kinsmen, compadres, and friends. The analysis by

Bennett and Despres suggests that the interaction between the organization of family life and the economic institutions of the society need not result in the adjustment of the family to the "needs" of the economic institutions.[39]

In contrast to the view that the small, independent nuclear family in Western society has emerged as an adaptation to industrialization, Greenfield suggests that the independent nuclear family had an earlier existence in Western Europe and in the American colonies. He contends that the family may be responsible for the particular form of social organization developed in Western industrial society. According to Greenfield, the small nuclear family existed in Western Europe and notably in England before the seventeenth century.[40] Calhoun indicates that colonization of America facilitated the growth of independent nuclear families. Without a background of feudalism and populated by migrants with Protestant views from towns and cities, the American colonies in general readily accepted civil marriage, easy divorce, and a subordination of parental authority to "the interests of the community."[41] Colonial origin and Protestantism rather than industrialization may be responsible for the predominance of the nuclear family as an independent unit in America.

[39] John W. Bennett and Leo A. Despres, "Kinship and Instrumental Activities: A Theoretical Inquiry," American Anthropologist, 62 (1960), pp. 254-267.

[40] Sidney M. Greenfield, "Industrialization and the Family in Sociological Theory," American Journal of Sociology, 67 (1961), pp. 312-322. See also Parsons, loc. cit., p. 249.

[41] Arthur W. Calhoun, A Social History of the American Family, New York: Barnes and Noble, 1960, Vol. I.

The interactionist scheme does not suggest specifically that when contradictions in norms and difficulties in social conditions arise, individuals will give priority to family commitments over nonfamily commitments. However, the family is a "primary" group for the individual in which many of his values, sentiments, and personal attachments are formed. Hence, generally people will tend to take into account family relations when they try to extricate themselves from predicaments.

THE FORECAST: INTERACTIONIST APPROACH

The trends in American life listed earlier in this chapter present problems for family members. In handling these problems, family members develop strategies to organize their family life to maintain the personal commitments they value. The idealist, functionalist, and interactionist explanations of social change can be regarded not only as independent conceptual schemes, but also as strategies for organizing family life. As strategies, these explanatory schemes are subsumed under the interactionist approach. (Perhaps one reason that students of the family cannot agree upon a single explanatory scheme is that various segments of the population derive their strategies of family organization from different motivations.)

The three explanatory schemes of social change can be described in terms of the kinds of family organization strategies they motivate. Briefly, the interactionist explanation describes individuals who, when they plan action either within or outside the family, try to increase the personal welfare of the members of their family (with whom they prefer to maintain a high personal commitment). This approach to organizing family life is the *welfare strategy*. The functionalist explanation provides a picture of those families which utilize an *efficiency strategy* in new situations. The idealist explanation, based on the retention of a particular kind of family organization, appears to describe the *conservative strategy* of family organization. The three kinds of strategy for organizing family life will be described below in terms of their implications for lineage, production of children, rules of residence, rules of marriage and divorce, and the most significant grouping in the family.

The welfare strategy

The welfare strategy evolves as a result of the commitment of individuals to their family. There are two factors in this commitment. The first factor: In contemporary society, numerous conflicting demands are made upon family members and their resources. The school, the work organization, the commercial recreation industries, and sometimes the church demand commitment and participation which conflict with one another and may exceed the individual's personal or economic resources. The incapacity of the individual to manage his activities in connection with several institutions would be especially severe at times of uncertainty or personal crisis. A family group whose members were deeply committed to assist each other would be mobilized for action in time of need. This mobilization would generate norms relating to the welfare of family members. The second factor: Tension and emotional pressures are built up outside the home. Many institutions in American society magnify competition and conflict (for example, the child in school, the parents at work, the political party system, international relations). Sometimes the home becomes the only place where commitments that are not based primarily on competition, conflict, or a rationalized division of labor exist. The adequacy of the family as a tension-reducing agency depends upon the good will of its therapist members. Heightened demands are made upon each member of the family to develop courses of action for promoting the welfare of his fellow family members.

The welfare strategy of family organization consists of norms and values focusing on assistance and emotional support. Specific family and kinship norms appropriate to the welfare strategy of family organization will now be described.

With respect to lineage, the bilateral kinship system appears appropriate to the welfare strategy because this system provides members of the nuclear family with a maximum number of kindred who can provide the identity and sources of assistance needed to support and supplement family resources. When specific kin do not exist, the bilateral system simplifies the process of complementary filiation. This simplification occurs through a lack of specificity in the rights and duties as well as in the identification of particular classes of kin in the bilateral system. For example, in societies where the bride "belongs" to a lineage, it is incumbent upon the father or other specified representative of the lineage to "give the bride away." In the bilateral system, however, "giving the bride away" is an honorific rather than symbolic act and is often performed by a close friend. Thus, in the bilateral system, it is easy to become an "honorary relative" to someone who has no "blood" kindred.

The number of children also becomes a matter for welfare norms. Each family can determine the number appropriate for itself, perhaps as pledges to the permanence of the marriage. However, as the birth of children is a matter of choice, the parents may also respond to fads and group pressures; at different times varying numbers of children per family are in vogue (about three children being the current fashion).

Residence of the married couple also becomes a welfare concern. In a bilateral kinship system it is irrelevant where the married couple live so long as they are available to kindred in time of need either as givers or receivers of aid. In general, a tendency for bilocal residence is appropriate (although with modern transportation facilities, proximity loses its crucial importance). In the past, although the American family has had patrilineal tendencies, some people have observed a tendency toward matrilocal residence. Perhaps the combination of patrilineal and matrilocal tendencies has fostered the development of the bilateral system.

Marriage and divorce in the bilateral kinship system are both evaluated in terms of welfare and therapy norms. Under welfare norms, marriage of a couple whose personal welfare will not be furthered by the marriage is generally frowned upon. Correspondingly, when a marriage appears to be harmful to the mental health of one of the spouses, a divorce is considered appropriate. As long as the marriage (or divorce) is interpreted as based upon the welfare of the husband and wife, the creation (or dissolution) of the marriage is encouraged. However, marriage or divorce for economic stability or for reasons of family pressure is considered improper.

With personal welfare as the basic criterion for judgment by family members, the families utilizing the welfare strategy are undergoing a constant re-formation of family norms in the process of transmitting these norms from one generation to the next. (Families organized on the basis of the welfare strategy are described in a later chapter as home-oriented.)

The efficiency strategy

The functionalists such as Parsons have conceptualized trends in family organization on the basis of the efficiency strategy. As was indicated in a previous section, their contention is that the organization of family life adjusts itself to maintaining or improving the community position of the members of the nuclear family. The basic relationship exists between the family and the occupational activity of the breadwinner. Family life is organized to meet the needs, routines, and limitations of the breadwinner. As the occupational structure of society changes, the breadwinner's relationship to his family changes accordingly. As the breadwinner's relationship to the family shifts, the organization of family life is modified.

Lineage plays little part in the efficiency strategy. The fewer lineage commitments, the more the couple can make its decisions in terms of occupational advancement and economic position. Thus, kinship elimination rather than the bilateral system appears to be appropriate for the efficiency strategy. However, job sponsorship and financial aid by parents and in-laws to the young married couple to maintain economic status suggest that the family of orientation has an obligation to give the married children a secure place in the community as its final obligation to them. Other than that assistance, the efficient norm is that of nonkinship rather than that of bilateral kinship.

Children are both an economic impediment and a drain upon the time and energy of the parents. The efficiency strategy implies that the number of children appropriate to the family is the minimum number needed to maintain the personnel needs of the society in populating the succeeding generation. Children impede both residential and upward social mobility.

Neolocal residence appears suited to the efficiency criterion. In neolocal residence, the married couple and children would face few kinship restrictions in attaining or maintaining their economic position.

The most efficient marriage is one in which the husband and wife are partners or colleagues and marriage or divorce is considered by the couple on that basis. However, since the norm is for love to precede marriage, the wife chosen as the love object should at least not impair the ability of the husband to get ahead. Because marital problems ordinarily interfere with economic productivity, the marriage should be free from strife. Where strife occurs, divorce is an acceptable remedy.

Insofar as the orderly replacement of kinship and family patterns is frequently inimical to adaptations fostered by "efficiency," this strategy is not conducive to the orderly transmission of family norms from one generation to the next. This negation of continuity emphasizes the antikinship element of the efficiency strategy. (Families organized on the basis of the efficiency strategy are described in a later chapter as parent-oriented.)

The conservative strategy

The conservative strategy is aimed at the development or retention of a stable kinship system. As was indicated earlier, conditions in contemporary society operate to inhibit a stable kinship system. Even so, families in contemporary society may sometimes attempt to use the conservative strategy.

Whereas the bilateral kinship system appears appropriate to the welfare strategy and nonkinship to the efficiency strategy, unilineal kinship seems appropriate to the conservative strategy. Either patrilineal or matrilineal patterns are consistent with the conservative strategy. Although past tradition in America has leaned toward the patrilineal system, Murdock suggests that the trend toward control of American wealth by women fits the possibility of a future matrilineage.[42]

With the continuity of the lineage at stake, the conservative strategy requires a maximum number of children per family. For families employing the conservative strategy, children are not a handicap to the parents. A maximum number insures the transmission of family culture intact even though some of the children may depart from family practices and loyalties.

In order that control over the generation of grand-

[42] George Peter Murdock, public lecture at University of Illinois, 1962.

children be maintained, residential mobility of the children's families of procreation should be kept at a minimum. Matrilocal residence facilitates the stability of matrilineal descent and patrilocal residence is appropriate for patrilineal descent.

Marriage and divorce rules under the unilineal system depend upon the line of continuity. Under the matrilineal system, divorce does not affect the lineage and the frequency of divorce and remarriage is irrelevant to the problem of maintaining the lineage. Under the patrilineal system, since the mother-child bond is close, divorce does ordinarily affect family continuity (with the child being with the mother but belonging to the father's lineage). Hence, solutions to the problem of divorce would depend upon the particular unilineal system.

In a society as heterogeneous as the American society, there is no reason to suppose that the conservative strategy could not be practiced in various segments of the society. The conservative strategy could probably operate to sustain a particular family culture in the lowest social classes as well as the highest social stratum of the contemporary society. Moreover, with health and vigor sustained in the later years of life, grandparents can play an active role in their children's families. This trend in health and longevity may also make the great-grandparent commonplace. The prominence of the aged in family life may promote the conservative strategy. (In a later chapter, families utilizing a conservative strategy of organization are characterized as child-oriented.)

Table 5 summarizes the characteristics of the welfare, efficiency, and conservative strategies. The continued co-

Table 5

APPROPRIATE CHARACTERISTICS OF STRATEGIES OF
FAMILY ORGANIZATION IN CONTEMPORARY SOCIETY:
THE WELFARE STRATEGY, THE EFFICIENCY STRATEGY,
AND THE CONSERVATIVE STRATEGY

Characteristics	Strategies of family organization		
	The welfare strategy	The efficiency strategy	The conservative strategy
1. Rules of lineage	Bilateral system	No kinship system	Unilineal kinship system (patrilineal or matrilineal)
2. Appropriate number of children	Individual decision as "pledge" or commitment	Minimum number	Maximum number
3. Rules of residence	Bilocal or neolocal, but family available to kindred	Neolocal with maximum mobility	Matrilocal or patrilocal (highly stable)
4. Rules of marriage and divorce	Marriage and divorce based on welfare and therapy considerations	Marriage and divorce based on impedance and facilitation of economic and social status "needs" of each partner	Marriage in accordance with parental wishes. Patrilineage: minimum divorce. Matrilineage: divorce based on personal decisions

(continued)

Table 5 (continued)

Characteristics	Strategies of family organization		
	The welfare strategy	*The efficiency strategy*	*The conservative strategy*
5. Basic family unit	Life careers of entire nuclear family as mutually contingent	Husband and wife dyad	Patrilineal: father and child dyad. Matrilineage: mother and child dyad

existence of these strategies in organizing family life acts to perpetuate the cultural pluralism of our society.

The Conceptual Model of the Contemporary Family (Chapter 4), suggested that the American kinship system is becoming increasingly bilateral in its structure, that viewing marriage as a personal commitment which is potentially temporary (permanent availability) is consistent with objective data in family life, and that regarding children as "pledges" to maintain the commitment explains trends in birth rate more adequately than "functional" explanations. These trends indicate that the welfare strategy of family organization is becoming increasingly prominent in American society. The prominence of the welfare strategy is consistent with increased attention given to mental health and adjustment problems in family life.

The consequences to be anticipated for the conservative strategy and the efficiency strategy in coping with trends of American society have been described above in the sections on the idealistic explanation and the functional explanation. What additional forecasts can be made with respect to the welfare strategy?

1. *The anticipated higher standard of living occasioned by the increase in productivity through automation, higher average income, and higher educational levels will obviate the need for individuals' concern over subsistence.* With a surplus of income and leisure, families will have numerous opportunities for choices in style of life. A forecast would thus anticipate less emphasis upon "efficiency" and less concern with adaptation to occupational and economic requirements. This change will promote the welfare strategy in the future as a desired approach to family life. However, automation may bring the growth of a proletariat who for lack of training or ability will remain close to subsistence levels of living and will choose a conservative or efficiency strategy in family organization.

2. *With an increase in general health, income, and longevity, the population will have more opportunities for planning.* Morgan and his colleagues report that:

In general, younger persons more frequently feel able to plan than do older persons. About half of those under thirty-five feel able to plan, while less than a third of those sixty-five and older express this attitude. The decline in feeling of ability to plan results both from increasing realism and from a narrowing of the alternatives available to persons as their age increases. Older people may find that their plans miscarry and report that they are unable to plan as a consequence; younger people have had less experience and have seen fewer of their plans fail. . . . Feeling able to plan is not a function of age

alone, however. Married couples with children are less likely
to feel able to plan than married couples without children.
Least able to plan are single persons with children. This may
reflect the generally low incomes of that group, and the difficulty in arranging employment and child care jointly. . . .
Spending unit heads who have incomes in excess of their
estimated needs feel much more able to plan than spending
unit heads whose incomes are barely sufficient to meet their
budget requirements.[43]

Increased length of life, health, income and education may permit or promote an increase in planning in all
facets of life. Even now, the majority of couples in American society practice contraception as a facet of family
planning. In general, the higher the educational level of
the wife, the greater is the probability that she will use
contraceptives prior to her first pregnancy.[44] As the educational level of American women increases, it is realistic
to expect even greater control over conception and more
planning in general.

3. *Increased longevity and increased planning will
themselves foster family crises.* As long as people do not
plan, they are prepared to accept almost any occurrence
as an act of fate. Planning carries with it some confidence
that the individual can control his own destiny, that he
can produce the events he desires. However, with increased life spans, people will have more opportunity to
encounter tragedy and uncertainty in connection with

[43] James N. Morgan, Martin H. David, Wilbur J. Cohen, and
Harvey E. Brazer, *Income and Welfare in the United States,* New
York: McGraw-Hill, 1962, p. 432.

[44] Freedman, Whelpton, and Campbell, *op. cit.*

their interpersonal commitments. For example, physiologists have suggested that the contraceptive pill which inhibits menstruation may prolong the reproductive life of women. The basis for this view is that at each menstruation the ovary is scarred and menopause occurs when the ovaries are covered with scarred tissues. However, the probability of giving birth to a deformed child increases with the age of the mother. The future may see a marked increase in the number of families having to cope with severely handicapped children.

4. *As health, longevity, and economic status are increased, the prospect is for a greater participation of the parents in the family life of their married children.* Sussman and Burchinal indicate that parental aid in money, goods, and services is widespread in American society.[45] This fact suggests that the parents are operating with a welfare norm in their interaction with their married children. The trends in health, life expectancy, and income will promote the increased use of welfare norms in the future.

5. *With high marriage rates and high survival rates for children, if present family growth plans are realized, population growth will be rapid.* Freedman, Whelpton and Campbell predict that on the basis of current mortality and marriage patterns, present fertility practices will provide a United States population of 312 million by 2000 and of 600 million by 2050.[46] Even if these estimates are

[45] Marvin B. Sussman and Lee Burchinal, "Parental Aid to Married Children: Implications for Family Functioning," *Marriage and Family Living*, 24 (1962), pp. 320-332.

[46] Freedman, Whelpton, and Campbell, *op. cit.*

too high, they suggest a continued population increase. Several alternative strategies in family life may result from this growth in population:

(a) Given a population of such immense proportions as well as the technological means for mobility and communication, social density will increase. A unilineal system seems to be difficult to maintain in a population of high social density. Yet, given the high standard of living anticipated in the major segment of the society, the efficiency norm would not be necessary for family organization. Thus, it appears that the population explosion under conditions of a high standard of living will promote bilateral characteristics in American kinship.

(b) There is a possibility that organizations (giant corporations, estates, special interest groupings, "total institution" arrangements) may wrest control over orderly replacement of family culture in the middle-class population from the kindred. Organizational control may be made possible by the huge labor surplus which will probably exist under conditions of extreme automation of industry and services. Conformity in family life may become a requirement for continued employment.

(c) The highly specialized knowledge needed in an automated industrial and professional society will leave a large unemployed segment unsuited for work unless the conception of productive occupation is broadened. Many activities which are now regarded as unpaid family pursuits, leisure-time activities, and household maintenance chores can be redefined as productive occupations. The number and kinds of professionals in sports, child-raising, household maintenance, theatricals, and other activities can be expanded. Broadening the occupational base will expand the middle class and with it the application of bilateral norms in family life.

Difficulties in Long-Run Forecasting

Three factors make the forecast of a long-run trend in American family life difficult. These factors are: new elements (technical inventions and social innovations), the future structure of the society, and the strategies of family organization which may be preferred.

Technical inventions and scientific discoveries which are now unfolding through such mechanisms as the electronic digital computer, the electron microscope, and the radio telescope may have far-reaching implications for the distant future. As scientific tools continue to improve, knowledge gained may change the basic philosophies and religions guiding social life. As astronomical knowledge increases, man's ideas about the destiny of the galaxy and the universe may change. As the codes embodied in the genes are deciphered, controlled modification of human heredity will be possible. As the minute elements of the electron are discovered, the potentialities of chemistry will accelerate. Possibly the "soma" pills in Huxley's *Brave New World* will become a reality to help people maintain youthfulness and glamour for permanent availability. The potentialities are infinite.

The structure of society in the distant future introduces a second uncertainty in long-run forecasting. General trends are indeterminate. At some future time, American society may be devastated by hydrogen-bomb warfare or, equally possible, world government may dissolve national boundaries. The economic system may cease to exist on the basis of scarcity of goods and be concerned only with ascertaining that all persons get their share. On the one hand, living space on earth may become a scarcity (perhaps the only scarcity); on the other hand, colonization of the moon and satellites surrounding the earth may occur. Again, it is difficult to forecast long-range trends in family life in the face of these uncertainties.

Finally, the organization of family life in the distant future may take various forms. It is possible that there will be communal rearing of children; it is equally possible that two-way television and other inventions may reintroduce into the home activities relating to education (so that schools become obsolete). The time may be reached when people decide that further change would be harmful for society and that conservative strategies in family organization (rather than efficiency or welfare strategies) would be appropriate. Moreover, controlled modification of human genetics may be applied to the entire population in regulating marriages or it may be used only to eliminate certain characteristics related to physical, mental, and metabolic aberrations. Here again, a long-run forecast would be fraught with uncertainty.

Given the many risks in forecasting long-range trends in family life, concentration on short-run trends seems appropriate. In the short run, the most probable trend is the further elaboration of norms and values associated with bilateral kinship systems. This trend could extend into the more distant future.

Selected Readings

Change in family organization and social structure is discussed in:

Greenfield, Sidney M. "Industrialization and the Family in Sociological Theory," *American Journal of Sociology,* 67 (1961), pp. 312-322.

Habakkuk, H. J. "Family Structure and Economic Change in Nineteenth-Century Europe," *Journal of Economic History,* 15 (1955), pp. 1-12.

Lee, Shu-Ching. "China's Traditional Family, Its Characteristics and Disintegration," *American Sociological Review,* 18 (1953), pp. 272-280.

Schorr, Alvin L. "Family Policy in the United States," *International Social Science Journal,* 14 (1962), pp. 452-467.

Sjoberg, Gideon. "Familial Organization in the Preindustrial City," *Marriage and Family Living,* 18 (1956), pp. 30-36.

Talmon-Garber, T. "Social Change and Family Structure," *International Social Science Journal,* 14 (1962), pp. 468-487.

Trends in American family life are described in:

Glick, Paul C., David M. Heer, and John C. Beresford. "Family Formation and Family Composition: Trends and Prospects," in Marvin B. Sussman (ed.), *Sourcebook in Marriage and the Family,* Houghton Mifflin, 1963, pp. 30-40.

Jaco, E. Gartley, and Ivan Belknap. "Is a New Family Form Emerging in the Urban Fringe?" *American Sociological Review,* 18 (1953), pp. 551-557.

Nimkoff, M. F. "Biological Discoveries and the Future of the Family: A Reappraisal," *Social Forces,* 41 (1962), pp. 121-127.

PART THREE

Interaction between Family Members

8 Predicaments in
Family Organization

The previous chapters in this book explored the relationship between family and society. The chapters in Part Three will deal with interaction between family members. The present chapter discusses persistent problems in the organization of family interaction. The following chapters investigate transitory problems associated with the family life cycle, family crises, general predicaments in the socialization of children in the contemporary family, and mental health as related to family interaction. Part Three will attempt to explain the relevance of interaction between family members to the orderly replacement of family life in contemporary society.

This chapter will first discuss ways of conceptualizing persistent problems in family organization (in the section on Dilemmas versus Predicaments). Four family pre-

285

dicaments will then be described and a typology pertaining to solutions of predicaments will be presented.

Dilemmas versus Predicaments

Merton has suggested that many situations arise in which the participants are "socially ambivalent."[1] He regards social ambivalence as the presence of two contradictory sets of possible courses of action, either of which is recognized in the culture as desirable and permissible. This ambivalence accumulates readily in relationships which last a long time. A result of the persistence of social ambivalence is that in a relationship which may endure (for example, the nuclear family), the ambivalence may be incorporated into the norms by which the family organizes its activities.

Families might incorporate social ambivalence into their norms and rules either by permitting the specific ambivalence-evoking situations to dictate which of the courses of action should be followed or else by determining a series of priorities for deciding which courses of action are preferred in ambivalence-evoking situations. The former policy, in which the *situation* dictates the alternative chosen, implies a loosely defined family organization wherein decisions made cover only the specific events occurring at that particular time. The latter policy, in which the *consensus of the family members on a set of values* determines the alternatives chosen in particular situations, implies a clearly defined organization of courses of action

[1] Robert K. Merton and Elinor Barber, "Sociological Ambivalence," in Edward A. Tiryakian, ed., *Sociological Theory, Values, and Sociocultural Change,* New York: Free Press, 1963, pp. 91-120.

over a period of time. Both policies, however, reflect a spirit of compromise; without compromise, each family member would choose his own alternatives in ambivalence-evoking situations and the family would no longer exist as an enduring relationship. Some of the implications of viewing the family as organized on the basis of each of these policies are indicated in the following discussion.

SITUATIONAL DECISIONS: DILEMMAS

In his characterization of family organization, Kirkpatrick concentrates upon situational decisions in encountering social ambivalence. Kirkpatrick has suggested that the character of family life is determined by the choices made in specific situations with respect to a series of dilemmas. Dilemmas present contradictory alternatives that are substantially equal in their cost-consequences and in their desirability. Family dilemmas included in Kirkpatrick's list are: freedom (in family roles, mate selection, personal interaction, and breaking of uncongenial family ties) versus order and efficiency; personal expression for parents versus child-raising obligations; family activities geared to work-achievement versus those consonant with love-reproduction; family loyalty versus community loyalty; extensive casual interaction with many people versus restricted intensive interaction within the nuclear family; love experiences versus love safety; and free sex expression versus sex as linked to family stability.[2] Presumably, the family members must choose between these mutually exclusive alternatives as they encounter situations involv-

[2] Clifford Kirkpatrick, *The Family as Process and Institution,* New York: Ronald, 1955, pp. 86-92.

ing the particular dilemmas. The choice made depends more upon the demands and desires present in the situation than upon maintaining a consistent pattern of action in the family.

Certain difficulties become apparent in the attempt to apply the concept of dilemma to the study of family organization. Three of these difficulties will be described. First, Kirkpatrick does not consider the relationships between dilemmas systematically. He does not integrate his list of dilemmas into a scheme. His list contains many overlapping dilemmas and, paradoxically, suggests that each dilemma is independent. Second, Kirkpatrick's discussion, focusing on situational decisions, implies that the cost of a particular choice cannot be changed through the development of additional norms or techniques. But is the cost unchangeable? Third, Kirkpatrick assumes that individuals are necessarily faced with the dilemma of choosing between alternatives which are equally desirable to them. Yet people may have a clear preference in choosing between alternatives. In short, although the concept of dilemma appears to be useful for analyzing the family organization process, Kirkpatrick does not make sufficient allowance in his formulation for interaction between dilemmas for the effects of experimentation and creativity in developing norms which maximize gains and minimize cost, or for developing a system of priorities in resolving social ambivalences.

PRIORITY DECISIONS: PREDICAMENTS

Perhaps the difficulties found in the dilemma view can be avoided by regarding the contradictions in norms and the variety of problems in family life as *predicaments*. A predicament refers to a situation characterized by the presence of a perplexing problem. The various kinds of family organization represent different solutions to these predicaments.

Several advantages may be gained through the use of the concept of predicament rather than that of dilemma. The concept of the dilemma implies that the price or cost of goal a is equal to the price of goal b, otherwise there would be no dilemma. The term predicament carries the assumption that prices of goals a and b do not necessarily have an equal valence for the individual. If the individuals rank one goal over another, their solutions to predicaments are not arbitrary or capricious. Instead, solutions to predicaments are based upon choices which minimize the price (as a symbolic or subjective cost) and maximize the gain to the family members.

This discussion will focus upon the priority solution to the problem of social ambivalence. There are probably numerous priorities to be established for meeting the changing circumstances of family life. In order to reconcile the choices made in these predicaments, families develop additional norms. The patterns of choices are strategies for solving predicaments. Family organization accordingly is strategically structured—with respect to authority, division of labor, daily routine, and the like—to solve the maximum number of predicaments in the family.

The changing situations in which families find themselves may sharpen the focus of the family members upon certain ends (such as companionship or the healthy socialization of children). If a sufficient number of families is faced with similar decisions of organization and chooses similar strategies in meeting these predicaments, the resulting pattern becomes the cultural norm.

The solution to predicaments (what) involves the content or kind of family interaction (how the members interact), the time period (when), the location of interaction (where), and the family personnel involved in interaction (who). Other social scientists have applied these categories in their work (for instance, Lasswell defined politics as who gets what, when, and how[3]).

The concern of the chapter with family organization evolves from a more general interest in the predicament of reconciling orderly replacement of generations with permanent availability of persons as mates for all others of the opposite sex (regardless of marital status). The predicaments that concern content of interaction, time period, location of interaction, and personnel therefore must be defined in terms of their relevance to the problem of orderly replacement versus permanent availability.

The four sections that follow discuss four persistent predicaments in family organization which appear to be relevant to orderly replacement and permanent availability. Then the last section of the chapter indicates how patterns chosen in these predicaments reflect particular forms of organization of interaction between family members. The four predicaments comprise the choices of priority for (a) social-emotional versus instrumental values and norms in the *content* of interaction, (b) short-run versus long-run *time* considerations in interaction—role orientation versus career orientation, (c) family commit-

[3] Harold D. Lasswell, *Politics: Who Gets What, When, How.* New York: Meridan, 1958.

ments versus community commitments in the *location* of interaction; and (d) gratification of parents' needs and desires versus gratification of children's needs and desires in determining *personnel* priorities. The discussion assumes that ideally family members wish to maximize *all* of the alternatives, but they consider some alternatives as more important than others.

Social-Emotional (Personal Relations) versus Instrumental (Family as an Institution) Values and Norms

This section is concerned with the content of family interaction. Social-emotional values and norms generally are related to the development of a system of personal relationships between family members. Social-emotional valuation is manifested in a high preference given to values and expectations related to companionship, personality development, emotional security, and affectional satisfaction. In contrast, from the viewpoint of the family as an institution, instrumental values and norms pertain to the continuity of the family unity through generations, administration of family affairs, and the place of the family among other institutions. Instrumental valuation is manifested in a high preference given to values and expectations related to economic security, physical health of the family members, a respected place in the community, and adherence to moral and religious principles in developing role expectations.

One of the issues regarding family organization is whether companionship and affectional relations are positively or negatively related to specialization of roles in the division of household labor. Opposite views are held by Parsons and by Burgess. According to Parsons, in the small, independent nuclear family, the complementarity of husband-wife roles becomes accentuated and differentiation of roles by sex is increasing in importance for socialization of children and stability of the family. Moreover, evidence elicited by Bales in his studies of small discussion groups and by Zelditch in his cross-cultural analysis of sex-role differentiation in nuclear families is cited as an empirical basis for assuming that role differentiation is efficient for sustained group behavior. At the same time, Parsons emphasizes that affectional relationships and companionship are basic ingredients for solidarity in the family. Hence, for Parsons, companionship and role *specialization* in the family are positively correlated.[4] In the Burgess conception of the companionship family, on the other hand, specialization in division of labor and affectional relationships are negatively interrelated. According to Burgess, the change in the status of women has occasioned an equalitarian basis for marriage. This equalitarian basis is associated with a tendency toward sharing tasks and decisions. The condition most favorable to the equalitarian marriage is the presence of a high degree of companionship and affectional relationships. Hence, the Burgess position is that companionship and role specialization in the family are negatively correlated.[5] These positions are presented in terms of community-oriented com-

[4] Talcott Parsons and Robert F. Bales in collaboration with James Olds, Morris Zelditch, Jr., and Philip E. Slater, *Family, Socialization and Interaction Process*, Glencoe, Ill.: Free Press, 1955.

[5] See Ernest W. Burgess, Harvey J. Locke, and Mary Margaret Thomes, *The Family from Institution to Companionship*, New York: American Book, 1963; and Ernest W. Burgess and Paul Wallin, *Engagement and Marriage*, New York: Lippincott, 1953.

panionship (Parsons' position) and commitment-oriented companionship (Burgess' position).

COMMUNITY-ORIENTED COMPANIONSHIP

The Parsons view of companionship assumes that, with the isolation of the nuclear family from kinship supports and constraints, the husband and wife must concentrate their affectional interaction within the family and must act jointly to establish the place of the particular nuclear family in the community. Companionate relationships between husband and wife thereby become a means appropriate to the establishment of the nuclear family as a going concern. Blood and Wolfe utilized the Parsons view of companionship in their studies of an urban community. They defined four types of companionship.[6]

1. *Organizational companionship*, which consists of joint participation of husband and wife in such formally organized groups as P-TA, church-connected organizations, or neighborhood improvement associations.

2. *Informative companionship*, which involves imparting information about events which occurred while the couple were apart. The question used by Blood and Wolfe in their study was: "When your husband comes home from work, how often does he tell you about things that happened there?" Responses to this question were highly associated with responses to: "When you've had a bad day, do you tell your husband about your troubles?"

3. *Colleague companionship*, which involves direct contact with the husband's work role and frequent interaction with the husband's colleagues.

[6] Robert O. Blood, Jr. and Donald M. Wolfe, *Husbands and Wives*, Glencoe, Ill.: Fress Press, 1960.

4. *Friendship companionship,* which was based upon the question: "About how many of your husband's friends are men that you personally know quite well?"

Each of the Blood and Wolfe questions on companionship makes relevant for the marital relationship some aspect of the person's life not ordinarily associated with marital roles—participation in community organizations, communication of events in the daily routine, contact with the spouse's work role, and interaction with the spouse's friends. The kind of companionship emphasized by Blood and Wolfe incorporates into family relationships numerous activities related to the family's place in the community. This kind of companionship may be regarded as community-oriented companionship.

The findings by Blood and Wolfe support the expectation that community-oriented companionship is positively associated with high division of labor.[7] They found that:

1. The higher the socioeconomic status, the greater was the relative amount of household work performed by the wife as compared with the husband. When change in socioeconomic status was analyzed (by comparison of the husband's occupation with his father's), the finding was that upward mobility was *positively* related to the relative amount of household work performed by the wife (according to her report). In addition, the higher the socioeconomic status, the greater was the relative power of the husband in decision making. At the same time, the higher the socioeconomic status, the greater was the *in-*

[7] *Ibid.*

tensity of companionship, especially in the organizational and colleague categories. Hence, the Blood and Wolfe findings suggest that in precisely those socioeconomic categories in which there is a marked specialization of family role in dominance and performance, the intensity (or amount) of community-oriented companionship tends to be high.

2. The division of labor in families in which the wife was employed was more equalitarian than in families in which only the husband worked. Employed women reported less performance of household tasks than nonworking wives except in those families in which husbands performed only traditionally masculine tasks—lawn mowing, snow shoveling, repairing, and the like. (Similarly, in her study of 324 Detroit children, Lois Hoffman found that working mothers made fewer decisions and performed fewer routine tasks in the household than did nonworking mothers.[8]) Employed wives reported a greater amount of influence in family decisions relative to their husbands than did nonworking wives. The amount of relative power of the wife was positively related to the number of years she had been working. Along with less specialization in family roles, employed women reported a *lower* intensity of community-oriented companionship than nonworking wives.

The types of companionship described by Blood and Wolfe thus reveal little conflict between community-oriented companionship and the division of labor in the home.

[8] Lois W. Hoffman, "Effects of the Employment of Mothers on Parental Power Relations and the Division of Household Tasks," *Marriage and Family Living*, 22 (1960), pp. 27-35.

The same power and work roles assumed by the husband and wife in the home can be extended to community-oriented companionate activities. In fact, the couple probably could make efficient use of its internal division of labor by extending familial roles to the joint activities necessary to establish itself in a community of friends, colleagues, and associates in formal organizations. A positive association between community-oriented companionship and specialized familial division of labor is therefore to be anticipated.

COMMITMENT-ORIENTED COMPANIONSHIP

In contrast to the Parsons-Blood-Wolfe conception of companionship, the Burgess view of companionship implies mutual participation in giving and receiving affection, in confiding, in common experience, and in family decisions. Instead of being a means for establishing the family as a going concern, companionship in the Burgess conception is regarded as interaction which is carried on to stimulate further social relationships and thereby to maintain high personal commitment between family members. The concept of companionship as used by Burgess resembles the concept of expressive behavior as used by Parsons, in that both concepts refer to ways of maintaining personal relationships. Several conditions are necessary for a high degree of companionship to occur. These conditions define the kinds of interaction which will take place.

The first condition for companionship is that formal behavior be at a minimum. Formal conduct is dictated by conventional, categorical relationships with another person. If interaction is guided mainly by conventional etiquette, there is little to stimulate further interaction. Conversation, conduct, and values must be *personal and intimate* for the relationship to be companionable.

A second condition for companionship is that the interests and aims of interacting persons be congenial. If the persons antagonize one another by working at cross-purposes, there is little to stimulate further interaction except to eliminate the other's opposition. In a casual acquaintanceship the aims and interests of the persons do not affect the interaction and therefore cannot be uncongenial. While there are few marriages in which there is a congeniality of all aims and interests, in most marriages the participants work toward the development of the *congeniality of aims and interests.*

A third condition for companionship is that the interaction be exciting for the participants. The role of a common interest is not the furthering of a career or skill, but the *mutual stimulation* through which each person gains in excitement by sharing an event with another. Reinforcement of each other's responsiveness, mutual perception of critical features of the event, and discussion of the event's meaning serve to create a stimulating effect on both persons.

A fourth condition for companionship is that the interaction must be *expansive* for the participants. In repartee, in new interests, and in developing congenial strategies, the person develops new techniques of sociability. The interaction of the couple becomes exploratory and additional interpersonal techniques are continually developed to meet this exploration. This exploratory interaction also requires that the individual not conceive the relationship as threatening. If the person regards the relationship as threatening to his self-esteem, he cannot interact with the other person in an exploratory manner. The other person may characterize him as stubborn, moody, easily angered, suspicious, or highly sensitive.

For companionship to increase interpersonal commitment, probably the conditions of congeniality, interest, informality or intimacy, and expansiveness must be present. To the extent that these conditions are absent, companionship in the relationship seems to decline. The couple may then define their relationship as lacking companionship or they may try to maintain a fiction of companionship. That is, the couple may participate in common activities without becoming more intimate or informal; they participate as "companions" because it is expected of them. In the absence of companionship, the relationship can be characterized as antagonistic, routine, formal, or threatening.

The preceding discussion provides a basis for distinguishing four sets of polar factors in commitment-reinforcing companionship: congeniality versus antagonism, interest versus routine, informality versus formality, and expansiveness versus threat or hostility. Activities which maintain a high personal commitment between family members cannot ordinarily rely for their performance on "efficient" role bargains in which each person maximizes his personal gains while doing as little as possible for others.[9] Nor can commitment-reinforcing companionship thrive when family members are isolated from one an-

---

[9] See William J. Goode, "A Theory of Role Strain," *American Sociological Review*, 25 (1960), pp. 483-496.

other. These activities require congeniality, interest, informality, and expansiveness in interpersonal relations. They flourish in interaction characterized by intimacy and by joint participation on an equalitarian basis. Hence, commitment-reinforcing companionship appears to be inimical to segregation in division of labor and power relations, giving formal authority to one family member (regardless of the efficiency of the role specialization for getting the work done). A negative association between commitment-reinforcing companionship and division of labor is to be anticipated.

Just as empirical findings supported the Parsonian view that community-oriented companionship and highly specialized family division of labor are positively associated, other findings are consistent with the Burgess view that commitment-reinforcing companionship and division of labor are negatively associated.

The Blood and Wolfe investigation substantiates the cluster of characteristics which identify commitment-reinforcing companionship.[10] They found that joint decision making was associated with the wife's satisfaction with her husband's love, her satisfaction with the extent of companionship with her husband, and the husband's sympathetic response to his wife's problems. Conversely, the wife who did not know any of her husband's friends well tended to be dissatisfied with the extent of her husband's love. Breakdown in role specialization was related to intimate interaction. More employed wives than housewives confided their problems to their husbands.

The negative relationship between commitment-rein-

[10] Blood and Wolfe, *op. cit.*

forcing companionship and division of labor is also suggested by findings related to equalitarian decision making in marriage. Some of these findings are:

1. Analyzing responses of couples in the Burgess and Wallin study, Yi-Chuang Lu found that the equalitarian decision making is associated with high marital adjustment.[11]

2. In the Blood and Wolfe investigation, syncratic decision making (making decisions together) was associated with high marital satisfaction of wives. On the other hand, the number of household tasks performed by the husband was *not* found to be linearly related to marital satisfaction.[12]

3. In his comparison of happily married and divorced persons, Locke found that in describing their marriage, the happily married persons reported democratic relationships more frequently in making family decisions and in affectionate behavior.[13]

Since the Burgess position is that intimacy of interaction and the breakdown in role specialization are related to companionship, the findings on equalitarianism and intimacy provide confirmation of this conception of companionship as an empirical entity.

THE COMPANIONSHIP PREDICAMENT
AND ORDERLY REPLACEMENT

Although the Parsons and Burgess views of companionship in marriage appear contradictory, they refer to two

[11] Yi-Chuang Lu, "Marital Roles and Marriage Adjustment," *Sociology and Social Research,* 36 (1952), pp. 364-369.

[12] Blood and Wolfe, *op. cit.*

[13] Harvey J. Locke, *Predicting Adjustment in Marriage,* New York: Holt, 1951.

different kinds of activity—community-oriented companionship and commitment-oriented companionship. The two types of companionship do not necessarily conflict; extensive joint activities in community affairs may sometimes reinforce personal commitment of husband and wife. However, the couple that spends most of its time in community events may lack the time for commitment-reinforcing companionship. Just as joint community participation may preclude intimate interaction, the amount of time spent in intimate interaction may interfere with community-oriented companionship. The possible conflict implies that the two types of companionship reflect different kinds of joint participation of husband and wife.

The companionship predicament can be stated as commitment-oriented companionship versus community-oriented companionship and/or emphasis upon instrumental activities. Emphasis upon instrumental activities conflicts with commitment-oriented companionship whether or not community-oriented companionship is also present. Possibly the joint occurrence of community-oriented companionship and emphasis upon instrumental activities provides a more stable family organization than the presence of either alone; they may sustain one another.

The companionship predicament is related to the problem of orderly replacement versus permanent availability. Commitment-reinforcing activities carry the implicit assumption that without them, people tend to drift apart and to place emphasis upon self-gratification. Hence, persons who emphasize commitment-reinforcing activities implicitly presuppose a tentativeness in social relations. In marriage, this tentativeness is one of permanent availability. Like community-oriented companionship, however, instrumental activities are directly associated with maintaining family life. A clearly defined division of labor in performing activities instrumental to the continuity of the family (coupled with community-oriented companionship) promotes the orderly transmission of norms from one generation to the next.

Role Orientation versus Career Orientation—the Short Run versus the Long Run

The preceding section investigated the content of family interaction. This section turns to the time dimension in family interaction.

A *role* can be described as the organization of an individual's activities in an institution such as the family at any particular time. A *career* is regarded as progession by an individual through a series of roles.

Problems faced by family members necessarily change during crises and in the normal course of the family life cycle. The succession of problems stimulates changes in roles of the family members. Insofar as the family exists as a system of careers, a marked shift in one career in the system affects the other careers. With respect to each career in the system, the sequence of role changes can be orderly as opposed to haphazard from an observer's viewpoint and anticipated as opposed to unanticipated from the family members' perspective. In part, the orderliness of the development of the career system depends upon the anticipations of the family members with respect to future role changes within each career. Hence, the extent to which the family members are oriented toward potential role changes may affect family organization.[14]

[14] See Bernard Farber, "The Family as a Set of Mutually Contingent Careers," in Nelson N. Foote, ed., *Household Decision-*

One manner of developing roles is for family members to consider only short-run consequences and immediate personal gain. This kind of development can be considered as "role oriented"—that is, the members focus upon problems in the current family situation and minimize possible long-term consequences. A second way of developing roles is for family members to give minimal consideration to short-run consequences in the family and maximum consideration to long-run effects in planning. This kind of development can be described as "career oriented."

PLANNING FOR THE FUTURE

The distinction between role and career orientation does not necessarily imply that in career-oriented families the members consider alternatives more carefully than do the members in role-oriented families. Rather, the emphasis here is on the kind of perspective given priority. Career-oriented persons plan for the future to a greater extent than do role-oriented persons.

The tendency to plan does not occur at random. Various characteristics related to socioeconomic status, family life cycle, and social background are associated with the tendency of people to plan.

SOCIOECONOMIC STATUS

People in lower socioeconomic classes of the population do not plan ahead as readily as do those in the higher socioeconomic levels. Morgan and his associates found that the lower the income and education, the less did the respondents feel that they were able to plan for the future.[15] Planning usually implies a commitment to a particular line of action, a strategy to be followed regardless of the particular circumstances which may occur. In low socioeconomic classes either the individual may be unwilling to work out the details of the social process which defines the long-term line of action or he may believe that he has so little control over future circumstances that he cannot realistically devise a workable strategy. For example, a parent at a low socioeconomic level may want to send his children to college when they eventually mature. He may lack resources for planning. ("We just live from hand to mouth—there's never enough to put anything away.") Even given a sufficient income so that by careful saving he can at least partly finance the children's college education, the lower-class parent may not be willing to defer more immediate gratifications, he may not investigate college costs in order to formulate a savings plan, or he may dream that he will "strike it rich" some day—any of these actions would inhibit his working out the details of a planned line of action. Even if the parent is motivated to develop a detailed strategy, he may regard his life situation as very precarious and regard the future as almost completely uncertain. ("Governments keep bickering back and forth and you can never tell what's going to happen.")[16]

FAMILY LIFE CYCLE

People at different stages in the course of their lives show diverse inclinations to plan. Morgan found that younger

[15] James N. Morgan, Martin H. David, Wilbur J. Cohen, and Harvey E. Brazer, *Income and Welfare in the United States,* New York: McGraw-Hill, 1962.

[16] *Ibid.*

persons have greater confidence in planning in family life than do older persons. Married couples without children reported that they were able to plan to a greater extent than couples with children. Divorced or widowed parents were least able to plan. Perhaps as individuals mature, have children, and grow older, they experience the countless ways in which circumstances over which they have little or no control create crises and make the execution of plans impossible.[17]

RELIGIOUS AND ETHNIC-GROUP BACKGROUND

Religious and ethnic-group background is associated with the inculcation of the values and practice of planning. For example, in Detroit, Mayer and Sharp found that Jews and Eastern Orthodox persons showed the greatest achievement in advancing their socioeconomic status when the level of their parents was held statistically constant.[18] Viewed ethnically, the Jews and Eastern Orthodox (primarily Syrians, Lebanese, and Greeks) are traditionally traders, shopkeepers, merchants, and entrepreneurs. These occupations are associated with rationalization and planning. In addition, Mayer and Sharp found that Protestants showed greater achievement than Catholics. Another Detroit-area study (by Miller and Swanson) revealed that Protestants were more likely than Catholics to inculcate norms of responsibility in children at an earlier age. Moreover, the Protestants were more prone to use symbolic reward and punishment rather than direct re-

[17] *Ibid.*

[18] Albert J. Mayer and Harry Sharp, "Religious Preference and Worldly Success," *American Sociological Review,* 27 (1962), pp. 218-227.

ward and corporal punishment.[19] The inculcation of responsibility and the use of symbolic reward and punishment are indicative of the development of the ability to delay direct gratifications. The delay of direct gratifications involves an orientation toward future events, and, in turn, the orientation toward the future facilitates confidence in planning.

THE TIME DIMENSION AND ORDERLY REPLACEMENT

What are the consequences for orderly replacement when priority is given to career orientation over role orientation? By itself, priority of career orientation over role orientation does not appear to imply a priority of norms associated with orderly replacement over those of permanent availability. Yet, depending as it does upon the tentativeness of interpersonal relations, permanent availability suggests that family relationships are capricious and as a result of this capriciousness, people cannot have much confidence in long-run plans. Short-run planning in family life is more consistent with the view of marriage as a voidable relationship and remarriage as a perennial possibility than is long-run planning. To have confidence in long-range planning, individuals must regard their social relations as relatively stable and orderly. Career orientation implies that family relations are predictable over long periods of time. Career orientation is therefore more consistent with orderly replacement from one generation to the next than is role orientation.

[19] Daniel R. Miller and Guy E. Swanson, *The Changing American Parent*, New York: Wiley, 1958.

Commitment to Internal (Family) versus External (Community) Organization

This section discusses the location of activities by family members: Which factors determine where they carry on their activities?

In a society based primarily upon kinship considerations, the predicament of choosing between nuclear family commitments and kindred commitments may occur.[20] Similarly, in contemporary urban society, parents can develop strategies for maintaining or increasing their commitment and consequent participation in other institutions and thus give priority to the development of a successful career in these institutions rather than to the nuclear family. Or the parents can develop a different set of strategies for withdrawing from a good many activities in the community and thereby give priority to their domestic careers.

The relationship between the family-community predicament and the predicament of orderly-replacement versus permanent availability depends upon the norms of the community in which the family exists. If the family exists in a community whose norms promote orderly replacement, then involvement in community matters reinforces a conventional domestic life oriented toward orderly replacement. However, participation in a community oriented toward permanent availability would not be conducive to orderly replacement. The extent to which family life is privatized thus depends upon the extent to which family members view the norms of the community

[20] Max Gluckman, *Conflict and Custom in Africa*, Glencoe, Ill.: Free Press, 1955, pp. 54-80.

as hostile to the continued existence of their mode of living.

The hostility of the community to domestic life is a comparatively recent development in Western society. Halmos regards the growth of privacy with respect to the nuclear family as a part of a general trend.[21] Many sociologists (including Max Weber) have pointed out that this privatization of family life occurred with the separation of the place of work from the residence in the course of the rise of the factory system and urbanization. The home could then become a more or less independent sphere of activity. Taking an extreme position that privatization occurred in all nonproductive aspects of society (for example, family life and recreation), Halmos has described the privatization process vividly in terms of dancing and drinking as aspects of the decline of ceremonies and rituals connected with communal solidarity.

The choral dance was widely practiced in medieval Europe until the sixteenth and seventeenth centuries. It had begun to decline earlier, toward the end of the feudal era. In the period marking the decline of feudalism and the rise of industrial society, choral dances and couple dances persisted together especially in couple dances performed within a choral framework (for example, the minuet, the square dance, the allemand). The waltz and the polka ended the popularity of the choral dances. By the beginning of the twentieth century, the dance had become almost exclusively an activity performed for purposes of courtship and sexual titillation. According to Hal-

[21] Paul Halmos, *Solitude and Privacy*, New York: Philosophical Library, 1953.

mos, the dance "is no longer an important formaliser of social skill, of manners, and it has become arid, business-like or downright erotic, and non-social."[22]

Halmos also pointed out that drinking ordinarily took place as a part of social participation. In the Middle Ages, there were few people who avoided intoxicants. There was heavy drinking and conviviality on almost all social occasions. Participation was expected as a duty to one's association, and membership in an association (or corporate body) was a necessity; the unattached person could be dispossessed, exploited, robbed, or murdered. "To exist, one had to belong to an association: a household, a manor, or monastery, a guild; there was no security" except in a corporate life.[23] Each corporate body had social occasions for business and celebration. In contrast, the contemporary pub and tavern draw as clientele an anonymous population who drink and seek conviviality for *private* reasons rather than as participation in communal events.

The trend in dancing and drinking is but part of a general movement toward privatization. Charles Madge has indicated that "with the growth of urban forms of social organization, links of kinship and of feudal dependency become less vivid and the house as headquarters of the family becomes more focal. Each family became an organization in its own right, with its own private space."[24] Halmos regards the turning inward toward the family for

[22] *Ibid.*, p. 30.
[23] *Ibid.*, p. 37.
[24] Charles Madge, "Private and Public Spaces," *Human Relations*, 3 (1950), p. 192.

friendship and companionship to the exclusion of extra-family attachments as an ideological and even obsessional affirmation of family ties.

Whereas Halmos has viewed the development of family life in terms of withdrawal of family members from a chaotic or even hostile world, other writers such as Whyte are concerned with the kind of family life that large-scale organizations select as "the fittest." As was indicated in Chapter 6, Kinship and Social Criticism, modern corporate life, like that of its medieval counterparts, requires of its personnel congenial relations and conformity to conventional standards for its efficient operation.

The "progressive" corporation encourages community-oriented companionship in its member-families and tends to be paternalistic toward its executives (both senior and junior). Whereas the privatized family is frequently organized in terms of the welfare of its members, the family in a bureaucratic structure develops an organization appropriate to the demands of the large-scale organization.[25]

The middle-class suburb, developed since World War II, represents the style of family life appropriate to the large-scale organization. According to Whyte, in the middle-class suburb (such as Levittown, Pennsylvania, or Park Forest, Illinois), "privacy has become clandestine." Instead, neighborliness, the reliance upon friends (rather than kin) for good will and exchange of favors, having to get along in a community in which everyone is a migrant—all of these characteristics reinforce the emphasis placed upon congeniality and the development of a sociable personality.

The extreme of privatization described by Halmos

[25] William H. Whyte, Jr., *The Organization Man*, Garden City, N.Y.: Doubleday, 1956.

and the extreme of community involvement discussed by Whyte indicate the internal-external predicament in organization of the contemporary family. Insofar as the large-scale organization and residential community provide order and security for the family, the family members may orient their lives around the demands of the organization and community. However, should the large-scale organization and residential community cease to shelter the family, families may choose a privatized existence.

Problems of family privatization versus integration into the community may be presented in terms of conventionality of norms. Conventional norms are those prevalent in the community and considered appropriate for maintaining a stable domestic life.

Three situations describe the relationship between family and community in contemporary society: (a) both the family and community may be oriented toward conventional family norms; (b) the family with a deviant member (or members) may exist in a community dominated by conventional norms; (c) family members may try to carry on a conventional domestic life in a disruptive community. Where both family and community are oriented toward conventional norms, community participation is supportive of domestic life. In the other two situations, the norms and values of the community are hostile to the domestic life of the particular family.

CONVENTIONAL FAMILY AND CONVENTIONAL COMMUNITY

As the discussion of community-oriented companionship in an earlier section indicated, the participation of the married couple in congenial communities of friends, colleagues, and civic associations need not disrupt the personal commitment of the husband and wife to each other. Insofar as both husband and wife agree on their participation, this involvement in the life of the community may actually increase family solidarity. Burgess and Wallin found, for example, that devotion to a common cause, active community service, and similar professional interests had a considerable binding effect on married couples.

Burgess and Wallin concluded that socially active persons, in addition to being more religious and more conventional than the socially inactive, are also more determined to make a success of marriage.[26] Their findings are buttressed by results of other investigations. For example, Zimmerman and Broderick reported that "successful" families not only have a larger number of intimate family friends but also have more in common with their friends than unsuccessful families do.[27]

DEVIANCE IN THE FAMILY

Whereas the conforming family apparently thrives through community activity, the family with a deviant member does not. Families with a handicapped child tend to limit interaction with others in the community. For example, K. S. Holt found that in his English sample, outside-the-home activities of parents of severely mentally retarded children were limited in many of the families.[28]

[26] Burgess and Wallin, *op. cit.*

[27] C. C. Zimmerman and C. B. Broderick, "The Nature and Role of Informal Family Groups," *Marriage and Family Living,* 16 (1954), pp. 107-111.

[28] K. S. Holt, "The Home Care of the Severely Mentally Retarded," *Pediatrics* 22 (1958), pp. 744-755.

Similarly, Tizard and Grad found that in London about half of their families with a retarded child living at home reported that their social contacts were limited by his presence.[29] In Australia, the investigation by Schonell and Watts showed that about half of their families with a retarded child reported restriction in such social activities as visits to other people's homes.[30] In the United States, the results are comparable.[31] Investigations consistently indicate a tendency for parents of handicapped children to be less sociable and more withdrawn, and for these mothers to be less likely than other mothers to take employment outside the home. In many ways, the parents of the severely handicapped appear similar to the aged in their disengagement from community activities in which they had previously participated. To be sure, withdrawal of parents from community participation results in part from the exhausting problems of caring for some of the severely handicapped. However, more than the immediate care of the severely retarded child seems to be involved. The withdrawal of the parents from "normal" community participation signifies that such participation is incompatible with family demands. Moreover, this withdrawal further signifies that the community of "normal" families is not supportive of the revised norms of child care that must

[29] J. Tizard and Jacqueline C. Grad, *The Mentally Handicapped and Their Families,* New York: Oxford University Press, 1961.

[30] F. J. Schonell and B. H. Watts, "A First Study of the Effects of a Subnormal Child on the Family Unit," *American Journal of Mental Deficiency,* 61 (1956), pp. 210-219.

[31] For example, Bernard Farber, "Effects of a Severely Mentally Retarded Child on Family Integration," *Monographs of the Society for Research in Child Development,* 24 (1959), No. 2 (Serial No. 71).

be established by families with a severely handicapped child. In effect, the norms and values regulating participation in the community of "normal" families are hostile to the demands made upon the parents of a severely handicapped child.

The fact that there is a tendency for families with severely handicapped children to withdraw from community involvement and commitment does not imply that all families with handicapped children do so. Indeed, the family may live in a community which chooses either to regard the handicapped child as irrelevant in interaction with the family or to develop services which free the family from unusual duties. In either instance, the family can then cease to regard the community as hostile and can give priority to community commitments over family commitments.

THE DISRUPTIVE COMMUNITY

"Differential association" has been applied to explain conformity of delinquents and criminals to a "criminal" way of life.[32] Similarly, the internal organization of the family is disrupted by intensive interaction in groups that do not support those norms and values which promote orderly replacement. Some recreational interests and activities appear to be divisive in marriage when husbands or wives regard them as a major interest. These activities tend to be segregated from domestic life (a) by their requirement for a special physical setting and clothing (as

[32] Daniel Glaser, "The Differential-Association Theory of Crime," in Arnold M. Rose, ed., *Human Behavior and Social Processes,* Boston: Houghton Mifflin, 1962, pp. 425-442.

swimming, night clubs, theater); (b) by their restriction to specific short seasons and locations (sports), (c) by their conventional definition as traditionally masculine or feminine recreation (as hunting, tea parties, poker playing), (d) by involving little sentiment or personal projection, but depending mainly on competition through skill or luck (as games, sports, gambling), or (e) by facilitating little in the way of interaction of the couple (as reading). The greater the portion of activities set apart from the normal domestic life of the couple, the lower tends to be the marital adjustment. Strong involvement by husbands or wives in these activities seems to impair their commitment in the marriage.[33]

One of the institutions which frequently conflicts with the domestic way of life is the gang. By a gang is usually meant a group, ordinarily of the same sex, which exists through a period of time and in which the individual finds companionship and maintains significant personal relations. Adult gangs exist as quasi families—the work gang, the bottle gang, the poker club, the tavern gang, the gossip circle, the bookie-joint gang, the corner gang, the clique. All of these manifest a way of life which, if the person invests much of his time and self-esteem in the particular activity, conflicts with the domestic style of living.

Unconventional occupations may also impede domestic life. Becker has pointed out the dilemma of the professional dance or jazz musician:

[33] Burgess and Wallin, *op. cit.;* Purnell Benson, "The Interests of Happily Married Couples," *Marriage and Family Living,* 14 (1952), pp. 276-280.

If he is to achieve financial success, he must give up some of his artistic autonomy; if he chooses to remain an artist, he renounces financial security, for steady work does not come to those who make that choice. The expectation that a man will have a regular and sufficient income governs most marriages, and a musicians' decision to remain an artist would violate that expectation. Consequently, marriage often causes a crisis in which the musician begins to reshape his career toward more "commercial" goals or, alternatively, breaks up the marriage over this issue.[34]

COMMUNITY, FAMILY, AND ORDERLY REPLACEMENT

A predicament between family and community commitments emerges as a problem related to orderly replacement and permanent availability when the community relations do not provide the kind of social criticism which supports the norms of family life. The benevolent community situation, rather than threatening the integrity of the family, would reinforce orderly replacement. Given a community situation which is hostile to family life, the family members can maintain themselves by withdrawing their community commitment and thereby facilitate the transmission of family values and norms from one generation to the next. Given deviance in the family living in a conventional community, the family also tends to withdraw into itself in order to continue to exist in a hostile environment.

[34] Howard S. Becker, "The Implications of Research on Occupational Careers for a Model of Household Decision-Making," in Nelson N. Foote, ed., *Household Decision-Making*, New York: New York University Press, 1961, p. 248.

Priorities in Career Gratification:
Parents versus Children

The preceding sections dealt with the content, time dimension, and location of family activities. Personnel considerations in family organization will now be discussed. Many parents subordinate their own needs and desires to those of their children. These parents organize not merely their daily routine and recreation in accordance with the child's needs, but also their long-range financial and educational planning. Other parents believe that their own career needs should assume priority over those of their children when there is a conflict. In any particular family, the parents may agree or disagree on whose career is to be given priority in long-range planning—parents or children.

The perennial conflict between parents and their children can be resolved only by giving priority either to parental gratifications or to children's gratifications. Traditionally, the ideal in American society is that children's needs are to be given priority over those of the parents. Parents are expected to delay their gratification for their children's sake, but children are not expected to reciprocate. Duvall's study of traditional and developmental conceptions of parenthood provides corroborating evidence for the priority given by parents to children's wants and "needs." In both the traditional and developmental conceptions, the good parent gives priority to the child's needs. The good traditional mother keeps house (washes, cooks, cleans, mends, sews); she takes care of the children physically; she trains them to live on a regular schedule; she disciplines them and makes them good (teaches obedience, instructs in morals). The good developmental mother, among other things, sees to the emotional well-being of the children (keeps them happy and contented, makes a happy home, makes the children welcome and secure); she helps them to develop socially (plays with them, supervises their play, provides companions); she guides them with understanding (sees their point of view, gears her life to their level); and she relates herself lovingly to them (shows them love and affection, enjoys them, spends time with them, is interested in them).[35] Thus, whether traditional or developmental, parental norms have been geared to give priority to the children's socialization. Priority of the children's socialization over immediate parental gratification implies an emphasis upon the orderly replacement of one generation by the next.[36]

In spite of the emphasis given to gratification of children's needs in conceptions of the "good parent," the expansion of socializing and child-minding agencies suggests that many parents subordinate the children's needs to their own. Halpern sees a trend toward greater freedom of parents from the "directly personal, deeply intimate, minute-by-minute total involvement in the child's development" that has long characterized the parental role. The proliferation of parent-surrogate institutions such as nursery schools, day camps, after-school programs, and community centers has enabled (and sometimes driven)

[35] Evelyn Millis Duvall, "Conceptions of Parenthood," *American Journal of Sociology*, 52 (1946), pp. 193-203.

[36] The parents frequently justify giving priority to children's needs and desires on the basis of vicarious satisfaction in seeing the children grow into responsible and happy adults.

parents to spend their time in adult formal and informal community activities. For example, without surrogate institutions, mothers could not enter the labor force in large numbers. These institutions "offer the children guidance, instructions, impulse control, socialization, warmth and a sense of belonging, and they afford for the parents a sense of dutiful involvement with their children from a comfortable and liberating distance."[37] Hence, by relegating traditional parental activities to surrogate institutions, parents can give priority to their own life-career gratifications.

The predicament concerning parent gratification and child gratification is related to that of orderly replacement of generations versus the permanent availability of the parents for subsequent marriages. Insofar as the parents give priority to the gratification of the children's needs, they may be concerned directly with the transmission of norms and values associated with family life from one generation to the next. However, giving priority to gratifying desires of the husband and wife over gratifying those of the children is consistent with norms associated with permanent availability. The belief that married couples, regardless of their personal feelings, should stay together for the sake of the children is giving way to the belief that a happy remarriage is better for both parents and children.[38] With this change in belief, parents can divorce

[37] Howard Halpern, "Alienation from Parenthood in the Kibbutz and America," *Marriage and Family Living*, 24 (1962), pp. 42-45.

[38] William J. Goode, *After Divorce*, Glencoe, Ill.: Free Press, 1956; F. Ivan Nye, "Child Adjustment in Broken and in Unhappy Unbroken Homes," *Marriage and Family Living*, 19 (1957), pp. 356-361.

and remarry without feeling that they are depriving their children of proper socialization and can at the same time gratify their own desires. Perhaps this justification explains at least in part the steady rise in the number of divorces involving children.

Strategies of Family Organization

The preceding discussion has suggested that the priorities chosen in predicaments of family organization are not necessarily discrete choices. Instead, the combinations of priorities selected reflect strategies by which family members organize their interpersonal relations to handle social ambivalence. This section presents a typology of family organization based upon the choices made in the predicaments described in the previous sections. Several studies in which this typology was used will then be described briefly. Finally, several unresolved problems pertaining to the typology will be indicated.

TYPES OF FAMILY ORGANIZATION

The types of family organization resulting from the combination of alternatives chosen as solutions to four predicaments in family relations will now be presented.[39] These predicaments are concerned with ambivalence in family interaction with respect to content, time, location, and personnel. Each combination of alternatives determines a particular type of family organization. However,

[39] Reported in Bernard Farber, "Types of Family Organization: Child-Oriented, Home-Oriented, and Parent-Oriented," in Arnold M. Rose, ed., *Human Behavior and Social Processes*, Boston: Houghton-Mifflin, 1962, pp. 285-306.

the combinations differ as to effectiveness for maintaining high family integration as a condition enabling orderly transmission of family culture from one generation to the next.

For the purpose of the typology of family organization, the content of family careers is defined in terms of the structuring of family life in middle-class American society. The starting point in developing this typology is the assumption that the wife's role revolves around the home while the husband's role is primarily aimed at relating the home to the community. That is, the wife is generally responsible for the internal relations of the family, whereas the husband is responsible for keeping the family a going concern in relation to the rest of the community. Insofar as this division of roles occurs, the wife is in the position of balancing the demands of the husband with those of the children. Successful mediation by the wife of the husband's and children's demands and needs is necessary for the smooth coordination of activities within the family. (These traditional family role assumptions are employed because the concern in this particular typology is with orderly replacement.)

Effective solutions to the family predicaments depend upon the coalitions formed by the husbands and wives to formulate decisions to resolve or minimize crisis or conflicting demands. Generally, the task of the husband in achieving high marital integration is to adapt his family role in such a way as to minimize contradictory demands made on his wife. Theoretically, crisis and conflicting demands can be resolved or minimized in one of three ways: (a) by instituting a sharp division of labor, (b) by a coalition between husband and wife giving priority to social-emotional activities in structuring family life, and (c) by a coalition between wife and husband giving priority to achieving goals in the community social structure. These three strategies are described below as child-oriented, home-oriented, and parent-oriented. Since all three of these strategies are concerned with consistency in the allocation of priorities over time, they all tend to be career-oriented rather than role-oriented. Failure to resolve any of the predicaments in a consistent manner would affect the extent of integration.

With respect to solutions of the predicaments, the *child-oriented* family gives priority to instrumental (family as an institution) over social-emotional (personal relations) norms and values, to community-status commitments over home-life commitments, and to children's gratifications over parents' gratifications. These solutions to the predicaments can be accomplished through a sharp division of labor between husband and wife. Under this division of labor, community-status commitments do not conflict with the priority of children's over parents' gratifications. The activities related to community status can be delegated to the husband and those related to children's gratification to the wife. The rationale for this kind of organization is provided by giving priority to norms supporting the family as an institution over the norms and values of personal relations; the parents agree that the most important task in family life is the maintenance of the family unit as an ongoing concern vis-à-vis all other social groupings.

The *home-oriented* family gives priority to social-emotional (personal relations) norms and values over instrumental (family as an institution) norms and values, to home-life commitments over community-status commitments, and to children's gratifications over parental gratifications. Inasmuch as ordinarily little conflict can occur between home-life commitments and children's gratification, there is little need for specialization to implement the home-oriented solution: both parents concentrate on structuring congenial interpersonal relations in the home. The middle-class model of the family described earlier places the wife in the position of mediating between demands of the husband and children. With both parents concentrating on social-emotional relations, possibly the wife may lose her status as the social-emotional leader and the husband may then become *the* central figure in the family.

In the *parent-oriented* family the priority system is as follows: social-emotional (personal relations) norms and values take priority over instrumental (family as an institution) norms and values, community-status commitments over home-life commitments, and parents' gratification over children's gratification. Ordinarily, there is little conflict between community status and parents' gratification as priorities. However, in order to carry through the solution of predicaments in the face of the priority of personal norms over familial norms, the parents would have to develop an equalitarian organization to make their set of solutions internally consistent. This equalitarian organization places stress upon the personal development and social skill of all members of the family. In this organization, the primary activities of the wife become those of (a) reinforcing such goals as the acquisition of artifacts and social contacts symbolic of success in middle-class society, and (b) developing skills to collaborate with her husband in his work or social contacts in the community. To compensate for the wife's assumption of achievement functions, the husband has to perform some of the social-emotional activities ordinarily performed by her.

In each of the above three types, a clear-cut focus of the parents upon a single aspect of family life is implied. Families falling into a fourth or residual category, however, are either (a) lacking in focus or common orientation in career priorities, or (b) organized in their systems of roles in such a way as to impede gratification pertaining to a common orientation. Hence, the residual category in this typology is considered tentatively as the grouping of kinds of family organization not conducive to high marital integration in critical situations and to orderly replacement.

In the studies reported below, the primary aim was to explore consequences of applying the three family types for interpersonal relations. Thus, little analysis was made of the cases falling into the residual category. A systematic analysis of these residual families might reveal other strategies of family organization. Analysis of the residual category of families is also discussed later in the section on unresolved problems of the typology.

EMPIRICAL INVESTIGATION OF THE FAMILY TYPES

In order to be a useful research tool, the family-orientation typology should make possible predictions regarding various aspects of family behavior not directly associated with the family types.

Farber applied the family-orientation typology in his study of families with mentally retarded children. He found that regardless of whether the retarded child was at home or in an institution, the parents in the child-, home-, and parent-oriented families were characterized by higher marital integration than were parents in residual-category families.[40]

Liebman studied children's perceptions of their parents' dissatisfaction with their behavior in certain activities.[41] The activities included were: (a) individual instrumental activities such as household chores, (b) group family activities such as helping care for siblings, and (c) extrafamily activities such as working, dating, or staying out late. Her findings were as follows:

1. Children in child-oriented families showed the highest performance level in individual instrumental activities; the consequence of failure to perform particular individual instrumental activities, however, was related to the sex of the child in the child-oriented family. When a boy reported low performance, he generally did not perceive much parental dissatisfaction. However, girls in child-oriented families perceived much dissatisfaction

[40] Bernard Farber, "Family Organization and Crisis: Maintenance of Integration in Families with a Severely Mentally Retarded Child," *Monographs of the Society for Research in Child Development*, 25 (1960), No. 1 (Serial No. 75).

[41] Carol S. Liebman, "Family Type and Child's Perception of His Mother's Satisfaction with His Behavior," Master's thesis, Department of Sociology, University of Illinois, 1960.

when their performance of individual instrumental activities was low.

2. In home-oriented families, the performance level of individual instrumental and extrafamily activities was low; performance of group family activities was high. Even when performance of individual instrumental activities was low, little parental dissatisfaction was perceived by the child.

3. In parent-oriented families, the performance level of individual instrumental activities was especially low and that of extrafamily activities especially high. Furthermore, when the child's performance level of extrafamily activities was low, he generally perceived much parental dissatisfaction with his performance.

4. Among families in the residual category, regardless of the level of performance, the children generally perceived a higher degree of parental dissatisfaction than did the other children.

The results of the Liebman study suggest that pressures or difficulties in a particular area of activity could have quite different meaning to families of different orientations.

Farber and Jenné found that children in child-, home-, or parent-oriented families perceived a greater distinction between instrumental and social-emotional behavior (especially in their impressions of their mother's expectations) than did children in residual-category families.[42]

[42] Bernard Farber and William C. Jenné, "Family Organization and Parent-Child Communication: Parents and Siblings of a Retarded Child," *Monographs of the Society for Research in Child Development,* 28 (1963), No. 7 (Serial No. 91).

Jenné has found that the types of family orientation are related to the parents' life goals for their children.[43] His findings indicated that there was greater similarity in parents' preferences in life goals for their children between home-oriented and parent-oriented families than between either of these types and child-oriented families. Characteristically, parents in child-oriented families placed greater emphasis upon the importance of their children's success in business than did parents in home-oriented or parent-oriented families. The stress on business success is consistent with the emphasis by child-oriented parents upon economic security as a criterion for successful family life. However, some differences were found between home-oriented and parent-oriented families. For example, home-oriented parents generally considered it more important than did parent-oriented parents for their children to learn not to take life too seriously. This finding apparently reflects the tendency for the home-oriented family to focus upon intrafamily personal relations rather than community relationships.

The results of the studies relating to the types of family organization suggest that the typology may be useful in the study of marital relations, parent-child relations, and socialization of children.

UNRESOLVED PROBLEMS RELATING TO
THE FAMILY TYPOLOGY

Although the studies which have been cited indicate that the classification of families as child-oriented, parent-ori-

---

[43] William C. Jenné, "Parental Life Goals for Children," unpublished Ph.D. dissertation, University of Illinois, 1964.

ented, or home-oriented may be a useful research tool in gaining insights into family organization, the findings were not wholly unequivocal. Several problems were raised:

1. *The conceptual scheme upon which the typology is based has not been fully exploited.* Logically, eight rather than three family types can be depicted by the scheme. These are shown in Table 6. A refinement of indices relating to the combinations of priorities established as solutions to the predicaments discussed earlier would make it possible to study the associations of solutions X_1 to X_5 in Table 6 with marital integration and parent-child relations.

2. *Are the family types related to particular stages in the family life cycle?* In separate analyses involving 57 Champaign (Illinois) families with normal children and 55 Chicago families with a retarded child, Farber examined the relationship of type of family orientation with (a) the age of the youngest child and (b) the age of the husband.[44] The youngest child in the parent-oriented family was much younger than the youngest in the home-oriented or child-oriented family. The youngest child in the parent-oriented family was generally of preschool age. Similarly, the age of the husband in the parent-oriented families was generally lower than that in the child-oriented or home-oriented families. The chances of the parent-oriented husband's being under forty were much greater than those of the child-oriented or home-oriented husband. Further investigation might determine more

[44] Reported in Farber, "Types of Family Organization," *op. cit.* at note 39.

Table 6

TYPES OF FAMILY ORGANIZATION AS THE ESTABLISHMENT OF
PRIORITIES IN ALTERNATIVE COMMITMENTS CONSTITUTING
PREDICAMENTS IN FAMILY LIFE

Types of family organization	*Alternative given priority in particular type of family organization**		
	Social-emotional (personal relations) versus instrumental (family as an institution) norms and values	*Family-group commitment versus community commitment*	*Personnel priorities: parents versus children*
Child-oriented	Family as an institution	Community	Children
Home-oriented	Personal relations	Family group	Children
Parent-oriented	Personal relations	Community	Parents
X_1	Personal relations	Community	Children
X_2	Family as an institution	Family group	Children
X_3	Family as an institution	Family group	Parents
X_4	Family as an institution	Community	Parents
X_5	Personal relations	Family group	Parents

* In all of these assignments of priorities as solutions to predicaments, the priority of career orientation over role orientation is assumed. Career orientation is considered as necessary to permit the maintenance of high family integration in a crisis. This assumption too should be tested.

adequately the extent to which age (or stage of family life cycle) and type of orientation are related.

3. *How stable are the types of family orientation?* Do they persist over a long period or do they fluctuate as situations involving social ambivalence arise? In reinterviewing families (after one year in Champaign and after three years in Chicago), Farber found that many of the families had apparently shifted in orientation. However, the shifts may have reflected the unreliability of his indices rather than changes in value priorities.

4. *How are the types of orientation related to permanent availability?* Perhaps parent-oriented families are more vulnerable to divorce than are the child-oriented and home-oriented families. Moreover, families which emphasize short-run planning (those in which parents are role-oriented rather than career-oriented) may also be highly vulnerable to divorce.

The unresolved problems of the typology of family organization indicate the tentativeness of its adequacy as a tool for understanding family life.

Summary

This chapter has presented implications of viewing family organization in terms of predicaments which family members face. These predicaments reflect social ambivalences in family life. Specific predicaments were discussed which were considered particularly relevant to the problems of orderly replacement and permanent availability. The predicaments investigated were those of giving priority to (a) social-emotional versus instrumental values and norms in the *content* of interaction, (b) short-run versus long-run *time* considerations in interaction, (c) family commitments versus community commitments in the *location* of interaction; and (d) gratification of parents' needs and desires versus gratification of children's needs and desires in determining *personnel* priorities.

The priorities chosen for solving the predicaments of family organization are not necessarily discrete choices. The combinations of priorities selected reflect strategies by which the family members organize their relations with each other. As an illustration, a typology of family organization strategies was presented which had been developed to study families with handicapped children. The types included the parent-oriented strategy, home-oriented strategy, and child-oriented strategy. Findings of investigations utilizing this typology suggested that marital integration and socialization of children were related to the development of these organization strategies. Perhaps the formulation of other typologies based upon family predicaments will provide additional insight into the process of family organization.

Selected Readings

Discussions relevant to persistent problems in family organization may be found in:

Aberle, David F., and Kaspar D. Naegele. "Middle-Class Fathers' Occupational Role and Attitudes Toward Children," *American Journal of Orthopsychiatry*, 22 (1952), pp. 366-378.

Benson, Purnell. "The Interests of Happily Married Couples," *Marriage and Family Living*, 14 (1952), pp. 276-280.

Herbst, P. G. "The Measurement of Family Relationships," *Human Relations*, 5 (1952), pp. 3-35.

Komarovsky, Mirra. "Functional Analysis of Sex Roles," *American Sociological Review*, 15 (1950), pp. 508-516.

Komarovsky, Mirra. "Class Differences in Family Decision-Making on Expenditures," in Nelson N. Foote (ed.), *Household Decision-Making*, New York University Press, 1961, pp. 255-265.

Leik, Robert K. "Instrumentality and Emotionality in Family Interaction," *Sociometry*, 26 (1963), pp. 131-145.

Nye, F. Ivan, and Lois W. Hoffman (eds.). *The Employed Mother in America*. Rand McNally, 1963.

Riesman, David, and Howard Roseborough. "Careers and Consumer Behavior," in Lincoln H. Clark (ed.), *Consumer Behavior*, New York University Press, 1955, II, pp. 1-18.

Spiegel, John P. "The Resolution of Role Conflict within the Family," in Milton Greenblatt, Daniel J. Levinson, and Richard Williams, *The Patient and the Mental Hospital*, Free Press, 1957, pp. 545-564.

Zelditch, Morris, Jr. "Role Differentiation in the Nuclear Family: A Comparative Study," in Talcott Parsons and Robert F. Bales, *Family, Socialization and Interaction Process*, Free Press, 1955, pp. 307-351.

9 The Course of Family Commitments

Chapter 8 dealt with persistent predicaments in family organization. This chapter focuses upon changes in family organization over time. First, a general statement concerning time as a factor in family relationships will be presented. This statement is concerned with the family as a set of mutually contingent careers and with the concept of the family life cycle. The chapter will then investigate temporal aspects of the marital relationship and the relationships between family members of different generations. The discussion of the marital relationship includes the creation of marital commitments, the creation of commitments versus the maintenance of commitments, commitments and contingencies in divorce, and remarriage. The section on interaction between generations emphasizes youth-parent relationships and parent-grandparent relationships. The concluding section in the chapter will compare marital and intergenerational commitments.

Time and Family Commitments

This section discusses two related conceptions relevant to the time dimension in family commitments—the family as a set of mutually contingent careers and the family life cycle. Both conceptions refer to the development of family organization. The family as a set of mutually contingent careers emphasizes the process by which development occurs; the family life cycle provides descriptive categories for indicating development.

THE FAMILY AS A SET OF MUTUALLY CONTINGENT CAREERS

The conception of the family as a set of mutually contingent careers appears useful in the analysis of the family both in crisis and under normal circumstances.[1] The set refers to the members of the nuclear family. The major concepts used to describe the family as a set of mutually contingent careers—the concepts of career and career contingencies—have been used in analyzing occupational decision making. These concepts may be applied to the study of family life.

A *career* can be regarded as a progression of statuses or roles "which unfold in a more or less orderly though not predetermined sequence in the pursuit of values which themselves emerge in the course of experience."[2] A person's life or whole career may be described as his progression through the various statuses he occupies (or roles he

[1] Bernard Farber, "The Family as a Set of Mutually Contingent Careers," in Nelson N. Foote, ed., *Household Decision-Making*, New York: New York University Press, 1961, pp. 276-297.

[2] Nelson N. Foote, "The Movement from Jobs to Careers in American Industry," in *Transactions of the Third World Congress of Sociology*, International Sociological Association, 2 (1956), p. 31.

undertakes). This life career can be analyzed into special careers—occupational career, domestic career, recreational career. These special careers, in turn, can be analyzed into subcareers. The special careers refer to the course of the individual's development within specific institutions (the family, the agencies of economic activities, the school).

The *career contingencies* of an occupation have as their counterparts in family life critical events which upset norms and values at any time. It is only through a high family integration that control can be exerted upon individual members so that orderly replacement of generations can occur.

The concepts of career and career contingency thus seem applicable to family life. A marked shift in the domestic career of one family member should affect the careers of the other family members, provided the family members have a high personal commitment to each other. To the extent that the other family members adjust their careers in a predictable manner in response to this stimulation, the family does in fact exist as a system of mutually contingent careers.

Ordinarily, family careers develop predictably in ways which facilitate orderly replacement of the family. If the career patterns of each member of the group are coordinated with the others in the family, the career of the individual member will be furthered through (a) an efficient division of labor, (b) constant reinforcement of norms and values by significant others, (c) existence of a nonthreatening arena for relaxation and discussion, and (d) reinforcement of motivation through personal obligations toward other family members. Thus, for all members, career facilitation will take place when there is high family integration at any time.

In this conception of the family, the unit which describes the state of a career at a given point in time is the person's role. A *role* is regarded as a patterned sequence of intended courses of *action* to be performed by a person in an interaction situation. For example, in her domestic career in the family of procreation, a woman will develop through a series of roles—wife without children, wife-and-mother with preschool children, wife-and-mother with preadolescents, and so on.

There are many sources of role content. The source may be (a) roles in the previous families of orientation, (b) roles in families of friends or relatives, (c) roles as observed in mass communication media, or (d) roles created out of the unique situation of the particular family.

The development of roles is seen as potentially a creative process. In working out strategies of organization, the actors write their coordinated script out of a variety of materials. However, only the roles derived from the parents' families of orientation are directly involved in the transmission of the family culture from one generation to the next. The roles derived from other sources may (or may not) be incorporated into the family culture to be retained as the children grow to adulthood.

The careers seem to develop in response both to critical events and to mutual adaptation. It is assumed here that roles are not fixed but that as situations change the roles played must also undergo change. In the uncertainty of contemporary society, each family is faced repeatedly by changing situations that demand decisions which will affect the future course of family life. Various choices must be made either deliberately or through default. The choice of the number of children; the choice of residence; choice of occupation of husband, wife, and children; the choices of recreation; the choices of friends; the choices in the accumulation of material goods; and the choices in the education of children—all these are only a few of the foreseeable indeterminacies of contemporary life.[3] Although various social pressures influence choices, each of these events has to be faced at the time it arises. The decision thereby provides a stimulus for the shift in roles of the family members.[4] The stimuli for role changes come not only from the parents, but also from children as they develop in their biological changes. If the career of an individual is defined as his development through a series of roles, the definition attributes to the perfectly integrated family the character of a closed system with complete control over the life careers of its members. Ideally, the closed system implies a duplication of descendant families; actually, it merely means that the probability is high that this family *is* maintaining control over its present members in such a way as to increase the chances of its younger generation's assuming the norms and values of the parent system.

THE FAMILY LIFE CYCLE

What is the life cycle of the family? In the rhythm of life from generation to generation, events take place in a cyclical pattern. People marry, have children, raise these

[3] Nelson N. Foote and Leonard S. Cottrell, Jr., *Identity and Interpersonal Competence,* Chicago: University of Chicago Press, 1955.

[4] See Nelson N. Foote, "Matching of Husband and Wife in Phases of Development," in *Transactions of the Third World Congress of Sociology,* International Sociological Association, 4 (1946), pp. 24-34.

children, lose these children through death or marriage; finally, the family dissolves following the death of one spouse. Social scientists have attempted to classify the regularities in this repetitive series of events. This section pertains to attempts to describe the stages in the series. First, the section indicates the relationship between the family life cycle and the family as a set of mutually contingent careers. Second, difficulties encountered in trying to characterize the cycle stages are presented. Finally, social scientists' definitions of the stages in the cycle are portrayed.

The family life cycle and the family as a set of mutually contingent careers

The concept of the family life cycle appears to be useful for analysis of changes in family commitments over time. From the viewpoint of the family as a set of mutually contingent careers, the family life cycle develops through changes in participation in institutions and these changes bring about an orderly predictable change in the family. A stage in the family cycle can be defined by marked changes in the career of any family member. Any marked change in the career of one member entails an adjustment of roles of the other family members. The entire patterning of roles thus requires modification. The reference for describing movement in the family life cycle may be the father, the mother, or the child, whoever undergoes a marked shift in his career line. If the child starts school, his new activity is the stimulus for movement in the family cycle; if the father retires, the shift in his career is the stimulus; as the child takes over the roles of the adolescent, again the other members of the family must modify their conduct and their identifications of self. Through such interaction of careers, the family life cycle proceeds from one stage to the next.

Problems in characterizing stages of the family life cycle

Although the rhythmic pattern of family life is apparent, social scientists encounter several kinds of difficulty in their attempts to characterize the different stages of the family cycle. These difficulties pertain to classification problems concerning children in the family, turnover in personnel, the complexity of modern society, and cross-cultural analysis.

If each family had only one child, the task of describing each stage in the family life cycle would be relatively simple (although several other difficulties might exist). However, since families generally have more than one child, the task is more complex. Three problems in classification arising from number of children are:

1. In which stage of the family life cycle is a family with several children to be placed? Is the oldest child, the youngest, or the middle child to provide the basis for classifying any particular family?

2. Should the age range of the children be taken into account in describing stages?

3. Should the childless couple who have been married many years be classified in the same category as the recently married couple? The older childless couple may present characteristics which are very different from both

the older couple with children and the recently married couple.[5]

The turnover in family personnel introduces a second complexity into the task of classifying stages of the family life cycle. Three problems resulting from turnover in personnel are:

1. How should the family be classified when divorce or death of one of the parents occurs in the early years of marriage while the children are small?

2. Should a family in which an only child has died be regarded in the same way as a newly formed marriage? What if this family then adopts an older child?

3. How is remarriage to be handled in classification? What effects on family characteristics are there when the new family includes children from the first marriage and also children born into the present marriage?

A third source of problems in classifying stages of the family life cycle is the complexity of modern society. For example, lower-class culture is marked by frequent family break-ups (with or without marriage and divorce), occasional doubling-up of families, and a large number of female heads of households; the school drop-out rate is high and children generally marry shortly after leaving school. Middle-class culture, on the other hand, is characterized by higher family stability and a predominance of married couples present in households; the school drop-out rate is low and (especially in college or university) children may marry while still attending school. Can the same cycle

[5] See Robert O. Blood, Jr. and Donald M. Wolfe, *Husbands and Wives,* Glencoe, Ill.: Free Press, 1960.

stages be applied to families in both of these segments of society?

The fourth series of problems in the classification of stages in the family cycle emerges in cross-cultural analysis. Problems in cross-cultural analysis are:

1. Are the stages of families with different marriage groups comparable (polygynous versus monogamous families)?[6]

2. Is a particular stage in the life cycle of an independent nuclear family comparable to a stage in the life cycle of a nuclear family within an extended family whose members occupy the same household (examples: married children living independently versus married children and their families living with parents; the elderly living with their married children)?[7]

3. Wide variations in institutional participation in different societies also affect the definition of life-cycle stages. In one preliterate society, preparation for initiation into adulthood may last a few months; in another preliterate society, the preparation may last for years.[8]

Definition of stages in the family life cycle

Because of the enormous number of combinations which could be developed on the basis of variations in family life cycle, the definition of the stages of life cycle has depended upon the specific problems investigated. Table 7

---

[6] Charles P. Loomis, "Study of the Life Cycle of Families," *Rural Sociology*, 1 (1936), pp. 180-199.

[7] *Ibid.*

[8] For example, see C. W. M. Hart and Arnold R. Pilling, *The Tiwi of North Australia*, New York: Holt, 1960.

shows the various ways in which researchers have classified stages in the family cycle.[9]

According to Hill, at each stage in the family cycle,
family life grows more complex in role expectations within
the family as well as in the relations of its members to external agencies.[10] In consequence, more problems are created than are solved in the course of the family cycle.

The increasing complexity of family relationships occurs partly because initial relationships between husband
and wife are *intragenerational* whereas later family relationships are also *intergenerational.* Interaction between
people of the same generation would not change markedly
over time. Although variations in the rate of development
of persons of the same generation may exist, these differences are not so profound as variations for persons of different generations. Change in interpersonal relations of
persons of the same generation would result from persistent problems in the family life cycle mainly in the husband-wife relationship whereas single-stage problems
would tend to occur in the intergenerational relationships.

[9] One possible solution to the problem of complexity in classification caused by variations in family composition is to view each
family as a series of triads. If the family is regarded as a series of
child-mother-father triads then it becomes possible to handle a
variety of configurations in family cycle and development. With
respect to one child, the family can be at a preschool stage and
with respect to another child the family can be at the grandparent
level. It is then a matter of empirical investigation to determine
the interaction effects of these triad variations upon socialization of
children, family integration, or other family variables.

[10] Reuben Hill, "Patterns of Decision-Making and the Accumulation of Family Assets," in Nelson N. Foote, ed., *Household Decision-Making, op. cit.* at note 1, pp. 57-102.

Table 7

STAGES OF THE FAMILY LIFE CYCLE DESCRIBED IN EMPIRICAL INVESTIGATIONS

Stage in family life study	Glick study[a]	Lansing and Kish study[b]	Blood and Wolfe study[c]	Reiss study[d]	Rohrer and Schmidt study[e]
1. Premarital stage		Young single		The unmarried	
2. First couple stage	Entrance into first marriage	Young married couples with no children	Honeymoon stage: childless couples married less than 4 years		Alone family: married couple alone
3. Parenthood stage (general)	Birth of last child			Two phases: (a) child-bearing phase, married 15 years or less; (b) child-raising phase, majority of children still at home, over 15 years of marriage	
3a. Preschool phase		Young married couples with youngest child under 6	Preschool stage: oldest child under 6		Young-family type: youngest child under 6
3b. Elementary-school phase		Young married couples with youngest child 6 or older	Preadolescent stage: oldest child 6-12		Middle-family type: youngest child 6-11

(Continued on next page)

343

Table 7 (continued)

Stage in family life cycle	Glick study[a]	Lansing and Kish study[b]	Blood and Wolfe study[c]	Reiss study[d]	Rohrer and Schmidt study[e]
3c. High-school phase		Continuation of 3b	Adolescent stage: oldest child 13–18		Mature family type: youngest child 12 or over
3d. College phase					
3e. Post-school phase (child's unmarried stage)			Unlaunched stage: oldest child 19 or over and still at home		
4. Second couple stage (general)	Marriage of last child	Older married couples, no children	Postparental stage	Period after the children have left home	
4a. In-law phase (child in first couple stage)					
4b. Grandparent stage (child in parenthood stage)					

5. Dissolution stage		Older single	Retired stage: non-employed husbands 60 or over	Widowerhood or widowhood
5a. Widowhood and remarriage	Death of spouse			
5b. End of cycle	Death of surviving spouse			

[a] Paul C. Glick, "The Life Cycle of the Family," *Marriage and Family Living*, 17 (February, 1955), pp. 3–9.

[b] John B. Lansing and Leslie Kish, "Family Life Cycle as an Independent Variable," *American Sociological Review*, 22 (October, 1957), pp. 512–519.

[c] Robert O. Blood, Jr. and Donald M. Wolfe, *Husbands and Wives*, Glencoe, Ill.: Free Press, 1960. In most respects similar to Evelyn Millis Duvall, "Implications for Education through the Family Life Cycle." *Marriage and Family Living*, 20 (1958), pp. 338–341.

[d] Paul J. Reiss, "The Extended Kinship System in the American Urban Middle Class," Ph.D. dissertation, Harvard University, 1960; and Paul J. Reiss, "The Extended Kinship System: Correlates of and Attitudes on Frequency of Interaction," *Marriage and Family Living*, 24 (November, 1962), pp. 333–339.

[e] W. C. Rohrer and J. F. Schmidt, *Family Type and Social Participation*, College Park, Md.: Agricultural Experiment Station, University of Maryland, Miscellaneous Publication 196, 1954.

Marriage Relationships

This section will describe the course of marriage relationships during the family life cycle in terms of (a) the creation of marital commitments, (b) the creation of commitments versus the maintenance of commitments in marriage, (c) commitments and contingencies in divorce, and (d) remarriage.

THE CREATION OF MARITAL COMMITMENTS

In American society, love is supposed to be a prelude to marriage. There have been various attempts to characterize the sentiment of love in courtship. Burgess and Locke have analyzed love into components of sexual desire, physical attraction, rapport or attachment, satisfaction of basic personality needs, companionship, stimulation and excitement, freedom of communication and action, emotional reassurance, and heightened self-esteem.[11] Waller has regarded love as a habit of propulsive force which has been blocked. The blocking of sexual impulse creates an idealization of the love object, mental agony or mental conflict, a sense of euphoria, an ennobling stimulus in personal development.[12] Kephart has described the sentiment of love as "(1) a strong emotional attachment toward a person of the opposite sex; (2) the tendency to think of this person in an idealized manner; and

[11] Ernest W. Burgess and Harvey J. Locke, *The Family from Institution to Companionship,* New York: American Book, 1960. The 1963 edition of Burgess and Locke (with Thomes) does not present a definition of love.

[12] Willard Waller, *The Family, A Dynamic Interpretation,* New York: Dryden Press, 1938.

(3) a marked physical attraction the fulfillment of which is reckoned in terms of touch."[13]

How does the person recognize the sentiment of love? The signs of love are not developed in community but rather in individual experience. Examples of conceptions of love held by young married persons, which are presented below, indicate the private symbolism involved in the sentiment of love.[14]

Woman: I found out that I loved him on the Fourth of July. I was sunning on the beach at the lake and he had gone somewhere for a few minutes. He didn't come back when I wanted him to. *I felt lost without him.* There were lots of people around, but I wanted *him.* When he got back, I practically wrung his neck bawling him out; I knew I loved him though.

Woman: I thought he was nice, but I was not in love with him even when we were going steady. Suddenly, it hit me. There was no special thing. At first, I thought he was nice and then I was sure of it.

Man: I fell in love with her several weeks later, after my furlough when I returned to the Army. First, I began to think about her quite a bit. I missed her very much. I would wander off in a daydream thinking about her.

Woman: First, I'll tell you what love used to mean. Love used to mean chills running up and down my spine whenever I saw the person. That is why I wasn't sure about Sam when I met him. Instead of making chills run up my spine, he made me feel contented and happy to be with.

[13] William M. Kephart, *The Family, Society, and the Individual,* Boston: Houghton Mifflin, 1961, p. 321.
[14] From life histories collected by Bernard Farber.

Woman: Love is intangible. I was not in love with Steve at first sight. I am there now. I could fall out of love and in again. There has to be mental and physical stimulation and response, feelings of security, of being wanted and to want in return. The realization of being in love came after he told me he loved me. There is no love which is not returned. The problem of love is certainty.

Chance appears to play a large part in falling in love. An event or series of events defines the cross-sex individual as someone who is unique and whose relationship must be maintained. A woman feeling lost and alone for a moment: a girl believing she had found something essentially "nice" in her boy friend; a soldier daydreaming about a girl he had met on his furlough; a woman finding contentment; a girl feeling wanted—these are the signs of love upon which marital commitments are based. One question which cannot be answered is: If the particular events which signified being in love had not occurred when they did, would other events have taken their place for the couples?

Having decided that they are in love, the couple then redefine their relationship to one another. They apply further tests of love (and make demands upon one another to reinforce the original signs) and if everything goes as anticipated, they are married.

Burgess and Wallin have suggested that two kinds of commitment formation in courtship exist: the telescoped courtship and the extended courtship. In the telescoped courtship, the couple's emotional involvement with one another is rapid and intense. The extended courtship is marked by companionship and a slowly emerging love.[15] Several prediction studies have shown that the longer the courtship and engagement period, the greater the chance of marital adjustment.[16] Apparently, in the extended courtship, the couple can work out a mutual accommodation. Following a telescoped courtship, the couple may or may not develop a workable mutual accommodation.

THE CREATION OF COMMITMENTS VERSUS THE MAINTENANCE OF COMMITMENTS IN MARRIAGE

Being in love creates the interpersonal commitment of the couple. But do the same factors which created the couple relationship sustain it after marriage? If complementarity of basic personality needs were the primary factor in mate selection, as Winch suggests, then no decline in interpersonal commitments would be anticipated as the years pass. However, if a capricious sentiment of love is responsible at least in part for mate selection, then continuance of love may be a matter of chance (or of reinforcement through companionship in commitment-maintenance activities).

Dentler and Pineo investigated changes in marital adjustment of men in the Burgess and Wallin sample from the early years to the middle years (approximately fifteen) of marriage. They found that when adjustment in marriage changed, it tended to decrease rather than in-

[15] Ernest W. Burgess and Paul Wallin, *Engagement and Marriage*, New York: Lippincott, 1953, pp. 162-169.

[16] Ernest W. Burgess, Harvey J. Locke, and Mary Margaret Thomes, *The Family from Institution to Companionship*, New York, American Book, 1963, p. 318 .

crease.[17] In another analysis, Pineo reported the following trends: (a) a decrease in confiding, kissing, and reciprocal settling of disagreements, (b) an increase of reports of loneliness, (c) decrease in reported frequency of sexual intercourse, (d) smaller amount of sharing of activities, and (e) little change in personal adjustment and description of personality characteristics. Pineo attributed this change to the high selectivity of mates. With random selection, according to Pineo, increase in confiding, kissing, sharing, and sexual intercourse would occur as often as would decrease. Merely by chance, the mean amount of these activities would remain fairly constant. However, since these individuals "chose" one another *because* of their desirability in performing these activities, chance effects would tend toward the population mean. The married couples may have started near the upper limit of activity, and, if they changed, there could be only one direction—to decrease in amount of this activity.[18]

This discussion will follow the trends in marital commitment through the family life cycle. Because of lack of comparability in defining the stages of the family life cycle, the results from one study cannot be compared for any particular stage with results for another study. However, despite the lack of agreement regarding definitions of specific stages in the life cycle, general trends can probably be discerned in the division of labor and style of interaction.

[17] Robert A. Dentler and Peter C. Pineo, "Sexual Adjustment, Marital Adjustment and Personal Growth of Husbands," *Marriage and Family Living*, 22 (1960), pp. 45-48.

[18] Peter C. Pineo, "Disenchantment in the Later Years of Marriage," *Marriage and Family Living*, 23 (1961), pp. 3-11.

Trends in the development of stages in the family life cycle are described below in terms of companionship relations, division of labor, and community participation. These aspects of family life were discussed in Chapter 8 in relation to predicaments in family organization.

Companionship relations

Personal relationships between husband and wife have been designated in various places as manifestations of companionship, intimacy, affection, and love. With each successive stage of the family life cycle, the following trends were found in the Blood and Wolfe study:[19]

1. Except for the period when the children have left home, the wife's satisfaction with her husband's companionship tends to decrease.

2. The amount of discussion between husband and wife (as reported by the wife) of daily personal events tends to decrease.

3. Wives tend to report less satisfaction with the amount of their husband's love and affection.

4. The amount of satisfaction with marriage reported by the wife tends to decrease.

5. The frequency with which wives tell their husbands personal troubles after a bad day tends to decrease.

Similarly, in his study of value convergence in marriage, Keeley found that although value convergence was positively correlated with length of marriage for people married less than two years, the correlation was negative

[19] Robert O. Blood, Jr. and Donald M. Wolfe, *Husbands and Wives, op. cit.*

for his entire sample.[20] Although his correlations were small, Keeley's findings suggest that specialization and divergence set in after a period of mutual convergence.

Various interpretations have been offered concerning the tendency for companionship in marriage to decline. Waller has suggested that many marriages begin at a high level of optimism and euphoria. However, after experiencing the initial excitement, enjoying the novelty of a sustained erotic relationship, and learning to know one another, the married couple settles down to a routine of domestic life. Companionship activities decline and the marriage tends to attain a "dead level of interaction."[21] Another interpretation is that as persons live together in marriage they encounter many situations in which personal differences previously considered unimportant produce conflict and disagreement.[22] To avoid open conflict, the husband and wife develop a highly specialized division of labor and thereby segregate their activities. This segregation operates to reduce the companionship and solidarity of the married couple.[23] A third interpretation is that in marriage the only tie initially possible is that between husband and wife. With the birth of children, however, there is a rearrangement of the couple's emotional attachments and personal involvements. The children then become the focus of family activities and husband-wife

[20] Benjamin J. Keeley, "Factors Associated with Value Convergence in a Social System with Special Reference to the Marriage Group," unpublished Ph.D. dissertation, University of Nebraska, 1954.

[21] Waller, *op. cit.*

[22] Burgess and Wallin, *op. cit.*

[23] See Philip E. Slater, "Parental Role Differentiation," *American Journal of Sociology,* 67 (1961), pp. 295-308.

roles are subordinated to parental roles. This subordination would imply a diminution of companionship activities for the couple. This third interpretation is the one most consistent with the view of the family as a set of mutually contingent careers. Possibly all three interpretations are relevant for understanding the tendency for companionship in marriage to decline.

Division of labor

Division of labor in the family refers generally to the style of daily life and specifically to the handling of daily routine affairs in maintaining family personnel. Although there are probably numerous nonlinear variations within life-cycle development, the trends enumerated below refer to steady (linear) increase or decrease of activity with each successive stage in the family life cycle. The Blood and Wolfe study indicates that as the family cycle proceeds through its various stages:[24]

1. The wife's power relative to the husband's in decision making tends to increase.

2. The amount of role specialization by husband and wife in household tasks tends to increase.

3. More families tend to acquire their own homes. (Home owners probably spend more time than tenants in caring for the property.)

4. There is a decline in the number of mothers report-

[24] Blood and Wolfe, *op. cit.* Findings on increased role specialization and decreased companionship with length of marriage are supported in a study of 454 married women in Helsinki: see Kalevi Heinila, "Family Companionship and Family Cohesion," *Yearbook of Population Research in Finland,* 7 (1961-1962), pp. 75-100.

ing that they have problems pertaining to children (illness, personal restrictions, worries).

5. Except for the period after the children have left home, mothers in families in which the husband's income exceeds $5,000 tend to become less satisfied with their standard of living. For families in which the husband's income is less than $5,000 there is no consistent trend.

Community participation

Several changes were also found with respect to participation with others outside the nuclear family. Studies of relationships outside the family indicated that:

1. With each successive stage in the family life cycle there is an increasing tendency to report "companionship" as an advantage of having kin.[25]

2. In families in which the husband's income is over $5,000, after a sharp drop following the birth of the first child, the proportion of working wives tends to increase steadily as the children grow older. No consistent trend appears in families in which the husband's income is under $5,000.[26]

3. The following results were reported by Rohrer and Schmidt in their study of participation in formal organizations as related to family life cycle: (a) Spouses in the couple stage reported low activity in formal organizations and a low number of intrafamily activities. (b) Spouses in families with a preschool child reported low activity in formal organizations but high intrafamily activities. (c)

---

[25] Paul J. Reiss, "The Extended Kinship System in the American Urban Middle Class," Ph.D. dissertation, Harvard University, 1960.

[26] Blood and Wolfe, *op. cit.*

Spouses in which the youngest child was aged six to eleven reported high activities in both formal organization and within the family. (d) Spouses in families in which the youngest child was a teenager reported high formal-organization activity and low intrafamily activity.[27]

Thus, with the stabilization of the family in the community, there is an increase in seeking personal gratifications and meaningful participation outside the nuclear family. There is also an increasing use of formal organizations as compared with intrafamily activities, kin are seen from the point of view of companionship rather than in terms of assistance they can offer, and there is a greater tendency for wives to work when there is dissatisfaction with the existing standard of living.

General trends in the family cycle

Various inferences can be drawn from the findings regarding trends in division of labor, companionship, and community participation as related to the family life cycle.

1. With successive stages in these family life cycles, the mutual contingency of husband and wife careers tends to decline. With the rise of the wife's relative power in decision making, declining companionship, and increasing role specialization, there is a growing independence of the wife's activities from her husband's. This trend suggests that without counteracting strategies, the marriage tends to disintegrate even when no dramatic crises occur. The tendency to fall apart supports the contention made

[27] W. C. Rohrer and J. F. Schmidt, *Family Type and Social Participation*, College Park, Md.: University of Maryland Agricultural Experiment Station, Miscellaneous Publication 196, 1954.

earlier that the bilateral kinship system in contemporary society is geared to the phenomena of divorce and remarriage. Without special institutions such as family corporations or a strong kinship system to reinforce the mutual contingency of careers of family members, there is a decline in integration of values and organization of marital roles in the nuclear family.

2. With a greater emphasis upon stability of community position in the later stages of the family life cycle, there is a change in the types of critical situations which would probably disrupt family life. In these later stages, those critical situations which would threaten the stability of the family in the community would probably be more disruptive than crises which disarrange the relationships within the family but have little direct effect on the community relationships of individual family members. Hence, in the later stages of the family life cycle, job loss, public disgrace, and downward social mobility would probably be critical. In early stages of the family cycle, internal difficulties such as a child's handicap would be more severe.

3. With the lessening of the husband-wife mutual contingency, there is probably an increase in the stake which parents have in their children's careers. As the role-integration factors become more important than companionate factors in marriage, the reason for the family's continued existence is to be found in the relationship to children and grandchildren rather than in the relationship to the spouse. The greater stress on companionship with the children and grandchildren that accompanies increasing age indicates the strengthening of the generational mu-

tual contingencies at the expense of the husband-wife contingencies.

4. The increasing stress on stability of community position suggests that two major types of crises can occur. In the early stages of the family cycle, with most of the future life of the family still to come, consensus on values relating to the *future* would be most important. Hence, one type of crisis that would be especially stressful at the early stages would be one which would interfere with future *attainment* of these values. As the individuals continue in their development and the increase in stability and role differentiation occurs, the critical events of major importance would be those which interfered with the *current* division of labor. In Chapter 10, these two types of problems will be discussed in terms of tragic crisis and role-organization crisis.

COMMITMENTS AND CONTINGENCIES IN DIVORCE

Divorce may terminate a marriage but it does not end the relationship between husband and wife. Throughout their lives, they will be known both as someone's ex-husband or ex-wife and also as the husband or wife in their current marriage. Generally, a relationship of formality and avoidance is expected to exist between a divorced couple. The major tie in the relationship between ex-husband and ex-wife lies in their rights and obligations to their children. As time passes, new roles and social relationships give rise to changes in the person's own self identify from "ex-wife" or "ex-husband" to new personal commitments.

The residue of the husband-wife relationship is characterized by the kind of affect felt by the man or woman toward the ex-spouse. In his study of divorced women, Goode found positive affect (feelings of love and friendliness) as well as negative affect (hatred, indifference, and punitive wishes). Both positive and negative affect were influenced by the passage of time.[28]

In general, the positive affect of divorcees toward their ex-husbands tends to decrease with time. This decline in affect is related to the contact between husband and wife. Goode constructed an index of contact intensity based on (a) whether the divorcee dated her ex-husband, (b) whether she sought information about him, (c) whether she saw him, and (d) whether she would not avoid seeing him. He found that when a divorcee with positive feelings toward her ex-husband maintained a high level of contact intensity, these feelings persisted. However, when a woman with positive feelings did not maintain intense contact, her feelings toward her ex-husband dissipated. There is a sex difference in the decline of positive feelings. Bernard found that by the time of remarriage men were generally slightly more friendly toward their first wives than were women toward their first husbands.[29]

The slow dissipation of the wife's commitment to her ex-husband may restrict the woman's availability for another marriage. Goode found that divorcees who had positive feelings toward their ex-husbands tended also to view the ex-husbands as having a positive feeling toward them.

[28] William J. Goode, *After Divorce*, Glencoe, Ill.: Free Press, 1956. Unless otherwise indicated, the material in this section is based upon Goode.

[29] Jessie Bernard, *Remarriage*, New York: Dryden, 1956.

In effect, they still had hopes for reconciliation. Women with a positive attitude toward their ex-husbands tended to report that changes in themselves or their ex-husbands following the divorce made reconciliation attractive. As might be expected, women who were not in love with another man prior to the divorce were more reluctant to remarry than those who had an extramarital love affair.

Interpersonal contingencies exist not only when there is positive affect but also when there is negative affect. For most wives in the Goode study, divorce was a trauma which induced difficulty in sleeping, poor health, and loneliness. The amount of trauma was great when (a) the woman was mature in age (especially 35 or over), (b) the husband first suggested divorce, (c) the decision to divorce had been uncertain or ambivalent, and (d) the divorce involved financial hardships or family disapproval. About one-third of the high-trauma women wanted to punish their husbands at the time of divorce, but few of the women to whom divorce was not a trauma wanted to punish them. The majority of women who wanted their ex-husbands punished at the time of divorce still wished them punished at the time of the study.

In contrast with the situation of divorcees who report positive feelings toward their ex-husbands, the passage of time does not dissipate negative feelings. Goode found that, on the average, negative affect increased with time. When there was a low intensity of contact, the amount of negative affect generally remained constant through the years. However, with a high intensity of contact, negative feelings toward the ex-husband increased. Bernard reported that the marriage partner who did not seek divorce may become extremely jealous after divorce and may constantly check up on the former spouse. The intensity of contact may thus reflect both an expression of negative feelings and a reinforcement of these feelings.

The findings on divorce trauma suggest that when the woman perceives her position after divorce as inferior to her life situation during the marriage, trauma is greatest and negative feelings increase. Three or more years after the divorce, women who were neither remarried nor going steady more often had negative feelings toward their ex-husbands than did women who had remarried or were going steady. The proportion of women with negative feelings toward their ex-husbands was especially high not only where the woman was not remarried or going steady but also where the ex-husband had not continued support payments *and* the wife reported that she had few opportunities to meet people. The isolation and financial difficulties would reinforce negative feelings toward the ex-husband.

Perhaps the major bond between divorced husbands and wives is the children of the marriage. In approximately 90 per cent of divorces, the mother has custody of the children. There is thus a continuity in mutual contingency of the careers of the divorced mother and children. The relationship between the divorced father and his children, however, is highly complex. The divorced father's relationship with his children is defined legally through his obligations to support the children and his privileges to visit the children. Goode found that divorced women viewed the privilege of paternal visit as one to be earned. They wanted to restrict paternal visits when the father failed to continue support payments or when they wished to punish the father. As the major means of interaction between the father and children, the visit provides the opportunity to effect a change in the relationship with the ex-spouse. The mother may see in the visit a chance for re-establishing the marriage. The visit may create conflicts of loyalty for the children and, after paternal visits, the mother may have difficulty in handling the children. With the passage of time, divorcees prefer that their ex-husbands visit the children less often. Chances for reconciliation dwindle or the amount of hatred may increase. The women tend to regard the children as their own, and paternal visits interfere with this possessiveness. Moreover, the Bernard study indicated that in remarriage, an affectionate relationship tends to develop between stepfathers and children; visits from the divorced father detract from this relationship. The father may fall behind in support payments or he may be involved with his new wife and children. Hence, a variety of forces tends to bring about a decline in paternal visiting. This decline tends to reinforce the ties between the divorced mother and her children and, at the same time, to weaken ties with the father.

In summary: divorce generally produces a slow dissipation of the personal commitments developed in the marriage; and when the divorce is traumatic, negative sentiments may arise which bind the couple by generating spiteful acts. Intensive contact maintains hope for reconciliation when the divorced person has positive feelings toward his ex-spouse; this contact may intensify negative feelings. Negative feelings develop especially when the divorced person believes that his or her life situation has been worsened by the divorce. However, perhaps the greatest tie between the divorced couples is their children. Virtually all children of divorced couples are placed in the custody of the mother. Major ties between the father and his children are maintained through his visits (or their visits to him). The frequency of these visits depends upon various factors—feelings of the mother, hopes for reconciliation, continuing support payments by the father, conflict in the children's loyalties. On the whole, these factors operate to decrease the amount of paternal visiting. Hence, in the long run, the divorced father tends to be frozen out of association with his ex-wife and children.

REMARRIAGE

Remarriage differs from first marriage not merely because the persons are older and more experienced but also because more people are involved in family relations. In a first marriage, generally only the husband and wife are involved. In remarriage, the children are involved directly and the previous spouses indirectly.

As individuals who are directly involved in remarriage, minor children's attitudes and wishes are generally considered when the parent contemplates remarriage. Goode found that the more children a divorced woman had, the less time she spent in dallying with men who were not serious in their intentions to marry. Although the children interfered with the frequency of dating, within two years after the divorce 60 per cent of mothers with three or more children were married as compared with 45 per cent of mothers with one child. In addition, more than 90 per cent of the remarried mothers reported that their children's lives had either improved or remained the same. Only 8 per cent of the remarried mothers considered the remarriage as detrimental to the child. Since the presence of children apparently influenced the decision to remarry and the choice of mate, very likely the kinds of commitments made between husbands and wives in remarriages differ markedly from personal commitments in first marriages.[30] Even though a woman may choose a second husband who resembles her first husband in some ways, the second relationship, involving children, necessarily begins on a different basis from the first one.

The closeness between the stepparent and his ready-made family depends upon various factors. Bowerman and Irish found that children usually prefer their natural parent to their stepparent. Moreover, the sex of both stepparent and child influenced their relationship markedly.[31] With respect to the sex of the parent, Bernard found that children in remarriages are more friendly toward a new father than toward a new mother.[32] Bowerman and Irish also reported that stepmothers were faced with more problems than stepfathers. Children of both sexes with stepmothers reported more often than children with stepfathers that their stepparent discriminated against them and that they wished they were living with a different family. With respect to the sex of the child, Bernard found that the remarriage had a better chance of success if the stepchildren were all male. Bowerman and Irish,

[30] Goode, *op. cit.*

[31] Charles E. Bowerman and Donald P. Irish, "Some Relationships of Stepchildren to their Parents," *Marriage and Family Living*, 24 (1962), pp. 113-121.

[32] Bernard, *op. cit.*

however, reported that for children of previously divorced parents, if the sex of the stepparent and child were the same, the relationship was closer than for cross-sex stepparent-child pairs. (The boy-girl differences with respect to a stepfather are greater than boy-girl differences with respect to a stepmother; thus, the presence of a boy is more important to the new stepfather-son relationship than is a girl to the new stepmother-daughter relationship.)

In addition to the sex of child and stepparent, other factors also affect the relationship. Bowerman and Irish found that the younger the children, the better they are able to accept the new stepparent. Bernard found that adult children, like the very young, accepted the stepparent. Success in remarriage was also related to the previously divorced wife having exclusive custody of the children, to an affectionate attitude of the husband toward his stepchildren, and, in reciprocation, to a friendly attitude of the children toward their stepfather.

Considered together, the findings on children and their stepparents suggest that when a man marries a woman with children, his commitments to his wife are intimately connected with commitments to his stepchildren. Inadequate performance with respect to either his wife or her children would affect the entire arrangement. In remarriage, then, a person does not start afresh as an equal partner; he begins with a highly complex set of interpersonal relations existing independently prior to the marriage. People who divorce a first time have a greater chance of a subsequent divorce according to various investigations. This greater risk may in part result from the greater complexity of interaction in remarriage than in first marriage.

In remarriage, the person enters with lingering commitments from the previous marriage. For example, Goode found that when a woman believed her ex-husband still loved her she was more likely to have arguments with her second husband over him. Moreover, when the ex-husband continued seeing the children, the likelihood of arguments was greater. However, on the whole, husbands of previously divorced women tended to be indifferent toward the wife's first husband. Wives of previously divorced men showed a tendency to either friendliness or resentment toward the husband's first wife.[33] These findings suggest that the lingering commitments of previous marriages are of greater concern to women than to men in remarriages. The men tend to be more independent of the previous commitments; this independence is consistent with the earlier conclusion that the ex-husband tends to be frozen out of the divorced family.

SUMMARY: THE COURSE OF MARRIAGE

Implicit in the notion of permanent availability is the assumption by individuals that they might be able to "do better" in another marriage. They may begin the new marriage with the belief that this marriage, because of high personal commitment, is the best of all possible marriages for them. However, the factors which create the commitment and those which maintain the personal commitment are not the same. There is then a tendency for

[33] Goode, *op. cit.*

personal commitments to wither with the passage of time. Generally, this decline in personal commitments does not proceed at the same rate for both husband and wife. In time, the personal commitment of at least one of the spouses may reach the point where he wishes to terminate the marriage. The other spouse, who continues to maintain a high personal commitment to the marriage, reacts to the divorce either by desiring a reconciliation or by developing negative sentiments toward the instigator of the divorce. After the divorce, the positive feelings slowly disintegrate. Generally, the more intense the contact between the divorced couple, the longer the positive feelings linger. Negative feelings, in contrast, are intensified by contact with the ex-spouse.

The probability is high that divorced persons will marry again. In remarriage, new complexities enter the husband-wife relationship. If the wife has children, the man must create a congenial relationship not only with his new wife but also with the children. If the children are young boys and the husband does not resent their greater attachment for their mother, there is a good chance that family solidarity will develop. However, if the children's loyalties are split between their mother and divorced father, and this conflict in loyalties is sustained by continual interaction with the divorced father, the new husband-wife relationship is weakened. Not only the presence of children but also the mother's feelings toward her ex-husband complicate remarriage. If the wife believes her ex-husband still loves her, she tends to have arguments with her second husband over him. Wives of previously divorced men tend to be either more friendly or more resentful of first wives than are husbands of previously divorced women toward first husbands. Thus, in remarriage, a residue of personal commitments from the first marriage remains and the complexity of interpersonal relationships may be much greater than that in first marriages. This complexity may interfere with the stability of remarriages.

The discussion has followed the paths of the careers of the married couples to suggest how they merge and diverge in the course of the family life cycle. The tendency for careers to diverge over time suggests that marital problems tend to persist and solutions to the predicaments of family life which would permit maintenance of high personal commitments in marriage are not developed. Instead, couples appear to give priority to solutions which are inimical to sustained personal commitments in the family.

Interaction between Generations

It was suggested earlier that whereas those problems in family interaction that are connected with marriage tend to be persistent, major problems arising from interaction between generations tend to be related to particular stages of the family cycle. This section will deal with interaction between generations first in terms of the emerging youth and then in terms of the older person. The discussion of youth focuses upon problems generated by failure to perform independently activities which the parents sponsor and by independent performance of acts which the parents do not sponsor (and in fact oppose). The discussion of the older person concerns problems in the two last stages of the family cycle—the postparental married couple and the terminal stage.

YOUTH

Many people regard youth's major task in contemporary Western society as the attainment of autonomy from his nuclear family of orientation. The role of parents in this endeavor is to foster independence. For example, Kenkel suggests that parents can help their child to achieve independence by teaching him to allocate budgetary resources, to make selections and purchases, and to develop his own life plans.[34]

Do people really mean complete autonomy from the family when they discuss youth's independence from the family of orientation? Probably they have in mind the fact that as children mature they are supposed to assume adult roles. But parents do not try to foster *all* kinds of independence in youth. The parent who rewards his child for allocating budgetary resources independently would punish the child for independently deciding to spend his time with a gang of delinquents. In one instance, the parent sponsors the independence of the child while in the other instance the independence is unsponsored.

The distinction between sponsored and unsponsored independence is reflected in two kinds of problems which social scientists investigate: one kind concerns dependence versus independence (pertaining to activities sponsored by parents); the other concerns conformity versus devi-

[34] William F. Kenkel, *The Family in Perspective*, New York: Appleton-Century-Crofts, 1960.

ance (pertaining to activities not sponsored by parents). The youth who does not perform the autonomous activities ordinarily sponsored by parents is generally considered as too dependent. The youth who performs autonomous activities not sponsored by parents is called deviant.

In regard to sponsored independence, parents play an active role in trying to make the child self-reliant. In sponsoring independence in certain areas, parents guide the child, offer him advice, and grant him autonomy in certain areas, all the while retaining the power to withdraw this grant of "independence." In contrast, the parents play a passive role in the child's unsponsored independence. Unsponsored independence arises through lack of supervision, guidance, and control.

Sponsored and unsponsored independence appear to be related to social stratification. Kohn investigated parental values in child raising in lower and middle socioeconomic classes.[35] His interpretation of his findings was that middle-class parents value the development of self-control and self-reliance in children whereas lower-class parents emphasize conformity to rules. Middle-class parents punished children not so much for the damaging consequences of acts (like breaking furniture) as for the child's intention, and they tried to understand the child's motivations. With their emphasis upon understanding the child's intentions, the middle-class parents would be able to guide him in developing responsibility and initiative in performing activities which they sponsor. Lower-class par-

[35] Melvin L. Kohn, "Social Class and Parent-Child Relationships: An Interpretation," *American Journal of Sociology*, 68 (1963), pp. 471-480.

ents, however, valued children's conformity to rules. They punished children by the most direct means (such as spanking). The severity of the punishment was generally proportional to the gravity of the transgression. The parents viewed their roles as constraining the child and teaching him limits of permissible activities. In the lower-class situation, independence from the parents would occur when the child overreached the limits and participated in unsponsored activities.

The differences in parental values in child raising in middle and lower socioeconomic classes suggests corresponding differences in the meaning of "independence." Ordinarily, for middle-class children, independence from the family has the meaning of maturing into adulthood while for lower-class children independence from the family means deviance from conventional standards through committing delinquent acts.

Research on the emerging independence of the child will be examined below in terms of the distinction between sponsored and unsponsored independence.

Sponsored independence

Generally, research on sponsored independence is performed with middle-class samples in comparison with lower-class samples and emphasizes the maturation of the child into a responsible, respected adult who strives for prestige or for material wealth or for both in conventional society. The studies dealing with sponsored independence indicate that:

1. Although both the adolescent peer group and parents are influential in stimulating boys to pursue a profes-

sional career (rather than a blue-collar career), the parental pressure is more effective than the peer-group pressure.[36]

2. Children of working mothers are more highly motivated to achieve goals presumably associated with occupational success than are children of mothers who are not gainfully employed.[37] Apparently, parental values related to economic and social mobility are more effectively transmitted to the child when both parents act as models.

3. Children of employed mothers perform more household chores than do children whose mothers are not employed.[38] With boys performing household tasks and children seeing *both* parents working, children would find little sex differentiation in family roles. There would be an implicit expectation that each family member be responsible for maintaining the family as a domestic unit and as an economic cooperative group.

4. McClelland and his associates found that Catholic parents expect their children to achieve sponsored activities of independence at a later age than do Protestant and Jewish parents.[39] The sponsored activities investigated

[36] Richard L. Simpson, "Parental Influence, Anticipatory Socialization, and Social Mobility," *American Sociological Review*, 27 (1962), pp. 517-522.

[37] Kathryn S. Powell, "Maternal Employment in Relation to Family Life," *Marriage and Family Living*, 23 (1961), pp. 350-355. See also Marian Radke Yarrow, Phyllis Scott, Louise de Leeuw, and Christine Heinig, "Child-Rearing in Families of Working and Nonworking Mothers," *Sociometry*, 25 (1962), pp. 122-140.

[38] Prodipto Roy, "Maternal Employment and Adolescent Roles: Rural-Urban Differentials," *Marriage and Family Living*, 23 (1961), pp. 340-349.

[39] David C. McClelland, A. Rindlisbacher, and Richard de Charms, "Religious and Other Sources of Parental Attitudes toward

include the child's knowing his way around the city, trying new things for himself, doing well in competition, and making his own friends. Since Protestant and Catholic American families have generally originated in different countries, it is difficult to determine the effect of religion separately from effects of national culture. There are differences in age of expected independence even within the Catholic group. On the whole, Catholic parents of Italian descent expect their children to achieve independence in the mentioned sponsored activities at a later age than do Catholic parents of Irish descent. McClelland and his associates suggest that parent sponsorship of activities related to the child's independence from the nuclear family promotes the child's achievement of economic and occupational success. On the basis of these findings as well as similar ones by Miller and Swanson, one would expect that children in Protestant and Jewish families are more pressured into independence in sponsored activities than are children in Catholic (especially Italian) families. Catholic parents may give greater attention to the prevention of unsponsored independence.

5. In their study of gifted children, Getzels and Jackson distinguished between parents who were vigilant about their children's behavior and academic performance and those parents who focused on their children's development of interests, new experiences, and "enthusiasm for life."[40] They found that the children of vigilant, pressur-

---

Independence Training," in David C. McClelland, ed., *Studies in Motivation,* New York: Appleton-Century-Crofts, 1955, pp. 389-397.

[40] Jacob W. Getzels and Philip W. Jackson, *Creativity and Intelligence: Explorations with Gifted Students,* New York: Wiley, 1962.

ing parents tended to have high general intellectual ability but little creativity whereas the children of less vigilant parents were more highly creative. This finding suggests that the kinds of activities sponsored by parents may be highly individuated.

6. Miller and Swanson have suggested that, with the spread of large-scale organizations in our society, parents may give less attention to sponsoring independent activities in children and more attention to maintaining stable social relations.[41] Miller and Swanson argue that fostering independence and responsibility in children was appropriate to training children to be individualistic entrepreneurs. However, with the decline in independent enterprises, child raising must be oriented toward developing adults who will not be highly individualistic. The trend in child raising will probably be toward increased sociability and mental health and away from responsible independence. Viewed in combination with the Getzels and Jackson findings, the Miller and Swanson study suggests that sponsored independence in the future may take on recreational and mental-health purposes rather than occupational training.

In summary: the various studies of sponsored independence of youth take the stance of "conventional" society and regard the performance of sponsored activities as training for adulthood—*parents* are more influential than adolescent peers in stimulating boys to pursue a professional career, families in which both parents work stimulate children to achieve occupational and financial success and require the children to perform family mainte-

[41] Daniel R. Miller and Guy E. Swanson, *The Changing American Parent*, New York: Wiley, 1958.

nance tasks, parents sponsor children's activities in conformity with their own considerations of "the important things in life," and the independence-inducing activities sponsored by parents reflect the parents' work setting and religious and ethnic background.

Unsponsored independence

Problems relating to unsponsored independence appear in lower socioeconomic families and in families without close ties binding the parents and children together. Various investigators have found that problems in the home are related to delinquent behavior in children, to alcoholism, and to other deviant behavior.[42] Moreover, when children center their activities around the home, they tend to view their parents as satisfied with their behavior even when the parents are dissatisfied; however, children who spend much time away from home tend to underestimate their parents' satisfaction with them.[43] Unsponsored independence then not only entails actual deviance from parental expectations but also magnifies this deviance in the eyes of the children. This magnification in turn probably stimulates further deviance.

Unsponsored independence includes not only delinquent acts but also other acts which might meet with parental disapproval. These acts are related to the loss of parental supervision and control of children's conduct. Findings related to unsponsored independence in courtship behavior reveal that:

[42] For example, F. Ivan Nye, *Family Relationships and Delinquent Behavior*, New York: Wiley, 1958.

[43] Bernard Farber and William C. Jenné, "Family Organization and Parent-Child Communication," *Monographs of the Society for Research in Child Development*, 28 (1963), No. 7 (Serial No. 91).

1. Parents are more ignorant of their sons' love life than their daughters'. Various studies have indicated that girls are more closely bound to their parents and discuss courtship problems with them (especially with the mother).[44] Perhaps cross-sex inhibitions associated with the incest taboo operate to diminish son-mother communication; possibly the sons have more than the daughters to hide; or boys may merely be less communicative about their affective life. In any case, sex differences in independence are reflected in parental knowledge about the child's love life as well as about other activities of the child.

2. The separation of mother and daughter when the girl goes to college affects the girl's attitude toward love behavior that is deviant from parental expectation.[45] Until college, the girl and her mother are similar in their attitude toward virginity prior to marriage. However, after the girl enters college, she frequently becomes more liberal in her attitude toward premarital intercourse. The more liberal attitude does not necessarily mean that the girl herself is participating in premarital erotic activity, only that she revises her views concerning the conditions under which intercourse is permissible before marriage. Going away to college is a special instance of the loosening of family ties that increases the probability of unsponsored independent behavior.

[44] For example, Carlfred B. Broderick and Stanley E. Fowler, "New Patterns of Relationships between the Sexes among Preadolescents," *Marriage and Family Living*, 23 (1961), p. 29 (Table 4).
[45] Robert R. Bell and Jack V. Buerkle, "Mother and Daughter Attitudes to Premarital Sexual Behavior," *Marriage and Family Living*, 23 (1961), pp. 390-392.

Types of adult-youth relationships

This discussion has distinguished between two kinds of independence achieved by youth in their development—sponsored and unsponsored. It has not, however, related these modes of independent behavior to each other. Pairing modes of independent behavior establishes four extreme types of youth-adult relations:

The *emancipated youth* (high sponsored independence, high unsponsored independence) is one who, in the process of achieving a successful position in accordance with parental wishes, deviates from many of the norms held by his parents. The individual who is highly socially mobile (as through sports, dating popularity, academic achievement) and who is assimilated into a different segment of society is typical of the youth emancipated from the family.

The *All-American boy* or girl (high sponsored independence, low unsponsored independence) is one who achieves success in the areas in which the parents promote achievement while, at the same time, he avoids behavior which deviates from parental wishes. The individual who is a star in sports, very popular in dating, or achieves academic success (if these are the activities promoted by the parents) and who stays out of trouble with adults typifies the All-American boy or girl.

The *deviant* (low sponsored independence, high unsponsored independence) is one who achieves little in the activities promoted by his (or her) parents, but deviates considerably from parental expectations by performing unsponsored acts (for example, truancy, premarital sex activity, brawls, belonging to a gang). In middle-class segments of society, the hipster and the beatnik are characterized by low sponsored independence and high unsponsored independence.

The *passive individual* (low sponsored independence, low unsponsored independence) is one who is highly dependent upon his parents for the performance of many activities which are ordinarily done by the child himself. The passive individual does not get into trouble, yet neither does he (or she) achieve independence in sponsored activities ordinarily associated with his age-sex role.

An evaluation of the usefulness of this typology must await its application to particular problems. Getzels and Jackson studied social factors in high intelligence and creativity in children. The vigilant and nonvigilant families in their study appear to reflect family relations associated with the All-American child (high-IQ child) and the deviant (highly creative child) respectively. The vigilant family applies pressure for achievement to the child while giving him close supervision to prevent deviant behavior. The nonvigilant family offers little pressure and permits the child to develop as he will, thereby risking much deviance and nonachievement in school. The Getzels and Jackson formulation, however, does not take into account family relations associated with the emancipated youth. Similarly, the Miller and Swanson entrepreneurial family appears to be associated with the All-American child whereas their bureaucratic family seems an appropriate environment for developing a sociable, affable, passive individual. Possibly, the other two parent-child relationship types can also be incorporated into the Miller and

Swanson scheme. In any case, the distinction between sponsored and unsponsored independence of youth may provide various insights into the development of family relations.

THE OLDER PERSON

The increase in average life span during recent years produces a situation which was not faced by people of previous generations. In past generations, ordinarily the life of the parents did not last very long past the marriage of the last child. In 1890, in most families, one of the parents died before the marriage of the last child and the other parent generally died 10 or 12 years later. There was then little need to plan for a domestic career after the children had married. By 1950, both parents could expect to survive a median period of 14 years after the marriage of the last child and the remaining parent another 6 years.[46] The family life of the older person in contemporary society thus has two stages: (a) the postparental marriage and (b) the period of terminal widowhood (or widowerhood).

The first stage is that of the postparental married couple whose children have families of their own. The postparental married couple retain an active adult status —living independently, helping their children, and generally maintaining an elder-statesman relationship with their children. The second stage is the terminal stage in the family life cycle, in which the older persons no longer have personal or economic resources for maintaining an active adult status. In the terminal stage, the parent is or-

[46] Paul Glick, *American Families,* New York: Wiley, 1957.

dinarily nonmarried and requires assistance in housing or self-maintenance. The terminal stage is often marked by desolation and despondency.

Chapter 6 on kinship relations discussed the first stage of the family life of the older persons—after their children marry. It was noted that parents wish to continue to grow and develop with their married children, receive the companionship of their grandchildren, and provide whatever help they can to promote the welfare of their children's families. However, since the grandparents are no longer exclusively responsible for maintaining and providing for their married children, there is less pressure upon them to act upon specific problems. Axelson has noted also that couples in the postparental stage show a *decline* in specific concerns regarding their children's welfare, fewer financial difficulties, and fewer marital difficulties. There is an increase in loneliness and subsequently in community activities.[47] Domestic life apparently becomes simpler again.

The extension of the postparental period of marriage has another consequence. Earlier in American history, when both parents generally did not survive the marriage of the last child, the personal commitment of the older husband and wife toward one another made little difference in their decision, if they made any at all, as to the kind of life they would lead as retired parents. Their marriage could not be expected to endure much longer. Hence, the postparental period could be accepted by the

[47] Leland J. Axelson, "Personal Adjustment in the Postparental Period," *Marriage and Family Living*, 22 (1960), pp. 66-68.

parents and their married children as a temporary arrangement during which parental whims could be humored and
hostility held in abeyance. Retired parenthood could be
regarded as a kind of sick role which must be endured.
In the middle of the twentieth century, with a protracted
postparental stage, the parents and their married children
realize that this period may occupy a long time. Unless the
parents look forward to a companionate existence, they
may divorce. However, should they decide to remain together, when they withdraw from active participation in
work and other community activities, they may become
extremely attached to each other. Thompson and Streib
suggest that as a result of extreme attachment to the
spouse in very old age, the death of one may lead to the
desolation and despondency of the other. The despondency of the aged upon widowhood may increase in the
future and suicide rates among the aged may reflect this
increase in despondency. (Some older persons appear to
prepare for widowhood by "disengaging" from interaction
with the spouse as well as with others. Others may meet
the problem of desolation by remarriage.[48])

In the terminal stage of family life, the older person
no longer has an active adult status. He is reduced to being a nonmarried person, his roles are defined by his children, and his economic and personal resources degener-
ate. Thompson and Streib report that the older person adjusts his activities to fit in with those of his children and
grandchildren. His age roles and personal identity are in
their hands. This dependence upon children and grand-

[48] E. L. Cumming, L. R. Dean, D. S. Newell, and I. McCaffrey,
"Disengagement—A Tentative Theory of Aging," *Sociometry,* 23
(1960), pp. 23-35.

children is especially characteristic of the nonmarried older woman. Schorr reports that an older nonmarried woman is more likely to live with one of her children and more often with a daughter (with whom she has a close relationship) than with a son. Similarly, nonmarried older women are more likely to receive contributions from their children than are nonmarried men or married older couples.[49]

The preferred way of living for older persons is to have an independent residence but to receive companionship and affection from the children and their families. However, the older person may not have the personal competence or economic resources to live apart from the children. The major problem precipitating referral of an older person to a social agency is that of housing.[50] There appears to be little relationship between social class, social mobility, and the tendency to incorporate aged parents into the home.[51]

Thus, following the postparental stage, in which the parents maintain a dominant position by providing advice and assistance to the married children, the parent-child roles are reversed in the terminal stage of family life. The parent is no longer available as a potential spouse; his role

[49] Alvin L. Schorr, "Current Practice of Filial Responsibility," in Robert F. Winch, Robert McGinnis, and Herbert R. Barringer, eds., *Selected Studies in Marriage and the Family*, New York: Holt, 1962, pp. 417-435.

[50] Paul H. Glasser and Lois N. Glasser, "Role Reversal and Conflict between Aged Parents and Their Children," *Marriage and Family Living*, 24 (1962), pp. 46-51.

[51] John Kosa, Leo D. Rachiele, and Cyril O. Schommer, "Sharing the Home with Relatives," *Marriage and Family Living*, 22 (1960), pp. 129-131. See also Glasser and Glasser, *op. cit.*

is no longer one of adult responsibility; his physical capabilities are limited. The cycle has been completed.

SUMMARY: INTERACTION BETWEEN GENERATIONS

Although the trend during the course of marriage tends to be a divergence in the life careers of husband and wife, interaction between generations is not clear-cut. There is an ebb and flow in the course of family commitments between generations.

The section on youth indicated that children are expected by their parents to achieve an autonomy in their life careers—but not really. Generally, parents—mainly in the middle-class household—want their children to become autonomous only with respect to certain activities related to achievement of success in occupation and social life. In any case, the position of the parents in society and the values they hold important determine the kind of independence they tend to sponsor for the child. The term unsponsored independence applies to those activities which the child performs but which the parents would prohibit. Unsponsored independence refers not only to delinquent acts but also to moral and ethical attitudes disapproved by the parents.

The section on the older person again indicated that the parents do not intend that the child's life career be completely independent of their own (especially among middle-class parents). The intention of the older parents to grant only partial independence is revealed by the acts of assistance offered by parents to their married children in exchange for companionship. The mutual contingency of life careers of parents with their children also enters into parents' expectations that children will care for (or at least care about) them in the terminal stage of the family cycle. Thus, there is a tendency for the family to exist as a set of mutually contingent careers in intergenerational relations.

Marital versus Intergenerational Commitments

The foregoing analysis of the course of personal commitments of family members in the family life cycle revealed that although marital commitments tend to disintegrate through the years, personal commitments between parents and children (and grandchildren) tend to be sustained. There is probably much fluctuation in the personal commitments between parents and children. During the early years of their marriage, children who wish to develop strong personal commitments in their own family of procreation frequently isolate themselves from parents and in-laws. In adolescence, youths take advantage of their partial autonomy. In the postparental period, parents take advantage of their own independence from the responsibilities of child raising. Even so, there is generally the implicit assumption (often rousing guilt feelings) that an individual has obligations to his parents (or children). However, weakened commitments to husband or wife are ordinarily regarded as unfortunate but not as moral transgressions.

There is no moral equivalent in marriage relationships to the sponsored independence in relationships between generations. The popular ideal in marriage is not the fostering of autonomy in particular areas of family life. The ideal American marriage is one of joint decision making, common interests, and companionship. Departures from this ideal are not generally promoted by the marriage partners. These departures are instead considered as deviant behavior, frequently as ground for divorce. In relationships between generations, however, beginning in childhood there is preparation for the child to form his own family of procreation and to take on responsibilities for maintaining that family. Hence, the parents sponsor certain activities requiring autonomy on the child's part. With adolescence, this sponsored autonomy is increased; with marriage, still more. The autonomy is probably greatest in the period required by the child to establish his own family of procreation as a cohesive operating unit. However, with the birth of grandchildren, the child's family of procreation becomes a recognized establishment and a closer liaison can again be maintained with the parents and in-laws. After the establishment of the child's family of procreation, parents and children are expected to participate in mutual assistance and sometimes in recreational activities. The grandparents are expected to develop an indulgent relationship with grandchildren. Finally, the assistance expected is reversed when the parents reach the terminal stage of the family cycle. Thus, sponsored autonomy develops as a necessity in intergenerational relationships to permit the establishment of the child's family of procreation; once the child's family of procreation has been established, the life careers of members of different generations again merge.

The presence of moral prescriptions to sustain a relationship with parents (or children) long after the marriage of the children and the absence of similar moral precepts with respect to marriage suggests that even in American society parent-child relationships take precedence over marital relationships in the long run. If this priority of parent-child obligations exists after the child's family of procreation has become established, then the forecasts in Chapters 4 and 7 of increased characteristics of bilateral kinship in American society would be supported. With continued intergenerational commitments between family members, kinship arrangements could survive the practice of multiple marriage and divorce.

Selected Readings

Many writers have used the time dimension as a basis for organizing information about family life. Paul Glick, "The Life Cycle of the Family," *Marriage and Family Living*, 17 (1955), pp. 3-9, has provided general categories for the analysis of American family relations in terms of time. Jack Goody (ed.), *Developmental Cycle in Domestic Groups*, Cambridge University Press, 1958, has viewed the time aspects of family organization from a cross-cultural perspective.

Discussions of changes in marital relations over time include:

Blood, Robert O., and Donald M. Wolfe. *Husbands and Wives*. Free Press, 1960.

Dentler, Robert A., and Peter C. Pineo. "Sexual Adjustment, Marital Adjustment, and Personal Growth of Husbands: A Panel Analysis," *Marriage and Family Living*, 22 (1960), pp. 45-48.

Foote, Nelson N. "Matching of Husband and Wife in Phases of Development," *Transactions of the Third World Congress of Sociology*, 4 (1956), pp. 24-34.

Pineo, Peter C. "Disenchantment in the Later Years of Marriage," *Marriage and Family Living*, 23 (1961), pp. 3-11.

Data on divorce and remarriage are reported in:

Bernard, Jessie. *Remarriage: A Study of Marriage*. Holt, 1956.

Glick, Paul C. *American Families*. Wiley, 1957.

Goode, William J. "Marital Satisfaction and Instability: A Cross-Cultural Class Analysis of Divorce Rates," *International Social Science Journal*, 14 (1962), pp. 507-526.

Hillman, Karen G. "Marital Instability and Its Relation to Education, Income, and Occupation: An Analysis Based on Census Data," in Robert F. Winch, Robert McGinnis, and Herbert R. Barringer (eds.), *Selected Studies in Marriage and the Family*, Holt, 1962, pp. 603-608.

Monahan, Thomas P. "The Changing Nature and Instability of Remarriages," *Eugenics Quarterly*, 5 (1958), pp. 73-85.

Relationships between youth and parents are discussed in:

Davis, Kingsley. "The Sociology of Parent-Youth Conflict," *American Sociological Review*, 4 (1940), pp. 523-535.

Muuss, Rolf E. *Theories of Adolescence*. Random House, 1962.

Smith, Robert J., Charles E. Ramsey, and Gelia Castillo. "Parental Authority and Job Choice: Sex Differences in Three Cultures," *American Journal of Sociology*, 69 (1963), pp. 143-149.

Strodtbeck, Fred L. "Family Interaction, Values, and Achievement," in David C. McClelland, Alfred L. Baldwin, Urie Bronfenbrenner, and Fred L. Strodtbeck, *Talent and Society*, Van Nostrand, 1948, pp. 135-194.

Family relationships of the elderly are described in:

Burgess, Ernest W. "Family Living in the Later Decades," *Annals of the American Academy of Political and Social Science*, 279 (1952), pp. 106-114.

Cavan, Ruth Shonle. "Family Tensions between the Old and the Middle-Aged," *Marriage and Family Living,* 18 (1956), pp. 323-327.

Simmons, Leo W. "Social Participation of the Aged in Different Cultures," *Annals of the American Academy of Political and Social Science,* 279 (1952), pp. 43-51.

Streib, Gordon F. "Family Patterns in Retirement," *Journal of Social Issues,* 14 (1958), pp. 46-60.

Thompson, Wayne E., and Gordon F. Streib. "Meaningful Activity in a Family Context," in Robert W. Kleemeier (ed.), *Aging and Leisure: A Research Perspective into the Meaningful Use of Time,* Oxford University Press, 1961.

10 Crisis and the Revision of Commitments

The study of family crisis has been stimulated mainly by practical concerns over family disorganization. As Kirkpatrick has suggested, the term "crisis" is applied most readily to the atypical or premature event for which particular customs or agencies have not been devised to alleviate suffering.[1] Fashions in research on family crisis have followed problems for which alleviating or therapeutic institutions have been considered insufficient. Hence, in the latter part of the depression, effects of unemployment on family relationships were investigated;[2]

[1] Clifford Kirkpatrick, *The Family as Process and Institution*, New York: Ronald Press, 1955, p. 503.

[2] See Samuel A. Stouffer, Paul F. Lazarsfeld, and A. J. Jaffe, *Research Memorandum on the Family in the Depression*, New York: Social Science Research Council, 1937; Robert C. Angell, *The Family Encounters the Depression*, New York: Scribner, 1936; E. W. Bakke, *Citizens without Work*, New Haven: Yale Univer-

in time of war, the effects on family adjustment of the husband's departure to military service and his return to family life were studied;[3] with increasing concern over mental health, this kind of family crisis has become an object of study.[4]

Studies of crisis have produced many insights into the functioning of the family. Indeed, if adequate research design is to be applied to family study, families which deviate from the normal must provide the many statistical controls (as well as interesting configurations of factors) necessary for an adequate investigation of family interaction.

This chapter examines family crisis from the viewpoint of family process. The first section compares conceptions of family crisis used in research. In particular, it compares the stimulus-response approach to family crisis with the process approach. The second section describes the characteristics of the crisis process. Stages in this process are suggested. The third section applies the characteristics of the crisis process to families with a handicapped child. This application illustrates the process in terms of a particular kind of family crisis. Finally, the fourth section relates the family crisis process to problems in orderly replacement.

---

sity Press, 1940; Ruth S. Cavan and Katherine H. Ranck, *The Family and the Depression*, Chicago: University of Chicago Press, 1936; Mirra Komarovsky, *The Unemployed Man and His Family*, New York: Dryden, 1940.

[3] Reuben Hill, *Families under Stress*, New York: Harper, 1949.

[4] John A. Clausen and Marian Radke Yarrow, Issue Editors, "The Impact of Mental Illness on the Family," *Journal of Social Issues*, 11 (1955), No. 4.

Conceptions of Family Crisis

The inadequacy of present working conceptions of family life is indicated in the current views of family crisis. These conceptions focus upon disorganizing stresses and, by definition, the family in the throes of crisis is inadequate in the performance of its functions.

Many typologies have been constructed to describe and study crises in the family. Generally, these typologies follow a stimulus-response conception of family life. In each of these conceptions, there is an original state which is interrupted by an external or internal stimulus. This stimulus disorganizes the activity of the family. As a response to this disrupting stimulus, the family must devise ways to reorganize itself. For example, Burgess, Locke, and Thomes indicate that: "A crisis is any decisive change which creates a situation for which the habitual behavior patterns of a person or a group are inadequate. What are the typical situations resulting in family crises? What factors determine the way in which family members react to crises?"[5]

Burgess, Locke, and Thomes list as types of crisis-provoking situations: conflict in role expectations, disgrace, economic reverses, and family disruption. Among deviations from role expectations, they include problem behavior of children, major emotional disturbances in parent-child relations, and the transitional period of adolescence. They regard crises between husbands and wives as having two kinds of stimuli: (a) the shattering of il-

[5] Ernest W. Burgess, Harvey J. Locke, and Mary Margaret Thomes, *The Family from Institution to Companionship*, New York: American Book, 1963, p. 415.

lusory role conceptions and (b) the development of divergent conceptions of role expectations.

Hill suggests that an event will become a crisis (a) when it produces hardships and complicates the family situation, (b) when the resources of the family are such that it cannot cope with these hardships, and (c) when the family defines a particular event as the source of threat to its initial situation.[6] Hill then enumerates the kinds of situations which ordinarily (a) produce hardships for which the family's resources are inadequate and (b) are readily identified as a source of hardship. Hill classifies crisis stimuli as being extrafamily versus intrafamily in origin, as provoking or not provoking change in status within the family, and as having to do with accession of new members or dismemberment.

The conception of crisis by Hill involves the concept of equilibrium. Following Koos, he diagrams crises as beginning with an initial equilibrium, which is succeeded by disequilibrium, whereupon the family seeks to attain a new level of equilibrium. Hill appears to equate equilibrium with the adequacy with which the family performs its "functions." Other classifications of crisis stimuli include the nature of the stimulus as dramatic versus slowly emergent and sudden riches as compared with sudden impoverishment. The major concern of Hill, however, is whether certain crisis stimuli are more provocative of disequilibrium than are other stimuli.

In the stimulus-response conception of family crisis, the crisis proneness of the family indicates the extent to

[6] Reuben Hill, "Generic Features of Families under Stress," *Social Casework*, 39 (1958), pp. 139-150.

which the responding organism has "crisis-meeting" resources. Included as pertinent information regarding family adequacy in a crisis situation are flexibility of roles, feelings of affection, and past experiences with meeting crisis. These make the family more adaptable in meeting new potentially disruptive situations.

Inasmuch as the stimulus-response approach to crisis seeks to explain family behavior in crisis mainly on the basis of reaction to classes of stimuli, it tends to regard adjustment reactions to crisis as more or less unique. The major elements in schemes relating to family crisis refer to pressures (other stimuli) impinging upon the family as it reacts to the crisis. The ways by which families *meet* critical events are not generally as well conceptualized as are the stimuli.

One purpose of this chapter is to indicate an alternative way of viewing family crisis which permits a more adequate conceptualization of the manner by which families counteract the disruptive aspects of crisis.

The stimulus-response conception of family crisis suggests that social order is disrupted with the advent of crisis. It would be equally plausible to suggest that the crisis situation is one which induces a process in family life which is counter to the ordinary organization of the norms and values of the family members. For example, studies of disaster in communities indicate that rather than relapsing into utter chaos people begin to show concern over their family members and attempt to save them from discomfort.[7] Similarly, the Komarovsky study of the fam-

[7] Lewis M. Killian, "The Significance of Multiple-Group Membership in Disaster," *American Journal of Sociology*, 57 (January, 1952) pp. 309-314.

ily in the depression indicated that there was a change in authority pattern when the husband lost his job.[8] This change in authority pattern is not to be confused with chaos but rather with the introduction of a new process in family life which is not in accordance with the wishes of the family members.

What difference does it make to regard crisis as being the initiation of a new process rather than as a disorganization? One answer is that complete disorganization implies an infinite number of ways in which a crisis stimulus can affect the family. If the crisis stimulus merely produces disorganization, then there is little that can be done to predict the nature of the patterns of family reorganization. However, if crisis is regarded as inducing a certain type of distorting process to the initial organization, then this new process can eventually be identified. With this identification of the distorting process, the researcher can predict types of strategies developed by families to handle this new process. With a smaller number of alternatives to investigate, he can restrict the number of hypothetical reorganization patterns to a workable number. For example, if the effect of loss of a job is the lowering of the husband's authority, then ways can be determined to reinstitute authority (if reinstitution is desired). The deviations in authority then are not *reactions* by family members to the crisis stimulus but rather the institution of *new* distorting processes against which the family must reorganize its power and role structure if it is to survive.

A second answer is that the stimulus-response conception of crisis focuses attention upon the precipitating

[8] Komarovsky, *op. cit.* at note 2.

event. But the importance of the study of crisis lies in the insights it provides for advancing knowledge about processes of family interaction and organization. The stimulus-response conception thus isolates family crisis as a unique set of events; the alternative conception characterizes crisis as a class of interaction process in family life.

A third answer is that from a therapeutic viewpoint, the process view seems more adequate than the stimulus-response view. The stimulus-response view focuses upon the inadequacies existing in family structure which disrupt family life when a critical event occurs. The process view emphasizes what action is to be taken to counteract a series of events over which the family members are concerned.

Because the process approach to crisis offers advantages over the stimulus-response approach in terms of identification of what is occurring, attention to more general knowledge about family interaction, and potential effectiveness for use in family therapy, this discussion will concentrate on family crisis as a process.

The Crisis Process

This section will outline the crisis process in family relations, first reviewing major investigations into family crises emerging from different problems, and then abstracting features from these studies which present a description of the sequence of events significant for the understanding of family interaction in problem situations.

PAST STUDIES OF FAMILY CRISIS

As was indicated earlier, there has been little attempt to describe the processes which induce deviation from desired division of labor and companionate interaction in the family. Yet it would be impossible to determine effective strategies for maintaining integration without an adequate description of the deviant process. Perhaps an analysis of reports on strategies for maintaining family life in the face of crisis will provide us with a basis for describing processes which distort conventional norms and values associated with normal family arrangements. There have been numerous studies of family crises.

The husband in military service

Hill studied the adjustment of families to the entrance of the husband into military service in World War II and then the family adjustment to reunion.[9] An analysis of case studies revealed that in families making a good adjustment to separation or reunion, or both:

1. In the absence of the husband, the wife made decisions and managed the home without advice from the husband by letter or telephone.

2. Grandparents and relatives were available for interaction and assistance and did participate in family life.

3. Children carried on various responsibilities in the home. This feature was important for adjustment to separation.

4. Freedom from illness or financial difficulty facilitated adjustment during the separation.

5. Adequate personal communication by letter and visiting maintained during separation was related to good adjustment to both separation and reunion.

Generally, good adjustment to separation was related

[9] Hill, *Families under Stress, op. cit.*

to good adjustment to reunion. If conflict existed prior to separation, it was resumed upon reunion.

The husband who is mentally ill

Clausen, Yarrow, and their associates investigated crises associated with the institutionalization of psychiatric male patients.[10] The respondents were 33 wives of patients diagnosed as psychotic or psychoneurotic. The investigators schematized the trends in the wife's reactions prior to institutionalization as follows:

1. After the accumulation of various kinds of behavior (deviations from routines of behavior, bizarre thoughts, delusions, physical complaints) which are not readily understandable or acceptable to her, the wife reaches a threshold for initially discerning the presence of a problem.

2. This accumulation of unusual behavior ultimately forces upon the wife the necessity for reexamining and adjusting behavioral expectations for herself and her husband in such a way as to permit her to find some way to account for his unusual behavior.

3. The wife finds herself in an "overlapping" situation. She cannot without professional validation determine whether her husband's behavior represents a problem. Her interpretations shift back and forth from seeing a problem to viewing her husband as normal.

4. Adaptations to the atypical behavior of the husband must occur if the couple is to continue to live together. The wife continues to test and wait for additional cues before coming to any definite interpretation. In adapting to her husband's behavior, the wife mobilizes

[10] Clausen and Yarrow, *op. cit.*

strong defenses against defining the husband's behavior as deviant. These defenses take the form of denying the existence of abnormal behavior, attenuating its abnormality, and normalizing the husband's problems.

5. Eventually the wife reaches a threshold point at which her defenses collapse and she comes to a relatively stable conclusion that her husband's problem is a psychiatric one or that she cannot cope with his problem without assistance.[11]

After the husband's admission to a mental hospital, the wife faces additional problems in social relations:

1. The wife of the mental patient experiences altered relationships with her family and friends. Not only is she a "single" person, but she also becomes "special" because of her problem. At the same time, she is involved in new relationships such as those with the mental-hospital staff.

2. With the departure of the husband from the functioning family, the wife's roles within the family ordinarily expand. She has to take over many of the activities previously performed by her husband.[12]

The birth of the first child

In his exploratory study of parenthood as a crisis, LeMasters found that 38 of his 46 couples reported marked dif-

[11] Marian Radke Yarrow, Charlotte Green Schwartz, Harriet S. Murphy, and Lelia Calhoun Deasy, "The Psychological Meaning of Mental Illness in the Family," in Clausen and Yarrow, *op. cit.*, pp. 12-24.

[12] John A. Clausen, Marian Radke Yarrow, Lelia Calhoun Deasy, and Charlotte Green Schwartz, "The Impact of Mental Illness: Research Formulation," in Clausen and Yarrow, *op. cit.*, p. 8.

ficulty in adjusting to the first child.[13] Almost all of these crisis families rated their marriages as at least good in adjustment (with ratings confirmed by friends). The 38 couples had romanticized parenthood and had defined the parental role in an idealistic manner. The mothers reported the following difficulties: loss of sleep, chronic tiredness, extensive confinement to home, curtailment of social activities, accumulation of household chores, concern over personal appearance, and dissatisfaction over giving up gainful employment. The fathers reported: decline in the wife's sexual response, economic pressures, curtailment of social life, and concern over a possible second pregnancy. Although the LeMasters discussion did not trace a trend in crisis behavior, he did indicate problems in the division of labor and companionship.

The alcoholic husband

Jackson investigated the crisis which arises in family relations through alcoholism of the husband.[14] In her study, she made a distinction between *acute crises* such as spending money for drinking instead of necessities and *habituated crises* such as prolonged diminished support. Moreover, Jackson pointed out that behavior in the earlier phases of the crisis affects the form of the habituated crisis and sets limits on alternatives that can be taken later. She attempted to identify the stages in the crisis situation.

[13] E. E. LeMasters, "Parenthood as Crisis," *Marriage and Family Living*, 19 (1957), pp. 352-355.

[14] Joan K. Jackson, "The Adjustment of the Family to Alcoholism," *Marriage and Family Living*, 18 (1956), pp. 361-369. Jackson studied the wives of Alcoholics Anonymous members and of hospitalized alcoholics.

Stage 1. Concern grows over extent of drinking and the couple attempts to deny that drinking is a problem. The couple is concerned with the "social visibility" of drinking, but friends and the husband assure the wife that the husband's drinking behavior is not abnormal.

Stage 2. As the family becomes socially isolated (both voluntarily and through avoidance by others), drinking is then identified as the "cause" of family difficulties. With the definition of drinking as a problem, attempts are made to decrease its visibility. Unable to control the problem of drinking, the husband and wife experience increased shame and resentment. Both husband and wife regard themselves as failures.

Stage 3. The drinking behavior is then regarded as a permanent part of the situation and attempts at hiding this problem are relinquished. Even so, the family has not yet become habituated to the father as an alcoholic. Instead, the father's role in the family is revised slightly to accommodate his drinking. However, since the others in the family cannot rely on him to carry on conventional father-husband roles, the alcoholic's family role becomes superfluous. Additional conflict arises over the husband's refusal to abdicate his previous father-husband rights.

Stage 4. In this stage, the husband is effectively isolated from the rights and duties associated with the husband-father status. Instead of being acknowledged as a husband-parent, he is now treated like a recalcitrant child by the wife and children. In effect, he is demoted socially in generation. The acute difficulties of the husband now shift to violent behavior, illness, imprisonment, unemployment. The husband's sense of being unmarried is indicated by his committing adultery openly.

Stage 5. With the husband's shift in generational position socially, separation or divorce generally follow. However, the wife often regards drinking as an illness and cannot abandon the alcoholic.

Stages 6 and 7. These stages deal with the two alternatives in reintegration of the family. Stage 6 deals with the reshuffling of family roles after divorce or separation. Stage 7 deals with problems of introducing the father again into roles that preceded his alcoholism: breadwinning, control over budgets and children. In addition, Stage 7 often brings with it a high involvement with other nondrinking alcoholics and/or with alcoholics the husband is helping.

The husband's unemployment

Bakke studied patterns of family adjustment to the unemployment of the father during the economic depression of the 1930's.[15] He suggested five stages in the adjustment cycle:

Stage 1. Momentum Stability. In this stage, the patterns of family relationships are relatively undisturbed; the old patterns of family life continue under the momentum of accustomed ways. There is little anxiety over financial instability. Few disciplinary problems arise.

Stage 2. Unstable Equilibrium. A change in household division of labor occurs. The husband begins to withdraw from familial responsibilities. As the husband's status declines, the wife's status increases. The mother assumes more responsibilities and is more powerful in family deci-

[15] E. Wight Bakke, *Citizens without Work, op. cit.* at note 2.

sions. She may procure outside employment. Children may also become supplementary earners. Mutual activities tend to diminish. The parents tend to use authoritarian disciplinary techniques to a greater extent. Anxiety over financial matters increases.

Stage 3. Disorganization. This stage is an intensification of the unstable equilibrium that precedes it. The dominant position of the wife is unchallenged. The parents regard themselves as failures, with the supplementary earners resentful of their contribution to the family. There are definite discipline problems and much reliance upon authoritarian means.

Stage 4. Experimental Readjustment. Unless it breaks up in the disorganization stage, the family sooner or later begins to pull itself together. Although the wife is regarded as the dominant individual in management and planning, the husband begins again to participate in decisions. There is more acceptance of the new routines; the supplementary earners have become accustomed to contributing and are less resentful.

Stage 5. Permanent Readjustment. This stage is merely a continuation and strengthening of trends in Stage 4, experimental readjustment.

This section has presented a brief review of major studies of family crisis. To insure a broad spectrum of kinds of problem situations, and social backgrounds of families, it has described studies dealing with wartime separation, mental illness, birth of a first child, alcoholism, and unemployment. Families in these investigations included a variety of ethnic groups, urban and rural backgrounds, and various socioeconomic classes. The following section abstracts from these descriptions features which appear to characterize the crisis process.

CHARACTERISTICS OF THE CRISIS PROCESS

The studies on family crisis presented various distortions in family relationships but not a general description of the crisis process in family life. Which of these distortions are relevant in the description of the crisis process?

In family crisis, the organization of the values of family members and the arrangement of their roles shift so that the coalitions among family members also change. The event which precipitates the crisis is important in that (a) it triggers a change in values and roles, (b) it cannot be controlled by merely erasing its effects and continuing life in the manner which had gone on before its occurrence, and (c) the potential distortions in interpersonal coalitions which it is capable of inducing are considered as "undesirable" at least by the parents. In the terms of the family as a set of mutually contingent careers, the end product of the crisis process is the freezing-out of one or more members from the set.

The investigations of family crisis exhibit several regularities that appear relevant to the series of events which culminates in this freezing-out. These regularities will be described briefly and then will be applied to an illustration of the crisis process. The regularities observed in the crisis investigations are identified as: attempts to handle deviance within existing family arrangements; coalition distortion as a basis for definition of the problem; revision of coalitions with extrafamily individuals and groups; rearrangement of age, sex, and generation roles; the freezing-out.

I. Attempts to handle deviance within existing family arrangements

The crises in some of the studies reviewed centered on the deviant behavior or condition of one family member. In such cases, the remaining family members generally make an effort to handle this deviance through existing arrangements.[16] The wife of the alcoholic or mentally ill husband attempts to deny and to "explain" his problems in such a way as not to threaten existing family organization. Patterns in the family of the unemployed man continue under the momentum of accustomed ways. In discussing disavowal of deviance in interaction with the visibly handicapped, Davis stresses the point that in order to maintain a fiction of normality in overlooking or minimizing the handicap as an impediment to social relations with "normals," the handicapped person himself must carry off this fiction.[17] Denying the deviance and "explaining" the deviance are accordingly parts of a complex of efforts to elicit from the deviant person a comparable fiction of normality. If the deviant person can carry off this fiction of normality, there is no need to revise the existing coalitions: he can maintain his current expected roles and no new course in family process is initiated. The deviance

[16] Exceptions to this effort were the separation of the husband from the rest of the family because of military service and the birth of a first child. However, as in the case of death or divorce, the absence of the spouse or the presence of an infant makes impossible any sustained attempt at normality. Crises growing out of changes in family composition would ordinarily omit this stage of the crisis process.

[17] Fred Davis, "Deviance Disavowal: The Management of Strained Interaction by the Visibly Handicapped," *Social Problems,* 9 (1961), pp. 120-132.

or handicap is considered as an individual or personal problem rather than as a family problem. However, if the fiction of normality is to be effective, both the deviant person and the others in the family must cooperate. Otherwise, as Komarovsky's study indicates in the case of the unemployed man whose authority rests upon his position as breadwinner, claims for maintaining normal family relations in the face of failure are disregarded by the other family members.[18]

II. Coalition distortion as a basis for definition of the problem

The studies of crisis indicate that family members do not define the crisis-provoking event as a problematic situation until the initial coalitions among family members have already been affected. Thus: (a) families of mentally ill men regard themselves as having difficulties only when the husband's atypical behavior is identified as a permanent feature of the relationship, and the wife reaches the threshold point of regarding him as a psychiatric problem; (b) among couples who have romanticized parenthood, the marked change in husband-wife relations with accompanying dissatisfaction over these changes produces the parenthood crisis; (c) the husband in military service cannot come home at will, and (d) shame, resentment, and a sense of failure as *husband and wife* accompany the realization that the husband's drinking or unemployment is a problem. Hence, the initial husband-wife coalition, which involved specific arrangements regarding authority, obligations, and companionship, can no longer

[18] Mirra Komarovsky, *op. cit.* at note 2.

operate; the couple cannot merely wave aside "the problem" and revert to their previous coalition.

III. Revision of coalitions with extrafamily individuals and groups

In "normal" family life, participation in organizations with friends outside the family ordinarily supports the norms and values associated with everyday life. For the family in crisis, these ordinary community relationships do not support norms and values pertinent to handling "the problem." On the other hand, other extrafamily coalitions do provide means for handling the crisis. Women with husbands in the military service shift reliance to grandparents and relatives; the wife of the mental patient withdraws from family and friends and forms coalitions with the mental-hospital staff; parenthood ordinarily involves a curtailment of social activities (especially activities with friends who have no children); attempts are made to decrease the social visibility of drinking and eventually coalitions are formed with doctors, social workers, psychologists, and the like, and with nondrinking alcoholics; the family of the unemployed tends to withdraw from friends at the old social level and to find new friends at the lower socioeconomic level.

IV. Rearrangement of age, sex, and generation roles

Whereas the initial critical situation developed with the realization of a shift in coalitions among family members, the continuation of family life in the crisis situation is sustained through a rearrangement of age, sex, and generation roles in the family. The drinking husband is eventually demoted in generation to the role of a recalcitrant child; the mother retains her coordinating role in the various family relationships and assumes the husband's responsibilities. Similarly, the unreliable behavior of the mentally ill husband causes a comparable demotion. The unemployed husband withdraws from planning and management; children assume adultlike roles, contribute financially, and demand a change in power structure in the family. In all of these instances, the family members have departed from conventional age, sex, and generation roles. The family organization itself becomes deviant.

V. *The freezing-out*

The effect of the rearrangement is to acknowledge that the domestic career of the deviant member—such as the drinking husband, the mentally ill husband, the husband or wife who refuses to adjust to the new child, or the unemployed husband—has been ended or indefinitely interrupted. Inasmuch as it has been one in the set of mutually contingent careers which is the family, that set is disrupted and needs to be reconstituted without that member; the individual's career line is no longer associated with those of the other family members. Nor does he continue to promote the career development of the others. He cannot remain in the contingent set. The alternative is to freeze him out.

Families with a Handicapped Child: An Illustration of the Crisis Process

The preceding section indicated generic characteristics of the crisis process. In this section, the crisis process is applied to a specific family problem.

The family with a handicapped child offers the opportunity to observe family interaction under severe enduring crisis. The presence of a child who is severely mentally retarded, blind, deaf, or afflicted by cerebral palsy presents the family with the potential of highly dramatic interaction. In a highly dramatic crisis, the dynamics of ordinary life are magnified enormously and the family encounters exaggerated problems of amount and kind of interaction.

Investigation of handicapped children and their families is of interest not only because of the knowledge to be gained about family interaction but also because handicaps in children constitute an ever-present problem. Roughly 10 percent of school-age children are sufficiently handicapped to require special education facilities.[19] Possibly half of these handicaps are temporary and others may not interfere appreciably with family life. However, with more than 50 million school children in the United States, even 5 per cent represents at least 2.5 million children. Moreover, there may be handicaps which do not require special education facilities but which do interfere with family life. For example, several studies have indicated that 7 or 8 per cent of school children show signs of emotional disturbance.[20] (These results are consistent

[19] Samuel A. Kirk, *Educating Exceptional Children,* Boston: Houghton Mifflin, 1962, pp. 21-25.

[20] Eli Bowers, *Early Identification of Emotionally Handicapped Children in School,* Springfield, Ill.: Thomas, 1960; Charles E. Ullman, *Identification of Maladjusted School Children,* Public Health Monograph Number 7, Washington: Government Printing Office, 1952. However, only about 2 or 3 per cent are severely disturbed according to the Wishik and Farber studies. See S. Wishik, "Handicapped Children in Georgia: A Study of Prevalence, Disability Needs, and Resources," *American Journal of Pub-*

with findings on adults. In Baltimore, 11 per cent of the
adults were found to have mental disorders; in midtown
Manhattan, 23 per cent of the adults had mental impair-
ments; American military rejections and discharges for
mental disorders for World War II were about 18 per
cent.[21]) Since the prevalence of emotional disturbance is
likely to increase rather than decrease from childhood to
adulthood, estimate of childhood emotional disturbance
at 7 to 8 per cent does not seem unreasonable. Concededly,
not all emotionally disturbed children require special education facilities. Even so, if to the pool of handicapped
children those children are added who may interfere with
family life even though they do not show severe educational disabilities, possibly one family in ten may have a
child who generates family difficulties.

This discussion will examine families with handicapped
children in terms of the crisis process. It will follow the
family through (a) its attempts to handle the handicap
within existing family arrangements, (b) its definition of
problems on the basis of distortions in family coalitions,
(c) its revisions of relationships with extrafamily individuals and groups, (d) its rearrangement of the age, sex,
and generation roles taken by family members, and (e)
its freezing-out of the handicapped member. Findings on
alternatives to freezing out the handicapped individual

lic Health, 46 (1956), pp. 195-203, and Bernard Farber, The
Prevalence of Exceptional Children in Illinois in 1958, Springfield,
Ill.: Superintendent of Public Instruction, 1959.

[21] Adult data cited in Leo Srole, Thomas S. Langer, Stanley T.
Michael, Marvin K. Opler, and Thomas A. C. Rennie, Mental
Health in the Metropolis: The Midtown Manhattan Study, Volume
1, New York: McGraw-Hill, 1962, p. 141.

will then be presented. Because of the extensiveness of research on the severely mentally retarded child as compared with other handicapping conditions, most findings will pertain to the family with a retarded child.

I. ATTEMPTS TO HANDLE DEVIANCE WITHIN
EXISTING FAMILY ARRANGEMENTS

The existence of a family crisis depends upon the extent to which the family members regard an event as changing present or future family life in an undesirable way. If the event is defined by the family members as *no different in any way* from the situation they had expected to encounter and if these individuals believe that the family routines they have developed will meet the situation, there is no crisis. A retarded child (as defined medically and psychologically) thus injects the *potentiality* of crisis rather than actual crisis into the family relationships. Once the parent considers his child as severely mentally retarded, he must then reevaluate the efficacy of the family's norms and roles for coping with the child. Only when the parents perceive this child as mentally retarded and define their present norms and roles as inadequate does the crisis process develop.

The parents can maintain a fiction of normality either by blaming the child's inability to perform activities ordinarily expected at his age level upon slow maturation or by attributing his difficulties to an easily remedied illness. As long as the parents can maintain this fiction of normality, no family crisis will develop. Some parents can continue for a long time to regard the child's deficiency as resulting from a lack of vitamins, insufficient endocrine secretion, or late development. However, eventually the diagnosis of severe mental retardation is confirmed by a physician or a psychologist. Wanting to maintain a fiction of normality, parents of retarded children frequently "shop around" for a hopeful diagnosis. They will "go from doctor to doctor, to psychologists, to social workers, to teachers, and to friends looking for someone who will reassure them that the child is not mentally retarded."[22]

The impact of a handicapped child on family relationships begins with the parents' definition of the child as a deviant individual. This definition is taken as a starting point in most studies of effects of a handicapped child on the family. It might be interesting to determine how the presence of a child who is identified as handicapped by a physician, teachers, or playmates but *not* by the family affects family relationships. The family would have to compensate in some ways to avoid regarding the child as handicapped or perhaps would assign a lesser handicap. For example, the father may define his mongoloid child as merely having a speech impediment.

Zuk found that parents tended to overestimate the social quotient of retarded children but that this distortion was most pronounced when children were relatively normal in motor functioning.[23] This finding suggests that parents tend to minimize the amount of deviance in evaluating development of social roles by the child. However, Schulman and Stern indicate that parents are fairly realis-

[22] Samuel A. Kirk, Merle B. Karnes, and Winifred D. Kirk, *You and Your Retarded Child,* New York: Macmillan, 1955, p. 3.

[23] Gerald H. Zuk, "Autistic Distortions in Parents of Retarded Children," *Journal of Consulting Psychology,* 23 (1959), pp. 171-176.

tic in their judgments of the IQ of their children.[24] In their study, the correlation coefficient between test and estimated Stanford-Binet IQ was .67 at the time that the parents first sought help.

The severity of handicap appears to be related to the extent of redefinition. Hall found that mothers with severely cerebral-palsied children reported more feelings of continued guilt, denial, and futility than did mothers of less severely handicapped cerebral-palsied children.[25] In his study of children who had contracted polio, Davis indicated how the parents initially react to the child's illness.[26] The parents initially try to diagnose the child's illness in terms of symptoms of a less serious, more familiar disease. Generally, only when the child does not have all the symptoms of the less serious illnesses or does not respond to remedies do the parents call the physician. In another paper, Davis also indicated that physicians sometimes report falsely that prognosis is uncertain in order to maintain the hopes and morale of the parents.[27] Indeed, Murstein found that the more information given to the parents of leukemia victims, the worse was the emotional adjustment of the parents as contrasted with that of par-

[24] J. L. Schulman and S. Stern, "Parents' Estimate of the Intelligence of Retarded Children," *American Journal of Mental Deficiency*, 63 (1959), pp. 696-698.

[25] W. T. Hall, "Family Disorganization as Associated with Severity of Handicap (by Cerebral Palsy) of a Minor Child," unpublished doctoral dissertation, University of Minnesota, 1961.

[26] Fred Davis, "Polio in the Family," unpublished doctoral dissertation, University of Chicago, 1958.

[27] Fred Davis, "Uncertainty in Medical Prognosis, Clinical and Functional," *American Journal of Sociology*, 66 (1960), pp. 271-274.

ents of children with nonfatal diseases in which a legitimate basis of hope existed.[28] A question might be raised here with respect to the value of ignorance in meeting a situation which is defined by the expert as a hopeless situation.[29]

The definition of the child as deviant is probably related to age of the child: The more severe the deviance, the earlier in the child's life is the diagnosis made. Many physicians, psychologists, teachers, and social workers try to promote early recognition by parents that their child is retarded. The rationale is that early recognition of mental retardation will facilitate adjustment and, sometimes, remediation. Other professional people suggest a delay for as long as possible in defining the family situation as abnormal:

It is fortunate for many retarded children that their mothers are incapable of recognizing their retardation until the time when the difference between their chronological age and intellectual development becomes obvious—because by being in the care of their mothers through the period of their early development, they are more likely to acquire speech and motor skills than if they had been admitted to an institution for the mentally retarded.[30]

[28] Bernard I. Murstein, "The Effect of Long-Term Illness of Children on the Emotional Adjustment of Parents," *Child Development*, 31 (1960), pp. 157-171.

[29] See Louis Schneider, "The Role of the Category of Ignorance in Sociological Theory: An Exploratory Statement," *American Sociological Review*, 27 (1962), pp. 492-508.

[30] Leo H. Bartemeier, "Fundamental Problems with Retarded Children," in *Heuristic Hypotheses about the Variant Child in our Culture*, Langhorne, Pa.: Woods Schools and Residential Treatment Center, 1961, p. 38.

Seeing no differences between their own children and others, the mothers treat their children as normal and the children can to some extent respond as normal and thereby avoid debilitating sheltering.

II. COALITION DISTORTION AS A BASIS FOR
DEFINITION OF A PROBLEM

There is an accumulation of evidence that the presence of a handicapped child in the home creates many hardships for the nonhandicapped family members. For example, Roe found problems of adjustment among families with a cerebral-palsied child.[31] In a study on an Australian sample, Schonell and Watts uncovered many "family upsets" in families with a child with an IQ of 55 or under.[32] In London, Tizard and Grad found that 70 per cent of the very young retardates below school age and an additional 25 per cent between ages six and fifteen generated severe management problems in the family.[33] Various other studies report feelings of frustration, projection, doubts, fears, guilt feelings, favoritism of the handicapped child, and other behavior indicating personal maladjustment of parents of handicapped children.

Variations in family life stimulated by the presence of the handicapped child will be reflected in all other family relationships. Yet these distortions in family relation-

[31] H. Roe, "The Psychological Effects of Having a Cerebral-Palsied Child in the Family," unpublished doctoral dissertation, Columbia University, 1952.

[32] F. J. Schonell and B. H. Watts, "A First Study of the Effects of a Subnormal Child on the Family Unit," *American Journal of Mental Deficiency*, 61 (1956), pp. 210-219.

[33] J. Tizard and Jacqueline C. Grad, *The Mentally Handicapped and Their Families*, New York: Oxford University Press, 1961.

ships do not occur in a random fashion. The ways in which the parents regard their children as deviant affect interaction among family members. Factors in the definition of the child as deviant include etiology ascribed by the parents, socioeconomic status, sex of parent and child, and religion.

Korkes investigated reactions of the parents who regarded the child's mental illness as resulting from their own behavior as opposed to extrafamily factors.[34] She found that parents who accept personal responsibility for the child's illness, in contrast with those who do not, more often undergo relatively profound changes in personal values, marital relationship, and child-raising behavior. She found that the parents who regard themselves as responsible for the child's illness also more often perceive the child as "a human being with comprehensible responses" and that these parents tend to include the patient in their future family plans. The distortions in coalitions in the family, thus, appear to depend upon the extent to which the parents regard their handicapped child as "human" or comprehensible. The definition of the child in terms of his being "human," in turn, depends upon parents' perceptions of their role in his illness.

Another perspective upon the relationship between the parental role and the definition of the child as deviant is presented in terms of types of crisis as related to socioeconomic status. In a study by Farber, two kinds of crisis were considered: the tragic crisis and the role-organiza-

[34] Lenore Korkes, *A Study of the Impact of Mentally Ill Children upon Their Families,* Trenton: New Jersey Department of Institutions and Agencies, 1956.

tion crisis. These types represent different ways in which the parents perceive disruption in family life.[35]

In the tragic crisis, the aims, aspirations, and anticipated "happy" family life are frustrated. Families of relatively high socioeconomic status generally place much emphasis upon future aims and aspirations. This emphasis makes the family of high socioeconomic status especially vulnerable to tragic crises. The child's handicap is regarded by the parents as an uncontrollable event preventing fulfillment of their hopes and aspirations. Since the handicapped child himself is identified as the reason for their frustration, hostility tends to be directed toward him.

The direction of hostility toward the child in the family of high socioeconomic status is facilitated by the parents' view that socialization is primarily a matter of internalization of norms rather than mere "obedience." For example, a study by Kohn indicated that the higher the mother's social status, the greater was her emphasis on the development of consideration for others, of curiosity, and of self-control in the socialization of children.[36] Hence, in the family of high socioeconomic status, socialization is primarily the child's activity rather than the parent's.

While the parent of high socioeconomic status regards a handicapped child as the precipitator of frustration,

[35] Bernard Farber, "Perceptions of Crisis and Related Variables in the Impact of a Retarded Child on the Mother," *Journal of Health and Human Behavior*, 1 (1960), pp. 108-118.

[36] Melvin Kohn, "Social Class and Parental Values," *American Journal of Sociology*, 64 (1959), pp. 337-351.

various factors prevent the parent from acting aggressively against the child. First, the parent cannot regard the child as having become retarded intentionally. Second, the parent may even view the child's retardation as only one link in a chain of events resulting from the parent's own activity or personal attributes. Hence, the parent of high socioeconomic status cannot easily rationalize his hostility toward the child; he is motivated to continue in his parental role of providing love and care for the child.

From the preceding discussion, it appears that two opposing tendencies are present in the parent of high socioeconomic status. On the one hand, the parent regards the child as the direct cause of personal frustration. On the other hand, the parent feels a strong obligation to continue care for the child. The resolution of this conflict lies in the priorities assigned by the parent to his conformity with conventional norms and obligations as compared with personal gratification. In families of high social status, there is a tendency for individuals to give a higher priority to conformity with expectations and obligations than to expression of impulsive personal gratification. Hence, the hostility tends to become subdued and parental responsibilities toward the retarded child tend to be emphasized in families in a tragic crisis.

In the role-organization crisis, in contrast, the predicament facing the parents is not one of frustration of aims and aspirations but one of coping with a seemingly interminable care problem.

Essentially, whereas the tragic crisis develops mainly through the emergence of problems regarding ends of family life (aims, aspirations, values), the role-organization crisis is concerned with the inability to organize a system of workable roles or means. The presence of a system of workable roles implies an ability to control activities of the individual members. Hence, unlike tragic crisis, role-organization crisis occurs in the realm of what is regarded as controllable by the family members.

The probability of the occurrence of a role-organization crisis is accordingly high among those groups in which emphasis upon parental control is great but in which long-range ends of family life are not especially stressed. According to a study by Kohn, working-class mothers emphasize such parental control—obedience and responsiveness to parental authority—as values in the socialization of children.[37] Role-organization crisis would be pronounced, therefore, in working-class families.

Continued constant care and attention by the parent implies for the handicapped child an inability to achieve self-control in his activity. The greater the behavior problems of the child (either dependence or erratic behavior), the greater is the problem of control as seen by the parent and the more attention and involvement of the parent with the child is required. The greater the involvement of the mother with the retarded child, the more she withdraws from conforming to the expectations of others in the family. She tends to become alienated from the other family members. Hence, the greater the demands of the retarded child upon the mother (in her perception of the situation), the greater is the probability of her alienation

[37] *Ibid.*

from the rest of the family, and the worse the effect on the family system.[38]

In several respects, the Korkes study is consistent with Farber's distinction between tragic crisis and role-organization crisis. However, according to the tragic-crisis formulation, the parent does not blame himself for the child's handicap but instead blames himself for rejecting the child. The Korkes study found some parents who blamed themselves for the child's handicap. In both cases, however, there is an element of guilt which functions as a basis for maintaining a social relationship with the child and for including the child in future family plans.

Other parents in the Korkes study disavowed responsibility for the child's handicap and regarded the child as incomprehensible or uncontrollable. These parents tried to cope with the handicap even though they could find no set of roles which were capable of managing the child. The situation of these parents was like that of the parents in the Farber study confronted with a role-organization crisis. In both studies, parents in such a situation were very willing to hospitalize or institutionalize the child.

The distortions in family coalitions described by Korkes and by Farber are related to other factors besides etiology and socioeconomic status. Two other influences in organizing family relations generally are sex role and religion.

Sex of parent and child appear to be important in determining how coalitions in the family will be distorted.

[38] See Talcott Parsons and Renee C. Fox, "Illness, Therapy, and the Modern Urban American Family," *Journal of Social Issues,* 13 (1952), pp. 31-44.

In his study of eighty families with severely mentally retarded children in the San Francisco area, Tallman found
that fathers tended to be more highly motivated in coping
with problems of retarded boys than of retarded girls.[39]
Similarly, fathers were better able to cope with nonmon-
goloid children than with mongoloid children.

Tallman also found that whereas the mother's ability
to cope with the child was associated with factors which
were intrinsic to the parent-child relationship (child's IQ
and social competence), the father's ability to cope with
the child was related to the child's sex and diagnostic
classification. These findings suggested to Tallman that
the fathers' expectations for their retarded children were
influenced more by nonfamily social factors than were the
mother's.

Farber, Jenné, and Toigo found that the initial impact
of the diagnosis of severe mental retardation appears to
be somewhat sex-linked, with the mother indicating a
slightly greater impact if the retarded child is a girl and
the father a markedly greater impact (regardless of socioeconomic status) if the retarded child is a boy.[40] In the
low-status families, where sex differentiation in family
roles is probably greatest, mothers suffered a much greater
initial impact when the retarded child was a girl. How-

[39] Irving Tallman, "A Study of the Effects of Community and
Institutional School Classes for Trainable Mentally Retarded Chil-
dren," report issued by San Francisco State College, June, 1961,
Leo F. Cain and Samuel Levine, Co-directors of Research Project.

[40] Bernard Farber, William C. Jenné, and Romolo Toigo, "Fam-
ily Crisis and the Decision to Institutionalize the Retarded Child,"
*Council of Exceptional Children, NEA, Research Monograph
Series*, No. 1, Series A, 1960.

ever, with the passage of time, the nature of the impact on the mother shifted so that mothers of retarded boys tended to find the problems of coping with the child more severe than did the mothers of girls. Hence, the Farber-Jenné-Toigo findings suggest that the problems of living vicariously through the children and other emotional factors in identification are associated with the early tragic crisis and feelings of guilt while the later problems are associated with the life-cycle development of the family. In the family life cycle the retarded boy may provide more difficult role problems than the retarded girl.

Distortion of family coalitions is also influenced by the religious and moral principles of the parents. The problem of guilt feelings has been investigated by Zuk.[41] Zuk found that Catholic mothers were more "acceptant" than non-Catholic mothers and that mothers of younger retarded children were more "acceptant" than mothers with older retarded children. As compared with Protestant mothers, Zuk found that Catholic mothers were also more faithful in church attendance, more loyal to the religious training of their own parents, more prone to attend church when everything was going well (not just in crisis situations), and more consistent in prayer practice. Unfortunately, he was not able to hold religiosity constant statistically in the comparison between Catholic and Protestant mothers. Hence, it is uncertain whether religiosity or Catholicism was responsible for the Catholic-Protestant differences. However, there is a suggestion in a study by Ray that Catholic parents are helped in their

[41] Gerald H. Zuk, "The Religious Factor and Role of Guilt in Parental Acceptance of the Retarded Child," *American Journal of Mental Deficiency*, 63 (1959), pp. 139-147.

denial of responsibility for the child's handicap.[42] The study by Ray indicated that the majority of the Catholic mothers felt that God had given them a handicapped child as a "cross to bear." Similarly, in the Zuk study, 60 per cent of the Catholic mothers and 30 per cent of the Protestant mothers agreed with the item, "Having a slow child is the cross I must bear." On the other hand, the Protestant mothers in Zuk's investigation more readily agreed with the statement, "My greatest mission in life is to care for my slow child."[43] There are numerous contradictions in the findings on the role of religion in families with handicapped children.

The apparent contradictions regarding the effects of religion on the crisis process may occur because the investigators fail to concentrate on specific aspects of religion in the lives of the parents of handicapped children. For example, Saenger found that Jewish parents were more overprotective and less likely than Catholic parents to institutionalize their retarded child.[44] The basis for this difference, however, is open to much speculation. Little is known about the specific relationships between the belief system, religious practices, sense of guilt over the responsibility for the child's illness or guilt over rejecting the child, and kind of parental activities concerning the child.

This section has reviewed the results of studies dealing

[42] I. Ray, "A Study to Develop a Guide for Education of Parents of Cerebral-Palsied Children," unpublished Master's thesis, University of Iowa, 1951.

[43] Gerald H. Zuk, "The Religious Factor and Role of Guilt in Parental Acceptance of the Retarded Child," *op. cit.*

[44] Gerhart Saenger, *Factors Influencing the Institutionalization of Mentally Retarded Individuals in New York City,* Albany: New York Interdepartmental Health Resources Board, January, 1960.

with kinds of definitions of the handicapped child as related to ways in which existing family coalitions are influenced. In terms of etiology, Korkes indicated that regarding the child as incomprehensible is associated with severe care problems and tendencies in the parents to dissociate themselves from the child. Socioeconomic status affects the definition of the problem through variations in the emphasis placed on ultimate ends in child raising by different social classes. These variations lead parents to view their difficulties as a tragic crisis or as a role-organization crisis. Since sex role and religion are important in the organization of family relationships, these also enter into the definition of the family problems generated by the handicapping condition. Problems related to sex role develop through the parents' frustrated ambitions to live vicariously through their child (as would be expected in tragic crisis) or through their difficulties in handling boys (as would be expected in role-organization crisis). The effects of religion upon the definition of the problem are numerous. However, these effects are highly complicated and will require much refinement in future investigations.

III. REVISION OF COALITIONS WITH EXTRAFAMILY INDIVIDUALS AND GROUPS

One of the most important ways of adjusting family life to cope with the handicapped child is the limiting of parents' participation in extrafamily relationships such as organization membership or recreation. Evidence of withdrawal by family members from participation with others in the community was presented in an earlier chapter. In addition, coalition distortion seems to be related to extent of withdrawal. Pocs reported that mothers whose family relationships were most affected by their retarded child belonged to fewer organizations, were less socially mobile, and attended church less frequently than other mothers of retarded children.[45] In his study of cerebral-palsied children, Hall found that mothers of the more severely handicapped group were more likely to remain in the home than to take employment.[46]

In many ways the parents of the severely handicapped appear to act like the aged in their disengagement from role activities in which they had previously participated. There are, however, differences between the notion of disengagement that applies to the aged and the withdrawal of the parents of a severely handicapped child from community participation. For the aged there is no new role within the family to occupy the individual's time (unless it be that of a grandparent), whereas in the family with a severely handicapped child there is much pressure upon the parents to reorganize their activities to cope with the problem of the handicapped child. Holt reported that about 20 per cent of his mothers and 5 per cent of his fathers regarded themselves as being physically exhausted.[47] Boles indicated that not only were mothers of young cerebral-palsied children more socially withdrawn than mothers of older cerebral-palsied children but that

[45] Olgert Pocs, "Community Participation of Mothers with Mentally Retarded Children," unpublished Master's thesis, University of Illinois, 1960.

[46] Hall, *op. cit.* at note 25.

[47] K. S. Holt, "The Home Care of the Severely Mentally Retarded," *Pediatrics,* 22 (1958), pp. 744-755.

mothers of cerebral-palsied children were more preoccu-
pied with their children than were mothers of the nonhandicapped.[48]

The tendency to withdraw from relationships with
others in the community does not imply that parents lose
contact with all outsiders. The primary withdrawal is from
relationships which reveal norms (if not attitudes) which
are "hostile" to the kind of family life the parents of severely handicapped children may have to lead. Parents
of normal children require support to stimulate further
development of *conventional* family norms. Various studies have found that high community participation is conducive to healthy family life. However, the parents of a
retarded child require support for a *different* kind of role.
These parents' interests and routines differ from those of
parents of normal children of the same chronological age.
Discipline, play, development, and the like are not comparable for the retarded and the normal. Ordinarily, kinship, friendship associations, and activity in formal organizations are based on the dominant values and norms of the
community; and community participation gives support to
these values. Such participation would not, however, give
support to parenthood norms revolving around the mentally retarded. On the contrary, these groups and associations may be used for escaping problems, duties, and responsibilities connected with the retarded child. In evaluating his home life, the parent with high participation in
these associations may adopt a point of reference prevalent in them. These same associations would foster values

[48] G. Boles, "Personality Factors in Mothers of Cerebral-Palsied
Children," *Genetic Psychological Monographs*, 59 (1959), pp. 159-
218.

which are inappropriate for the parent whose child is mentally retarded. For the parent of the retarded child, these community relations are thus nonsupportive.[49]

To determine the effects of nonsupportive community relationships on families with a handicapped child, Farber divided the families in his sample into two groups on the basis of a battery of questions drawn from marital-prediction studies: families in which marital integration had been low prior to the birth of the retarded child, and families in which early marital integration had been high. Farber found that the estimated level of early marital integration in combination with nonsupportive community participation did affect the level of marital integration at the time of the study. Results relating to nonsupportive community relationships were especially clear-cut for families in which the early level of marital integration had been low. In these families, wives who had a high degree of neighborliness tended to have a lower marital-integration score at the time of the study than wives who were relatively isolated from their neighbors. In addition, with respect to husbands in families of low early integration, high activity in formal organizations tended to produce a disruptive effect on the marriage. It is probable that the parents whose early marital integration had been low were precisely the ones who required much support for family behavior from their friends, from neighbors, and from participation in organizations. These parents would be more vulnerable to the effect of nonsupportive interaction than would other parents. Participation in formal or-

[49] Bernard Farber, "Effects of a Severely Mentally Retarded Child on Family Integration," *Monographs of the Society for Research in Child Development,* 24 (1959), No. 2 (Serial No. 71).

ganizations for the husbands and in neighborly and friendly interaction for the wives possibly provided a means of escape from the burdens of the home. In these families the presence of a role-organization crisis may well have been the normal state of affairs.

In contrast to nonsupportive community relationships, certain individuals and groups can provide understanding and sympathy necessary for the development of new roles as parents of a retarded child. A major supportive relationship is that between the wife and her mother (maternal grandmother of the retarded child). One of the clearest findings in the Farber study was that when the parents of the retarded child were in frequent contact with the wife's mother, their marital integration tended to be high. However, when they were in frequent contact with the husband's mother, marital integration tended to be low. A review of case material provided insight into the findings. Ordinarily, the wife's mother showed much sympathy and understanding for her daughter's situation whereas the husband's mother generally blamed the wife for the retarded child. Sometimes, the mother-in-law implied that the child's retardation was punishment to the daugher-in-law for an earlier wrongdoing. To gain additional information on the relationship between the wife and her own mother, Farber examined the extent to which the parents regarded the retarded child as highly dependent. Presumably, if the contact with the wife's mother were related simply to the degree of the child's dependence, a good deal of the supportive relationship might be expected to come from physical assistance provided by the grandmother. Such was not the case. The findings suggested that the effect of seeing the mother rather than her assistance had a noticeable influence on marital integration.

Associations of parents for promoting the welfare of the handicapped reputedly provide another source of supportive interaction for parents of the handicapped. In his study of the development of such parents' groups, Katz suggested:

Participation in the groups may provide an outlet to parents for feelings of frustration and of inability as isolated individuals to cope with the adjustment problems of their family members and themselves. As such, the groups have a socializing and therapeutic value. Participation in the groups is of an intensive nature as compared with participation in other types of voluntary health and welfare organizations.[50]

However, Katz found that only a minority of the parents who join the association are active in its operation. Moreover, as the association becomes well established, much of the work is taken over by professional personnel such as social workers, psychologists, and teachers. Hence, the parents of handicapped children as a whole do not form a deviant community capable of exchanging sustained support. Instead, they must either withdraw socially from a hostile environment or seek support from people who are sympathetic (as the wife's mother).

IV. REARRANGEMENT OF AGE, SEX, AND GENERATION ROLES

In the crises described in an earlier section, there was a shifting in age, sex, and generation roles in the family—the alcoholic father was demoted to a child role; the work-

[50] Alfred H. Katz, *Parents of the Handicapped*, Springfield, Ill.: Thomas, 1961, p. 5.

ing children of the unemployed father demanded adulthood family status to accompany their support. Similarly,
among families with handicapped children, roles are ab-
dicated and reassigned. In these families, major problems
tend to arise when the handicapped child is unable to
perform parent-sponsored activities related to his independence. Veznedaroglu, in a study of mothers of asthmatic children, indicated that conflicts in handling situations occurred at those times in which the dependency
of the asthmatic children was the greatest.[51] These were at
mealtime, at bedtime, and while preparing for school. The
mothers had conflicts in handling naughty behavior at
these times and were unable to be consistent and firm.
Difficulties between mother and child also occurred during asthmatic attacks. However, the mothers generally
were intolerant toward aggressive behavior of the child
and used withdrawal of love rather than physical punishment as a means of controlling the child. This maternal
behavior suggests the infantilization of the handicapped
child.

The presence of a severely handicapped child in the
family is a factor that arrests the family life cycle.[52] This
effect has several features:

In their interaction with their children, parents tend
to assign a status to the child commensurate with the capabilities they impute to the child. The roles embodied in
the status are classified on the basis of an age grading. By

[51] K. N. Veznedaroglu, "A Study of Mothers' Discipline and
Control of Asthmatic Children," cited in "Abstracts of Theses,"
Smith College Studies of Social Work, 32 (1961), pp. 69-70.
[52] Farber, "Effects of a Severely Mentally Retarded Child on
Family Integration," *op. cit.*

definition, normally, mental age is approximately equal to chronological age. Age grading in a culture is regarded as a psychological and social activity rather than a chronological variable. (For example, the chronologically middle-aged severely retarded individual is generally regarded as a "boy" or "girl" by those with whom he interacts. According to Eaton, one religious group, the Hutterites, excludes the mentally retarded from adult responsibility by canceling baptism requirements, thereby giving them a moral status of children.[53])

As the normal child proceeds in his career, the parents normally tend to shift correspondingly in their self-conceptions and roles. With respect to their normal children, ideally, parents continually redefine their roles, obligations, and values to adjust to the changing role of the child. As the normal child performs new parent-sponsored activities, he moves toward adulthood. With respect to their retarded children, the parents' role is fairly constant. Regardless of his birth order in the family, the severely handicapped child eventually becomes the youngest child socially. This progressive movement of the retarded child toward the youngest-child role is indicated by Farber's study of sibling interaction.[54] He found that interaction between the retarded child and a normal child approximately the same age tends to be on an equalitarian basis when the retarded child is young; as the children grow

[53] Joseph W. Eaton and R. J. Weil, *Culture and Mental Disorders*, Glencoe, Ill.: Free Press, 1955.

[54] Bernard Farber, "Family Organization and Crisis: Maintenance of Integration in Families with a Severely Mentally Retarded Child," *Monographs of the Society for Research in Child Development*, 25 (1960), No. 1 (Serial No. 75).

older, the normal sibling, especially the sister, tends to assume a superordinate position in the relationship. In addition, like the oldest child in large families, the normal sibling tends to be placed in a position of caring for the severely handicapped child. Shere found that, where one twin is cerebral-palsied, the normal twin tends to be given many responsibilities in caring for the handicapped twin and is under pressure to perform his own school and home duties well (more than the amount Shere thought was appropriate for the age and sex of the child).[55]

The severely handicapped child at home does not engage in dating and courtship, belong to organizations, seek part-time employment, or take part in other activities characteristic of adolescents. In his progressive movement to the youngest-child status in the family, the severely retarded child thus tends not merely to slow down movement in the family cycle but also to prevent the development of the later stages in the cycle. Hence, because of his inability to perform his age-sex roles, the handicapped child stimulates a revision of age, sex, and generation roles of other members of the family.

V. THE FREEZING-OUT

The distinction between the domestic group and the family appears useful in discussing the freezing-out of the deviant family member. The end product of the freezing-out process (when the deviant family member is a handicapped child) is the permanent hospitalization or institu-

[55] Marie Orr Shere, "Socio-emotional Factors in Families of the Twin with Cerebral Palsy," *Exceptional Children*, 22 (1955), pp. 197-199, 206, 208.

tionalization of the child. The act of placing the child in an institution or a hospital takes the child out of the domestic group but not out of the family. His dual status (being an outsider with respect to domestic group and an insider with respect to family) presents the parents of a handicapped child with another predicament: Should the family continue to treat the institutionalized individual as a member?

Factors in institutionalization of the mentally retarded were studied by Saenger.[56] In his investigation of 1050 families in New York City, Saenger found that:

1. The greater the degree of mental retardation, the higher was the probability of institutionalization.

2. Secondary physical handicaps are not important factors in commitment. Persons with severe problems in coordination, cerebral palsy, and epilepsy were institutionalized only slightly more often than others.

3. Although there appears to be no difference in the incidence of severe mental retardation among various income levels and ethnic groups, the majority of persons institutionalized came from low-income families and from Negro and Puerto Rican families.

4. Among the severely retarded from middle-class families, adjustment problems of the child in the home (not the community) were a major factor in commitment to an institution.

Downey investigated both the willingness to institutionalize the retarded child and the effects of institution-

[56] Saenger, *op. cit.*

alization on the parents.[57] He found that those parents of high socioeconomic status who do institutionalize the child do so early and then afterwards "forget" about the child, whereas parents of low socioeconomic status try to delay placing the child, and after the child is placed tend to continue their contact with the child. Downey's findings also indicated that parents of low socioeconomic status tend to report that intrafamily considerations were foremost in their institutionalizing the retarded child; families of high socioeconomic status give as reasons for placing the child extrafamily considerations such as neighborhood relationships of the entire family, career and educational aspirations of other family members, and advice of friends and physicians.

The findings in Downey's study are consistent with those of Farber, Jenné, and Toigo in their investigation of families with retarded children at home.[58] They studied effects of socioeconomic status upon parents' reported willingness to institutionalize their retarded child. In families at low socioeconomic levels, the mother was generally more willing than the father to place the retarded child in an institution. However, in those low-status families in which marital integration was low, husbands were also willing to institutionalize the retarded child. In high-status families, degree of marital integration did not affect the willingness of the husband to institutionalize the retarded child, but there was a linear, positive relationship

[57] Kenneth Downey, "Parental Interest in the Institutionalized Mentally Retarded Child," unpublished doctoral dissertation, University of Illinois, 1962.

[58] Farber, Jenné, and Toigo, *op. cit.*

between the number of children at home and the husband's willingness to institutionalize a child.

On the basis of the findings on socioeconomic status in the Downey and Farber-Jenné-Toigo studies, it appears that social status influences institutionalization and its consequences through the definition of family problems. In the families of high socioeconomic status, planning and concern for the future life of the normal children are factors in institutionalization. These factors are consistent with the delayed-gratification patterns generally found in families with fathers who are professionals or proprietors. Delayed-gratification norms, in turn, are related to the maintenance of status. On the other hand, the closer relationship between low marital integration and willingness to institutionalize in the low-status family suggests institutionalization as a strategy to counteract a more immediate family problem. After the child has been institutionalized, he can still be considered as a family member or can be deemed separated. Among families of low socioeconomic status, with immediate problems solved by institutionalization, the family can regard the child as a member living away from home. For families of higher socioeconomic status, with emphasis upon aspirations of members of the domestic group (where sponsored independence can be stimulated and supervised), the parents often regard institutionalization as exempting them from all but legal responsibilities.

The influence of religion upon the decision to institutionalize the retarded child was also investigated by Farber, Jenné, and Toigo. Their findings suggest that Protestant husbands in families with low marital integration were more willing to place their retarded child in an institution than were Protestant husbands in more highly integrated families. On the other hand, Jewish husbands, regardless of marital integration or degree of emotional impact, showed much reluctance to place the retarded child in an institution. (Saenger also found Jewish families the most reluctant to commit their children.[59]) Catholic husbands showed only a very slightly greater tendency to commit the retarded child when marital integration was low than when marital integration was high. Generally, the willingness for Catholic husbands fell between that of Protestant fathers and that of Jewish fathers.

The Jewish mothers generally showed even greater reluctance to commit the retarded child than did their husbands. No clear pattern was found for Protestant and Catholic mothers. For mothers in all three religious groups, those with marital-integration scores in the middle range indicated a greater willingness to institutionalize the child than did mothers in the more extreme high and low marital-integration ranges. More study is needed to explain the effects of religion on institutionalization practices.

In summary: Various factors are related to the institutionalization of the retarded child. The greater the degree of mental retardation in the child, the higher was the probability that he would be institutionalized. The lower the socioeconomic level of the family, the higher was the likelihood of institutionalization. However, families of different socioeconomic levels also differed in their reasons for placing the child in an institution. Families at the

---

[59] Saenger, *op. cit.*

lower socioeconomic levels tended to place the child to solve immediate problems in family relations. They tended to institutionalize the child at a later age than did those of higher socioeconomic levels, but they also remained in contact with the child after institutionalization. Families of higher socioeconomic level tended to commit the child on the basis of the relationship of the rest of the family to the community. The families of higher socioeconomic level considered opinions of others as important and took into account the careers of the other children. Religion also played a role in willingness of parents to institutionalize retarded children. In Protestant families, as in families of lower socioeconomic level, degree of marital integration was a factor in the willingness of parents to institutionalize them. Jewish families were generally very reluctant to institutionalize their retarded children. Catholic families fell between Protestant and Jewish families in their willingness to place their children in an institution.

ALTERNATIVES TO FREEZING OUT

In Chapter 8 on predicaments in family organization, it was noted that many families with mentally retarded children were able to establish priorities to maintain a congenial, integrated family life. A part of this inhibition of the freezing-out process might be attributed to the creativity and adaptability needed to develop strategies of organization. However, the freezing-out process was also inhibited by a minimal amount of disruption of family roles. For example, marital integration of the parents at the time of the study was high under the following combination of conditions: marital integration prior to the birth of the retarded child had been high, the retarded child was a girl and was not the first-born, and the family was in a low socioeconomic position.

Various alternatives to institutionalization of retarded children have been proposed to limit the disruptive effects of a severely retarded child on the family.

One strategy which has been developed to minimize the disrupting effects of the retarded child on the family (as well as to teach the child habits of self-care) is that of sending him to a day school. Many parents are frank in stating that they favor day schools for handicapped children as a benefit to themselves as well as to the children. However, studies by Hottel and by Goldstein[60] suggest that, after a temporary euphoria in the first year of the school program, there is little general effect upon family relations. On the other hand, Guenther found a decrease in the emphasis of parents of trainable retarded children on academic skills.[61] The study by Tallman indicated that the day-school strategy should be regarded in terms of its interaction with other characteristics of the parents to determine its effects upon the child.[62] Tallman found that only among the highly adaptable mothers did an increase in the child's social competence occur. How-

[60] John V. Hottel, "An Evaluation of Tennessee's Day Class Program for Severely Mentally Retarded Children," Nashville, Tenn.: George Peabody College for Teachers, 1958; and Herbert Goldstein, *Report Number Two on Study Projects for Trainable Mentally Handicapped Children,* Springfield, Ill.: Superintendent of Public Instruction, 1956.

[61] R. J. Guenther, *The Michigan Demonstration Research Project for the Mentally Retarded,* State Advisory Board for Michigan Demonstration Research Project, 1956.

[62] Tallman, *op. cit.*

ever, if anything, there was a tendency for both mothers and fathers to drop in adaptability ratings over the two-year study period. Yet, since Baldwin's investigations with the Fels scale suggest a lessening of tolerance of deviance with age of the child, perhaps the Tallman data actually represent a relative elevation of adaptability over what might have occurred without day-school classes.

The influence of the day school upon the role of the father in the family with a handicapped child is suggested in findings by Tallman.[63] He found that the time fathers spent with their retarded children was associated with the mother's adaptability in handling the child. The effect of the fathers was not merely that of a surrogate. When Tallman compared children whose fathers were present in the home with children whose fathers were absent, the father-present group showed greater gains in social competence during the child's period of training in a special group. This finding suggests that day-school attendance facilitated the ability of the father to play a supportive, integrative role in the family. If so, day-school attendance by the retarded child may enable families to develop consistent child-oriented, home-oriented, or parent-oriented patterns of family organization.

Another strategy which has been applied to minimize the disruptive effects of the retarded child is to limit the number of siblings to those already born. The parents' concern with coping with the handicapped child, as well as fear of another defective child, tends to limit births in families with a retarded child. In his study of 201 families with retarded children in England, Holt indicated that

[63] *Ibid.*

although additional pregnancies were theoretically possible in 160 of the families, 101 families did not want more children.[64] In 90 of these 101 families, the restriction appeared to stem directly from the presence of the retarded child. Similarly, Tizard and Grad found that there was a tendency to avoid having additional children.[65] In each group, however, there was a very small percentage of families in which other children were wanted because of the defective child. Perhaps a survey of size of families with handicapped children would show a relationship between severity of handicap and propensity toward family limitation when appropriate statistical controls are made for socioeconomic status, religion, and age of the parents.

Still other strategies have been developed to inhibit the freezing-out process. These include community day-care and training centers which accommodate handicapped residents on a short-run basis, housekeeping assistance to lighten the work load of the parents and siblings, assumption of the grandparents' role by elderly persons in the community to provide emotional support and baby-sitting services, and short-term institutionalization during periods of family stress. These other strategies, however, have not yet been evaluated in terms of their effects on family relations.

Family Crisis and Orderly Replacement

The previous sections have indicated that the crisis process involves (a) attempting to handle deviance within

[64] K. S. Holt, "The Influence of a Retarded Child on Family Limitation," *Journal of Mental Deficiency Research*, 2 (1958), pp. 28-36.

[65] Tizard and Grad, *op. cit.*

existing family arrangements, (b) defining the nature of the problem in terms of the ways in which the deviance distorts and disrupts previous coalitions in the family, (c) revising coalitions with extrafamily individuals and groups, (d) rearranging age, sex, and generation roles in the family, and, finally, (e) freezing out the deviant member.

Ways in which the crisis process is related to process of orderly replacement can be elicited by asking the question: What would happen to norms and practices of family maintenance if the crisis process were not permitted to run its course? Imagine what would happen if the crisis process were inhibited at any stage.

(a) If a particular deviance can be handled within existing family arrangements, then the deviance remains an individual problem but is irrelevant with respect to family organization. Hence any deviance which can be handled through existing family arrangements does not interfere with orderly replacement.

(b) If the deviance distorts and disrupts previous coalitions in the family and the crisis process is held at that stage, congenial family relationships will tend to disintegrate and life careers of family members will lose their reciprocal influence upon one another. With the disintegration of the family as a set of careers, orderly replacement will be impeded.

(c) If the deviance has distorted previously existing family relationships and has forced a revision of extrafamily interaction, but the crisis process does not develop into the next stage, then the family members generally find new extrafamily commitments to replace family commitments. These extrafamily commitments may accelerate the disintegration of the family. However, some extrafamily commitments may stimulate movement to the next stage.

(d) If the family has readjusted its age, sex, and generation roles to cope with the deviant individual, the family can remain integrated (perhaps even more highly integrated) as a set of careers. However, the family can no longer operate as a bearer of norms for maintaining nuclear family life from one generation to the next. It will have introduced new norms into family life. As Farber and Jenné found, siblings who interact constantly with their retarded brothers or sisters are more oriented toward humanitarian and welfare life goals than are siblings who do not interact frequently. The *in*frequent interactors are more interested in maintaining congenial interpersonal relations in the future.[66] Thus the family in which age, sex, and generation roles are revised will continue to exist but with somewhat different norms and values than its neighbors.

(e) If the deviant individual frozen out is a child, then the normal individuals in the family can assume those roles which they regard as appropriate to the family life cycle, and orderly replacement is sustained.

The total effect of the crisis process on orderly replacement is then: After the family finds it cannot handle the deviant individual within existing family arrangements, possibilities of orderly replacement are small unless the deviant individual is frozen out.

[66] Bernard Farber and William C. Jenné, "Interaction with Retarded Siblings and Life Goals of Children," *Marriage and Family Living*, 25 (1963), pp. 96-98.

Selected Readings

General statements regarding family problems are found in:

Brim, Orville G., Jr., Roy W. Fairchild, and Edgar F. Borgatta. "Relations between Family Problems," *Marriage and Family Living*, 23 (1961), pp. 219-226.

Goode, William J. "Family Disorganization," in Robert K. Merton and Robert A. Nesbit (eds.), *Contemporary Social Problems*, Harcourt Brace, 1961.

Hill, Reuben. "Generic Features of Families under Stress," *Social Casework*, 39 (1958), pp. 139-150.

Specific kinds of family crises are discussed in:

Bakke, E. Wight. *The Unemployed Worker*, Yale University Press, 1940.

Clausen, John A., and Marian Radke Yarrow (Issue Editors). "The Impact of Mental Illness on the Family," *Journal of Social Issues*, 11 (1955), No. 4.

Day, Barbara R. "Alcoholism and the Family," *Marriage and Family Living*, 23 (1961), pp. 253-258.

Jordan, Thomas E. "Research on the Handicapped Child and the Family," *Merrill-Palmer Quarterly*, 8 (1962), pp. 243-260.

Parsons, Talcott, and Renee Fox. "Illness, Therapy and the Modern Urban American Family," *Journal of Social Issues*, 8 (1952), pp. 31-44.

Shere, Marie Orr. "Socio-emotional Factors in Families of the Twin with Cerebral Palsy," *Exceptional Children*, 22 (1955), pp. 197-199, 206, 208.

Vogel, Ezra F., and Norman W. Bell. "The Emotionally Disturbed Child as the Family Scapegoat," in Norman W. Bell and Ezra F. Vogel (eds.), *A Modern Introduction to the Family*, Free Press, 1960, pp. 382-397.

11 *Socialization in the Contemporary Family*

The relationship between culture and personality has long interested social scientists. Insight into this relationship can lead to an understanding of "the intergenerational transfer of culture ('enculturation' or socialization), culture change, the institutionalization of modes of coping with individual diversity, and the like."[1] Without reference to the relationship between culture and personality, it is not possible to answer even apparently simple questions such as: What is mental retardation? What is mental illness? What is competence in interpersonal relations? Each of these questions can be answered in a meaningful way only if concepts of norms, values, and institutions prevalent in a society are introduced as a base line for describing central tendencies or variations in personality among members of the society.

[1] Anthony F. C. Wallace, *Culture and Personality*, New York: Random House, 1961, p. 3.

Many anthropologists assume the replication of one generation by the next in personality. Gorer believes that there is sufficient social continuity in any particular society so that "the observable adults shared experiences and vicissitudes of childhood similar to those which observable infants and children are now undergoing; and further, that observable infants and children will grow up to have shared predispositions and characters similar to those of observable adults."[2] Hence, rituals, ceremonials, family patterns and other cultural characteristics, like genes, carry within them the genetic information to make "of each cohort a replica of its adult predecessor."[3] Implicit in the replication viewpoint is the assumption that each parent wishes his children to become adults of the same kind as himself.

Often the rituals involved in socialization of the young occupy a long time. These rituals, carried out generation after generation, act to replicate the experiences of successive cohorts of members of the society. The initiation rituals of the Tiwi of Australia, described by Hart, illustrate the stabilizing influence of fixed practices on socialization in successive generations.

For females there were no initiation ceremonies, but for males it was a long drawn-out and elaborate affair, marked by successive stages or grades which began with the status of *Marukumarni,* which a boy entered when he was about fourteen, and did not end finally until he was around twenty-four. . . . The group of men, necessarily older than himself, who

[2] Cited in Wallace, *op. cit.,* p. 112.
[3] *Ibid.*

initiated a youth thereby put him under obligation to them the rest of his life. They "did something for him" and years later would bring it up if his subsequent behavior seemed to be directed against their interests. The obligations contracted in initiation, like obligations contracted at burials or mourning ceremonies, were woven into the kinship and influence systems; indeed the relation of a youth to the men who initiated him was often the beginning of a satellite-patron relationship that lasted half his life.

. . . It was the duty of male cross-cousins to initiate their wives' little brothers, but in true Tiwi style the father had to request them to do it, and they [the male cross-cousins] counted it in their tallies of what they owed him [the father] and what he owed them.

Though the father instigated and stage managed the whole affair, he and his household were always thunderstruck when the cross-cousins—armed to the teeth and painted like a war party—arrived at his camp one evening and proceeded to carry off forcibly the yelling 14-year-old. . . . From then on, until the the final stage (*Mikingula*) at age 24-26, the boy was completely under the authority of the men who carried him off. During these approximately ten to twelve years, he spent much of the time along with them in the bush where the group lived a monastic existence, as a small band of isolates, speaking to no one (especially not females) and obtaining their own food. During these phases the tutors guarded the boy as if he were literally a prisoner and taught him all the things—chiefly ritual matters—that grown men should know. At intervals the youth was allowed to go home, on weekend leaves so to speak, but when at home he had to observe all the silences, the modest demeanor, the taboos and the austerities of the isolated life. In monastic language, he was under a strict rule of obedience to his tutors.

Breaking in on the long years of austerity, spent either in seclusion in the bush or in *pukimani* at home, were periodic collective ceremonies when the youth was ritually advanced from one stage of initiation to the next. . . . At these ceremonies the youths were handled in batches or classes, all the boys in one grade being ritually advanced to the next grade, and the top grade or final class being formally graduated as fully initiated men.[4]

With the strict regime in maturation of males of each succeeding generation, socialization was such among the Tiwi that: (a) men regarded women mainly as chattels to be used in gaining influence and power in their "games" of exchange of obligations, (b) there was "an enormous frequency of disputes, fights, duels, and war parties arising directly or indirectly out of cases of seduction," and (c) men made alliances with other men but apparently established few close personal relationships with them.[5] Thus, among the Tiwi (at least until the coming of outsiders) the long initiation process sustained a continuity in personality characteristics through stable socialization practices from generation to generation.

The wide spectrum of experiences in contemporary families offers a sharp contrast to the homogeneous experiences in the ritualized socialization process among the Tiwi. This chapter will deal mainly with the variations in socialization practices in contemporary America and their implications for orderly replacement. However, socialization of children in all societies occurs in the context of a

[4] C. W. M. Hart and Arnold R. Pilling, *The Tiwi of North Australia*, New York: Holt, 1960, pp. 93-94.
[5] *Ibid.*

small intimate group.[6] The small group generally involves at least one mother and children. Because of the composition of the small socializing group, some factors in socialization are common to most sectors of modern society. The first section will investigate family-group factors in socialization. Factors to be discussed include sex and birth order of children, mothering and fathering behavior, and the relationship between the parents. The second section will indicate cultural factors in socialization in the United states from a historical perspective. The third section will study cultural factors in socialization from a cross-sectional view, with attention to differences in socioeconomic levels, ethnic character, and religious preference. The discussion of cultural factors will be restricted to those bearing on socialization within the family.

Family-Group Factors in Socialization

Despite the variations among the various contemporary societies in ways of socializing children, there are also similarities arising mainly from the biological character of the family group—the long period of maturation in humans, the sex of individuals, and the birth order of siblings.

Parsons characterized the basic pattern of family life as resting on two axes—a generational axis providing a basis for power differentiation, and a sex-role axis.[7] Parsons then regarded as the essential problem in socializa-

[6] M. J. Levy, Jr. and L. A. Fallers, "The Family: Some Comparative Considerations," *American Anthropologist*, 61 (1959), pp. 647-651.

[7] Talcott Parsons and Robert F. Bales, *The Family, Socialization and Interaction Process*, Glencoe, Ill.: Free Press, 1955.

tion the attainment of appropriate sex-role identification within the nuclear family. The generational axis is mainly a means for enabling the parents to control the socialization of children.

The Parsonian emphasis on sex-role development is reinforced by results of several investigations. Sears, Maccoby, and Levin found that mothers of five-year-old boys have more often than mothers of girls applied physical punishment, but less often (a) placed high demands on the child for table manners and neatness, (b) praised the child for "good" behavior, or (c) threatened withdrawal of love for "bad" behavior. Mothers of boys placed greater emphasis on the child's attending college and encouraged the child "to fight back if another child started a fight."[8] Koch's study of 360 five- and six-year-old children from native-born white intact two-child families in Chicago showed that boys more often than girls viewed their mothers as siding with the sibling. Teachers in this study rated girls as more affectionate, more obedient, and less resistant than boys.[9] Zelditch found comparable tendencies in masculine-feminine differentiation in family relations in his cross-cultural analysis of role specialization in the nuclear family.[10]

In contrast to the emphasis upon sex-role differentiation by Parsons, Bossard indicated that "one of the most

[8] Robert R. Sears, Eleanor E. Maccoby, and Harry Levin, *Patterns of Child Rearing*, Evanston: Row, 1957, p. 403.

[9] Helen L. Koch, "The Relation of Certain Formal Attributes of Siblings to Attitudes Held toward Each Other and toward Their Parents," *Monographs of the Society for Research in Child Development*, 25 (1960), No. 4 (Serial No. 78).

[10] Morris Zelditch, in Parsons and Bales, *op. cit.*, pp. 307-351.

obvious forms of specialization of role in a large family is that which results from order of birth."[11] Bossard classified types of role specialization in terms of birth order as: (a) the eldest as the responsible child, (b) the second as the sociable or popular child, and (c) the last child as the spoiled child. He indicated that other role specialties existed in the sibling group but he did not ascribe a modal birth order to these roles. The other sibling role specialties were (a) the socially ambitious child, (b) the studious type, (c) the self-centered isolate, (d) the irresponsible child, and (e) the special-problem child.[12] Koch also found birth-order influences on socialization. First-born children tended more often than second-born to view their mother as favoring the sibling and to see the father as impartial in his treatment.

Sex and birth order have combined effects on socialization that are perhaps even more significant than either of them alone for the transmission of family roles and values. In Koch's study, boys with an older brother were increasingly close to the mother as difference in age between the two boys widened. However, with greater age disparity between a boy and an older sister, the boy was less close to his mother.

Vuyk, in a replication of the Koch study in Europe, reported differences in the personality of a boy with a younger brother as compared with a boy with a younger sister.[13] Vuyk, like Koch, found much jealousy in same-

[11] James H. S. Bossard and Eleanor S. Boll, *The Large Family System*, Philadelphia: University of Pennsylvania Press, 1956, p. 221.

[12] *Ibid.*, pp. 201-221.

[13] Rita Vuyk, *Das Kind in der Zweikinder Familie*, Bern: Verlag Hans Huber, 1959.

sex pairs. Moreover, when Brim reanalyzed the Koch data, he found that "cross-sex siblings tend to assimilate traits of the opposite sex, and that this effect is most pronounced in the younger of the two siblings."[14] These findings point toward a greater differentiation between masculine and feminine personality traits and role performance in those societies in which boys and girls are segregated than in societies permitting much cross-sex interaction of children.

The generation "axis" supplements sex and birth order as determinants in socialization.

The major activity between generations relevant for socialization is "mothering." The term "mothering" has been applied to the large variety of activities normally found in child raising.

Sewell has found that the particular practices in mothering of young children appear to have little influence on later personality.[15] Specifically, Sewell's study indicated that later personality adjustment and personal traits were not related to the following infant experiences: breast feeding versus bottle feeding, demand feeding versus regular schedule, gradual weaning versus abrupt weaning, early versus late bowel training, early versus late bladder training, punishment versus nonpunishment for toilet-training accidents, sleeping with the mother versus sleeping alone, high versus low personal security, and favorable versus unfavorable toilet-training and feeding experiences.

In spite of the negative results in the Sewell study,

[14] Orville G. Brim, "Family Structure and Sex-Role Learning by Children: A Further Analysis of Helen Koch's Data," *Sociometry*, 21 (1958), pp. 1-16.

[15] William H. Sewell, "Infant Training and the Personality of the Child," *American Journal of Sociology*, 58 (1952), pp. 150-159.

other investigators who focused upon grosser variations in mothering have discerned some effects of mothering on socialization of children. For example, Kagan and Moss found that the mother's education was a more important factor than the father's in determining the tested intelligence (IQ) of children.[16] Casler reviewed the results of investigations dealing with children who were deprived of mothering.[17] He found that emotional, physical, and intellectual malfunctioning occurs among children in institutions more often than among children living with their families. This malfunctioning, however, may not always be attributable to the deprivation of maternal love. Instead, he suggested "deprivation of maternal love can have ill effects only after specific affective responsiveness has been achieved by the child (usually at about the age of six months)." He attributed deviations in children maternally deprived before this age to the lack of stimulation. This deprivation of tactile, verbal, and other stimuli does not permit the child's perceptual processes to mature. The child does not develop the ability to perceive and utilize roles and values of family life in the ways intended by his parents. Hence, with absence or deprivation of "mothering," the child cannot become an efficient transmitting agent of family culture from one generation to the next. While the norms in some societies encourage mother-

[16] Jerome Kagan and Howard A. Moss, "Parental Correlates of Child's IQ and Height: A Cross-Validation of the Berkeley Growth Study Results," *Child Development*, 30 (1959), pp. 325-332.

[17] Lawrence Casler, "Maternal Deprivation: A Critical Review of the Literature," *Monographs of the Society for Research in Child Development*, 26 (1961), No. 2 (Serial No. 80).

ing of the child more than those of other societies, nowhere is mothering a forbidden activity.[18]

Mothering is not necessarily a constant attribute even within any family. Mothering depends upon a number of factors in the family group. For example, the Sears study suggests that both mothers and fathers in American families tend to be "delighted" less and less in each succeeding pregnancy with the prospect of another child. This decline in viewing pregnancy as a happy event is apparently reflected in the decreasing percentage of mothers who breast feed their children, in greater strictness about noise, in increased severity of weaning, and in greater permissiveness of aggression toward neighborhood children.[19] All of these tendencies suggest a decline in mothering behavior with each succeeding birth.

The decline in mothering behavior with increase in birth order is related to the interaction between the father and the child. Sears and his associates found that fathers shared the responsibility for determining policies in raising the oldest child, but not children later in birth order. Apparently the fathers' participation encourages various kinds of mothering behavior.

Paternal participation in helping with the oldest child may explain the finding that the eldest child receives more spankings than the other children (about equally by mother and father). For children later in birth order, the mother spanks more than the father, but at the same time,

[18] Beatrice B. Whiting, ed., *Six Cultures*, New York: Wiley, 1963, *passim*.
[19] Sears, Maccoby, and Levin, *op. cit.*

she is more demonstrative in her affection toward them. This difference displays how the increase in role specialization of the parents over the family life cycle influences socialization: there is a decline in spanking (a masculine mode of social control); there is an increase in demonstration of affection (a feminine mode of behavior); and the father withdraws from actively engaging in socialization practices. The study by Sears, Maccoby, and Levin utilized a sample of 379 mothers with one of their children in kindergarten. Their findings were supported by Henry's investigation of 1335 high-school students in Massachusetts and of 391 college students and 226 high-school students in Tennessee.[20] Both the Massachusetts and Tennessee samples indicated that the eldest child tends to view his father as the principal disciplinarian whereas the youngest child views his mother as the principal disciplinarian. The significance of these findings is suggested by another Henry study of 765 Air Force men on the tendency to blame one's self for things said in the heat of argument which hurt the feelings of others. He found that men who reported that "they would blame themselves and would not blame the other person are most likely to perceive mother as the principal disciplinarian."[21] Moreover, the authoritarian-personality studies indicated that an individual with a firm, authoritarian father would tend to project blame for problems on others.[22] These findings

[20] Andrew F. Henry, "Sibling Structure and Perception of the Disciplinary Roles of Parents," *Sociometry*, 20 (1957), pp. 67-74.

[21] Andrew F. Henry, "Family Role Structure and Self-Blame," *Social Forces*, 25 (1956), pp. 34-38.

[22] T. W. Adorno, E. Frenkel-Brunswik, D. J. Levinson, and R. N. Sanford, *The Authoritarian Personality*, New York: Harper, 1950.

suggest that the role of the father in the socialization of children also deserves consideration.

There has been less study of "fathering" behavior (what fathers do in the socialization of children) than of mothering behavior.

The question about what happens when the child is deprived of mothering has its analog concerning the effects of depriving the child of fathering. Tiller studied 80 Norwegian children, 40 of whom were sons and daughters of sailors at sea.[23] The other 40 were of comparable socioeconomic level in families with a father present. Tiller found that both the sons and the daughters of the sailors indicated greater maternal overprotection than did the control children. Moreover, the sailors' sons were more like the control girls in lack of aggression shown in doll play than they were like the control boys. Presumably, like those subjects in the Henry study who perceived their mothers as primary disciplinarians, the children of absent sailors would also tend toward self-blame. In addition to overprotection and lack of aggression, paradoxically Tiller's findings also indicate *exaggerated* masculine behavior of boys in father-absent families. Exaggerated masculine behavior occurs even *without* maternal overprotection in those urban lower classes in which families experience much turnover in husbands. From these studies, the role of the father appears to be the crucial variable in masculine identification of boys. Mussen and Distler found that if the father is very active in the son's upbringing (by tak-

[23] Per Olav Tiller, "Father Absence and Personality Development of Children in Sailor Families. A Preliminary Research Report," in Nels Anderson, ed., *Studies of the Family*, Goettingen: Vandenhoeck and Ruprecht, 1957, pp. 115-133.

ing care of the child and participating in child-raising policies), the boy is likely to develop strong identification with the father and to acquire masculine styles of action which the parents consider appropriate.[24]

The findings on the influence of fathering on socialization suggest a continuum in the socialization of boys. In the absence of fathering (in combination with a high degree of mothering), the boy child incorporates feminine styles of behavior. With both mothering and fathering minimized, he has difficulty in developing any kind of stable familial roles. With a high degree of fathering, the boy develops a strong masculine identification. Since the father participates more in the upbringing of the first child, masculinity in boys may well be related to birth order. Moreover, since in case of divorce, the children are awarded to the mother, divorce may also affect the masculine identity of boys (if the divorce occurred early in their lives and the mother-custodian's remarriage did not follow shortly thereafter).

Because the family in Western society normally includes both a mother and a father, the influence of marital interaction upon socialization of children assumes a measure of importance. Farber studied the relationship between marital integration and perceptions by children and their parents of the extent to which the parents were dissatisfied with the children's behavior.[25] His study suggested the following:

[24] Paul Mussen and Luther Distler, "Child-Rearing Antecedents of Masculine Identification in Kindergarten Boys," *Child Development*, 31 (1960), pp. 89-100.

[25] Bernard Farber, "Marital Integration as a Factor in Parent-Child Relations," *Child Development*, 33 (1962), pp. 1-14.

(a) There is a carry-over of role relationships in the marriage to the mother-child relationship and to the mother's development of a maternal role model for the children. In the family with a low-integration marriage, there appears to be a carry-over of conflict-role relationships from the marriage to the mother-child relationship and to the development of a mother-role model focusing upon hostility and frustration.

(b) The mother's role is essentially one of communicating the father's viewpoint to the children in the high-integration marriage in a positive, noncontroversial way (that is, buttressing the father's values and norms in the transmission). By an effective mediating role, the mother also reinforces the stature of the father as a masculine role model for the son. In general, the findings showed that the cross-sex parent acts as a mediator between the child and the other parent.

(c) The presence of a clear-cut consistent ordering of values in the family has a greater influence on the accuracy of a boy's perception of his parents' dissatisfaction with his performance of instrumental activities than on the accuracy of a girl's perception. The presence of parental consensus on domestic values then becomes an important factor in the transmission of family values and norms to boys.

(d) The child's perception of the mother's dissatisfaction with him is more a product of the quality of the marital relationship than of the parent's actual feeling toward the child.

In summary: several family-group factors influence socialization of children. When interaction between siblings is not limited by avoidance relationships, then sex and birth order influence personality development. Particular combinations of sex and birth order lead to jealousy (especially for first-born girls) and to the learning of roles and norms of behavior appropriate to the opposite sex (in cross-sex siblings). Although mothering as such may not be predictive of particular personality traits in children, the absence or deprivation of mothering may lead to failure of children to assume conventional roles and norms of behavior in adulthood. The amount of mothering behavior tends to decline for children later in the birth order. This decline is related to the amount of participation of the father in bringing up the child; the father's participation is highest for the oldest child. The father's participation in bringing up the child is negatively related to the child's tendency to introject guilt over mishaps and positively related to masculine identification in boys. The marital integration of the parents influences socialization through (a) providing role models, (b) transferring the kind of behavior directed toward the spouse to relations with children, (c) providing a coherent value system for the children (especially boys), (d) utilizing the mother as a communicator of the father's values to the children, and (e) permitting the cross-sex parent to act as mediator in situations of potential conflict between the child and the other parent.

Unlike other areas of family life such as marital relations, the relationship between family-group factors and socialization of children has received little systematic study. Hence, the inferences drawn here are to be regarded as suggestive rather than conclusive.

The discussion of family-group factors in socialization

assumed that the child could get along with only two parents. But are two parents enough? Many social scientists have been concerned with the problem of why there should be two parents instead of one; but in almost every society *more* than two adults are involved in the socialization of the child. These other agents, quasi parents, are generally outside the nuclear family. A previous chapter contended that social criticism can be best enforced by agents outside the nuclear family. The "third parent," whether he is a relative or teacher or minister, acts in the role of social critic in supervising the socialization of children. In some societies, this social-critic role is carried on at a school (among the Tiwi or in contemporary society) and in other societies by a relative (the mother's brother in matrilineal groups such as the Ashanti). In any event, the "third parent" serves to stabilize the socialization process and to counteract particular problems related to family crisis or to complexities of the family life cycle. Perhaps sociologists should attempt to determine systematically the number and kinds of persons who are directly involved in the socialization of children in contemporary societies.

Cultural Factors in Socialization in the Family: Historical Perspective

The preceding section indicated several family-group factors in the socialization of children. This section discusses changes in child raising over four periods of American history: (a) the colonial period to the Civil War, (b) the Civil War to World War I, (c) the years following World War I, and (d) the years following World War II.[26]

[26] See Daniel R. Miller and Guy E. Swanson, *The Changing American Parent*, New York: Wiley, 1958, pp. 3-29.

THE COLONIAL PERIOD TO THE CIVIL WAR

Historians of the American family tend to place in a single category the family life of the colonial period and that following the Revolutionary War. According to Calhoun:

Independence signified no fundamental revolution in the currents of social life, and colonial traditions passed on unbroken into the folkways of the republic; for until the Civil War the population was distinctly rural, and urban sophistication had acquired no dominant influence over the thoughts, standards, and habits of the major part of the inhabitants of the United States.[27]

This discussion will indicate briefly the family life of the different colonies and then touch upon trends following the Revolutionary War.

Even in the early periods of American history, child raising differed from one area to another and in the different social classes.

Child raising was considered as a family or kin activity, not one in the realm of public or governmental control. Calhoun reported that in the New England colonies, socialization took the form of disciplinary action: "Home discipline was relentless. Stern and arbitrary command compelled obedience, submissive and generally complete. . . . adults believed in the rod as an instrument of subjugation."[28]

Rationalization for stern disciplining came from Calvinist thought, which regarded the child's impulsive will

[27] Arthur W. Calhoun, *A Social History of the American Family,* New York: Barnes and Noble, 1945, Vol. 2, p. 11.

[28] *Ibid.*, Vol. 1, p. 112.

as a force which must be subdued for the child's own good and for the glory of God.

However, emphasis upon discipline in the colonies was based not only on religious ideas but also on popular notions of child raising. Calhoun indicates that John Locke's *Thoughts on Education,* which was published in 1690, was popular in the American colonies. Locke's *Thoughts* were suited to the harshness of pioneer life. Locke suggested that children be given cold baths, that their feet be soaked in cold water, that they go without hats, and that they engage in other activities to toughen them.

Yet, in the presence of the stern methods of discipline, New England colonial children took part in numerous playful and mischievous activities. Boys pulled the hair of girls "in the time of public worship" and pushed girls on the ice, played "at football" in the streets and played "idle tricks because 'twas first of April." Calhoun reports that there were many accounts of "mixt dancings, unlawful gamings, extravagence in dress, light behavior" and similar activities. Thus, in spite of (or perhaps because of) the harsh discipline, socialization of the New England colonial children permitted the development of a playful element in personality.

Among the Pennsylvania Germans, emphasis shifted from inhibition of impulse to the ethic of hard work:

Home discipline was rigid. When necessary the rod was used. Children received diligent home-training. They were taught early in life to work. The practice of binding children out to service so that they might learn trades or because the home family was so large as to render their services superfluous was followed quite generally in old Germantown. The

Pennsylvania Germans thought it no disgrace for a daughter to work in another family, where she might add to her knowledge of good housekeeping. Servants ate with the family on ordinary occasions and were well cared for. The servant and the master and mistress frequently were to each other as child and parents. Parents loved their home and their children and made the home attractive with proper games and privileges.[29]

In the southern colonies, plantations were large and families were isolated. Parents tended to be indulgent and discipline was relatively mild. The difference between socialization in the South and in the North was heightened by a more sharply defined class system in the South, where the aristocratic life of the landowners was in marked contrast to the life of indentured workers and slaves on plantations. The lower-class children were incorporated into the work force early in life.

Thus, even in colonial times, American society did not provide for a homogeneity of experience in childhood which could lay the basis for the socialization of a distinct national character.

The Revolutionary War stimulated an emphasis upon equalitarianism. Primogeniture (inheritance by the eldest son) and entail (settlement of property inalienably upon an individual and his descendants) were prohibited as prescribed norms because they fostered aristocracy. (Besides, free land was plentiful.) The principle of equal inheritance of property decreased the importance of sex and birth order in ascribing rights and duties to children. The emphasis upon equalitarianism facilitated the emancipation of children from parental control. Calhoun ob-

[29] *Ibid.*, pp. 203-204.

served, however, that the South was slower than the North in emancipating children. For the poorer population, early in the nineteenth century, household industry was beginning to give way to factory production. As the factory system developed, child labor was frequent; "women and children were frequently beaten with cowhides and otherwise abused."[30] However, the trends in family life of the post-Revolution period did not reach significant proportions until a large percentage of the population had moved to cities and was engaged in urban pursuits.

THE CIVIL WAR TO WORLD WAR I

The period between the Civil War and World War I was marked by the development of industrial society and the growth of the metropolis in America. Industrialization brought with it a rapid growth of population and a great surge of immigrants. The rapid social change accompanying industrialization made obsolete the emphasis on the pressure for obedience. Instead, parental focus in socialization turned to the child's development of abilities which would ensure his success in an industrial or commercial world. Hence, guidance, reasoning, and encouragement were substituted for corporal punishment. At the same time, in order to teach children to manage disappointments, pity and sympathy were avoided. To be sure, this shift in socialization practices represented a long trend starting from the colonial days and continuing into the industrial era. Moreover, the change occurred mainly in sectors of the population from which the professional persons, owners, and managers would emerge, that is, in the

[30] *Ibid.*, Vol. 2, p. 179.

emancipated middle class. For the most part, however, the bulk of the population retained an emphasis upon conformity in socialization. Calhoun quoted from the 1874 report of the Massachusetts Bureau of Statistics of Labor to indicate the enormity of problems related to the socialization of lower-class children:

> From what we have been able to learn, the law in relation to the employment of children neither is, nor can be, enforced. . . . The interest of parents, and, alas, too frequently the necessity of the case, compels the father or mother, or both, to register a falsehood, in order to keep the wolf from the door; but as long as children of tender age, more fit for the hospital than the mill, are allowed to have a place in our factories, their employment will be tolerated and the cheapness of their labor materially affects the wages of older persons. . . .
>
> It is safe . . . to say that, at least twenty-five thousand children between the ages of five and fifteen do not receive the slightest education either in our public or private schools.[31]

With the expansion in the use of child labor following the Civil War, humanitarian movements arose to eliminate abuses.

Thus began the era of factory legislation. Hours of labor were regulated, especially for women and children; some dangerous and unhealthy occupations were forbidden; and many similar matters were brought under public supervision and control. One particularly obvious evil, energetically opposed and with considerable success, was the employment of young children.

A campaign against child labor is negative and incomplete. If children must not work, what are they to do? Success in

[31] *Ibid.*, Vol. 3, p. 137.

child labor legislation led then, speedily and logically, to the necessary next step. This was emphasis on the education of these children. The training and education of future citizens began to be recognized as an imperative duty.[32]

Bossard suggested that the years following the Civil War and leading up to World War I can be regarded as the "child saving" stage in public concern for children. This period was marked by attempts to deal with "dependent and neglected children" including children with special handicaps (as blindness, deafness).

After the Civil War, the spread of industry in America created a large urban proletariat. The social-stratification system became more complex (with resulting increased diversity in child-raising practices). Immigrants poured into the country. A movement was under way to "save" the dependent, handicapped, and underprivileged children. In a way, the proposed "saving" of substandard children was a carry over from the older doctrines which equated achievement of economic success with a state of grace. The great difference between the post-Civil War and earlier views was that in colonial times the child had the "deviance" beaten out of him while industrial society precipitated the view that the forces of deviance may lie in social and biological systems not of the child's making.

THE YEARS FOLLOWING WORLD WAR I

In the years following World War I, emphasis upon independence in activities sponsored by the parents increased until the economic depression of the nineteen-thirties.

[32] James H. S. Bossard, *Marriage and the Child*, Philadelphia: University of Pennsylvania Press, 1940, p. 18.

Bossard indicated that people cannot be concerned with special problems without eventually becoming interested in the welfare of all children. *Child saving* gave way to *prevention of child exploitation* and concern for *child welfare* centered upon the family and home situation of the child. The young child was regarded as "not a thing detached and apart from his home, but . . . so much a part and parcel of that environment that child and home must be considered as a unity."[33] In the spirit of that view, interest increased in child raising based on scientific findings. After World War I, findings of behaviorist psychologists were applied to child raising for the purpose of promoting the efficiency of parents in the "manufacture" of responsible, socially striving adults. Watson developed a manual on *Psychological Care of Infant and Child:*

There is a sensible way of treating children. *Treat them as though they were young adults.* [Italics mine—B.F.] . . . Let your behavior always be objective and kindly firm. Never hug and kiss them, never let them sit in your lap. . . . If you expected a dog to grow up to be useful as a watch dog, a bird dog, a fox hound, useful for anything except a lap dog, you wouldn't dare treat it the way you treat your child.[34]

The emphasis upon creating useful and responsible adults required child training in self-reliance and in control over environment. Probably, because of the decline in child labor, the improvements in communication, and the universality of elementary education, there may have been a trend toward standardization in child-raising prac-

[33] *Ibid.,* p. 41.
[34] John B. Watson, *Psychological Care of Infant and Child,* New York: Norton, 1928, pp. 81-82.

tices. However, because of the continued immigration of diverse ethnic groups, because of internal migration especially to the cities, and because of continued specialization in occupations, many factors were at work to maintain heterogeneity in socialization of children in the different sectors of society.

THE YEARS FOLLOWING WORLD WAR II

With the economic depression of the nineteen-thirties, the situation changed. Emphasis upon collective action increased. Trends in mass production and labor-relations reform which had begun in the last part of the nineteenth century became more pronounced with the dramatic decline of the *petit bourgeoisie* in the 1930-1939 depression. At the same time, this depression marked an end to the high value placed upon upward economic mobility at the expense of kinship relationships. Perhaps the depression and the global war which followed awakened many people to a realization of the security and collective welfare found in maintaining relationships with family and kin. In terms of the earlier discussion of the trends of family life in American society, a shift occurred from using efficiency norms to applying welfare norms in organizing family life. Bossard indicated that the next step after considering *child* welfare is to emphasize the general welfare.[35]

Various explanations have been offered for the changes in child-raising practices from an emphasis on personal responsibility to a high valuation of competence in interpersonal relations.

Some social scientists suggest that the diffusion and

[35] Bossard, *op. cit.*

popularization of Freudian psychology was responsible for the recent change in child-raising practices. Play and expression became activities crucial to the development of mental health, and inhibition of "natural" impulses was considered harmful to the child's development. Other social scientists have regarded as the stimulus for this change the development of the affluent society following World War II, wherein consumption rather than production became a major interest of individuals. Part of the art of consumption is to indulge desires for luxuries and self-gratification without concern over the future; in an affluent society, there is little need to train children to endure hardships.[36] Still other social scientists indicate that, with the diffusion of large-scale organizations throughout contemporary society, the ability to get along with people has become more important than technical skills. The organization man depends upon his personality rather than his artisanship for his position in the company and the community. Thus, emphasis in child raising shifts from inculcation of responsibility to competence in interpersonal relations.[37] Perhaps all of these factors are important for explaining trends in socialization in the contemporary family.

This section has indicated how the child-raising practices in American society have been in continual flux. Initially, the various colonies, populated by immigrants from different countries and containing various kinds of eco-

[36] David Riesman and Howard Roseborough, "Careers and Consumer Behavior," in Lincoln H. Clark, ed., *Consumer Behavior*, New York: New York University Press, 1955, pp. 1-18.

[37] Miller and Swanson, *op. cit.*

nomic organization from the small New England farm to the southern plantation, were characterized by diversity in child-raising practices. With industrialization, problems in child raising changed and, in some ways, grew even more diverse. The child-saving movement developed to salvage physically or socially underprivileged children who could not meet bourgeois standards of ways of living. Following World War I, the emphasis shifted from child saving to child welfare. Efforts were made not only to improve the condition of the dependent and neglected child, but also to place *all* child raising on a scientific basis. The focus was still on bringing all children up to "standard" (as defined by educators and civic leaders). In the meantime, the American social structure became even more complex and there was still wider diversity in socialization practices. The 1930 Depression and World War II brought with them an emphasis on *collective* welfare; the emphasis on molding the *child* into a responsible, economic-achieving adult shifted to producing people who could participate and cooperate with others. Congeniality in social relations became an important aspect of socialization.

Cultural Factors in Socialization in the Family: Cross-Sectional View

The preceding section indicated that child-raising practices have shifted every two or three generations. Ritualized socialization practices cannot evolve under such circumstances. This section examines cross-sectional differences which, taken in combination with other influences of kinship and socialization, would further inhibit orderly replacement. It will discuss variations associated with

socioeconomic status as well as ethnic and religious variations. At an earlier period in American history, discussion
probably would have included rural-urban differences;
however, these differences in socialization practices are
rapidly disappearing.

VARIATIONS ASSOCIATED WITH SOCIOECONOMC STATUS

Heterogeneity in socialization practices in the United
States has accrued not only through changes in the rationale used in raising children but also through the diversity of life situations. In all four historical periods described, socioeconomic status provided a basis for differences in family life and, ultimately, in socialization practices. More than at middle-class levels, marriage at the low
socioeconomic levels is apparently based (often unsuc-
cessfully) upon seeking continual affectional and sexual
gratification. A study by Rainwater, Coleman, and Handel indicates that working-class wives are concerned with
the uncertainties of life, the dullness of daily existence,
and instability of affection. To counteract these concerns,
the wives try to enhance their attractiveness. A basic assumption in the thinking of working-class wives is the volatility of emotions. This impression of volatility interferes
with the stability of affectional relations.[38] Moreover, Rodman points out that members of lower-class families, because of their poor bargaining position in marriage, frequently must accept apparently diametrically opposed
norms of family life in order to maintain whatever stability they can. He points out that, although legal marriage

[38] Lee Rainwater, Richard P. Coleman, and Gerald Handel,
Workingman's Wife, New York: Oceana, 1959.

is preferred in lower-class West Indian families, the best that many women can hope for is a consensual marriage.[39] These studies suggest that less emphasis upon convergence of interests and value would be expected in low-status marriage than between partners at higher socioeconomic levels.

With convergence of interest regarded as being relatively unimportant at low socioeconomic levels, paradoxically neither conformity nor conflict is negatively valued as such. Kohn studied characteristics which parents desired in children. From a long list, parents were asked to select three as "most desirable" in a ten- or eleven-year-old. Middle-class mothers tended to choose as one of these three more often than lower-class mothers: "happiness of the child," "considerate of others," "has self-control," and "is curious about things." Lower-class mothers exceeded middle-class mothers in choosing: "obeys his parents well" and "is neat and clean." The findings for fathers were generally similar. Middle-class fathers tended more often to choose: "considerate of others," "dependable," and "has self-control." Lower-class fathers instead chose: "obeys his parents well" and "is able to defend himself" (for both boys and girls). Thus, the middle-class parents tended to select those items which would require much self-control whereas the lower-class parents tended to select items indicating conformity to standards but without giving up one's own personal feelings and attitudes. Conformity as construed by the lower-class parents appears to represent compliance with author-

[39] Hyman Rodman, "On Understanding Lower-Class Behavior," *Social and Economic Studies*, 8 (1959), pp. 441-450.

itarian decisions but does not preclude open conflict in the absence of external pressures. In sum, overt disagreement and dramatic display of disagreement appear to be acceptable at low socioeconomic levels.[40]

Similarly, in his summary of studies relating to socialization practices in various social classes, Bronfenbrenner finds working-class parents more often than middle-class parents intrusive into children's activities, irritable, punitive, ignoring the child, indulgent, in excessive contact with the child, more prohibitive in discipline, and in greater disagreement over child-raising policies.[41] Bronfenbrenner also reports that in middle-class families fathers were warmer toward the child, and that both parents more often share authority than in working-class families. These trends in child raising consistently appear through a range of studies covering thirty years. There appears to be sufficient evidence to characterize lower-class families as promoting aggressive spirit and affectionate display and relying on submission to authority to maintain a routine daily life. The middle-class families appear to demand in addition internalization of norms prohibiting conflict. Middle-class parents concentrate more on interpersonal competence.

Although the studies reported above describe the dominant tendencies in socialization practices as related to socioeconomic class, the complexity of American society

[40] Melvin Kohn, "Social Class and Parental Values," *American Journal of Sociology*, 64 (1959), pp. 337-351.

[41] Urie Bronfenbrenner, "Socialization and Social Class through Time and Space," in Eleanor E. Maccoby, Theodore M. Newcomb, and Eugene L. Hartley, eds., *Readings in Social Psychology*, New York: Holt, 1958, pp. 400-425.

mitigates their potency in explaining differences in child raising in various sectors of society. Variations in ethnic, racial, and religious composition of communities, in economic division of labor and size of communities, and in population dynamics all operate to complicate the relationship between socioeconomic position and socialization practices. The diffusion of fads and fashions in child raising from one class to another makes even more difficult the task of determining the influence of socioeconomic class on socialization. As a result of this complexity, inferences drawn from studies of socioeconomic position and socialization should be regarded as suggestive rather than definitive.[42]

VARIATIONS ASSOCIATED WITH RELIGIOUS AND ETHNIC DIFFERENCES

The influences of religion and ethnic-group connection are frequently highly intertwined so that we cannot be certain whether the cultural factor in socialization is primarily religious or mainly ethnic. There are wide variations in child training among different groups. In her study of immigrant parents in America, Wolfenstein found variations in the use of punishment among different ethnic groups. She reported that Chinese and Jewish parents tended to be moderate in their punishment. The Syrians, however, do not as a rule hesitate to apply punishment.[43]

[42] See William H. Sewell, "Social Class and Childhood Personality," *Sociometry*, 24 (1961), pp. 340-356.

[43] Martha Wolfenstein, "Some Variants in Moral Training of Children," in Margaret Mead and Martha Wolfenstein, eds., *Childhood in Contemporary Cultures*, Chicago: University of Chicago Press, 1955, pp. 349-368.

Similar results can be found in cross-nation comparisons. Rapp found that mothers in Germany tended to favor dominating and ignoring techniques in controlling children and to be more possessive of children than American mothers.[44] Hence, distinct family practices related to ethnic groups can be discerned.

Findings on religious and ethnic differences in socialization suggest that where parents sponsor activities related to independence and achievement of children, interpersonal competence is enhanced. Rosen has shown that Protestant, Jewish, and Greek mothers in the United States place a greater emphasis upon independence and achievement in children than do mothers with a Southern Italian or French-Canadian background. This sponsorship is reflected in the high motivation for achievement of children from Jewish and Greek homes.[45]

The discussion which follows is concerned only with the Jewish and Italian families. Strodtbeck compared the interaction process of Jewish and Italian families. He found that, in the Italian families, the father had very high power in contrast to both the mother and the son; in Jewish families, the differences were much less. There was more equality in Jewish families. The emphasis upon sponsored independence and achievement was maintained by minimizing status and power differences in the Jewish family. The lessening of power differences provided an opportunity for (a) increased interaction on the part of the

[44] Don W. Rapp, "Childrearing Attitudes of Mothers in Germany and the United States," *Child Development*, 32 (1961), pp. 669-678.

[45] Bernard C. Rosen, "Race, Ethnicity, and the Achievement Syndrome," *American Sociological Review*, 24 (1959), pp. 47-60.

Jewish son, and (b) with that interaction, practice in active participation in making decisions in a group situation.[46]

The findings by Strodtbeck are supported in a study reported by Maurice L. Farber in which differences in the socialization of English and American boys were investigated. Farber found that, whereas American boys stressed the adjustment of the child to other children (equalitarian interaction), English boys focused upon conforming behavior toward adults. The English boys appeared to be attuned to suppressing activities opposed by the adult world; the American boys were oriented to courting actively the approving attention of parents.[47] The American boys emphasized *congeniality* rather than merely *conformity* in relations with both adults and peers. Hence, the American boys would give greater attention to competence in interpersonal relations and to achievement.

The problem of competence in interpersonal relations and mental health as related to family interaction is investigated in the next chapter.

Summary

This chapter has shown how socialization practices in the United States have developed in a context of diversity of cultures and under rapidly changing economic and technological conditions. There are some regularities in social-

[46] Fred L. Strodtbeck, "Family Interaction, Values and Achievement," in D. McClelland, A. Baldwin, U. Bronfenbrenner, and F. L. Strodtbeck, *Talent and Society*, Princeton: Van Nostrand, 1958, pp. 135-194.

[47] Maurice L. Farber, "English and Americans: Values in the Socialization Process," *Journal of Psychology*, 36 (1953), pp. 243-250.

ization related to the fact that the family operates as a small group. Thus, sex and birth order of children, mothering and fathering behavior, and relationships between parents influence the course of socialization. In addition, however, various cultural trends are achieving prominence in family relations. Notable among these are the emphasis upon equality in the family and pressure by parents for children to achieve certain social-status goals in life. These changes in cultural emphasis are probably related to various events in the past quarter century that have generated much interest in the welfare of all family members. With these changes, a focus on competence in interpersonal relations has emerged, especially among middle-class families.

Selected Readings

General discussions of socialization in the family appear in:

Bettelheim, Bruno. "Does Communal Education Work?" *Commentary*, 33 (1962), pp. 117-125.

Elkin, Frederick. *The Child and Society*. Random House, 1960.

Maccoby, Eleanor E. "The Choice of Variables in the Study of Socialization," *Sociometry*, 24 (1961), pp. 357-371.

Wallace, Anthony F. C. *Culture and Personality*. Random House, 1961.

Historical trends in child-raising patterns are found in:

Calhoun, Arthur W. *A Social History of the American Family*. Barnes and Noble, 1945. (Originally published in 1917.)

Miller, Daniel R., and Guy E. Swanson. *The Changing American Parent*. Wiley, 1958.

Wolfenstein, Martha. "Trends in Infant Care," *American Journal of Orthopsychiatry*, 33 (1953), pp. 120-130.

Effects of social class on socialization in the family are described in:

Kohn, Melvin L. "Social Class and Parent-Child Relationships: An Interpretation," *American Journal of Sociology,* 68 (1963), pp. 471-480.

Rodman, Hyman. "On Understanding Lower-Class Behavior," *Social and Economic Studies,* 8 (1959), pp. 441-450.

Sewell, William H. "Social Class and Childhood Personality," *Sociometry,* 24 (1961), pp. 340-356.

Socialization in terms of sex role is discussed in:

Barry, Herbert, III, Margaret K. Bacon, and Irvin L. Child. "A Cross-Cultural Survey of Some Sex Differences in Socialization," *Journal of Abnormal and Social Psychology,* 55 (1957), pp. 327-332.

Brim, Orville G., Jr. "Family Structure and Sex Role Learning by Children: A Further Analysis of Helen Koch's Data," *Sociometry,* 21 (1958), pp. 1-15.

Hartley, Ruth E. "Some Implications of Current Changes in Sex-Role Patterns," *Merrill-Palmer Quarterly of Behavior and Development,* 6 (1959-1960), pp. 153-164.

Mussen, Paul, and Eldred Rutherford. "Parent-Child Relations and Parental Personality in Relation to Young Children's Sex-Role Preferences," *Child Development,* 34 (1963), pp. 589-607.

Findings relevant to problems of unsponsored independence appear in:

Davis, Kingsley. "The Sociology of Parent-Youth Conflict," *American Sociological Review,* 4 (1940), pp. 523-535.

Hoffman, Martin L. "Parent Discipline and the Child's Consideration for Others," *Child Development,* 34 (1963), pp. 573-588.

Middleton, Russell, and Snell Putney. "Student Rebellion against Parental Political Beliefs," *Social Forces*, 41 (1963), pp. 377-383.

Nye, F. Ivan. "Child Adjustment in Broken and in Unhappy Unbroken Homes," *Marriage and Family Living*, 19 (1957), pp. 356-361.

12 *Mental Health and Competence in Interpersonal Relations*

This book has been concerned with two tendencies of family life—the tendency to replicate the norms of family life in succeeding generations and the tendency in bilateral kinship systems for adults to be available for marriage to all other cross-sex individuals in the society regardless of marital status. This tendency for permanent availability operates at cross purposes with the tendency toward orderly replacement in contemporary society. Permanent availability interferes with the stability of the individual family and with the isolation of cultural subgroups in the society.

Socialization practices are related both to orderly replacement and to permanent availability. In a society based primarily upon ascribed status (rights and duties accruing to an individual because of the family or ethnic group into which he was born), lack of interpersonal competence has little impact upon the individual's destiny.

477

His destiny is determined by his ascribed position in society. However, in a society in which even family rights
and duties must be achieved (or earned), inability to
maintain congenial interpersonal relations may hamper the
individual's occupational, familial, or leisure-time career.
Permanent availability implies that all individuals are free
(and perhaps encouraged) to achieve a position in a new
family; hence, the individual cannot take his marriage for
granted. In turn, all members of society face a constant
pressure to be highly competent in interpersonal relations
if they wish to maintain their current marriage or remain
in a favorable competitive position in the perennial marriage market.

In recent years, social scientists have become concerned with social and cultural factors in mental health.
However, in spite of the broad interest in mental health,
persons involved in mental-health research and services
display little agreement as to the nature of mental health.[1]
The pragmatic definition of mental health in a society
must be congruent with the aims of socialization in that
society. The preceding chapter dealt with the emergence
in American society of a general interest in the socialization of children in ways that would enable them to maintain congenial social relationships. This interest affirms (as
Foote and Cottrell suggest) that competence in interper-

---

[1] Marie Jahoda, *Current Concepts of Positive Mental Health*,
New York: Basic Books, 1958; John Clausen, *Sociology and the
Field of Mental Health*, New York: Russell Sage Foundation,
1956; Leo Srole, Thomas S. Langner, Stanley T. Michael, Marvin
K. Opler, and Thomas A. C. Rennie, *Mental Health in the Metro-
polis: The Midtown Manhattan Study, Volume 1*, New York:
McGraw-Hill, 1962.

sonal relations is highly regarded in our society.[2] In this chapter, mental health is arbitrarily defined as competence in interpersonal relations. Although interpersonal competence is not the only criterion for determining whether someone is mentally ill, this competence does generally indicate medically defined "mental health."

Mental disturbance is detrimental to both orderly replacement and permanent availability. By definition, the deviant person would neither replicate family roles and norms in his family of procreation nor provide a generally acceptable role model for his children. Similarly, the mentally disturbed person is generally someone who is inept in maintaining congenial interpersonal relationships or has strange definitions of appropriate norms and values in family life or both. The management of the disturbed person represents an effort by the family members to cope with the deviant individual. As was indicated in a previous chapter, the inability of the family members to cope with the disturbed person develops into a role-organization crisis and eventuates in the freezing-out of the deviant. By the freezing-out process (if either a fiction of normality or actual normality cannot be achieved), the family members act to keep the family culture intact and to maintain their own marital availability.

This chapter will discuss problems related to mental health first from a *positive* perspective in terms of competence in interpersonal relations and then from a *negative* perspective in terms of family relations associated with

[2] Nelson N. Foote and Leonard S. Cottrell, Jr., *Identity and Interpersonal Competence*, Chicago; University of Chicago Press, 1955.

interpersonal incompetence (or mental illness). Presumably, family relations associated with mental illness are antithetical to those related to competence in interpersonal relations. The following sections will first discuss the definition of competence in interpersonal relations and procedures for increasing this competence, and then family factors in mental illness. In the section on mental illness, a distinction will be made between overcontrolling and undercontrolling families.

Competence in Interpersonal Relations

There has been a trend in recent years for popular and professional writers to focus attention upon the importance of congenial interpersonal relationships. The increasing emphasis upon competence in interpersonal relations has led to the study of the development of this competence. In 1955, Foote and Cottrell presented a statement in which they proposed applying to family research the concepts relating to interpersonal competence.[3]

In their initial description of interpersonal competence, Foote and Cottrell stated that "competence denotes capabilities to meet and deal with a changing world, to formulate ends and implement them." Moreover, competence implies that individuals are "capable of integrating their goals with those of others and collaborating" in the realization of these goals.

This section reports on studies testing propositions related to competence in interpersonal relations. These investigations include (a) a factor analysis to refine the defi-

[3] *Ibid.* Definitions and other brief quotations on the next several pages are variously from pp. 42 and 49-56.

nition of interpersonal competence, and (b) group discussion and role playing as techniques for increasing competence.

DEFINITION OF INTERPERSONAL COMPETENCE

Foote and Cottrell assume that social theory can develop along numerous paths. If the ultimate aim of the social sciences is to solve social problems, theory which develops from a direct concern with social problems will probably in the long run be the most useful in the solution of these problems. Hence, according to Foote and Cottrell, there should be a convergence between the concerns of the social scientists and those of the persons studied.

Briefly stated, the argument by Foote and Cottrell is that, with rapidly changing social conditions, family social structure itself is continually reorganized to meet new demands of society. Hence, older concepts in family research (such as adjustment), which are focused upon a particular kind of family organization with traditional roles and functions, are not appropriate to handle the new situations. Competence in interpersonal relations, however, should make possible the effective handling of family affairs in the face of changing social conditions. The concern of social scientists is with the developmental process and the measurement of competence; the concern of the interested population is with the achievement of competence.

As a goal for achievement in the population, competence in interpersonal relations is essentially a value. The characterization of the particular elements of interpersonal competence must then rest upon their formulation in the studied population. Foote and Cottrell regarded those elements of interpersonal competence described initially by the social scientist merely as a starting point. There is no commitment on the part of the social scientist to retain his initial definitions if these are contradicted by findings that competence is defined differently by the population. Tentatively, Foote and Cottrell defined the elements of competence in interpersonal relations as health, intelligence, judgment, autonomy, creativity, and empathy.

Foote and Cottrell regarded *health* as the capacity of the human organism "to exercise all of its physiological functions, and achieve its maximum of sensory acuity, strength, energy, co-ordination, dexterity, endurance, recuperative power, and immunity." They considered *intelligence* as the capacity of the human organism for such activities as "perception of relationships among events; the capacity to abstract and symbolize experience, to manipulate symbols into meaningful generalizations, and to be articulate in communication; skill in mobilizing the resources of environment and experience in the services of a variety of goals." By *judgment,* they meant "the ability, which develops slowly in human beings, to estimate and evaluate the meaning and consequences to one's self of alternative lines of conduct." Foote and Cottrell defined *autonomy* as an "acquired ability for handling those kinds of problematic interpersonal situations where self-esteem is threatened or challenged." *Creativity* was regarded as "resourcefulness in devising new and effective responses to problematic interpersonal situations." And *empathy* is involved in an "ability correctly to interpret the attitudes and intentions of others, in the accuracy with which they can perceive situations from others' standpoint, and thus anticipate and predict their behavior."

Farber investigated the extent to which the definitions of elements of interpersonal competence by Foote and Cottrell corresponded with those held by married men. He submitted the interview responses of 495 husbands in the twenty-year follow-up of couples in the Burgess and Wallin marital-prediction study to a factor analysis.[4] Items were selected on the basis of their apparent content as indicating empathy, autonomy, or creativity (104 items). As was anticipated, empathy, autonomy, and creativity emerged as orthogonal (or independent) factors. However, the results also suggested two revisions in the designation of elements of competence. First, an additional factor, not previously considered in the definition of interpersonal competence, emerged in the analysis. This factor emphasized items related to cooperativeness and to emotional support. Second, findings related to factors of perceived empathy, autonomy, and cooperativeness suggest both a generalized component and a component connected to a particular group. In each area, two factors were found, with one having reference to general empathy, autonomy, and cooperativeness of the individual and the other factor having reference to the application of the general capacity to a specific relationship (for instance, the person's empathy in the marriage).

[4] Bernard Farber, "Elements of Competence in Interpersonal Relations," *Sociometry*, 25 (1962), pp. 30-47. See also Ernest W. Burgess and Paul Wallin, *Engagement and Marriage*, New York, Lippincott, 1953. The couples were first interviewed in 1936-1939 during their engagement, then three to five years after marriage, and again about fifteen years after marriage.

Although modifications in concepts relating to inter-personal competence were indicated by the factor analysis, these modifications should be regarded as tentative, pending refinement of technique and replication studies.

DEVELOPING COMPETENCE IN INTERPERSONAL RELATIONS

A procedure which has been used in attempting to increase competence in interpersonal relations is a small-group, role-playing technique called participant experimentation. This technique is called *participant* experimentation because the participants themselves develop strategies to meet problems and unexpected shifts in family role. In acting out, observing, and discussing family or quasi-family situations, the participants develop techniques and insights which will assist them in their relationships outside the role-playing situation. The group is experimental in that it provides: (1) through unrehearsed role playing in typical family-life situations, the opportunity for the participants to formulate tentative strategies and to test their effectiveness in interpersonal relations; and (2) through discussion, the opportunity to study these strategies and thereby increase knowledge bearing on interpersonal relations. The group provides an atmosphere of spontaneity for creating alternative solutions to problems as well as for testing and increasing the insight of the participants through self-examination and evaluation. The aim of participant experimentation thus is to act as an agent for increasing self-awareness, broadening experience, and facilitating understanding in interpersonal relations.[5]

[5] Foote and Cottrell, *op. cit.*

The section which follows reports tests of interpersonal competence and attempts to increase competence through participant experimentation. Formal procedures for participant experimentation were devised under Foote's direction.

Increasing autonomy

In their conceptualization of the development of autonomy in interpersonal relations, O. Eggers and E. Eggers characterized a series of responses in role playing. In their characterization, autonomy develops through eight stages:[6]

1. *Anticipatory identification.* Prior to his interaction in the group, the participant views the group as being potentially useful in facilitating his ability to enter into personal relationships.

2. *Exploratory definitions.* The participant defines the work of the group as exploring in a variety of ways. This stage is a period of self-examination, searching through variations in role playing and discussion, and explorations into the motivations of other participants.

3. *Involvement identifications.* The individual becomes emotionally involved in group tasks and regards himself as a part of the group.

4. *Role-desire definitions.* The participant begins to *specify* the areas of life in which he wishes to increase autonomy.

5. *Concept applications.* As the participant verbalizes the autonomous modes of acting in various life situations, he begins to use the concept of autonomy as a per-

[6] Oscar Eggers and Eleanor Eggers, unpublished manuscript used at Family Study Center, University of Chicago, 1954.

spective for interpreting problematic events in his life and becomes mindful of the part played by autonomous activity in family situations.

6. *Role-playing identity applications.* The individual begins to carry over the acts learned in the role-playing scenes to those situations in which he has applied the autonomy perspective. He acts in "real life" as if he were "role playing." Although Eggers and Eggers did not compare their description to the George Herbert Mead approach to the development of the self, this stage may represent the transition from the "play stage" in which the individual imitates *others* to the "game stage" in which he takes account of others, but imitates his *own* earlier activity.[7]

7. *Challenge identifications.* The participant seeks out different areas of activity to test and reinforce his new skills in autonomy.

8. *Identity establishment.* Having met challenging situations successfully, the individual regards himself as autonomous.

When they had defined the various phases in the development of autonomy, Eggers and Eggers determined role-playing and discussion procedures to be instituted at various points in their role-playing series. Applying their techniques and autonomy tests to a group in a different section of the United States, Gillette found marked increases in autonomy in students who had undergone "training" in autonomy in a college course on marriage and the family. His results were especially noteworthy in that a comparable group in a conventional "functional"

[7] George Herbert Mead, *Mind, Self and Society,* Chicago: University of Chicago Press, 1934.

marriage course (using group discussion) showed little increase in autonomy over the same period of time.[8]

A test of autonomy in interpersonal relations

Stanton and Litwak reported findings based upon a role-playing test of interpersonal competence.[9] The score of the person tested consisted of ratings by the tester on twenty items related to lack of autonomy after the tester had completed role-playing a series of scenes with him. These scenes were: meeting a troubled friend, criticizing an old employee, and "parrying an interfering parent." The tester played the troubled friend, the old employee, and the interfering parent. In each scene, the tester introduced into his role playing "three or four points of interpersonal stress" in a standardized order. For example, in the troubled-friend scene, the person tested (a) had to pry into personal emotional problems, (b) had his advice requested and then refused, and (c) received considerable flattery.

This test was applied in a study of foster parents. The validity of the test was indicated by correlating the ratings by the relatively untrained testers with social case workers' evaluations of foster parents' autonomy. These correlations were fairly high. Interjudge reliability in using the autonomy-rating scale with the role-playing test was also high.

The test by Stanton and Litwak in an interview situ-

[8] Thomas L. Gillette, "Toward a Student-Centered Marriage Course: A Progress Report," *Marriage and Family Living*, 21 (1959), pp. 155-159.

[9] Howard R. Stanton and Eugene Litwak, "Toward the Development of a Short-Form Test of Interpersonal Competence," *American Sociological Review*, 20 (1955), pp. 668-674.

ation suggested that autonomy tests could be applied not only in evaluation of role playing in participant experimentation but also in survey research.

Increasing empathy

M. Flapan and D. Flapan developed role-playing procedures for increasing empathy.[10] They defined the problem of developing techniques under two headings. They developed, first, procedures for facilitating productive role playing and, second, special techniques for handling the problem of empathy. They regarded one of the difficulties in productive role playing as that of concealment of characteristic ways of behaving in the marital relationship. Some of the ways concealment occurs in role playing are: playing the part of a "perfect" husband or wife, playing a stereotype marital role, overplaying by "hamming" or caricature, or remaining detached and overly self-controlled. One technique developed to counteract such concealing role playing was to give the player the role of a person released from inhibition—for example, a drunk or a small child. Another technique was to stipulate a specific type of emotion to be displayed in playing the role.

The major concern that Flapan and Flapan had, however, was in developing specific techniques for increasing empathy. One technique developed by them was that of *retrospection:*

Imaginatively reviewing what had just taken place in a role-playing enactment, expressing what had not been expressed and formulating unverbalized thoughts or intentions, would enable a husband and wife to get a better understanding of the

[10] Mark Flapan and Dorothy Flapan, unpublished manuscript.

interaction in which they had just participated. Some of these retrospective techniques included the following:

1. *Reverie* consisted of a free association of thoughts as if the individual were by himself. In this technique, the number of distractions was minimized. The individual was seated in a soft chair, lights were lowered.

2. The individual was asked to think how he would have liked his wife to act if the role playing had been a *daydream*. Moreover, he was instructed to indicate the kind of situation he wanted to develop and to describe the desired outcome. Then, considering the role playing as a *nightmare,* the individual was asked to think of the worst possible things that could have happened in the role playing.

3. In *retrospective conversation,* each spouse was to elicit from the other the meaning of the other's role-playing behavior. Rather than focusing upon the problem which had been assigned for the role-playing enactment, the husband was expected to explain to his wife the behavior of the "husband" in the role-playing scene. At the same time the wife was to explain to her husband the role of the particular "wife" which she was playing.

4. In *retrospections in role-reversal,* the individuals were asked to imagine that they were the spouse in the previous role-playing scene and to think aloud from the perspective of the spouse. This ordinarily provided a way for a husband to determine how difficult it was for him to think of the situation as his wife may have perceived it.

Other techniques such as chum-talk, diary writing, letter writing, and projection into the future were also introduced as a form of reverie.

One of the difficulties with these techniques is the lack of evaluation of their effectiveness for developing empathy. There is as yet no experimental evidence to indicate that any of these techniques are effective for increasing empathy as a permanent trait in individuals.

A *test of creativity in interpersonal competence*

Stanton and Litwak and their associates reported a series of studies utilizing a role-playing test of creativity in interpersonal relations.[11] The test of creativity consists of two scenes. The tester participates in the role playing and an observer records interaction. In the first scene, the husband and wife, playing themselves, are asked to make a visiting, bashful cousin (played by the tester) feel at home. The respondents' actions in making the cousin feel at home are classified into four categories: (a) appeals for help (help with the dishes or help in care of the children), (b) offers of help or entertainment (take sight seeing or to the theater), (c) questioning behavior (ask questions regarding relatives or home life), and (d) rejecting behavior (be too busy working to spend time with cousin). For each response, the cousin-tester has prearranged answers. The closer the responses are to "appeals for help," the more at home the cousin-tester claims he feels.

In the test, creativity was appraised on two dimensions. The first dimension was the number of ways the respondent suggested to make the cousin feel at home. The second dimension was the time taken by the respondent to grasp the "correct" way of making the cousin feel at home.

[11] Stanton and Litwak, *op. cit.*; Howard Stanton, Kurt Back, and Eugene Litwak, "Role-Playing in Survey Research," *American Journal of Sociology*, 62 (September, 1956), pp. 172-176; Eugene Litwak, Gloria Count, and Edward M. Haydon, "Group Structure and Interpersonal Creativity as Factors which Reduce Errors in the Prediction of Marital Adjustment," *Social Forces*, 38 (1960), pp. 308-315.

In the second scene, the husband and wife, playing themselves, are at a party in which a prospective employer (played by the tester) is to be kept away from the competitors for the job. The task to be learned by the husband and wife is that of being silent. The prospective employer (tester) acts favorably when they are silent and unfavorably when they speak to him.

In both scenes, the task set for the respondents is one which is not ordinarily expected in the role of host or prospective employee. However, both scenes are played with a third person who is an outsider. Inasmuch as interaction with outsiders generally falls within the husband's expected activity, the role-playing test overemphasizes the husband's resourcefulness and underemphasizes the wife's.

Creativity and marital adjustment

Litwak, Count, and Haydon[12] found no simple relationship between marital-adjustment scores and score on creativity for husbands and wives (83 couples) in the middle-years follow-up in the Burgess marital-prediction study.[13] However, when the *relative* creativity of the husband and wife was examined, Litwak and his associates found that unless the husband's creativity score was lower than his wife's score in *both* role-playing scenes in the test just described, marital adjustment tended to be high. Using this cue, they examined errors in prediction of marital adjustment in the middle years on the basis of data gathered in engagement. By taking into account the relative creativity scores, the investigators increased the number of correct predictions markedly. They assumed that

[12] Litwak, Count, and Haydon, *op. cit.* at note 11.
[13] See Burgess and Wallin, *op cit.* at note 4.

this creative ability had been present in engagement (as a "cause") and had not developed in the course of achieving high adjustment in marriage (as an effect).

EPILOGUE: COMPETENCE IN INTERPERSONAL RELATIONS

The survey of research findings and theory regarding competence in interpersonal relations has avoided an evaluation of the potential achievements of the conceptual scheme and its applications in family research. One reason for this avoidance is that the conceptual formulations as well as research applications of interpersonal competence are still insufficiently developed to support speculation upon the ultimate utility of the competence approach to socialization and family life.

Parental Risk Taking and Mental Illness

The preceding section focused upon the influence of certain kinds of social relationships on the development of interpersonal competence. We shall now turn our attention to the other extreme—incompetence in interpersonal relations. Just as individuals can be trained to increase their ability to carry on sustained personal relationships, they can also be "trained" into an incapacity for congenial personal relationships. Clearly, although parents want their children to be highly competent in such respects, the children may deviate considerably from the parental aims. This section will be concerned, first, with the risk taking that socialization practices, regardless of their specific aims, impose on parents and, second, with ways in which the risk taking of parents is related to mental illness of their children.

PARENTAL RISK TAKING

Making judgments in interpersonal relations involves much risk of being wrong. Judgments in interaction with others are seldom made under ideal conditions. In parent-child relationships, the parent tries to control the socialization of the child without knowing for certain the long-run effects of his action upon the child. The risk of making wrong judgments is increased by the child's simultaneous attempt to control the parent. This section presents a theoretical statement regarding risks of mistakes in child raising.

Since individuals must make judgments in social relationships under vague and shifting conditions and cannot act "rationally" because of lack of information, then how do they minimize the risk of choosing the "wrong" alternative in making a judgment?

A mistake in social interaction may be defined as a misjudgment by the actor of the consequences of his act toward another person. There appear to be two types of mistakes in social judgment: technical mistakes and mistakes in implementation of acts. In the technical mistake, the misjudgment lies in a failure to determine under which conditions certain acts will control another individual in a particular way. The second type of error in judgment lies in misdiagnosing a particular situation to determine whether the appropriate conditions are present so that a particular act can be implemented effectively.

These two types of errors in social judgment are in the area of knowing *how* and knowing *when*. Knowing how is developed through the appropriation of social skills and sophistication in social relationships. Knowing when to implement an act depends upon the diagnosis of a particular social situation at a given time. This discussion is concerned mainly with knowing when.

In parent-child relationships, the parent always risks being wrong in his judgment concerning strategies in child raising. The extent to which the parent is willing to risk using too much or using too little of a particular kind of strategy becomes an important variable insofar as it affects socialization of the child. Determining the tolerance limits in performing too much or too little may provide a useful method for discovering ways in which parents socialize their children (and children socialize their parents). Would the parent rather risk the mistake of being too harsh than being too easy on a child? Would the parent prefer to risk the error of being overprotective rather than being underprotective in his actions? Would the parent rather provide too much affectionate behavior than too little? Would the parent prefer to err by imparting to the child too much or too little information regarding the world's vicissitudes?

These questions regarding parent-child relationships suggest that *no* parent *always* wishes to treat his child harshly, lovingly, punitively, protectively, or suspiciously. Instead, there are particular situations which the parent regards as appropriate for treating his child in these ways.

Kinship units, friendship networks, "how-to" literature, and families of orientation serve to define the critical points and establish norms for implementing behavior controls. Advice is frequently given in terms of: "If you want to be sure that . . ." or "If you don't want to take a chance that . . ." or "Chances are that if you do this,

Johnny won't do that again" or "A child learns by experience, so just let him do it until you think there is a good chance of his hurting himself." The individual parent thus does not develop patterns of risk taking in a vacuum. (The presence of two parents itself may introduce either conflict or reinforcement of preferred risk taking in making mistakes in child raising.)

The presence of norms relating to social judgment in families and religious, ethnic, and socioeconomic groupings tends to stabilize the practice of taking risks of certain types. For example, German mothers are more authoritarian and possessive than American mothers.[14] However, a second factor probably enters into the kind of risk taken in controlling others. This factor is the effectiveness of whatever strategy the parent employed to promote particular behavior in the child. If the child performed a desired act following the parent's behavior, this event would then affect the parent's behavior in the succeeding situations regardless of the realistic need for this strategy.

MENTAL ILLNESS

The concept of preferred risks in child raising may provide various insights into the development of mental disorders. No parent intends his socialization practices to result in the mental illness of a son or daughter. Mental illness or emotional disturbance is clearly unintentional. Some past studies of family relations view the family as an external environment to the child which somehow causes

[14] Don W. Rapp, "Childrearing Attitudes of Mothers in Germany and the United States," *Child Development*, 32 (1961), pp. 669-678.

his behavior to deviate from normal expectations. These studies have followed the pattern of taking mental patients (and sometimes normal controls) and attempting to determine deficiencies in their social environment. For example:

1. Lidz and his associates investigated the "pathologic" environment of 14 families as being adverse to the "normal" developmental process of a child's personality. This series of studies, based on interviews with all family members, suggested that marital discord, an ineffectual father, and a general failure to relieve tensions in the family facilitated the onset of schizophrenia. The role of the father was ineffectual in almost all of the cases even where marked schism in the marriage was not present. Where marital schism was present, the husband had little prestige in the home either because of his own behavior or because of his wife's attitude toward him. The husband tended to become an outsider who could not assert his leadership in the family and was forced more and more to assert himself in tyrannical ways. Lidz found that where marital schism was present there was a tendency for the parents' loyalties to be not with the spouse but with their own parents and siblings.[15]

[15] Theodore Lidz and Stephen Fleck, "Schizophrenia, Human Integration, and the Role of the Family," in D. Jackson, ed., *Etiology of Schizophrenia*, New York: Basic Books, 1959, pp. 323-345; Theodore Lidz, Alice R. Cornelison, Stephen Fleck, and Dorothy Terry, "The Intrafamilial Environment of the Schizophrenic Patient: I. The Father," *Psychiatry*, 20 (1957), pp. 329-342; Lidz, Cornelison, Fleck, and Terry, "The Intrafamilial Environment of Schizophrenic Patients: II. Marital Schism and Marital Skew," *American Journal of Psychiatry*, 114 (1957), pp. 241-248.

2. Vogel and Bell suggested that parents instil the emotional disturbance in the child by making him their scapegoat and by projecting their marital difficulties upon him.[16]

3. Giffin studied the problem of inadequate superego development among "acting out" delinquents and found that parents had transmitted lacunae or defects in their own superego to the children.[17]

4. Wynne reported on pseudo mutuality in family relationships of schizophrenics.[18] By pseudo mutuality he meant the strict conformity to a fixed set of behavioral expectations without recognition of individual needs, desires, or potentialities. According to Wynne, the family members view norms as holding the family together. They perceive divergence from these norms as leading to disruption of the family and, therefore, rigorously enforce conformity to norms. However, if family members suppress divergence, then growth of intimate relationships is im-

[16] Ezra F. Vogel and Norman W. Bell, "The Emotionally Disturbed Child as the Family Scapegoat," in Norman W. Bell and Ezra F. Vogel, eds., A Modern Introduction to the Family, Glencoe, III: Free Press, 1960, pp. 382-397.

[17] Mary E. Giffin, Adelaide M. Johnson, and Edward M. Litin, "Specific Factors Determining Antisocial Acting Out," American Journal of Orthopsychiatry, 24 (1959), pp. 668-684.

[18] Lyman C. Wynne, Irving M. Ryckoff, Juliana Day, and Stanley I. Hirsch, "Pseudo-Mutuality in the Family Relationships of Schizophrenics," Psychiatry, 21 (1958), pp. 205-220. See also the discussion of pseudo hostility. which is regarded as a split or alienation in the family functioning to maintain relationships in a fixed form, by Lyman C. Wynne, "The Study of Intrafamily Alignments and Splits in Exploratory Family Therapy," in Nathan W. Ackerman, Frances L. Beatman, and Sanford N. Sherman, Exploring the Base for Family Therapy, New York: Family Service Association of America, 1961, pp. 95-115.

peded. Wynne suggested that the families of persons who *later* develop schizophrenic episodes are characterized by a high degree of pseudo mutuality. Thus, Wynne viewed pseudo mutuality as a prior condition to schizophrenia.

It is probably true that often the family environment stimulates deviant behavior in the child. However, several writers have cast doubt upon the adequacy of the environmental view for explaining the connection between family relations and the persistence of deviant behavior. Klebanoff, using the parental-attitude research instrument developed by Schaefer and Bell, found fewer pathological attitudes among mothers of schizophrenic children than among mothers of brain-injured and retarded children and concluded that maternal attitudes have little to do with causing schizophrenia.[19] Escalona suggested that parents of children who present behavior problems are pressured by difficulty in handling the children into being inconsistent and autocratic in child-raising practices.[20] Peterson and his associates suggested that personality tendencies appearing early in the child's life may themselves have affected parent attitudes in child raising.[21] It may require

[19] Lewis B. Klebanoff, "Parental Attitudes of Mothers of Schizophrenic, Brain-injured and Retarded, and Normal Children," *American Journal of Orthopsychiatry*, 29 (1959), pp. 445-454. See also Earl S. Schaefer and Richard Q. Bell, "Development of a Parental Attitude Research Instrument," *Child Development*, 29 (1958), pp. 339-361.

[20] Sibylle K. Escalona, "Some Considerations Regarding Psychotherapy with Psychotic Children," *Bulletin of the Menninger Clinic*, 12 (1948), pp. 127-134.

[21] Donald R. Peterson, Wesley C. Becker, Leo A. Hellmer, Donald J. Shoemaker, and Herbert C. Quay, "Parental Attitudes

a sensible and lovable child to have sensible and lovable parents. Peterson also proposed that, by observing sequence of occurrence in parents' attitudes and personality trends in children, causal explanations can be established with respect to mental health.

As an alternative to the environmental view, this discussion will view parents as trying to manage a child who has deviated in his conduct. The child is behaving in a way defined as deviant by the parents. The parents face the problem of trying to eliminate or at least to minimize this deviance. Without "ritualized" procedures for increasing interpersonal competence, the parents must rely upon their own intuition regarding preferred errors in child raising. Some parents will be overstrict in their attempt to counteract the deviance; other parents will err in being too permissive.

Unlike the environmental approach, the management approach takes into account the role of other factors (physiological, social, and psychological) in precipitating mental illness or delinquent behavior. For example, Lu suggests that even when the onset of illness occurred in adulthood, the differentiation in the mother's relationship with the patient had occurred very early in the child's life.[22] She indicates:

One clue appears to be that the patient was an unusual or sick infant, cried more, and was more excitable than the non-

___

and Child Adjustment," *Child Development*, 30 (1959), pp. 119-130.

[22] Yi-Chuang Lu, "Mother-Child Role Relations in Schizophrenia," *Psychiatry*, 24 (1961), pp. 133-142.

schizophrenic infant siblings. Some such differences at birth and during infancy may have led the mother to pay more attention to the unusual or sick or more crying child than to the other child. Another clue is that the mother was undergoing severe hardships during the time of the patient's birth and infancy, but was not in the case of the non-schizophrenic sibling.[23]

(Some of these hardships included unemployment of the father, acute marital difficulties, illness.) Among emotionally disturbed children, a similar tendency for early differential treatment of the emotionally disturbed child and other children has appeared. Vogel and Bell found that emotionally disturbed children tended also to have had a physical abnormality, an early serious illness, or mental retardation.[24] Similarly, Nye found that delinquents far more than nondelinquents believed that their father was more lenient with their siblings in his discipline and that he was unfair in his punishment.[25] "Unfairness" here implies that the father erred by being excessively punitive. This "unfairness" might stimulate further deviance. These observations depict the development of mental illness or other personality difficulties in terms of willingness of parents to risk overcontrol or undercontrol of the child who has already manifested deviance.

Families which prefer to risk overcontrol in reacting to the child's deviance appear to have characteristics different from those of families undercontrolling the deviant

[23] *Ibid.*, p. 139.

[24] Vogel and Bell, *op. cit.*

[25] F. Ivan Nye, *Family Relationships and Delinquent Behavior*, New York: Wiley, 1958.

child. Characteristics of overcontrolling and undercontrolling families will be investigated in the following sections.

Overcontrolling families

The management view of mental illness regards parents who "overcontrol" the deviant child as doing so to counteract the variety of deviant behaviors manifested by the child. Deviant behavior is defined here as any action by the child which does not conform to parental expectations. In terms of the discussion on the course of the family cycle in Chapter 9, deviant behavior denotes unsponsored independence on the part of the child.

Families who overcontrol the deviant child regard this child as having at some time deviated from their expectations dramatically. This dramatic instance has apparently stimulated the parents to develop special control techniques to prevent or to counteract future deviance. Like the parents of retarded children, the parents of emotionally disturbed or delinquent children must guard against further deviance.

Parental tendencies to overcontrol children are manifested in authoritarianism and protectiveness. Past studies of parent-child relationships indicate that many parents of mentally disturbed children (and of children who grew into disturbed adults) tend to be highly protective and authoritarian in interaction with their children. In their tendency toward protectiveness and authoritarianism, parents of disturbed children risk imposing controls on the behavior of their "deviant" children even when these controls are not needed. Hence, the child does not have an opportunity to carry on interaction which would be conducive to the development of interpersonal competence.

Parental protectiveness. The child's dependence and parental protectiveness exist as a reciprocal relationship. Various investigations provide evidence of a heightened dependence-protectiveness relationship between the preschizophrenic child and his mother. Lu reported that the mother had insisted on controlling the schizophrenic patient as a child to a greater extent than the siblings and that, at the same time, the preschizophrenic child had increased his submission and dependency upon her. Lu found that the preschizophrenic child relies excessively upon his parents for guidance and support and, in the process, tends to be cut off from other potential sources of personal relations.[26] Vogel and Bell also reported that the emotionally disturbed child received special attention and was exempted from certain responsibilities which were expected of other children.[27] Thus, here too the child developed a sense of dependence upon the parent. However, Klebanoff reported that mothers of both schizophrenic and brain-injured children were higher in *over-posessiveness* than were mothers of normal children only.[28] In the Klebanoff findings especially there is a suggestion that the possessiveness of the mothers of mentally ill children may have been a reaction to the deviant behavior of the child.

Authoritarianism. Studies of social factors in mental illness find in addition that many parents tend to be au-

[26] Lu, *op. cit.*
[27] Vogel and Bell, *op. cit.*
[28] Klebanoff, *op. cit.*

thoritarian rather than equalitarian or permissive in their relationship with the child. Peterson and his associates found both mothers and fathers of problem children to be more autocratic and more concerned with discipline than parents in their control group.[29] Lu also reported that the mother was highly authoritarian in her relationship to the preschizophrenic child.[30] Myers and Roberts also reported a good deal of authoritarianism.[31] In authoritarianism as well as in emphasis upon the high relative power of the mother in the family, the families of preschizophrenic children resemble families of lower socioeconomic levels in their family relationships.[32]

If the overcontrolling family of the preschizophrenic child resembles the family of the lower socioeconomic levels in terms of power structure and authoritarianism, why do not *most* families at these levels produce schizophrenic children? This would be the most obvious question raised by the environmental view of family relations. A difference between lower-class authoritarianism and preschizophrenic authoritarianism can, however, be indicated if the management interpretation is followed. As was indicated earlier, in families at low socioeconomic levels, the parents tend to admire the retention of the child's spirit along with obedience. They do not generally regard aggression and physical violence as bad so long as the child is obedi-

[29] Peterson *et al., op. cit.*

[30] Lu, *op. cit.*

[31] Jerome K. Myers and Bertram H. Roberts, *Family and Class Dynamics in Mental Illness*, New York: Wiley, 1959.

[32] Melvin L. Kohn and John A. Clausen, "Parental Authority Behavior and Schizophrenia," *American Journal of Orthopsychiatry*, 26 (1956), pp. 297-313.

ent. For the overcontrolling parents of the preschizophrenic child, however, obedience is apparently not
enough. Having a child who has already manifested a severe deviance (or unsponsored independence), the parents must make special efforts through protectiveness and
rigorous control to prevent further deviance. Thus, it appears that in contrast to the ordinary authoritarianism of
families of low socioeconomic status, authoritarianism in
parents of the preschizophrenic child is intended to eliminate the initiative of the child in order to curb his deviance. The parents are faced with a role-organization crisis.
It therefore becomes important for them that the child adhere very closely to their restrictions. It may be significant
that, in Lu's study, the normal siblings of schizophrenics
reported that they had rebelled (and hence retained the
right to deviate) but the patients did not rebel. Since the
siblings were not regarded as a special problem, apparently their conformity was not so crucial to the mother as
that of the preschizophrenic.[33] Because of the necessity
for controlling the deviance, parents risk the error of applying repressive measures even when they are not needed.

The onset of mental illness. If parents' overcontrolling
behavior is regarded as an attempt to cope with the deviant child, what explanation is there for the onset of extreme deviance—such as schizophrenia or severe behavior
problems—in spite of the parents' continued efforts? The
most obvious situation for onset is a removal of the rigorous parental controls. A large number of the schizophrenics are found in nonfamily situations, with the onset of the illness following release from parental controls.[34]

[33] Lu, *op. cit.*
[34] S. Kirson Weinberg, "A Sociological Analysis of a Schizo-

Having been freed from the control of the parents and having been previously dependent on their parents, the individuals are unable to combat the onset of schizophrenic episodes. Thrust into new relationships in which failure is imminent, the preschizophrenic individuals have not developed sufficient self-controlling devices to prevent the onset of the illness. Lu reports another precipitating factor: schizophrenic episodes were frequently brought on by increased parental and community demands for achievement and responsibility.[35] Weinberg found there had existed among schizophrenic men, prior to onset, intensified desire for reassurance, aspiration to goals that were almost inaccessible, and a compulsion to attain whatever goals his parents had prescribed.[36] Weinberg also reported that the women in his sample were unable to cope with the "social techniques of male courtship" because of their ignorance of female courtship practices, inhibited aggressive tendencies, and inability to withstand termination of a courtship relationship. Faced with new predicaments and unable to fall back upon extreme parental controls for handling these predicaments, these individuals may resort to schizophrenic episodes.

In summary: The development of mental illness occurs in overcontrolling families through the interaction between a deviant child and his parents, and the onset of the illness may occur when the kinds of control instituted by the parents fail to provide a solution to a predicament

---

phrenic Type," in Arnold M. Rose, ed., *Mental Health and Mental Disorder*, New York: Norton, 1955, pp. 240-357.

[35] Lu, *op. cit.*

[36] Weinberg, *op. cit.*

in which the *child* finds himself. These kinds of control have included high protectiveness and authoritarian control even when these techniques were not needed. Obviously, if these techniques had been used prior to the child's deviance, the probability of their continued use would be large. The more extreme the repressive techniques, the more restricted the child's sphere of permitted activities becomes and the more incapacitated he is in interpersonal relationships.

Undercontrolling families

The authoritarian relationship in overcontrolling families reflects only one kind of parental reaction to the child's deviance. Myers and Roberts found that the close supervision by parents of the preschizophrenic occurred mainly in lower-middle-class stratum of their sample.[37] This stratum included proprietors of small establishments, office and sales workers, and a large number of skilled workers. Most of the individuals in this stratum of the population had completed high school. In contrast, Myers and Roberts found that among families in the lowest stratum of their population, the parents paid little attention to the preschizophrenic child and, in general, family life was highly disorganized. In the lowest stratum, almost all adults were unskilled or semiskilled workers and few of them had completed eight years of formal schooling. In general, the schizophrenics (especially females) from the lowest stratum appear to have encountered maternal deprivation.

The differences in overcontrol and undercontrol ap-

[37] Myers and Roberts, *op. cit.*

pear to be reflected in the symptoms shown by the Myers and Roberts subjects.[38] The lower-class (undercontrolled) schizophrenic patients were extremely suspicious and were convinced that other people were conspiring against them. They were violent and aggressive and displayed many psychosomatic symptoms. The lower-middle-class (over-controlled) schizophrenics, however, showed many feelings of superiority and had grandiose ideas. They displayed ritualistic behavior and believed that they were unclean and rotting away. Comparable symptoms were found in the neurotic patients in the Myers and Roberts study. The lower-class neurotic patients displayed many somatic symptoms (for example, pains); they were aggressive and suspicious. The lower-middle-class neurotic patients focused their complaints upon interpersonal problems; they had obsessive-compulsive symptoms and depressive reactions. Thus, the symptoms of patients apparently varied in accordance with the kind of parental control. In the sectors of society in which undercontrol would be expected, patients developed symptoms which would reveal their isolation and demand for attention. In the sector in which overcontrol would be anticipated, patients developed symptoms which would reflect restriction in activities.

Summary

Two kinds of risks in handling deviant children have been explored—overcontrol and undercontrol. With the lack of ritualized forms of socialization, the probability of error in implementing controlling behavior becomes great.

[38] *Ibid.*

Where the child himself has deviated appreciably from parental expectations, parents give up trying to apply any of the ritualized forms of control learned in experience or in child-development literature. The procedures developed in the interpersonal-competence studies of Foote and his associates are themselves attempts to institute new formal rituals in socialization. With the failure of even minimal rituals to socialize the child along "normal" lines, the parent tends to become extreme in either overcontrol or undercontrol of the child's activities. This extreme parental behavior appears to sustain the deviance, to inhibit the development of interpersonal competence, and, in doing so, to inhibit orderly replacement of family norms and values in the succeeding generation.

Epilogue: Mental Health in the Modern Family

This chapter ends with a value problem. The discussion of socialization in the previous chapter and of mental health in the present chapter points to the high degree of uncertainty and wastage in the "production" of the emerging family members. Given the current laissez-faire system of family life, the younger generation will deviate considerably from the norms and values of the older generation.

Much concern has been voiced over the lack of stability of the nuclear family. To try to maintain the stability and the orderly replacement of family life, various groups and institutions are competing to control family culture. Government, the religious institutions, social-welfare agencies, and the corporation are in constant competition with the kindred over the role of family critic to control socialization of succeeding generations of children. These agencies may be more efficient than the kindred in maintaining quality control in producing individuals with high interpersonal competence. Possibly, manipulation of the socialization process through the application of tested generalizations in child development, through extensive observation techniques (*à la* Orwell's *1984*), and through revision of genetic codes would create generations of such individuals.

The analysis earlier in this book indicated that the bilateral kindred continues to operate as a controlling influence on the nuclear family despite its inability to enforce sanctions for deviance. This inability to enforce sanctions weakens the effectiveness of the kindred in maintaining orderly replacement. In spite of this weakness, however, the bilateral kindred does provide some stability in socialization which cannot readily occur within the isolated nuclear family under conditions of permanent availability.

The agencies competing with the bilateral kindred tend to subordinate domestic life to their own interests. But is close supervision by these agencies over socialization practices compatible with democratic society? To be sure, because the bilateral kindred is less efficient than other agencies in communicating effective criticism of family relations, it may permit many socially incompetent persons to be produced. However, the choice lies between two alternatives: either the flexibility allowed by the bilateral system at the cost of some waste in personal development, or else the efficient utilization of people at the cost of centralized control over socialization practices.

Selected Readings

The relevance of interaction in explaining mental health and personal development is discussed in:

Foote, Nelson N., and Leonard S. Cottrell, Jr. *Identity and Interpersonal Competence.* University of Chicago Press, 1955.

Pollak, Otto. *Social Science and Psychotherapy for Children.* Russell Sage Foundation, 1952.

The findings in the following studies are also of interest:

Henry, Andrew F. "Family Role Structure and Self-Blame," *Social Forces,* 25 (1956), pp. 34-38.

Lu, Yi-Chuang. "Mother-Child Role Relations in Schizophrenia," *Psychiatry,* 24 (1961), pp. 133-142.

Wynne, Lyman C., Irving M. Ryckoff, Juliana Day, and Stanley I. Hirsch. "Pseudo-Mutuality in the Family Relations of Schizophrenics," *Psychiatry,* 21 (1958), pp. 205-220.

Temporal aspects of the relationship between the family and mental illness are suggested in:

Cleveland, E. J., and W. D. Longaker. "Neurotic Patterns in the Family," in Alexander H. Leighton, John A. Clausen, and Robert N. Wilson (eds.), *Explorations in Social Psychiatry.* Basic Books, 1957, pp. 167-200.

Fisher, Seymour, and David Mandell. "The Communication of Neurotic Patterns over Two and Three Generations," *Psychiatry,* 19 (1956), pp. 41-46.

Robins, Lee N., and Patricia O'Neal. "The Marital History of Former Problem Children," *Social Problems,* 5 (1958), pp. 347-358.

The relationship beween family and society as affecting the development of mental illness is indicated in:

Bettelheim, Bruno, and Emmy Sylvester. "Notes on the Impact of Parental Occupations: Some Cultural Determinants of Symptom Choice in Emotionally Disturbed Children," *American Journal of Orthopsychiatry*, 20 (1950), pp. 785-795.

Gronseth, Erik, and Per Olav Tiller. Section on "Father Absence in Sailor Families," in Nels Anderson (ed.), *Studies of the Family*, Goettingen: Vandenhoeck and Ruprecht, 1957, pp. 95-137.

Myers, Jerome K., and Bertram H. Roberts. *Family and Class Dynamics in Mental Illness*. Wiley, 1959.

Sanua, Victor D. "Sociocultural Factors in Families of Schizophrenics," *Psychiatry*, 24 (1961), pp. 246-265.

Index of Persons

513

Index of Topics